MUNICH 1923

MUNICH 1923

THE STORY OF HITLER'S FIRST GRAB FOR POWER

JOHN DORNBERG

HARPER & ROW, PUBLISHERS, New York

Cambridge, Philadelphia, San Francisco, London
Mexico City, São Paulo, Sydney

1817

In memory of Iain Macdonald (1927–1979), my friend and colleague, who first conceived of this book and who would have wanted, so much, to share and collaborate

FIRST EDITION

Designer: Sidney Feinberg

Library of Congress Cataloging in Publication Data

Dornberg, John.
  Munich 1923 : the story of Hitler's first grab for power.
  Bibliography: p.
  Includes index.
  1. Bavaria (Germany)—Politics and government—1918–1945.
2. Hitler, Adolf, 1889–1945. I. Title.
DD801.B42D67   1982   943.085'092'4   81-48670
ISBN 0-06-038025-X   AACR2

82 83 84 85 86 10 9 8 7 6 5 4 3 2 1

CONTENTS

A section of photographs follows page 152

A map of Munich appears on pages 16–17

MUNICH 1923

Today I can admit frankly that in the years 1920 to 1923 I thought of nothing but a putsch. It was the rashest decision of my life. . . . If today you could see one of our squads marching by, you would ask: "What workhouse have they escaped from?" But fate meant well with us in denying the success of an action which, had it succeeded, would have crashed in the end as a result of our movement's inner immaturity, weak intellectual foundation, and deficient organization in those days.

—ADOLF HITLER in Munich, 1936

In its imprecise goal and disorderly planning, his putsch was a folly. But it was of decisive significance for his nimbus. From 1919 until 1923 this Hitler had been but a "drummer," active largely only in Bavaria. But after November 1923, his reputation as a great popular leader spread to those parts of Germany where he had never even made a personal appearance, and for the first time, too, he became widely known abroad.

—HANS FRANK, Nazi governor general of Occupied Poland, before his execution as a war criminal at Nuremberg in 1946

I am rather vain about some of the political reports I made as acting consul general in Munich describing Hitler's raucous efforts; when I looked them up recently they seemed reasonably perceptive. But we never knew whether or not anybody in Washington read them. . . . During my Munich years I saw nothing to indicate that the American government or people were even mildly interested in the political developments which seemed so ominous and significant to us on the spot. Not once did our State Department . . . express concern over the developing Nazi movement. No comment came from Washington when I sent an eyewitness report of the Hitler group's attempt to overthrow the government of Bavaria in 1923, as a first step towards the national dictatorship which they eventually achieved. Yet, we were dealing with the origins of World War II.

—ROBERT MURPHY, U.S. ambassador and State Department official, in *Diplomat Among Warriors*, 1964

PROLOGUE

The men who met for tea on the afternoon of November 7, 1923, in the spacious Munich apartment of retired Lieutenant Colonel Hermann Kriebel did not look like revolutionaries or conspirators. Indeed, all were fairly prominent local grandees. They regarded themselves—and were considered by tens of thousands of their admirers and followers in those turbulent postwar days of Germany's degradation, political disarray, and economic deprivation—as paragons of patriotic virtue.

Like Kriebel, forty-seven, a large, heavyset veteran of twenty-four years' active service to the king of Bavaria and the Kaiser of the German Reich, given to wearing lederhosen and loden jackets when not garbed in his bemedaled old uniform, they thought of themselves as potential saviors of the nation and its honor.

Kriebel welcomed his guests.

There was Adolf Hitler, thirty-four, the Führer—leader—of the National Socialist German Workers party, not yet known by its later acronym "Nazi." In the scant four years since he had joined it, and thanks largely to his demagogic and magnetic oratorical performances, the party had mushroomed from a fringe sect into Bavaria's most powerful political force, with some 70,000 members.

He was accompanied by two of his closest associates. One was Dr. Max Erwin von Scheubner-Richter, thirty-nine, a Russian-born engineer who, like many émigrés, had come to Germany and settled in Munich after the Bolshevik revolution. The other was a World War flying ace, thirty-year-old Hermann Göring, already displaying some of the girth of his future years. Göring had won the Pour le Mérite order, Germany's highest medal for valor, as the last commander of the famous fighter squadron of Manfred von Richthofen, the "Red Baron." He was the head of Hitler's Sturm-Abteilung—SA—the party's private army of 15,000 uniformed storm troopers and street brawlers.

There was Dr. Friedrich Weber, thirty-one, a tall, thin, bespectacled veterinarian, who was not only a member of Munich's upper-crust Academic Guild but also the son-in-law of Julius F. Lehmann, one of the city's most prominent and successful book publishers. Weber was the "political" leader of the Oberland League, a paramilitary organization of 4,000 armed troopers, virtually all of them disgruntled war veterans. Calling themselves a "free corps," they had helped crush Bavaria's own short-lived Communist regime in 1919 and had then fought against Polish occupation of Silesia in 1920.

Sitting in Kriebel's study, too, that gloomy Wednesday afternoon, was Hans Streck, thirty-four, an ex-major who had been cashiered from the army for refusing to swear loyalty to the Weimar Republic that had succeeded the Kaiser's abdication.

And then, though he always afterward denied it, there was grim-faced, ramrod-straight ex-General Erich Ludendorff, fifty-eight, erstwhile imperial chief-of-staff, architect of Germany's early victories on the Eastern front and also of its final debacle in the West. After fleeing to Sweden following the armistice, Ludendorff had returned to Germany in 1919 and settled in a suburb of Munich to propagate his reactionary politics and fuzzy "Nordic" religion.

Together these seven men constituted the leadership of the Kampfbund. It was a battle league of ultra-nationalist, radically racist, virulently anti-Semitic, hysterically anti-Marxist, and militantly anti-democratic private armies, whose aim was to overthrow Germany's weak but legitimate and freely elected postwar government. They regarded the leaders of that government—in particular, President Friedrich Ebert, a moderate Socialist, and the succession of chancellors and cabinet members under him since 1919—as the "November criminals" responsible for Germany's defeat and for its humiliation and decline under the hated Versailles Treaty.

For months they had been discussing and preparing ways to achieve their goal. Hitler, for example, already being eulogized in his mass rallies as the "Mussolini of Germany," envisioned a coup d'état and "march on Berlin" similar to the Italian Fascist leader's March on Rome a year earlier, in October 1922.

The time certainly seemed ripe. The fledgling Weimar Republic was in crisis, the country in chaos. Political murder was commonplace. Inflation was rampant. The French had occupied the Ruhr to extract reparations. The government of Ebert and Chancellor Gustav Stresemann was threatened by revolt from both the extreme Left and Right. There had been Communist takeovers in Saxony, Thuringia, and the city-state of Hamburg. The loyalty of the Reichswehr, the 100,000-man postwar army, was in question, as was that of its strong-willed and authoritarian commander-in-chief, General Hans von Seeckt. Not only was Germany's first experiment in democracy clearly not working; it was apparent that the majority of Germans did not even want to try.

And Bavaria seemed the ideal pad from which to launch a coup. For the seven Kampfbund leaders it was a natural power base and safe haven, offering a perfect political climate in which to forge their plans. More than any other German state, this erstwhile kingdom had been traumatized by the revolution that swept the country in November 1918. A socialist mob had sent King Ludwig III fleeing from Munich and established a Red Republic that ultimately practiced terror. Six months later it had ended in a bloodbath of White terror and counterrevolution, staged largely by "free-corps" units of demobilized soldiers.

Ever since, Bavaria had been moving steadily to the political Right and to the past. It evolved as an enclave within Germany for reactionary monarchists, frustrated soldiers of fortune, and political opportunists. The free-corps veterans formed an array of "patriotic fighting societies." Led by retired officers, they were being armed and trained clandestinely by those on active duty with the local unit of the emasculated Reichswehr—the Seventh Division. They regarded themselves as auxiliary forces in waiting for the day when Germany could rearm. Increasingly, too, Bavaria was becoming disillusioned with the way the politicians in Berlin were running the country. Independent-minded by nature, conservative Bavaria began to regard itself as "a cell of law and order" within the muddled, turbulent body of Weimar Germany.

Extraction of that "healthy cell" from its "sick environment"—Bavarian secession from the Reich—became a mounting possibility. So did the imposition of Bavarian "order" on the Reich, by force of arms or a putsch. In September 1923, six weeks before the meeting in Kriebel's apartment, relations between Munich and Berlin had reached an impasse. Bavaria's prime minister, Eugen von Knilling, had declared a state of emergency. To implement it, he had appointed a former prime minister, Gustav von Kahr, as a "general state commissioner," a virtual dictator, whose powers were shared, and enforced, by the head of the State Police, Colonel Hans von Seisser, and the head of the Bavarian Reichswehr district, Seventh Division commander Lieutenant General Otto von Lossow.

This triumvirate in the classical Roman style suited the Kampfbund leaders perfectly. They had started almost immediately to pressure and cajole Kahr, Seisser, and Lossow into "extending" the dictatorship from Munich to Berlin by means of their combined forces: Lossow's Seventh Division, Seisser's divisional-strength Bavarian State Police, Hitler and Göring's SA, Weber's Oberland League, and the Reichskriegsflagge (RKF) Society, another private army of hardened combat veterans, headed by one of Lossow's own staff officers, Captain Ernst Röhm. They conjectured, moreover, that with the revered hero Ludendorff leading this formidable force northward, not a shot would be fired. The Germans, seeking salvation from their government of "November criminals," would greet them with open arms.

On the whole, the triumvirs and the Kampfbund leaders agreed in their political assessment of the German malaise and the Bavarian "cure" for it, though there were some differences of opinion, not to mention conflicts of ambition, among them. Kahr, for example, a stanch Bavarian monarchist deeply loyal to the dead king's eldest son, fifty-four-year-old Crown Prince Rupprecht, contemplated a secession that would restore the throne; better yet, Kahr envisioned a march on Berlin to make Rupprecht a new German Kaiser by substituting Bavaria's Wittelsbach dynasty for the hated, deposed Hohenzollern clan of Prussia. Ludendorff, on the other hand, as stiff a Prussian as imaginable and highly contemptuous of the Catholic Wittelsbach family, would have none of that. All, moreover, were suspicious of the ex-corporal Hitler, the upstart agitator who could mobilize frenzied masses. But mobilize them toward what end?

The greatest disagreement, however, was over how and when to strike. Lossow, cautious and prudent, wanted assurances that the coup would succeed, guarantees that Reichswehr units in the north of Germany would join forces with them. To him, but also to Ludendorff and Hitler, the thought of armed resistance by troops loyal to Berlin—tantamount to civil war—was abhorrent. Yet the prospects for such assurances diminished as the schism between Munich and Berlin deepened.

In response to the establishment of the Bavarian triumvirate, President Ebert had declared a state of emergency for all Germany, with dictatorial powers for War Minister Otto Gessler and Reichswehr chief von Seeckt. Kahr had rejected this as applying to Bavaria. When Berlin ordered Kahr to ban Hitler's daily newspaper, the *Völkischer Beobachter*, for its scurrilous attacks on Gessler, Seeckt, and Chancellor Stresemann, the Bavarian dictator had flatly refused to comply. Seeckt had then ordered Lossow to impose the ban; but the general, loyal to Kahr, had also balked. At this Seeckt had dismissed Lossow as commander of the Bavarian military district and of the Seventh Division, to which Kahr had replied with a stroke of the pen. He had placed the division and the district under his own dictatorial rule, leaving Lossow in charge of both. It was political and military rebellion.

Throughout that tense month of October 1923 the triumvirs and the Kampfbund leaders had met repeatedly to discuss their course of action; repeatedly Hitler had urged that they march on Berlin "before Berlin marches on us." But it was becoming increasingly apparent to him that the triumvirs were either losing heart or, even worse in his extremist, nationalist view, planning a separatist coup without him.

The triumvirs, for their part, feared Hitler might strike out on his own. He had given them frequent promises that he would not stage a putsch, but by early November his ability to keep that promise, if indeed he had ever meant it honestly, decreased from day to day. Time was running out. There was the possibility, first of all, that the Stresemann government, Germany's most effective since the war, might succeed in getting a grip on the country's turmoil and restore order. Like the sorcerer's apprentice, Hitler was also coming under mounting pressure of his own making as a result of his mass meetings and frenetic rallies. His followers and supporters, literally multiplying by the thousands every week that autumn, hungered for action. One day early in November, Wilhelm Brückner, an ex-lieutenant who commanded the SA storm troop regiment in Munich, warned him, "We have so many unemployed in the ranks, men who have spent their last on uniforms, that the day is not far off when I won't be able to keep a hold on them unless you act. If nothing happens, we will lose control."

Hitler had to take the initiative. But he also knew he could not take it against the Bavarian triumvirate—against Kahr's administration, Lossow's Seventh Division, and Seisser's State Police. Somehow, so Hitler, Göring, Scheubner-Richter, Ludendorff, Kriebel, Streck, and Weber reasoned, those three would have to be faced with a fait accompli, a public action of some kind that would force them to collaborate by integrating them into it—an action from which there was no turning back, which they could not repudiate. It was to concoct such a plan that these seven determined and fanatical men were meeting on Wednesday afternoon, November 7, 1923, in Hermann Kriebel's apartment on Sendlinger-Tor Platz.

Kriebel had an idea. The Kampfbund forces were planning a bivouac and training exercise the night of November 10/11 on a heath north of Munich. The date was symbolic: the fifth anniversary of the 1918 Armistice. The units would be present in full strength. Instead of training, they could march into the city, declare the nationalist revolution, kidnap Kahr, Lossow, and Seisser, and proclaim them members of a national dictatorship that would include Hitler, Ludendorff, and others. The elected members of the Bavarian government—Prime Minister von Knilling and his cabinet—would simply be arrested in their homes and prevented from interfering.

Hitler did not like the plan. There were too many risks. Who could guarantee that all the ministers of Bavaria's constitutional government would be in their homes or beds, or assure that Kahr, Lossow, and Seisser would be there? Besides, he argued, the scheme was too public. Though a weekend was good timing, the troops would be dispersed too thinly around the city.

The discussion dragged on. It had turned dark outside. Suddenly Hitler came up with an alternative proposal.

Kahr was planning to speak the following evening, November

8, in the Bürgerbräukeller, one of Munich's largest beerhalls, with an auditorium that could seat several thousand people. All prominent citizens—including Hitler and the other Kampfbund leaders—had been invited. In all likelihood, Seisser and Lossow would be on stage with Kahr, and the cabinet members were certain to be there too.

No one knew for sure what Kahr intended to say. The invitations, which had not been sent out until that morning, were vague. They indicated only that it would be an "important speech," spelling out the Bavarian government's position on "the domestic and international situation." But all prominent burghers, the editors of the key papers, German and foreign correspondents, diplomats, industrialists, and educational leaders had been invited. In fact, Hitler mused dourly, there was even the danger that Kahr might use the occasion to announce the restoration of the Bavarian monarchy and call for Rupprecht to take the throne—a potentially disastrous blow to his own plans. But why, he suggested, let matters go that far? The meeting provided a perfect setup and opportunity to strike.

SA and Oberland troopers could surround and seal off the beerhall and neutralize the police, many of whose high-ranking officers and officials were Nazi party members anyway. At that point, Hitler explained, he would go on stage and interrupt Kahr's speech, announce the national revolution, ask the triumvirs out of the hall into a side room for a conference, and assign them their roles in the future Reich government. They would then all return with him to the main auditorium.

"Triumphantly," he said, with mounting enthusiasm, "we will declare the Reich and Bavarian state governments as deposed and announce the march on Berlin.

"Everything will have to be perfectly timed, of course. But there is no way it can fail."

As he detailed the particulars, becoming increasingly excited, the others warmed to the plan.

They spent the rest of the evening working out the "military" steps. Finally, with a stiff shaking of hands all around, they left Kriebel's apartment around 10 P.M. to go out into the chilly night—the fifth anniversary of the monarchy's fall in Bavaria—to prepare for the putsch that they were all convinced would change the destiny of Germany and the world.

Interlude I
The City

Munich

Even before his coronation in 1825, Bavaria's King Ludwig I had vowed to make his capital a city that would "do honor to all Germany, of which all Germans will be proud." He envisioned it as "a new Athens," a metropolis stately in scope, as broad and spacious in its boulevards and architecture as in its attitude to life, a center of learning and of culture.

And thanks largely to his visionary and enlightened pledge, no other German city—in the scant century that the Bavarian monarchy was to endure—contributed as much to the country's arts, literature, music, and science.

It was here, at the foot of the Alps, on the banks of the Isar River, a torrential tributary of the Danube, that the genius of dozens of creative men and women unfolded: writers such as Henrik Ibsen, Paul Heyse, Thomas and Heinrich Mann, Oswald Spengler, Rainer Maria Rilke, Bertolt Brecht; composers Richard Wagner, Richard Strauss, and Max Reger, and musicians of such stature as Bruno Walter and Wilhelm Fürtwangler; the painters Carl Spitzweg, Vasily Kandinsky, Gabriele Münter, Paul Klee, Franz Marc, Lovis Corinth, and Max Liebermann; scientists, discoverers, and inventors of such fame as Justus von Liebig, Wilhelm Conrad Röntgen, Georg Simon Ohm, and Rudolf Diesel.

A magnetic, provocative, inspiring city: testimonials to it abound with superlatives.

Ibsen, who wrote his greatest plays during the fifteen years he spent there, declared shortly after arriving in 1874, "There are but two cities in which one can really live—Rome and Munich. And in Munich even reality is beautiful."

Kandinsky, who fathered abstractionism during the twenty years he was in Munich, described it as "a unique intellectual island of beauty that stimulates the world."

For Thomas Mann and his brothers and sisters, Munich was home from 1892—when their widowed mother moved there from Lübeck—until emigration in 1933, four decades that were the most decisive and productive of his life. Munich was where he met and married Katja, the daughter of a local professor, where their six children were born and raised, and where he wrote the greatest of his novels. In *Gladius Dei* he expressed his feelings about the city: "A heaven of blue silk radiates over Munich's festive squares and columned white temples, neoclassical monuments and baroque churches, playing fountains, palaces and parks. Art blooms, art reigns, art stretches her rose-clad sceptre over this city and smiles."

The American novelist Thomas Wolfe, who visited in 1925 on his tour of Europe, wrote in *The Web and the Rock,*

> Munich is a kind of German heaven. . . . A great Germanic dream translated into life. . . . The best beer in Germany, in the world, is made there, and there are enormous beer cellars that are renowned throughout the land. The Bavarian is the National Good Fellow. He is supposed to be a witty and eccentric creature, and millions of postcards are printed of him in his national costume blowing the froth away from a foaming stein of beer. In other parts of Germany, people will lift their eyes and sigh rapturously when you say you are going to Munich: *"Ach! München . . . ist schön!*

On Thursday morning, November 8, 1923, however, there was little of Munich that shone with beauty. Instead of blue silk, the heaven was a leaden gray—an adumbration of the winter soon to come but also somehow symbolic of the somber mood. The blooms of art had wilted and withered in the five postwar years since the fall of the monarchy, a half decade tormented by revolution, terror, assassinations, counterrevolution, hunger, poverty, mass unemployment, runaway inflation, hateful racism, frustrated chauvinism, pent-up anger, political extremism, and plotting. Art's scepter was not rose-clad but draped in the black of mourning for an era that seemed irretrievably lost.

Had Thomas Wolfe come that day, instead of two years later, he would have discovered a nightmare rather than a dream, a purgatory, not a paradise. A stein of that famous beer he loved would have cost him billions of marks, and the enormous beer cellars were not so much renowned as infamous for the demagogues, in particular Adolf Hitler, who harangued audiences of thousands there into hysterical frenzy. The Bavarian, feeling betrayed and cheated of the honor and glory that he considered his and Germany's rightful destiny, was in 1923 anything but a "National Good Fellow." Instead, he looked very much like a National Menace.

ONE

The Plan in the Making

1

    Adolf Hitler awakened on what was to be one of the most important days of his life—Thursday, November 8, 1923—with a throbbing headache and a persistent toothache. Friends had been urging him for several days to see a dentist, but Hitler said he didn't have time. Besides, he told them, there was going to be a revolution which would "change everything."

    If so, most of Munich's 640,000 inhabitants didn't seem to be aware of it. To the casual eye, the city appeared quite normal on that dismal, chilly morning.

    The streetcars clattered and clanged their way through narrow cobblestoned streets, along broad avenues, and beneath the window of Hitler's shabby little sublet apartment at No. 41 Thiersch Strasse, in a lower-middle-class district on the left bank of the Isar. Cars and trucks, such as there were, honked, chugged, and rumbled around horse-drawn wagons, pushcarts, and bicycles. Policemen, picturesque in their spike-topped leather helmets, struggled to direct this jumble of traffic: on Marienplatz in front of the neo-Gothic City Hall; on Karlsplatz, which Müncheners call "Stachus" because of a tavern that used to be located there; at stately Odeonsplatz between Ludwig Strasse and the monumental Feldherrnhalle; near the Isartor, one of Munich's few remaining medieval gates. Over on the Viktualienmarkt—the "Victuals Mart"—women vegetable sellers displaying their wares were bundled against the drizzly cold, butchers were opening their stalls.

    Those who had a job were hurrying to work. Among them

were two thirty-six-year-old lawyers, Dr. Hans Ehard and Dr. Wilhelm Hoegner, both recently appointed as assistant prosecuting attorneys: Ehard to his office in the Palace of Justice on the "Stachus," Hoegner to his in a courthouse in the Au district on the Isar's right bank.

Wilhelm Briemann, twenty-four, a publisher's representative but also a member of Adolf Hitler's rapidly expanding Nazi party and of its special bodyguard team, the Stosstrupp, started out on his round of bookshops to sell his company's wares.

Briemann's friend, the tough battle-hardened head of the Stosstrupp, ex-Lieutenant Josef Berchtold, twenty-six, hurried to open his little tobacco shop in the center of Munich on a street colorfully called Im Tal—"In the Valley."

Adolf Lenk, twenty, founder and leader of the Nazi party's first youth movement, the Jungsturm, made up of teenagers, didn't have far to go at all. Together with his father, he walked downstairs from their apartment to the family's main-floor piano-making shop at Jahn Strasse No. 20.

Heinrich Himmler, twenty-three, son of a prominent Munich high-school principal, recently graduated with a degree in agricultural science, went to his new job as a lab asssistant in a chemical fertilizer plant north of the city.

Dr. Ferdinand Sauerbruch, the famous surgeon whose appointment to Munich University's teaching hospital in 1918 had been a prestigious coup for the city, was operating.

The papal nuncio and dean of the diplomatic corps in Bavaria, Monsignor Eugenio Pacelli—later Pope Pius XII—was in his residence on Brienner Strasse.

Ex-General Erich Ludendorff, revered hero of the war who had settled in the Munich suburb of Solln-Ludwigshöhe, breakfasted leisurely that morning in his spacious house on Heilmann Strasse. He told his stepson, ex-Lieutenant Heinz Pernet, a student, that he was expecting important visitors from Berlin.

Former Prime Minister Dr. Gustav von Kahr, Bavaria's new "general state commissioner" with dictatorial powers, appointed six weeks earlier to enforce the state of emergency declared by the Bavarian government, walked somewhat absentmindedly through the cavernous corridors connecting his apartment with his offices at Maximilian Strasse No. 14, one of Munich's finest streets.

At about the same time, a gray Benz staff car sped down Ludwig Strasse, turned right into Schönfeld Strasse, then roared through the courtyard of what had been the Royal Bavarian War Ministry. On the back seat, sitting stiffly straight, a pince-nez clamped on his nose, was Lieutenant General Otto von Lossow, commander-in-chief of the German Reichswehr's Bavarian military district and the Seventh Division. This was his headquarters.

Two blocks away, on Türken Strasse, a similar car, but dark green, brought Colonel Hans von Seisser, chief of the divisional-strength Bavarian State Police, to his office in the Polizei Kaserne—the Police Barracks.

Not far from there, on Hofgarten Strasse, adjacent to the Army Museum, Major General Jakob von Danner, the Munich city commandant, Lossow's direct subordinate, was already at work in his garrison.

Meanwhile, Karl Mantel, Munich's municipal police chief, strolled into his second-floor office at the labyrinthine central station on Ett Strasse, near City Hall, and shut the door after mumbling a few words to his aides. Mantel, relatively new on the job, was a man with problems. Though politically a stanch conservative, he was strongly opposed to the burgeoning Nazi movement and Hitler's demagoguery, not to mention the violence of the SA storm troopers, who, increasingly, were taking the law into their own hands and terrorizing Munich burghers. To complicate Mantel's life, his predecessor in the post, Ernst Pöhner, an avid supporter of Hitler, continued to exert strong influence throughout the police hierarchy, and there was no way to stop him. As Mantel knew, a number of key officers were active Nazis. One, definitely, was Dr. Wilhelm Frick, chief of the internal security and political surveillance division. Two others were Matthäus Hofmann and Josef Gerum, both senior detective inspectors. Assigned to infiltrate the Nazi party as a police informer, Gerum had not only switched allegiance but joined that most elite group of Nazi toughs, the 120-member Stosstrupp.

But Mantel's worries were not those of most Müncheners that morning. Even cultural life seemed to be going on as usual. Thus, at 9 A.M.—it was barely light outside on that dismal day—Thomas Mann, in his routine and methodical way, sat down at a huge, heavy desk in the study of his three-story villa at No. 1 Poschinger Strasse, on the Isar's right bank in the fashionable Bogenhausen district, to read proof on his forthcoming book, *The Magic Mountain*.

At the opera house—the colonnaded National Theater on Max-Josef Platz, adjacent to the Residenz, the vast "winter palace" of Bavaria's erstwhile monarchs—Hans Knappertsbusch, recently appointed successor to Bruno Walter as chief conductor, called a rehearsal for that evening's seven o'clock performance of Beethoven's *Fidelio*. Elsewhere in the huge opera house, Lauritz Melchior, a young but already famous Danish tenor, was using one of the practice rooms to study his roles as Siegfried and Parsifal for the coming summer's Wagner festival in Bayreuth.

Knappertsbusch did not know that he would be conducting for considerably less than a full house that evening because the opera crowd—Munich's most prominent citizens—had received urgent, almost command-performance invitations to hear an important speech by General Commissioner von Kahr in the Bürgerbräukeller, the city's plushest beerhall, better known for its elaborate gingerbread auditorium than for its brew.

There, on Rosenheimer Strasse, a steep wide street leading from the Ludwigsbrücke and the right bank of the Isar, Korbinian Reindl, the innkeeper, came down early from his upstairs apartment to the office to prepare for the important event. But his was not the only Munich beer cellar that would be full that evening. Across town, in the Löwenbräukeller on Stiglmaier Platz, the cavernous main hall had been rented by Reichswehr Captain Ernst Röhm, head of the Reichskriegsflagge, a radical-rightist organization of "patriotic war veterans," for a "reunion" and "festive evening of comradeship." As the front-page advertisement in that morning's *Völkischer Beobachter*, the Nazi party daily, said, there would be music by a brass band, and, "during the course of the evening, our Führer Adolf Hitler will say a few words to us." Employees were busy cleaning and readying the hall.

Busy too that morning were Adolf Schiedt, managing editor of the daily *Münchener Zeitung*, who doubled as von Kahr's press spokesman, and Fritz Gerlich, editor-in-chief of the competitive *Münchner Neueste Nachrichten*. Both ultra-conservatives and of the same political mind, they had collaborated in the ghost-writing of Kahr's speech and were now making last-minute changes in it before delivering it to Kahr's offices on Maximilian Strasse.

Close by, in the Schauspielhaus, a commercial theater, unaware that he would soon become a witness to history, twenty-seven-year-old Carl Zuckmayer, a brilliant but as yet unrecognized playwright, was working part-time as an assistant director and acting coach. He had no premonition of impending drama that day.

Nor, for that matter, did Dr. Karl Alexander von Müller, forty-one, professor of modern history at Munich University and a prominent conservative political essayist, who arrived in his office to find an invitation for that evening's address by "His Excellency General Commissioner von Kahr." Among von Müller's students were a number of war veterans, including two former fighter pilots: ex-Lieutenant Rudolf Hess, then twenty-seven, and thirty-year-old ex-Captain Hermann Göring. Both, Müller knew, were highly active in the Nazi movement of Adolf Hitler, whom he had met socially and whose speeches he had heard: Göring as commander of the Nazi party's private army of storm troopers, the SA; Hess as Hitler's secretary and head of the SA's student battalion. But the fact that neither gentleman was attending lectures that day did not strike Müller as in any way unusual or ominous. They had a reputation for being absent more than in attendance.

Göring, in fact, was still at home, in his sumptuous suburban house in Obermenzing on the northern edge of Munich. He was trying to be solicitous to his rich, blue-blooded Swedish wife, Carin, recuperating—though still with fever—from a serious bout with pneumonia. "It may get late tonight," he told her apologetically. "There's an important meeting. If it should drag out too long, I'll call. But don't worry about me." Sighing with resignation, she said, "No, I won't worry." She, too, had no forebodings that morning.

Neither did Hess when, around 10 A.M., he received an urgent call asking him to come "at once" to Hitler's flat. Hess, who adored his Führer and obeyed him like a lapdog, "rushed there immediately."

In fact, if there was anyone that morning who might have had reason for thinking that something odd was going on, it was probably young Robert Murphy, twenty-eight, the acting U.S. consul general. Strangely, the city and his offices seemed to be

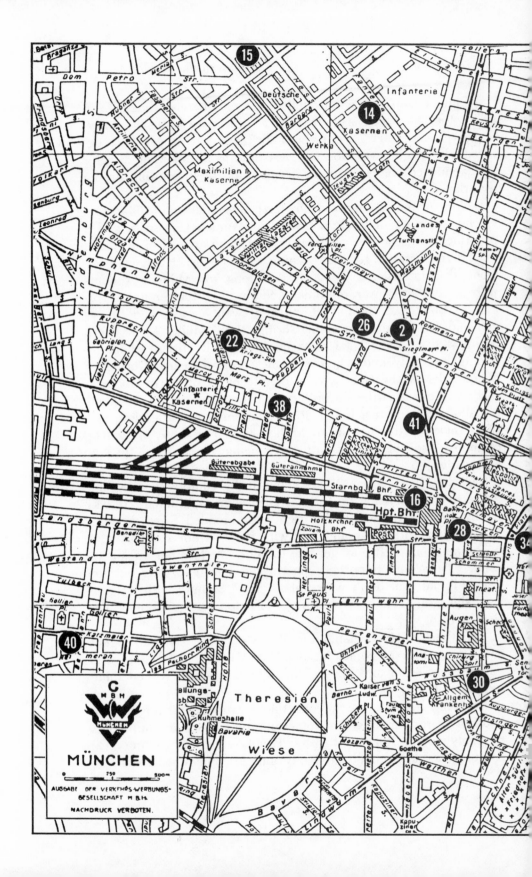

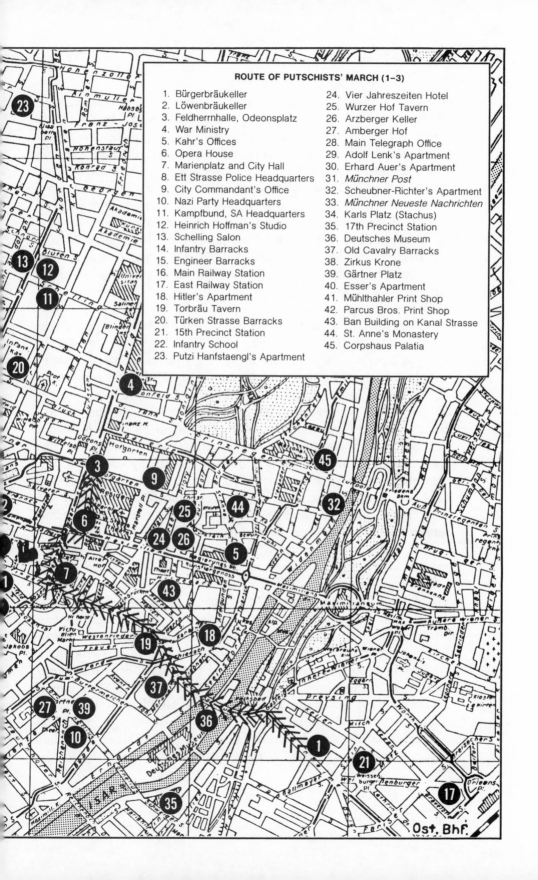

ROUTE OF PUTSCHISTS' MARCH (1–3)

1. Bürgerbräukeller
2. Löwenbräukeller
3. Feldherrnhalle, Odeonsplatz
4. War Ministry
5. Kahr's Offices
6. Opera House
7. Marienplatz and City Hall
8. Ett Strasse Police Headquarters
9. City Commandant's Office
10. Nazi Party Headquarters
11. Kampfbund, SA Headquarters
12. Heinrich Hoffman's Studio
13. Schelling Salon
14. Infantry Barracks
15. Engineer Barracks
16. Main Railway Station
17. East Railway Station
18. Hitler's Apartment
19. Torbräu Tavern
20. Türken Strasse Barracks
21. 15th Precinct Station
22. Infantry School
23. Putzi Hanfstaengl's Apartment

24. Vier Jahreszeiten Hotel
25. Wurzer Hof Tavern
26. Arzberger Keller
27. Amberger Hof
28. Main Telegraph Office
29. Adolf Lenk's Apartment
30. Erhard Auer's Apartment
31. *Münchner Post*
32. Scheubner-Richter's Apartment
33. *Münchner Neueste Nachrichten*
34. Karls Platz (Stachus)
35. 17th Precinct Station
36. Deutsches Museum
37. Old Cavalry Barracks
38. Zirkus Krone
39. Gärtner Platz
40. Esser's Apartment
41. Mühlthahler Print Shop
42. Parcus Bros. Print Shop
43. Ban Building on Kanal Strasse
44. St. Anne's Monastery
45. Corpshaus Palatia

virtually besieged by American newspaper correspondents, most of them normally posted in Berlin, who had flocked to Bavaria to check out rumors of an impending putsch, or possibly an armed drive northward, by ultra-rightist paramilitary units and von Lossow's Seventh Division into the neighboring German state of Thuringia, where a Communist government was entrenched in power. Among the correspondents were Larry Rue of the *Chicago Tribune,* Hubert Knickerbocker of the *Baltimore Sun,* Lincoln Eyre of the *New York Herald,* and free-lancer Dorothy Thompson.

Rue, an old hand who had been covering the German scene since his first assignment there in 1919, was eager to get in touch with a man he knew and who was close to Hitler: Ernst "Putzi" Hanfstaengl.

Hanfstaengl, a six-foot-four giant, was by far the most colorful character in Hitler's entourage. On his father's side he was the scion of a prominent Munich family of art printers and publishers; on his American mother's, of high-ranking Union officers in the Civil War, including General John Sedgwick. At Munich's prestigious Wilhelm Gymnasium, his principal teacher and mentor had been Gebhard Himmler, Heinrich's father. In 1905 he had gone to the United States to study at Harvard, graduated in 1909, and then managed the New York branch of the family's art reproduction business on Fifth Avenue. Ultimately he had opened his own art bookshop on West 57th Street across from Carnegie Hall. His New York friends in those years, especially at the Harvard Club, where he ate most of his meals, included Franklin D. Roosevelt.

In 1921, having married an American woman, Helene Niemeyer, Hanfstaengl decided to sell the shop and return to Munich. He soon met and befriended Hitler, helped him out financially, kept him in a good mood by playing Wagner on the piano for him, and provided him with connections to the right people. "Mine," he once boasted, "was the first Munich family of standing into which Hitler was introduced when he was still unknown" (thanks in large measure not to Putzi but his elder sister, Erna). By the morning of November 8, 1923, Hanfstaengl was one of Hitler's closest associates and advisers, a member of the young Führer's "kitchen cabinet."

After a late and leisurely breakfast with Helene and their three-year-old son, Egon, in their apartment in Schwabing, Munich's Latin Quarter, Hanfstaengl mounted his bicycle to pedal the dozen or so blocks to the editorial offices of the *Völkischer Beobachter* at No. 39 Schelling Strasse, also the headquarters of the SA and the Kampfbund. Hitler was the Kampfbund's "political leader," ex-Lieutenant Colonel Hermann Kriebel its "military chief." In recent weeks, as rumors of plots, counterplots, and putsches had multiplied, Hanfstaengl had taken to spending part of each day there to "keep track of developments."

It was shortly after 11 A.M. when he sauntered into the white-washed office of the paper's managing editor, Alfred Rosenberg, a man he disliked intensely. Rosenberg, thirty, a fanatic anti-Semite, was, like Dr. Max Erwin von Scheubner-Richter, another of Hitler's close advisers and cronies, a Baltic German who had grown up in Russia and emigrated in the wake of the Bolshevik revolution. Garishly and improbably dressed in a violet shirt, red tie, brown vest, and blue suit, Rosenberg had a pistol prominently displayed on his desk. He and Hanfstaengl were engaged in strained small talk when they suddenly heard doors slamming, feet stomping, and their angry Führer's voice in the hallway.

"*Wo ist Göring?*" Hitler shouted.

"Late as usual, probably clucking over his Carin," someone replied.

"Phone him, get him," snapped the Führer, obviously in no mood for jokes.

Suddenly Hitler, wearing a wrinkled, tightly belted trench-coat and holding a rhinoceros-hide riding whip—both virtual trademarks—yanked open the door and stormed into the room. Hanfstaengl and Rosenberg jumped to attention. With a wave of the whip he gestured them to sit down again.

"You must keep absolute secrecy," he said urgently. "Our time has come. Tonight we strike—in the Bürgerbräukeller where Kahr is giving a speech."

Briefly he spelled out the plan. While SA and Oberland units sealed off the beerhall and occupied key positions around the city, he would interrupt Kahr's speech to announce the "nationalist revolution" and the establishment of a new Reich government with himself as dictator. There would be posts in it for Lossow and Seisser. Ludendorff would be commander of the new German army, one of which all Germans could be proud. Kahr and Ernst

Pöhner, Munich's ex-chief of police, would head the Bavarian state government. The members of the existing one, as well as all Socialists, Communists, Jews, and other "enemies of the people," would be taken hostage. And then, all "patriots" together would march on Berlin from Munich.

"In case Kahr or the other gentlemen hesitate or resist, I will take them into a side room to negotiate," Hitler said, explaining that he had already ordered Rudolf Hess to rent a chamber in the Bürgerbräukeller from its manager, Reindl.

Göring and Kriebel, he went on, were responsible for the overall military operation, especially on the right bank of the Isar, and were already supposed to be busy mobilizing forces who would be handed arms at a secret location near the Bürgerbräu just before marching time. Röhm, holding his "comrades' re-union" in the Löwenbräukeller on Stiglmaier Platz, would an-nounce the revolution there and use the units at his disposal to obtain weapons from secret caches with which to occupy crucial points in the center of the city and on the left bank, such as the 19th Infantry Regiment and Army Engineer barracks and the Seventh Division headquarters on Schönfeld Strasse.

The Stosstrupp, his elite bodyguard unit under tobacconist Jo-sef Berchtold, would be assigned "special tasks," Hitler explained, adding, "An orderly is on the way to Berchtold's store to get him." Adolf Lenk's Jungsturm, the party's youth group, would be available for "auxiliary jobs."

As Hitler envisioned it, with Ludendorff at the helm and Los-sow and Seisser part of the operation, "the Reichswehr and State Police will surely be on our side. There will be no opposition, no resistance." And if there were? Well, in that case, he told the two, combined Kampfbund forces already being alerted would out-number the army and police by at least 4,000 men to 2,600.

The Führer then gave Hanfstaengl and Rosenberg their spe-cific assignments. Putzi, who harbored grave doubts about the plan, was to notify the foreign press "discreetly," make sure corre-spondents got into the Bürgerbräukeller to witness the great event, and look after their interests. Turning to Rosenberg, Hitler said, "You should start now to write the proclamations for posters and for the paper. Can you arrange with the printers for a special early edition of tomorrow's *Beobachter?* An extra?" Rosenberg assured him it would be done.

"The invitations to Kahr's speech are for seven thirty," Hitler mused. "He will probably start speaking at eight o'clock. I will make my move precisely at eight thirty. Rendezvous place is outside the Bürgerbräu—at seven sharp. I will drive from here. Rosenberg, you can accompany me in my car."

As he moved toward the door of Rosenberg's office, slapping the whip against his leg, Hitler looked back once more. "And, gentlemen, don't forget to bring your pistols."

2

Leaving the *Völkischer Beobachter,* Putzi Hanfstaengl's first thought was for his wife, pregnant with their second child, and little Egon. He rushed back to their apartment at No. 1 Gentz Strasse and, inventing a pretext, told Helene to pack up and go immediately to the country house they had bought in Uffing on the banks of Staffel Lake, 50 miles south of Munich in the Bavarian Alps.

Then he went in search of the American and British correspondents at the Bayerischer Hof on Promenade Platz and the Vier Jahreszeiten on Maxmilian Strasse, hotels where, in addition to visiting newsmen, the officers of the Allied military mission, responsible for enforcing the Versailles Treaty provisions against Germany's rearming, were living more or less permanently. But many of the reporters, expecting action three days later—on the fifth anniversary of Armistice Day—were out. Hanfstaengl left messages urging them to meet him outside the Bürgerbräukeller at seven o'clock that evening, without, however, telling them why.

He also tried the exclusive and expensive Hungaria Restaurant on Wittelsbacher Platz, where, to their joint relief and delight, he found the *Chicago Tribune*'s Larry Rue lunching sumptuously. Skillfully hemming and hawing, he induced Rue to go to the Bürgerbräu that evening, where he would be served "a journalistic delicacy" equal to, probably better than, any of the epicurean delights on the Hungaria's menu.

Göring, meanwhile, had finally arrived at the Schelling Strasse command post to bark orders at his subordinates—Stosstrupp leader Josef Berchtold, Jungsturm chief Adolf Lenk, and brawny Wilhelm Brückner, commander of the 1,500-man Munich regiment of the SA. Then, after calling Carin to tell her that it might, indeed, be a "very late" night, he went into conference with the other leaders: Hitler, the Kampfbund's Hermann Kriebel, the Oberland League's Friedrich Weber and Adolf Aechter, Max Scheubner-Richter, Ludendorff's stepson, Pernet, and a relative newcomer to the circle, thirty-year-old Gerhard Rossbach, an infamous free-corps leader who, after a brief prison stint in Berlin, had come to Munich to fish in muddy waters and regain control of his battalion of followers who had gone over to the SA.

It was the lunch period—a time sacrosanct for most people in Munich and usually of several hours' duration. But SA headquarters was a pandemonium of slamming doors, ringing phones, shouted commands, and whispered conspiratorial conferences. To Paula Schlier, a young typist at the *Völkischer Beobachter*, the atmosphere was "electrifying, disturbingly tense."

The tension was dictated by the need to improvise. Four key staging points were chosen where mobilized troops should meet at 7 P.M. All were inns and taverns that served as familiar haunts to the storm troopers: the Amberger Hof, near the Nazi party's Cornelius Strasse headquarters and business offices; the Wurzer Hof, just around the corner from the Vier Jahreszeiten Hotel; the Stosstrupp's favorite hangout, the bowling alley of the Torbräu Hotel in the "Tal" near Isartor Platz and Berchtold's tobacco shop; and the Arzbergerkeller on Nymphenburger Strasse, just a block from the Löwenbräu beerhall where Ernst Röhm would be holding his "reunion." Weapons would be handed out from trucks at secluded street corners close to the Bürgerbräu and from the secret caches where Röhm had been depositing them for months.

The urgency and tension were also compounded by the need to maintain absolute secrecy. The forces had to be alerted without telling them why. All storm troopers were to appear in the uniforms already familiar in Munich: gray windbreakers or greatcoats with red-white-and-black swastika armbands, gray ski caps or steel helmets, and weapon belts. But instead of red paper, the prearranged signal for "the real thing," orders went out all over the city on white slips indicating "just another practice."

Slowly—much too slowly, in Göring's opinion—these mobilization orders went out: by phone, hand-carried letters, and messengers on foot and bicycles. Not all they reached were elated, having made other plans for the evening—dancing, drinking, a movie, or the theater.

Thus Max Neunzert, an ex-lieutenant and "communications officer" of the Kampfbund, happened to be standing in the hallway at Schelling Strasse when Kriebel saw him and said, "You must be at the Bürgerbräukeller, in uniform, at seven thirty tonight. A car to take you there will be in front of your house."

Friedrich Mayer of the SA's 10th Company had just finished lunch when "the company clerk rang the bell" and handed him a message to report to the Amberger Hof in battle dress that evening.

The Stosstrupp's Wilhelm Briemann was leaving to resume his rounds as a book salesman when a messenger came to his apartment and told him to be at the Torbräu that evening.

Heinrich Himmler was back to working on fertilizer in his lab when someone phoned to say that attendance at Röhm's Löwenbräukeller "reunion" was no longer voluntary but mandatory.

Konrad Kiessling, a young police trainee and member of the Oberland League's First Battalion, led by Ludwig Oestreicher, was at his desk at police headquarters when he received a cryptic telephone message: "Be on Kohlen Insel of the Isar, behind the construction site for the new museum, at seven o'clock—in combat uniform."

For Hans Frank, a law student, it was late afternoon when he received a call instructing him to be at the Wurzer Hof tavern for "a special meeting of the Munich SA regiment."

Even some of the regiment's officers were getting the word late. Karl Beggel, a bank clerk in command of the SA's First Battalion, was just about to quit work at six o'clock when his orderly stormed into the office, stammering, "Göring says you are supposed to go to the Arzbergerkeller at once."

While Göring was frantically deploying and alerting the troops he would need, another man at the *Völkischer Beobachter* was making long-distance calls: the paper and party's business manager, thirty-two-year-old Max Amann, Hitler's wartime platoon sergeant. He was trying to notify the party's out-of-town leaders and supporters.

It was around noon when Amann got through to Nürnberg

and to a bald, stocky, mustachioed thirty-eight-year-old school-teacher there: Julius Streicher, the local Nazi leader and editor of a rabidly anti-Semitic tabloid, *Der Stürmer*.

"It is Adolf's wish, and of the utmost *patriotic* importance," Amann shouted over the crackling of static in the line, hoping that Streicher would get the hint, "that you come to Munich immediately. This afternoon! Yes. There is a one forty-five express train you can catch if you hurry. You must be at Schelling Strasse before seven o'clock. Do you understand?"

Streicher didn't. Though he made excuses to the principal of his school for skipping his afternoon classes, he ate an unhurried lunch and finally set off at 4 P.M. with Helmut Klotz and two other party members, by car.

The 100-mile drive along cobblestoned and unpaved country roads was a four- to five-hour journey. Streicher thought he was going to "just another party rally."

In Landshut, Gregor Strasser, thirty-one, a pharmacy owner and Gauleiter of the Nazi party in the district of Lower Bavaria, had been quicker on the uptake. He rented some trucks, alerted the 300 storm troopers in his area, and began moving his back-up force to a prearranged bivouac in the town of Freising, halfway between Landshut and Munich.

Quick to understand, too, were Hitler's sympathizers at the Infantry School on Blutenburg Strasse near the Löwenbräukeller and Stiglmaier Platz. With its 400 students, it was the nation's chief war and officer training college and under direct command of the Reichswehr and war ministry in Berlin, not von Lossow's Seventh Division. The students were cadets, enlisted men hoping to become officers and young lieutenants hurriedly commissioned on the battlefield during the war. They were undergoing advanced leadership and theoretical military training. Almost to a man—the exceptions being some of the field-grade officers who were their teachers—they were ardent supporters of the "nationalist patriotic" cause and adherents of Ludendorff and Hitler.

The most ardent by far was Lieutenant Robert Wagner. Between noon and 1 P.M. he had an unexpected visitor in his barracks room—his friend Heinz Pernet. "Come with me to the Schelling Strasse right away. I have a car waiting outside," Pernet said. "Rossbach wants to see you urgently."

Wagner hurried after Pernet to the open car waiting on Blutenburg Strasse. He was whisked to the Kampfbund headquarters, where Rossbach took him into a small office and explained, "Tonight, at eight-thirty, the new national Reich government under Hitler, Kahr, Ludendorff, Lossow, Pöhner, and others will be declared. The Reichswehr and the police are all behind it. But we will need the support of the cadets." Wagner, jubilant, promised to provide it.

By 2 P.M. he was back at the Infantry School and calling together his most trusted friends among the students—Siegfried Mahler, Hans Block, and others. He shut the door of his billet and told them excitedly, "Tonight is the X-hour for which we have all waited. Ludendorff will be the new commander-in-chief and Herr Hitler will take over the government. We are to march, under command of the famous Rossbach. We must keep as many of the students in the barracks as possible. Everybody must be ready when they call. No passes."

In the midst of all the flurry of confused and frenzied activity, Hitler himself was like the calm eye of a storm. After leaving the *Beobachter* with his trusty bodyguard Ulrich Graf, a horse butcher by trade, he waved at the driver of his new red Benz car to wait a little longer. Then he strolled a few yards up—and across—the street to No. 50 Schelling Strasse, the studio of his photographer friend, Heinrich Hoffmann. Making small talk and not giving a hint of his plans, he invited Hoffmann to drive with him to their favorite café at Gärtner Platz near party headquarters for some tea and sweet pastry.

There the two were bantering and engaged in light, meaningless conversation when Hitler asked Hoffmann, rather suddenly, "Would you mind coming with me to Hermann Esser's for a few minutes? I want to see how he's getting along."

Hermann Esser, twenty-three, handsomely blond and known about town as a Lothario, was one of Hitler's closest friends. More than that, he was one of the key figures in the Nazi leadership. An editor of the *Völkischer Beobachter*, he was in several respects the party's second-ranking man—in the number on his membership card and in his effectiveness as a propagandist and demagogic platform speaker. He had been in bed with jaundice for weeks.

Hoffmann, too, was a friend of Esser. But when they arrived

at Esser's apartment on Bergmann Strasse in Munich's fashionable West End around 3 P.M., Hitler emphatically told Hoffmann to wait outside, explaining that he wanted to talk to Hermann alone. Hoffmann, more mystified than miffed, did as commanded.

Once inside Esser's flat, Hitler spelled out the plan to his dumbfounded—and skeptical—friend, adding, "I don't care how ill you are or how rotten you feel. You must take my place on the podium at Röhm's rally in the Löwenbräukeller. The ads say I am to speak, so one of us has to be there. It starts at seven-thirty. Just keep the crowd going until you receive a call from us in the Bürgerbräu—between eight-thirty and nine—that everything is going according to schedule. The code words to Röhm will be 'Safe Delivery.' Then you announce the revolution over there. Röhm knows what to do after that."

Reluctantly, emphasizing plaintively that he was still running a temperature, Esser agreed. After all, it was the historic hour for which he too had been waiting.

"He feels much better," Hitler told Hoffmann on coming out of the apartment, suggesting they return to Schelling Strasse. But when Hoffman wanted to accompany him into the *Völkischer Beobachter*, Hitler tried to dissuade the photographer. Hitler's mood struck Hoffmann as oddly mercurial and conspiratorial— even more so when, in the building, Hitler suddenly mumbled an excuse, left Hoffmann standing in the hallway, and dashed into a room for a private conference with Göring.

Shrugging his shoulders, Hoffmann went to the nearby Schelling Salon, a popular coffeehouse with gaming tables, to play tarok. Strange secretiveness today, he thought to himself.

So did Ferdinand Schreiber, owner of a printing plant on Ismaninger Strasse, not far from the Bürgerbräukeller, when his office phone rang around four o'clock. It was Philipp Bouhler, Max Amann's assistant as business manager of the Nazi party, asking him to keep typesetters and pressmen on overtime for a late-night poster job. Two of Schreiber's competitors, Anton Schmidt and Hans Stiegeler, also received calls from Bouhler at about the same time.

"Very late," Bouhler told them on the phone.

Schreiber's company had done printing work for the party "almost since its founding," and he was used to peculiar requests.

But this one seemed unusually odd.

He wanted to know more: what the job entailed, when he would actually get it, and how many of his people it would require keeping in the shop, especially since normal quitting time was 5:30 P.M. and he planned to be out part of the evening, listening to von Kahr's speech in the Bürgerbräu. Unable to reach Bouhler again on the phone—the line was constantly busy—he took a streetcar across the river to Bouhler's office at the Cornelius Strasse party headquarters.

"Well," Bouhler lied, straining to sound as nonchalant as possible, "the posters are for a big rally in the Circus Krone on Sunday the eleventh. Very important." But unfortunately, he explained, the police had placed a variety of restrictive conditions on the meeting that were unacceptable to the party.

"The Führer and some of our leaders have an appointment later this evening with General Commissioner von Kahr and hope to have the police requirements changed," Bouhler said. "I don't know how long that will take. It may be after von Kahr's speech. But until they come back or I get the word, the copy for the posters won't be final and will not have a police clearance. You'll have to wait."

If the printers thought things a bit mysterious that afternoon, so did executives at the Schneider & Münzing bank when, shortly after four o'clock, one of their most valued customers, Dr. Gottfried Feder, walked in to close his account and demanded the portfolio of shares they managed and kept on deposit for him.

Gottfried Feder, forty, an affluent building contractor, was a founding member of the party and its "economic and financial theoretician." Indeed, it had been after hearing Feder discourse on global monetary and economic matters at a party meeting in September 1919 that Hitler decided to join the little group, then headquartered in the dingy Sterneckerbräu tavern in the Tal. Feder had also provided Hitler with vital connections and additional entree to Munich's socially and politically potent moneyed elite.

"On such short notice, Herr Doktor Feder?" the bank manager asked incredulously. "I am sorry, but we cannot do it. It is almost closing time. Not all your shares are here because they have not been validated, and I cannot get them tomorrow, either.

Come in Monday the twelfth, please, and we can settle the matter."

Angrily, Feder left. The ploy at the bank had been a calculated risk. If Hitler's plan succeeded—and how could it not? he mused—Feder would be Germany's new minister of finance that night. If not, having the packet of negotiable securities in his hand rather than locked away in a bank safe would certainly prove useful. But there was nothing to be done.

Meanwhile, over on Ett Strasse, in the labyrinthine five-story block-square Munich police headquarters, Karl Mantel, the chief, was preoccupied with deployment problems too: how to maintain order at Röhm's "comradeship evening" in the Löwenbräukeller and at another right-wing group's meeting in the Hofbräuhaus and, most important, provide security for Kahr and the members of the Bavarian government at the Bürgerbräu.

Mantel's position was unenviable, and not only because the force was laced with Nazi sympathizers and active Hitlerites. Almost as vexing was Mantel's ambiguous authority, limited by the convolutions and complexities of bureaucracy.

On the one hand, he was head of Munich's blue-uniformed municipal police, a contingent of 1,500 men. But its duties were limited to directing traffic, catching petty crooks, keeping drunks off the streets, settling family squabbles, issuing passports, resident permits, and all manner of licenses. Moreover, it was ill-equipped. Radio communication was in its embryonic stage and the telephone in its infancy, at least as a police tool. Though some police were mounted and some had bicycles, there were virtually no motor vehicles. Patrolmen did duty and chased criminals on foot, and when circumstances dictated that they really hurry, they hopped aboard one of Munich's blue-and-white trolley cars.

Simultaneously, Mantel was the local civilian director—within Munich's city limits—of Colonel Hans von Seisser's green-uniformed, division-sized and heavily armed Bavarian State Police, which was under the jurisdiction of Bavaria's ministry of interior. Virtually a successor to the old royal army, it had its own battle order of regiments, battalions, companies, and platoons commanded by officers with military ranks, the senior ones all field-grade veterans of the war. Its enlisted men and lower-ranking noncoms were billeted soldierlike in barracks and caserns, and they regarded themselves as soldiers, not policemen. Though its three Munich-based cavalry and infantry battalions, each with 400 men, and two mechanized and armored companies, could be called in for help by Mantel, with approval of the interior minister to whom he was also subordinate, he could not command or issue them orders. That was the prerogative of Seisser's colonels, lieutenant colonels, majors, and captains, a number of whom had their staff offices a flight above Mantel's second-floor suite in the Ett Strasse building.

Röhm's Löwenbräukeller rally and the meeting in the Hofbräuhaus were routine events that had been scheduled two days earlier with police approval. A few patrolmen, Mantel estimated, would suffice to keep order. But General Commissioner von Kahr's speech, to which the city's moneyed, journalistic, and political power brokers had been invited, seemed a knottier problem.

Mantel knew Kahr wanted protection and quick suppression of any disturbances by hecklers or brawlers in the beerhall. On the other hand, for political and image reasons, Kahr had opposed any overt or overbearing display of police power in and around the Bürgerbräukeller.

Seisser had offered a company of State Police troopers, and one of Mantel's aides had arranged with Korbinian Reindl, the Bürgerbräu innkeeper, to station them in a smaller banquet hall leading off the vestibule and main auditorium. But Kahr personally had rejected the arrangement that morning as "too obtrusive." Mantel was told to post the troopers more discreetly—in an old cavalry barracks on Morassi Strasse on the left bank of the Isar, some ten to fifteen minutes' march from the beer cellar—closer if they double-timed up the hill.

He also ordered two nearby precinct stations—one on Weissenburger Platz, the other on Zeppelin Strasse—to be augmented by fifteen additional "blue" patrolmen each. Beyond that, Mantel assigned twelve plainclothesmen for duty within the auditorium, though, unknown to him, several were hard-core Nazi party activists. Moreover, Seisser would be on the stage, and a number of his top officers, including Colonel Josef Banzer and Major Franz Hunglinger, would be in the hall. So would Mantel himself and a half dozen of his top civilian deputies.

In fact, so many of Mantel's aides intended to accompany him, among them the two most senior civil servants, Otto Bernreuther and Georg Rauh, that only one ranking official would be left at the Ett Strasse headquarters: Frick, the chief of political surveillance. Kahr's speech, he had said, didn't really interest him and would surely be printed in the papers next morning, so he would be glad to "stand in this evening" for the other gentlemen.

To be sure, there were others not going. Baron Sigmund von Imhoff, a State Police major, would be in the building teaching a class of younger officers the techniques of riot control. Friedrich Tenner, another ranking Ett Strasse civil servant, and State Police Lieutenant Colonel Wilhelm Muxel were both counting on quiet family dinners at home. So were von Lossow's three top subordinates: Major Generals Jakob von Danner, Munich city garrison commandant; Baron Friedrich Kress von Kressenstein, the Seventh Division artillery commander; and Adolf von Ruith, the division's chief of infantry. Kressenstein's chief-of-staff, Major Max Schwandner, was going to a lecture on German trade with America, and von Lossow's staff chief, Lieutenant Colonel Otto von Berchem, had a dinner engagement. Assistant District Attorney Hans Ehard, not particularly interested in politics, also would be staying home, with his wife, Annedore, and their small son, Carlhans. His fellow prosecutor, Wilhelm Hoegner, a rising star in the Social Democratic party, had an urgent meeting with the party's Bavarian leader, Erhard Auer, in the editorial offices of the SPD daily, the *Münchener Post*.

Many other Müncheners, of course, also had different plans— *Fidelio* at the opera, *Madame Pompadour* at the Operetta Theater, or perhaps a light comedy at the Schauspielhaus on Maximilian Strasse where Carl Zuckmayer was working behind the scenes. Indeed, not even two of Hitler's closest cronies, Heinrich Hoffmann and Dietrich Eckart, a middle-aged, virulently anti-Semitic writer known for his tomes on folkish Nordic and Teutonic themes, were going to the Bürgerbräu. Instead, they planned to play cards and drink beer at the Schelling Salon.

Nonetheless, Kahr could count on a full house—fuller than anyone had expected—and Hitler could bank on a lucrative catch. Considering that he had always believed a weekend to be the best time for a putsch because "everybody will be off his guard," he couldn't have chosen a better weekday night.

While Mantel was still busy with security arrangements, Gustav von Kahr himself was in his neo-Gothic official residence on Maximilian Strasse, rehearsing the speech his ghost-writers—editors Schiedt and Gerlich—had composed. But he was also waiting for the arrival of Seisser and Lossow, who would join him in a meeting with a man whose pressuring him to "act" had been making him more nervous and uncomfortable day by day: Erich Ludendorff. It was four o'clock when the stiff-backed, mask-faced general was driven up to the gate of Kahr's General State Commissariat in a Reichswehr staff car which Lossow had graciously sent out to Solln-Ludwigshöhe for him.

Ludendorff had requested the meeting—for himself and Hitler. But Kahr would see only him. Its purpose according to Ludendorff, and in his words, was "to find out from Kahr, personally and directly, just where he stood and what he intended to do." The aim according to Kahr, and in his words, "To convince His Excellency that the time was not yet ripe." But both really had a common goal: toppling the hated Reich government of President Friedrich Ebert and Chancellor Gustav Stresemann in Berlin and replacing it with a new "patriotic" regime to restore Germany's "honor and glory."

As Ludendorff saw it, "both gentlemen, Kahr and Lossow, were in total agreement with me, not only on the goal but the way to achieve it": by which he meant a march on Berlin. They disagreed, according to Ludendorff, only on the timing and the details, and he exhorted them to lose no time "because the yearning and need of the people are so great." But it was apparent to him that Kahr and Lossow "were hesitant, not yet ready, and wanted to procrastinate." As Kahr saw it, "the creation of a new Reich government from Bavaria was impossible" without the active support and cooperation of "nationalistic and patriotically minded forces in the North." If anyone could motivate and mobilize them, Kahr implied, it would be a Prussian such as Ludendorff.

Kahr feared that unilateral action by Bavaria would spark civil war. Ludendorff, convinced of his own charisma, believed that Reichswehr troops would not shoot or resist were he at their head.

The conversation, like previous ones between Ludendorff and the Bavarian triumvirs, reached an impasse, and the meeting broke up after five o'clock. On his way back to Ludwigshöhe,

Ludendorff told the driver to stop at Scheubner-Richter's apartment on Widenmayer Strasse, a quiet tree-lined boulevard on the left bank of the Isar. He dashed inside, gave Scheubner a quick summary of the discussion in Kahr's office, then came out—to be driven home. And to wait.

By then it was shortly past 6 P.M. The sun had never broken through the heavy gray clouds all day, and night had already fallen on the city. Under the cover of that gloomy darkness, strange things began to happen.

Patrolman Georg Alban, directing traffic at Isartor Platz, was startled when a passing bicyclist called out to him, "Haven't you heard yet? *Heute nacht geht's los*—Tonight it starts."

Three blocks away, on Cornelius Strasse, Patrolman Georg Christ was surprised by the "unusual amount of traffic and activity" at Nazi party headquarters. Phoning the desk sergeant at the 12th Precinct station from a nearby call box, he reported, "A lot of passenger cars and trucks have been stopping in front of the building. People in military uniforms have been hurrying inside, dashing out again after a few minutes, and driving off."

At the intersection of Cornelius Strasse and Gärtner Platz, Patrolman Josef Bömerl, on his way home in civilian clothes, spotted Josef Berchtold, whom he knew, with a number of Stosstrupp members. When he ambled over, he heard Berchtold giving the men "instructions to close off certain streets." Noticing Bömerl, Berchtold suddenly stopped talking.

Two miles north, at the Englischer Garten Precinct station, Wilhelm Pöhlmann, a carpenter, dashed in to tell Leo Günzer, the desk sergeant, "I just saw a group of SA men, carrying a swastika flag, marching down Biedersteiner Strasse. They stopped off at a store, went in, and from inside I heard someone say, 'Alarm!' "

Near the Maximilian Bridge, Detective Inspector Anton Zahner of the 13th Precinct, also on his way home, spotted "a company of 120 Hitler men, most of them in uniform," marching across the river and uphill in the direction of the Bürgerbräu.

All these officers tried to phone in their observations to the Ett Strasse headquarters and the main political department. Most had difficulty finding anybody left who seemed to be in charge. Those who did were told, "Just relax. There's nothing to worry about. The Hitler people have been invited to Excellency von

Kahr's meeting at the Bürgerbräu, so there is nothing unusual about their activities."

If the police leadership was not taking early warning signs seriously, Wilhelm Hoegner and Erhard Auer certainly did. They were meeting with Hans Unterleitner, a Bavarian Socialist member of the Reichstag, in Auer's office in the *Münchener Post* at Altheimer Eck, a short, narrow, cobblestoned street of steep-roofed houses within shouting distance of Ett Strasse, Marienplatz, and City Hall. The paper had reappeared that morning for the first time after an eight-day ban imposed by von Kahr for having criticized his dictatorship, in particular his edict to deport non-German East European Jews from Munich. Unterleitner was planning to return to Berlin later that evening. Suddenly, Auer was told that a man wanted to see him "urgently and privately."

The visitor was a Reichswehr officer in civilian clothes—never identified—who knew and outlined to Auer many of the details of the impending putsch, warning him also that, as Socialist leader of Bavaria, he was high on the list of those the Nazis planned to arrest. "It could be tonight, it could be on the weekend," the officer said. "I've heard two versions. But the Reich government and you, Herr Auer, are in very great danger."

Auer tried, to no avail, to phone through to President Ebert, then quickly drafted a message for him which Unterleitner could carry back to Berlin. He and Hoegner decided to accompany Unterleitner to the railroad station and have supper with him there before his train was to depart at nine o'clock.

As they were walking down the steps toward the building's courtyard, they heard the sound of booted marching feet and raucous singing on the street outside. Quickly Auer doused the lights.

The three groped their way down the darkened staircase, reaching the courtyard just in time to see a formation of helmeted, rifle-toting SA troopers pass the iron-grille gate. They waited a few minutes until the street seemed safe, then left the building hurriedly in the direction of Kaufinger-Neuhauser Strasse, there to catch a streetcar that would take them to the railroad station.

A half mile from the paper's offices, in the smoky bowling alley of the Torbräu tavern, tobacconist Josef Berchtold watched the members of the Stosstrupp-Hitler assemble. Among them were Ludwig Schmied, Wilhelm Briemann, Hans Kallenbach,

Emil Maurice, Heinrich von Knobloch, Walter Hewel, and more than a hundred others, all in the special uniform of the unit that was a precursor of the dreaded SS. Dressed in field-gray tunics with black belts and swastika brassards, a death's-head symbol on their Norwegian-style ski caps, they were the toughest of the tough, the most ruthless of Hitler's private army. All were hand-picked for their viciousness and brawling ways. They believed firmly that "might is right."

"Comrades," Berchtold announced, "the hour we have all yearned for is at hand. Tonight a new Reich government will be formed by our Führer Adolf Hitler and Herr von Kahr. Before I tell you more, is there anyone who for any reason wants to withdraw from the ranks? Now is your opportunity—no questions asked."

Not a single man moved or stepped back.

"All right," Berchtold said. "I will now swear you to absolute loyalty and unquestioning obedience to me and to the Führer, no matter what our orders." The ceremony completed, he marched his men out of the tavern, back toward Gärtner Platz and Cornelius Strasse, across the river, and up the Nockherberg to the corner of Balan and St. Martin streets, where trucks with rifles, machine guns, hand grenades, and ammunition would be waiting for them.

On Jahn Strasse, piano-maker and Jungsturm leader Adolf Lenk walked across the street from his father's shop to a school playground to inspect his motley troop of fuzzy-cheeked teenage Hitler youths.

In his official apartment on Maximilian Strasse, Gustav von Kahr stood stiffly awkward, trying to read through the speech once more as his daughter brushed lint from his frock coat.

At the university, Professor Karl Alexander von Müller, having just held his last lecture, walked into his office, took his hat and coat from the corner cloak stand, and left the building hurriedly to catch a trolley that would take him to the Bürgerbräukeller to hear Kahr's talk.

There, in the beerhall, Korbinian Reindl, irritated by the last-minute request, negotiated with a tall, thin, bushy-browed young man—Rudolf Hess—who insisted on renting "the little side room" that evening for Herr Hitler. Virtually every seat in the auditorium was already taken. Outside, on Rosenheimer Strasse, the crowd demanding admission was so large it overflowed across the streetcar tracks, prompting Chief Inspector Philipp Kiefer, the police officer in charge, to call headquarters for help and advice.

Captain Fritz Stumpf, the duty officer, promised to send reinforcements immediately—thirty more men. And Kiefer ordered the building closed for safety and fire reasons to all except those with written invitations.

Max Neunzert, the Kampfbund "communications officer," seeing that most people were wearing civilian clothes, felt embarrassed about being in uniform. He decided to "dash home to change." But the car that had brought him had disappeared. He took a streetcar.

Towering giantlike over the mob outside the entrance, a revolver bulging uncomfortably in his pocket, stood Putzi Hanfstaengl, with Larry Rue, Hubert Knickerbocker, Dorothy Thompson, and other foreign correspondents. I'll never make a revolutionary, he thought, wondering how he and the reporters would bluff their way through the police cordon without invitations. And where was Hitler? Why hadn't he arrived on time?

In fact, Hitler, wearing dark trousers and a formal cutaway coat, was still fidgeting nervously in his drab Thiersch Strasse apartment as bodyguard Ulrich Graf tried to pin the "EK-I"—his Iron Cross 1st Class—on that improbable-looking garment. "Hurry," he told Graf. "There is much to do. We have to return to Schelling Strasse and pick up the others."

And there, Julius Schreck, twenty-five, SA master sergeant and chief clerk, sat at his desk typing. The door burst open with a crash. It was Göring, wearing a belted rubber raincoat over his uniform, his Pour le Mérite on a ribbon around his thick neck, and a steel helmet with a huge painted swastika. "Schreck," he bellowed, "what are you doing, man? It is time. Get dressed! Get your pistol, quick!"

Interlude II:
The Maelstrom

November 1, 1923:

LONDON WARNS PARIS OF GERMAN PARTITION
—New York Herald

MONARCHIST FORCES AT THURINGIAN LINE

BAVARIAN SECURITY POLICE DRILLING RECRUITS
—New York Times

November 2, 1923:

LUDENDORFF ACTIVE IN MONARCHIST MOVE

General Named in Plot to Put Rupprecht on Bavarian Throne
—New York Herald

MARK PLUNGES AGAIN AS PEG IS REMOVED

Berlin Boerse in a Panic as the Rate Drops to 380 Billion to the Dollar
—New York Times

November 3, 1923:

FASCISTI MOBILIZE IN BAVARIAN HILLS

COOLIDGE FEARS FAMINE IN GERMANY THIS WINTER
—New York Herald

November 4, 1923:

**MARK SELLING HERE AT
420 BILLION TO THE DOLLAR**

—*New York Tribune*

RHINE SEPARATISTS PLAN NEW ATTACKS

—*New York Times*

November 5, 1923:

**UPRISING AGAINST REPUBLIC
PLANNED FOR WEDNESDAY**

—*New York Times*

November 6, 1923:

GERMANY SEEKS AMERICAN WHEAT

Cannot Pay Cash and Suggests Credits in U.S.

—*New York Herald*

BERLIN HUNGRY STORM BOERSE, RAID SHOPS

**Police Use Machine Guns to Disperse Mobs
Carrying on Pogroms in Jewish Quarter of Capital**

—*New York Tribune*

November 7, 1923:

700,000 IN RUHR FACE STARVATION

—*New York Herald*

BAVARIAN FASCISTI IMPATIENT

MUNICH (AP)—As Armistice Day approaches, the Bavarian military Dictator Dr. von Kahr is experiencing difficulty in his efforts to hold the Bavarian Fascisti in leash and the leaders of the moderate political factions there are inclined to view the approaching days with apprehension. . . .

The Bavarian insurgents along the Thuringian frontier are not taken seriously in competent quarters here, which believe von Kahr will be able to suppress them if the situation demands his intervention

—*New York Times*

On the morning of November 8, 1923, while the conservative *München-Augsburger Abendzeitung* was serializing the "exclusive story" of Benito Mussolini's successful takeover in Rome, the Social Democratic *Münchener Post* informed its readers that at current prices an old-age pensioner could afford to buy six loaves of bread, one pound of potatoes, and one candle per month.

The *Post*, a single copy of which cost 8 billion marks, reported the official exchange rate as 630 billion marks to $1 U.S. The price for a one-pound loaf of bread, it said, had increased nearly seventeen-fold in less than two weeks, from 1.8 to 32 billion marks, a quart of milk from 3 to 25 billion, a pound of meat from around 5 to 50 billion, and a one-liter stein of beer from 3.3 billion to 42 billion. Starting November 10, a ride on a Munich streetcar—depending on the number of zones—would cost from 5 to 10 billion marks. Unemployment compensation would also be raised—to a weekly 21 billion for men, 16.8 billion for women, and 6.2 billion a week for each dependent child.

"In recent days," the paper reported, "many bakeries have been closed all day long and it has been impossible to obtain bread." The reason: bakers could not afford to buy flour.

When bread was available, people had to carry money by the basketful to pay for it. Currency was inflating so rapidly, and prices rising so fast, that Germans in those autumnal days literally rushed to spend their paychecks, lest the money they had just received lost even more value before closing time. Money was being printed as quickly as the presses could turn, in increasingly giddying, astronomical denominations: millions, billions, trillions. It had no meaning.

How meaningless was revealed trenchantly by a cartoon in the satirical weekly *Simpliccisimus*, depicting a little girl sitting on the street beside two huge bundles of paper money, weeping pitifully. "Why are you crying?" a passer-by asked. Her reply: "Someone stole the straps off my money."

Munich, Bavaria, Germany were a city, a state, a nation abject, in turmoil and seething with anger. And not merely because of runaway inflation, economic chaos, hunger, or rampant unemployment which, in Munich, idled 25 percent of the work force.

In January, to extract reparations on which Germany had been in default, the French government of Premier Raymond

Poincaré had sent troops to occupy the industrial, vital Ruhr Basin. In response, President Friedrich Ebert's government had resorted, for nine months, to the weapons of general strike and passive resistance. Five years after the 1918 Armistice, France and Germany were virtually in an undeclared war.

The French were fomenting secession and openly supporting separatist movements in the Rhineland and in Bavaria's erstwhile territory, the Palatinate. Vest-pocket republics, forged by mercenaries and guerilleros, were sprouting like measles. In Saxony and Thuringia, meanwhile, Communist and left-wing extremist regimes had come to power. And Bavaria was in open defiance of the central government in Berlin.

Worst of all, though the 1918 revolution and armistice had brought Germany democracy and peace, a small majority or a large minority of the Germans—it being before the age of scientific poll-taking—wanted neither. Refusing to concede their old Empire's inner moral decay and military inferiority, they equated democracy and peace with defeat and humiliation, with a horrendous crime against the values, symbols, traditions, and institutions they regarded as quintessentially German and as Germany's historic due. In their eyes, the instigators and perpetuators of democracy and peace—whether Social Democrats such as President Friedrich Ebert or conservatives such as Chancellors Wilhelm Cuno and Gustav Stresemann—were criminals, traitors.

With such ideas rampant on November 8, 1923, Munich was a political, economic, and emotional maelstrom. The forces that created the turbulence had been at work for precisely five years.

Revolution had come earlier to Munich and Bavaria than to the rest of Germany—by some thirty-six hours—on November 7, 1918. It had begun, ironically, on the Theresienwiese, traditional site of the famous annual Oktoberfest, and at first it was less violent than that sudsy and raucous perennial beer bust—almost a comic opera. The leaders, many of them Jewish, were pacifist intellectuals and literati, most notable among them Kurt Eisner, a fearful-looking gnome of a man with a mop of unkempt shoulder-length hair, a wild and ragged red beard, and myopic eyes behind pince-nez. These men represented the Independent Socialist party, which held Germany to blame for the war and had broken with the moderate mainstream of the Social Democrats, headed in Bavaria by Erhard Auer, over the issue of support for the Kaiser's war effort.

That afternoon both Auer and Eisner had joined forces for a peace rally on the Theresienwiese that drew a crowd of many thousands. The demonstration was just about to culminate in a silent march through the city when one of Eisner's followers, carrying a red flag, jumped on the stage and shouted, "Off to the barracks! Long live the Revolution!"

Within a few hours—there was no resistance and not a shot was fired—Eisner's group occupied the military and police barracks, government ministries, and the Bavarian parliament building. There Eisner was proclaimed head of a "Workers' and Soldiers' Soviet" and named himself provisional president and prime minister of the "People's Republic of Bavaria."

Under cover of darkness, and without formally abdicating, septuagenarian King Ludwig III and his family fled the ornate Residenz by car for one of their castles near Berchtesgaden.

Nonviolent as its beginnings were, the revolution was to end in a massacre. Eisner headed a government that was a splinter faction within a minority. He had the reluctant support of Auer's Social Democrats and the Communists, all purporting to speak for the proletarian masses—of which, however, there were few. The majority of Bavarians were conservative farmers and craftsmen, loyal to the crown and the Wittlesbach dynasty and, though relieved that the terrible war was over, in no way sympathetic to Eisner's brand of militant pacifism and internationalism—especially not the soldiers returning from the front.

One of these was Adolf Hitler, who had wept bitterly when the Kaiser abdicated and Germany conceded defeat. Returning to his adopted Munich, still on active duty as a corporal in the Bavarian infantry, he found a city that was barely recognizable and swore to avenge what he considered betrayal.

Another was Wilhelm Briemann, then a nineteen-year-old lieutenant, who would soon join Hitler's fledgling party for reasons indelibly vivid to him ever since the day he was demobilized and walked out of the barracks, in his uniform, into the arms of "a mob of Red Guards who jeered at me and tried to rip the cockade off my garrison cap."

To Briemann, it was "a bitter, unforgettable experience. I had volunteered, faced death, fought for what I had been taught was right, and defended the fatherland with my life. And now, to be insulted, to have the colors of Germany, of Bavaria, torn from my tunic and cap? If that was the new order of things, it was not for me."

Nor was it for another young right-wing officer, Count Anton Arco-Valley. On February 21, 1919, as Eisner was walking from his office in the Montgelas Palace on Promenade Platz to the nearby parliament building, actually to offer his resignation after an embarrassing election defeat, Arco stepped out of a doorway and shot and killed him. Of Jewish background, Arco had hoped to gain acceptance among his anti-Semitic monarchist peers with a "patriotic deed—the elimination of that Jewish Bolshevist traitor." In fact he turned Bavaria's revolutionary comedy into a bloody tragedy.

Within an hour of Eisner's assassination, a member of the Revolutionary Workers' Council stormed into parliament, killed a conservative deputy, and gunned down Erhard Auer, hated by the far Left more than by the Right.

Thus began Bavaria's "second revolution," a ten-week nightmare of Red and White terror. The extremists on the Left proclaimed Bavaria a "Soviet Republic." Their leaders were members of the embryonic Communist party, among them one Rudolf Egelhofer, an ex-sailor in the Kaiser's navy, who was named "supreme commander" of the republic's "Red Army."

The spirit of that regime was best expressed by Egelhofer when he said, "It saddens me to come to Munich and not see an old capitalist or officer hanging from every lamppost in town." The killing was wanton and indiscriminate, especially during the month of April 1919, and did much to drive young men such as Adolf Lenk, then an apprentice to his father in the piano-making shop, to the other end of the political spectrum. He never forgot the morning his father told him, "They killed someone right in front of the house at dawn, for nothing." Lenk went out on Jahn Strasse and saw the body of a youth, no older than he, still lying there. "He hadn't done anything wrong. He had just been walking there when he was stopped by a Red Army patrol. They shot him for no reason at all. They didn't even know his name, and they left him there to bleed to death. It was horrible."

The ruthlessness of the "second revolution" triggered the counterrevolution—led by the Einwohnerwehr, a "burgher militia" that had recently formed; by free-corps *condottieri* under Major General Franz von Epp, the erstwhile commandant of the king's honor guard; and by Reichswehr units that included Captain Ernst Röhm, soon to become known as the "Liberator of Munich." On April 30, this "White Army" mounted an offensive against Engelhofer's Reds and invaded the capital. It was, in the words of one witness, Social Democrat Wilhelm Hoegner, "a full-scale civil war with hours of artillery bombardment, an outburst of abject hatred, and with the most incredible atrocities, especially against hostages that had been taken by both sides."

On May 2, when the shooting finally stopped, 58 White troopers, 100 Reds, and nearly 2,000 noncombatants had been shot, bayoneted, kicked, axed, knifed, or bludgeoned to death.

For a while, a moderate Social Democratic government took power; but as the hatred unleashed by the "Soviet Republic" and the civil war spread and perpetuated its poison, real power in Bavaria shifted to the Right.

On the Right were the Reichswehr and its officers, the monarchists, the bureaucrats and civil servants, the police, and the many other conservatives and reactionaries who still dreamed of a "Greater Germany" and who hated the new republic that had been pronounced in Berlin, the parliamentary democracy that the constitution of Weimar had established. It was they who believed the Reich had lost the war because of a *Dolchstoss*—"stab-in-the-back"—of the military by the Socialists, Communists, anarchists, pacifists, Jewish "profiteers," and other "November criminals" on the home front: President Ebert and even the conservative chancellors and ministers who constituted his government. And their biggest "crime," next to the *Dolchstoss* itself, was their acceding to the Versailles Treaty, with its crippling demands for reparations, its limitations on arms, its restrictions on science, technology, and industry, and its provisions that deprived Germany of territory and colonies. To the German Right, the treaty was "an unacceptable *Diktat*."

The Right also came to include that great mass of demobilized soldiers and erstwhile career officers for whom a world had collapsed in 1918. Men hardened, calloused, made ruthless and violent by war, they pined for the chauvinistic society that had cheered them to battle in 1914. Hungry, ragged, demoralized, unemployed and unemployable, they listened eagerly to any demagogue and were willing recruits for any freebooter forming an army who promised them full bellies, shelter, and a little glory.

And there was no dearth of armies to join in 1919 and 1920. "Free corps" were being equipped clandestinely by many in the Reichswehr, limited to 100,000 men, who dreamed of revenge and better days. These armies went by various names, such as the Oberland Corps, Einwohnerwehr, Freikorps Epp, Rossbach Battalion, and the Ehrhardt Brigade of ex-navy Commander Hermann Ehrhardt. At first, with the silent assent—some would say connivance—of the Berlin government, they were used mainly to regain disputed territories on Germany's eastern frontiers. Before long, however, they were backing plots and putsches to overthrow the republic itself.

One such putsch took place on March 13, 1920, when Ehrhardt's brigade occupied Berlin to establish Dr. Wolfgang Kapp, an ultra-right monarchist bureaucrat, as chancellor. While the Reichswehr, under General Hans von Seeckt, did nothing, Ebert and his ministers were forced to flee. It was only when the trade unions paralyzed Berlin with a general strike that the "Kapp Putsch" collapsed.

One day later, Munich had a mini-putsch of its own. The leader of the Einwohnerwehr, the Seventh Division commander, Police Chief Ernst Pöhner, and Gustav von Kahr, the ultra-conservative regional prefect, joined forces to present the moderate Social Democratic government with an ultimatum: either resign or accept establishment of a military dictatorship. Resign they did, and von Kahr became prime minister.

In his eighteen months as prime minister, Kahr endeavored to make Bavaria an *Ordnungszelle*—a cell of law and order—within the Reich. In the process, he made Munich a mecca for all those in Germany determined to overthrow the Weimar Republic, such as Ehrhardt, Rossbach, and Ludendorff. The city became a magnet for "philosophers" of Nordic and Teutonic purity who met in the secretive "Thule Society," for fanatical anti-Semites, and for exiles from Russia such as Alfred Rosenberg and Max von Scheubner-Richter. Munich also became the den in which the assassinations of Reich Finance Minister Matthias Erzberger and Foreign Minister Walter Rathenau were plotted. The murderers, linked to Ehrhardt's organization, were shielded from investigation by Police Chief Ernst Pöhner and his most loyal apprentice, Dr. Wilhelm Frick. Confronted with the charge that entire groups of political assassins were at large in and working out of Munich, Pöhner peered icily through his pince-nez and said, "Yes . . . but too few."

It was in this climate that a minimally educated Austrian ex-corporal in the German army turned the Deutsche Arbeiterpartei, little more than a debating club when he joined it, into Bavaria's most potent and feared political movement.

Historians with a socioeconomic bent maintain that Hitler was the right man with the right message at the right time. Local partisans contend that it could have happened only in Munich because "the city is so cosmopolitan and tolerant that any crackpot who comes along will find both a platform and an audience." There is a measure of truth in both claims.

More than that, Hitler knew how to tell people what they thought they wanted to hear. "My father took me to one of his first public appearances," Adolf Lenk recalled, "and what he said just made so much sense that I stood up and cheered." Rudolf Hess, who first heard him in May 1920, was almost in a trance afterward. "Everything was so logical, so clear."

He won the veterans by using the language of the trenches. Yet, corporal though he once was, he could also mesmerize colonels and generals—a Ludendorff, an Otto von Lossow, even a Crown Prince Rupprecht. The women in his audiences wept when he spoke of the shortages of bread and potatoes and the spiraling prices. The workers clenched their fists when he railed against capitalist "profiteers" exploiting them. The small tradesmen gnashed their teeth in angry agreement when he damned the Jewish department-store owners for "stealing your customers" and the bankers for charging high interest. The patriots and chauvinists cheered when he ranted against the "Red" traitors in Berlin. Moreover, he was magnetic, almost hypnotizing. And he spoke with a rhythm and sonority that left his audiences frenzied, ready to follow him over the edge of the world.

"I marvel at his ability to speak, without notes, without tiring, for two or more hours," Professor Max von Gruber, president of the Bavarian Academy of Sciences, observed in 1921. "He has complete control of and command over his audiences, a born leader."

Karl Alexander von Müller, who had met him socially but had not yet heard him speak in public, made notes the first time: "The mass seems to arouse him, give him strength, orgiastically—pale face, bulging and burning eyes—seems possessed—a fantasizing, hysterical romanticist with a brutal inner core—clear, manly voice—biting irony—sometimes like a dramatic actor—narcotic effect."

As his following multiplied, Hitler's power and influence grew. Awkward, bumptious, eccentric, slovenly, and provincially boorish as he was in private, it was nonetheless chic to be seen and identified with him. People, especially women, vied to have him as a guest for dinner, afternoon tea, coffee and cake.

By the spring of 1923, with his huge private army of SA storm troopers, tens of thousands of dues-paying party members, and a frenetic following, Hitler was not only a dominant figure on the Bavarian political stage. His power had been enhanced by the apparent alliances he had struck with Ludendorff, Ehrhardt, the chieftains of various "patriotic leagues," Röhm, and, through Röhm, with the Reichswehr and its local commander, General von Lossow.

Then began a nine-month period of ploys and counterploys, scheming, politicking, agitating, dreaming, planning, rabble-rousing, bluffing, and intimidation, all within the specific Bavarian context and Bavaria's intense hatred of Prussia and all things Prussian. As recently as 1866, Prussia and Bavaria had been at war with each other, and in 1871 Bavaria had most reluctantly agreed to German unity under the Prussian king as German Kaiser. Even today, the unconscious reflex of any good Bavarian is to add the prefix "pig" to the word "Prussian."

Given the chaos of the Reich, there were—as General von Lossow put it in those months—three possibilities: "Either we muddle on as we have until disaster comes; or Bavaria secedes from the Reich; or we march on Berlin to proclaim a national dictatorship."

The first solution being intolerable to everyone in Munich, that left the other two. But beyond that, there was total confusion.

In a sense, everyone was conspiring with and against everybody else. Many conservatives who shared some of Hitler's beliefs and aims, were repelled by the Nazi leader's rabble-rousing. They were also put off by Ludendorff's arrogant Prussian ways and strident anti-Catholicism. Yet Ludendorff—far more than Hitler, the upstart "drummer" with his leagues of the unwashed—was the one figure of national stature around whom the entire Right, not just in Bavaria, might rally. Simultaneously, those who detested and distrusted Hitler also feared him. Reluctant to move with him, they were afraid to move against him. For his part, Hitler was distrustful and contemptuous of the establishment members. At times he regarded them as too pusillanimous; at other times he suspected they might strike on their own without him. Concurrently, his incessant agitation and propaganda at mass rallies was creating a groundswell that even he might no longer be able to control.

The man he most needed, because he had the weapons and seemed most sympathetic to Hitler's stratagem, was von Lossow. "I agree with nine of ten things that Herr Hitler says," Lossow conceded. Hitler beseeched him to move, to summon the Reichswehr to revolt, to march on Berlin and establish a dictatorship. In April he called on Lossow almost every day, in an evident attempt to hypnotize or galvanize the general into action.

In Berlin, in August 1923, Wilhelm Cuno was replaced as Reich chancellor by Gustav Stresemann, a conservative democrat who recognized reality when confronted with it. Six weeks after taking office—on September 24—he called off the passive resistance to the French occupation of the Ruhr and agreed to pay the reparations.

That action brought an outburst in Germany from both the far Left and the Right. In Saxony and Thuringia, the Communists threatened—and soon carried out—rebellions that brought them to power. In Bavaria, Hitler seethed. To him it was capitulation and compliance at their worst. If ever there was a time to march, it was now. And he would do so, if the public mood was right.

To test that mood, he came up with a sudden plan that threw the Bavarian government into panic. In September, he mobilized his 15,000 storm troopers and announced that on September 27 he would hold fourteen mass meetings and would speak at each of them. That announcement was what prompted Prime Minister von Knilling to declare a state of emergency and name von Kahr, von Lossow, and Seisser as triumvirs to enforce it. In turn, this act precipitated Ebert's declaration of a national emergency and Bavaria's open defiance of Berlin.

Throughout September and October, the crisis mounted. While von Kahr was attacking the Reich government and openly calling for its overthrow, Hitler was waxing increasingly Napoleonic and Messianic, convinced more than ever that the people needed and wanted a revolution and that he was the one to lead it. "Only one question gnaws at the German people today," he shouted in speech after speech. "When does it start?"

In a sense it already had. With von Seisser's approval, Ehrhardt had massed his brigade of irregulars and *condottieri* on the Bavarian frontier with Thuringia as a kind of auxiliary State Police and was threatening to march against the Communist government there. In Munich, Kahr was insisting that Stresemann could be ousted only in an "atypical way," by which he meant, more discreetly, what Hitler was shouting. But von Kahr did not want to take the "atypical" way with the Nazi leader. He had repeatedly extracted promises from Hitler that he would not carry out a putsch, would not act on his own.

On Tuesday, November 6, Hitler realized he could not, and decided he would not, keep that promise. Kahr, Lossow, and Seisser met that afternoon with all the leaders of the "patriotic," "fatherland," and fighting societies except Hitler himself. Hitler's close associates, Hermann Kriebel and Friedrich Weber, who attended the meeting, exhorted the triumvirs to act. But the more Hitler's collaborators insisted, the more the three balked.

"Yes," Kahr reiterated, Stresemann would have to be removed the "atypical" way; "but it must be accomplished according to a united, sufficiently prepared and thought-out plan," especially with the help of "patriotic forces in the North."

"Yes," Lossow chimed in. "We want to march. By God, how I

want to march! But only when there is a fifty-one percent guarantee of success."

Then the trio warned, in no uncertain terms, that any unilateral action by any group would be "countered by all means at our disposal, including, if necessary, the force of arms."

When Kriebel and Weber reported back that Tuesday afternoon, Hitler made up his mind. If Kahr, Lossow, and Seisser could not be persuaded to move now, he would force their hand. In public—at the Bürgerbräukeller.

TWO

The Plot As Planned

3

Hitler's red Benz touring car jerked to a halt in front of No. 39 Schelling Strasse shortly after 7:15 P.M.

"Faster!" Hitler barked at Ulrich Graf as he rushed up the stairs to the second-floor offices of the *Völkischer Beobachter* and the Kampfbund. Storming down the corridor, he yanked open doors, slammed them again. "Rosenberg! Amann!" he shouted. "Is everybody ready to go? And where is Göring?"

Finding the paunchy, uniformed storm troop leader in Julius Schreck's little room, Hitler called him out for last-minute instructions. Then, impatiently, he snapped, "You must hurry. We are running late. Everything is behind schedule, Captain Göring."

Göring drew to attention. Beckoning to his adjutant, Walter Baldenius, and to Schreck, he strode downstairs, the two SA men in his wake, and into a waiting car.

"Where to, gentlemen?" asked Michael Ried, the driver.

"We'll show you," Göring snapped.

They sped through the city, across the river, and toward the grounds of a factory on Balan Strasse, just a few blocks from the Bürgerbräukeller, deliberately choosing a "roundabout way so that we would not have to drive past the beerhall." As the car thundered through an unusually dark side street, Schreck and Baldenius opened an oblong crate on the back seat. Gingerly they took out some stick grenades and two tommy guns.

At the secluded, dimly lit factory yard on the corner of Balan and St. Martin streets, tobacconist Josef Berchtold, Wilhelm Briemann, Ludwig Schmied, the other members of the Stosstrupp, and several hundred additional SA troopers were milling impatiently and nervously around four huge stake-body trucks loaded with rifles, heavy machine guns, and many boxes of hand grenades and ammunition. They were waiting for Göring, without whom the arms could not be passed out and who was to give the final orders and instructions.

"He's never on time," Berchtold grumbled to Jungsturm leader Adolf Lenk, who also had arrived with several dozen teenage troopers.

Hitler, too, was getting increasingly nervous as he conferred with Alfred Rosenberg and Max Amann at the Schelling Strasse headquarters.

"Have you drafted those proclamations and is everything set for a special edition?" Hitler asked the paper's editor-in-chief. "Are there enough typists and secretaries on night duty?" Testily, Rosenberg assured him that all was ready.

Turning to Amann, Hitler said, "I assume you've arranged for those extra offices on Kanal Strasse for the new government. Have the printers for the posters been notified?"

Amann nodded. "Everything is set, Adolf. Only Streicher is not yet here. If he took the one forty-five express from Nürnberg, he should have arrived nearly three hours ago. I told him to be here no later than seven o'clock. We can't wait for him any longer." The news disappointed Hitler. Julius Streicher's Jew-baiting had a special sting, and he was an effective platform propagandist. Hitler very much wanted him along. But it was really time to go.

Max von Scheubner-Richter stopped by briefly for last-minute consultations, accompanied as always by his faithful manservant, Johann Aigner. Then everybody left for the Bürgerbräu in two cars, Rosenberg, Amann, and Graf, his handlebar mustache specially brushed that evening, in Hitler's. As they drove off, Rosenberg peered at his watch, barely illuminated by a dim, flickering streetlamp. It was seven forty-five.

The 3,000-seat Bürgerbräu auditorium was jammed to bursting with a standing-room-only crowd. Tables and chairs had been pushed so close together that the buxom waitresses, clusters of beer steins clenched in their hands, could barely shove their way through the horde.

Ferdinand Schreiber, the printer, saw his competitor, Anton Schmidt, and asked to share his chair. They compared notes on the odd call from Philipp Bouhler that afternoon.

Georg Stumpf and Georg Ott, two off-duty police detectives present as invited guests and veterans of the 1919 Einwohner-wehr, hunted in vain for a seat on the balcony that ringed the hall. Finally they decided on the steps leading up to it as a good vantage point.

Georg Rauh, Otto Bernreuther, and other top police officials arrived together with their chief, Karl Mantel. Bernreuther and Mantel had reserved seats at the head table, but Rauh had to fend for himself. Turning to Chief Inspector Philipp Kiefer for help, he found him in conversation with Inspector Siegfried Herrmann. "Have you heard a rumor that Hitler plans to break up the meeting?" Kiefer was asking just as Rauh approached. Abruptly Herrmann changed the subject. "Ah, let me see if I can find a good place for Herr Rauh." He didn't answer Kiefer's question, and this troubled Rauh, but the thought passed from his mind as he hunted for a place to sit, finally settling uncomfortably atop a serving counter near the kitchen.

Karl Alexander von Müller, having squeezed through the throng outside and gotten past the police cordon thanks to his formal invitation, was luckier. A friend, Robert Riemerschmied, had saved a place for him near the platform. As he fought his way to it, he was perplexed by the strange mix and size of the audience: far more, he thought to himself, than Kahr had expected or even wanted. There was something ominously electric about the atmosphere.

Peering through the dense haze of acrid cigar, cigarette, and pipe smoke, he spotted many familiar and prominent faces: Prime Minister Eugen von Knilling and three members of his cabinet, Interior Minister Franz Schweyer, Justice Minister Franz Gürtner, and Agriculture Minister Johann Wutzelhofer; former Police Chief Ernst Pöhner; Count Josef Soden, Crown Prince Rupprecht's chef-du-cabinet.

It was an audience of the notable, important, and influential—an establishment crowd: many of the men stiffly uniformed and bemedaled, the women bosomy and bejeweled. There were even a few who were Jewish, though Kahr had originally asked Munich businessman Eugen Zentz, the meeting's sponsor and organizer, not to invite "any Jews." Zentz had balked at that, "considering, Excellency, that a number of them are your stanchest supporters."

But there were also hundreds of people who, von Müller was certain, had not been invited and who had streamed into the beer-hall before the police closed it off. He was surprised, especially, by the inordinate number of Kampfbund and Nazi party leaders. And hadn't he seen one of his students, Rudolf Hess, in the uniform of the old Bavarian army, standing awkwardly out in the cloakroom, apparently waiting? But waiting for what?

As von Müller surveyed the scene, scribbling notes for his diary as usual, the audience became increasingly impatient and annoyed. It was almost eight o'clock, and the invitations had read seven-thirty. Where was von Kahr? And why wasn't the beer getting around faster? There were angry shouts of "Down in front! We can't see!" and equally testy retorts of "Why? What's there to see? Didn't you come to hear?"

Outside, in the garden and on Rosenheimer Strasse, the crowd was growing larger by the minute and Putzi Hanfstaengl more nervous by the second. There was still no sign of Hitler, without whom he had no chance of entering the building. The police were letting in only invited guests and VIPs whom they recognized. Hanfstaengl and the foreign correspondents weren't in that league, and when German cops have their orders, he knew, no words will move them. On the other hand, he thought, there had been no sign of Kahr, Lossow, or Seisser either. He tried to keep up spirits and interest with small talk.

Suddenly a Reichswehr staff car pulled up: the triumvirate. And moments after it came Hitler's caravan—the red Benz in the lead, Scheubner-Richter's cabriolet behind it.

The rush of people pressed toward von Kahr, beseeching him to be let in, but without a word or even a look around, the stocky, swarthy little man strode through the aisle the police were cordoning for him. Then the crowd spotted Hitler and turned to him. Couldn't *he* do something?

"I am just a guest myself," he pleaded helplessly. But the size of the throng and the many police worried him. Would Göring and Berchtold get their trucks and troopers through that mob? Approaching an officer he knew, Hitler suggested that since the meeting was starting and the hall filled, he clear the street and reduce the security contingent. Gesturing toward Hanfstaengl, the correspondents, Rosenberg, Amann, Graf, and Scheubner, he added sharply, "And these people are coming in with me!" They trotted dutifully at Hitler's heels. In the entrance, relief written all over his face, stood Hess.

Hanfstaengl was bringing up the rear with Dorothy Thompson when suddenly the beerhall door slammed shut again. "But this lady represents an important American newspaper," he bellowed menacingly at the spike-helmeted guard barring the way. "If she does not get in to hear what Herr von Kahr is saying, there will be a tremendous scandal." The argument, despite Hanfstaengl's impressive height, fell on apparently deaf and impassive ears; but a proffered American cigarette, a luxury in the Munich of those days, persuaded the policeman to step aside.

The applause was cordial though subdued as Kahr, Lossow, and Seisser, accompanied by a retinue of waiting aides and adjutants, inched their way slowly forward to the stage. The *Chicago Tribune*'s Larry Rue and the *Baltimore Sun*'s Hubert Knickerbocker, still hoping to find a seat somewhere, followed behind them.

But Hitler and his party took up positions against a pillar near the auditorium's main door, some 30 yards from the platform. Hitler, still wearing his trenchcoat over the cutaway, nervously fingered the Browning revolver in his pocket. Clutching all the trillion-mark bills he had with him, Hanfstaengl strolled nonchalantly to a serving window and bought half-liter mugs of beer for his Führer, Amann, and himself. No use just standing around, he thought. Besides, with a beer in hand, Hitler would look less obvious.

As the drone of a thousand conversations muted into silence, Eugen Zentz walked stiffly to the rostrum to introduce von Kahr. "Your Excellency," he orated in a thick Bavarian brogue, "we want to welcome you in this gravest hour of our Fatherland, on the anniversary of the greatest crime ever committed against the

German people. No matter what differences there may be among us in this circle, three words unite us: 'Loyal,' 'German,' 'Bavarian.' Those words express what we honor in you, Your Excellency. We want to tell you that we all stand behind you loyally.

... A leader's strength is the loyalty of his following. Excellency! Be our leader on the road to a new, better, red-white-and-black Germany, and we shall follow you willingly, wherever you take us!"

"But without Jews!" someone shouted as a stormy ovation thundered through the hall.

Kahr, wearing an old-fashioned frock coat drooping at the shoulders and too long at the sleeves, his hair parted primly in the middle, his thick mustache at half-mast, his fat neck sunk into a high celluloid collar, strutted awkwardly to the lectern. All eyes were on him. In name he was a dictator. Zentz had just eulogized him as a great leader. But he was an administrator, a bureaucrat at heart, with, at best, the cunning mentality of a square-headed peasant. No statesman this, not even a politician. His small eyes peered nervously at the vast sea of faces. Then a hush fell over the audience as he began reading methodically, almost mumbling, from his voluminous manuscript. The only sounds in the huge auditorium besides his monotonous voice were an occasional slurping of beer and smacking of lips. The silence soon became the wordlessness of boredom. All had come to hear a decisive, epochal pronouncement. Instead, von Kahr bumbled on dryly, incomprehensibly, about the evils of Marxism as if reciting a doctoral dissertation.

Adolf Hitler, leaning against a pillar under the balcony in the back, gnawed at a fingernail and took a long, thoughtful swig of his beer. Briefly and disdainfully he glanced toward the platform and von Kahr, then looked expectantly at the enormous door to the auditorium.

Innkeeper Korbinian Reindl, rushing into the kitchen to speed up service, barely noticed the Nazi leader, but he was surprised to find two young men in storm trooper uniform—Wilhelm Kolb and Rolf Reiner—hovering over, almost guarding, the telephone there.

"We're waiting for a call," Kolb lied convincingly.

The crowd outside the Bürgerbräukeller had dispersed in disappointment and only a dozen blue-uniformed policemen remained on duty, among them Patrolman Johann Bruckmeier. The traffic was sparse. Periodically a streetcar creaked and rattled up or down the steep street. After the initial excitement, it seemed to Bruckmeier that it would be a quiet night after all.

Suddenly he heard the sound of jogging, booted feet. Looking up, he noticed two steel-helmeted men with submachine guns dash past the entrance to the beerhall. They looked around furtively, trotted downhill a few yards to where Rosenheimer Strasse curves toward Ludwig Bridge, stopped a moment, peered into a dimly lit side street, then double-timed back, past the Bürgerbräu toward Rosenheimer Platz.

They must be Reichswehr soldiers, Bruckmeier thought. But why at this hour? And why here?

"The quintessential evil of Marxism"—von Kahr was rambling on—"is that it raises man's expectations by pandering to his innate indolence on the one hand, and on the other by proclaiming that he has a right to all the material goods of our earth without work or any effort on his part."

Hanfstaengl yawned, bent down to the man standing next to him, and whispered, "Do you think a government like his can last long?" The man shrugged his shoulders. "Well, I'll tell you something." Putzi pressed the point. "I don't think it can last twenty-four hours more or even twelve. In fact, it cannot last even *one* more hour." Startled, the man looked up.

Hitler slowly walked out of the main hall to the vestibule and cloakroom, took off his trenchcoat, handed it to Graf, and went into a huddle with Amann, Rosenberg, Scheubner-Richter, Hermann Kriebel, and Friedrich Weber, who had been waiting there. Then, the beer mug in one hand, he fished for his pocketwatch with the other and began counting the minutes: 8:25 . . . 8:26 . . . 8:27 . . .

4

Hermann Esser barely recognized himself when he looked into the mirror to knot his tie; his face and eyes had the pronounced yellow tint of the jaundice that had kept him in bed for almost three weeks. The muscles in his arms and legs ached with every movement. He knew he was still running too high a fever to be going out into the cold, to stand on a platform and speak. Couldn't Hitler have picked another night? Yet he had promised to substitute for him at Röhm's Löwenbräukeller "reunion"—for appearance's sake and as a ruse.

But if this was going to be the night of Germany's rebirth and reawakening, he decided as he struggled into his coat, it would have to be without him. As soon as the message came—"Safe Delivery," wasn't that the code?—he would let Röhm take over and return home to bed.

When Friedrich Mayer of the SA's 10th Company arrived, as ordered, at the dingy Amberger Hof on Cornelius Strasse near Nazi party headquarters, he still did not know the purpose of the "alert" but found the tavern crowded with nearly 300 other storm troopers. Most of them seemed not to know each other. Mayer decided to have a beer.

Suddenly—it was around seven forty-five—Hans Knauth, commander of the SA's Third Battalion, called them to attention and told them to assemble on the street outside. "We are marching to the Arzbergerkeller near Stiglmaier Platz," he announced. "From there we will go to the Löwenbräukeller, where Ernst Röhm is holding a comradeship evening at which Adolf Hitler will speak. Fall in!"

Then, with swastika banners waving and everyone singing "battle songs loudly," Knauth marched the battalion through downtown Munich to their next staging point.

Karl Beggel, commander of the SA's First Battalion, had rushed to the Arzbergerkeller right after work but found the beer-hall almost empty. Only a few members of his battalion were there—at a table near a far corner—and he joined them to have a beer. None was in uniform and, like Beggel himself, none knew why he had been called. One beer led to a second and then a third.

"I can't figure what it's all about," he admitted to the little group. "But why don't we wait here for a while?"

Just then his orderly rushed in, breathless. "Direct orders from the high command—Göring. We are supposed to go to the Nineteenth Infantry Regiment barracks immediately, in uniform. They say that it's a special night training exercise and that we'll get arms there."

Beggel ordered his men to go home, change, and meet him at the barracks, then waited while the orderly brought him his SA cap, windbreaker, and pistol belt from his nearby apartment.

Feeling more properly dressed in the official regalia, he was just about to leave and walk the mile or so to the barracks near Munich's Oberwiesenfeld airfield when he heard Knauth's Third Battalion approach the Arzbergerkeller singing lustily. Not stopping to ask where they were headed, he dashed off with his orderly in tow.

The Wurzer Hof tavern, around the corner from the luxurious Vier Jahreszeiten Hotel, was a favorite hangout of the Munich SA regiment and was jam-packed with uniformed steel-helmeted storm troopers when Hans Frank of the Second Battalion arrived. Pushing his way through the carousing mob, he hunted for the battalion commander, Edmund Heines, to report for duty.

"We are on alert," said Heines, eyeing the young law student approvingly. Frank, he knew, was not an ordinary trooper but a veteran of the Epp Free Corps and one of the charter members of the party. "We shall be going to the Bürgerbräukeller, where the Führer personally will be awaiting us. There is to be an important national demonstration there."

Frank suspected that more was involved. Through the haze of smoke, he recognized some of the faces in the crowd: Kurt Neubauer, a member of the battalion, who was General Ludendorff's personal servant and orderly, and none other than Gerhard Rossbach, the former free-corps leader. As Frank ordered a foamy stein for himself, he watched Heines and Rossbach huddling in a corner.

"I need about a half dozen of your men—on loan," Rossbach was saying. "Special orders from Göring. I will take them to the Infantry School, where the cadets are already mobilizing and waiting for me to assume command."

"Choose the best," Heines replied.

Rossbach selected a small group. Hans Frank was not one of them. There would be other "special tasks" for him that night.

Three blocks from the Wurzer Hof tavern, in the National Theater, the curtain had just rung down on the first act of *Fidelio*, Hans Knappertsbusch had left the pit, and the audience—most of the men in white tie, the women in evening gowns—moved slowly toward the opulent foyers where buffet tables offered canapés and glasses of champagne, selling at almost 200 billion marks each.

Bavaria's Social Democratic leader Erhard Auer, Reichstag Deputy Hans Unterleitner, and Wilhelm Hoegner sat over their supper in the station restaurant, waiting for the departure of Unterleitner's train.

The ominous warning from Auer's visitor earlier that evening and the gang of storm troopers that had marched past the *Münchener Post* preoccupied the three men. Perhaps I'm overreacting, Hoegner thought. After all, Nazi toughs on the march—though not usually armed—had been a common sight on the streets of Munich for months. Yet he felt uneasy. There was something unusual about the evening—even the peculiar way a few of the waiters in the restaurant were eyeing Auer and Unterleitner, both well known in Munich.

Looking long at Auer, Hoegner said, "It might be prudent for you to spend the night at my place. The Nazis hardly know me and wouldn't think of hunting for you there. My wife would be pleased to put you up, and it will be no trouble at all."

"Let me think about that," Auer replied.

The 19th Infantry Regiment headquarters was almost deserted. Most enlisted men were out on pass, and the married noncoms and officers were in their quarters in the drab apartment blocks on Infanterie, Barbara, and Elizabeth streets. Only a handful were on duty, among them Gerhard Böhm, a chief warrant officer. His task for the evening was to give close-order drill to some 150 members of the Herrmann Bund, one of the less militant right-wing "patriotic fighting societies." The main drill hall, a cavernous building for indoor parading, was supposed to be available to them.

To his surprise and consternation, he found a contingent much larger than he had expected—by almost fifty men.

"Are you *all* from the Herrmann Bund?" Böhm asked.

"No, no. We're Oberland League." Some of the uniformed troopers laughed in indignant protest at being compared with such "amateurs." Their leader explained to Böhm that they had assembled there for a roll-call and would be leaving "on a night exercise as soon as our battalion commander, Captain Hans Oemler, arrives."

Böhm wondered how they had gotten into the barracks, but before he could explore the mystery more deeply, a gate guard rushed in, snapped to attention, saluted, and stammered, "Herr Chief Warrant Officer, there's an entire company of Oberland people without valid ID cards outside. They want their leader to come out and get them."

"Just for a roll-call? Tonight? Here?" Böhm asked incredulously, but finally gave orders to let them in.

Within the next half hour, as Böhm was trying to do his job, some 250 men in a motley assortment of uniforms sauntered into the building, among them Karl Beggel of the SA's First Battalion and 60 of his storm troopers. Turning to Beggel, who had been a 19th Infantry Regiment sergeant during the war, Böhm asked irritably, "What's going on, Karl? Your people and the Oberländers aren't supposed to be here tonight. I have my orders and they say I've got this hall to myself. There's no room left to drill."

"Don't get so ruffled," Beggel flashed back. "We have our orders too. We won't be here long. As soon as Oemler arrives, we'll be out of your way to go over to the Oberwiesenfeld for training."

"All right," Böhm grumbled. "But tomorrow morning I intend to make a report to the CO. Your people can't just wander in and out of the barracks whenever they please. You aren't regular army yet—just auxiliaries. There has to be some kind of control and order around here."

Angrily, he put the Herrmann Bund volunteers through their paces on the dwindling floor space left to him, hoping that Oemler, a much-decorated former army captain, would appear to take his ruffians away. After all, it was already 8 P.M.

Hans Oemler was having a different problem at that moment—just 50 yards away—on the dimly lit parade ground of the
Engineer Barracks. There, he and Max von Müller, an ex-major
who commanded another Oberland battalion, were arguing with
Reichswehr Captain Oskar Cantzler over the rifles and machine
guns with which Oemler's and Müller's troops were supposed to
hold their "night exercise."

As the 400 Oberländers listened incredulously to the loud exchange between "officers and gentlemen," Cantzler said emphatically, "I will *not* unlock that armory. I will *not* release your weapons."

Cantzler had good reasons. Thrice weekly for the past few
months—on Tuesdays, Thursdays, and Saturdays—Müller's and
Oemler's Oberländers, as well as members of Edmund Heines's
Second SA Battalion, had been training in the Engineer Barracks
as forbidden reservists of the Reichswehr. Technically, the weapons with which they exercised belonged to them "privately," not
to the army—a devious ploy to circumvent the Versailles Treaty
and hoodwink the Allied control officers in the Vier Jahreszeiten
Hotel. It was a clandestine arrangement in which Ernst Röhm had
played an instrumental role as Seventh Division ordnance officer.

As the Oberländers' training officer, Cantzler was responsible
for the safekeeping and safe deployment of their weapons. He
had strict orders, moreover, that the weapons used in training
must never be loaded and that the "auxiliaries" were not to be
issued ammunition. That afternoon, however, on a routine inspec-
tion tour, he had caught a squad of Müller's Oberländers belting
up with, and apparently squirreling away, machine-gun ammo. It
was a violation of regulations, not to mention, as Cantzler put it,
"a breach of faith and trust." By the time Müller and Oemler had
arrived with their troops for the scheduled "night exercise" on the
Oberwiesenfeld, Cantzler was livid—and adamant.

How often, he wondered, had the Oberländers and Nazi
storm troopers been in the armory without his knowledge, and
how much ammunition had they stashed away somewhere? "Because of what happened this afternoon," he told Müller and
Oemler sharply, "I will not permit those arms to leave this area.

You can either march your troops out of here and cancel tonight's session, or you can practice with the weapons indoors in the drill hall. But not outside."

Müller, an erstwhile career officer, was a highly excitable man. He railed, ranted, and hurled invectives at Cantzler. The more he blustered, the more Cantzler stood his ground. He was beginning to think that Müller had "ulterior motives"—other than "just a night exercise" on the nearby field.

"No man will leave this barracks with a weapon in hand," he barked, "and what's more, no weapon will be handed out until all of your men are inside that drill hall over there."

Thus began an impasse that was to last for hours, one that, in its seemingly trivial and coincidental way, was to change the course of history that night.

It was also eight o'clock when Gerhard Rossbach, accompanied by six of Heines's storm troopers, arrived at the Reichswehr Infantry School on Blutenburg Strasse.

The welcome mat was out for him, as he knew it would be. For weeks he had been carefully cultivating the cadets, candidates, and student officers, as well as those few instructors, such as Major Hans Fischbach and Colonel Ludwig Leupold, who were sympathetic to the Nazi cause. He had become a habitué of their favorite taverns, clubs, and dueling fraternities and had recruited some 80 to 100 of them as a core of loyal followers. They in turn had almost no difficulty in mobilizing virtually all the school's 400 students that evening.

Lieutenants Robert Wagner, Hans Block, and Siegfried Mahler were already waiting eagerly for Rossbach when he entered the red brick barracks complex. "We are ready for you to take command," Wagner said enthusiastically, clicking his booted heels and saluting snappily. Almost the entire school was lined up in companies, outfitted in combat uniforms and armed for battle with rifles, bayonets, hand grenades, and several light machine guns.

Passing out the Nazi flags and swastika armbands that he had brought with him, Rossbach announced cockily—and prematurely, "A new national government under Hitler and Ludendorff has been formed. Most of the Reichswehr stands behind it. You have the honor to be named a special storm detachment for His Excellency General Ludendorff." Hoarse shouts of wild approval thundered across the parade ground.

Most of the school's senior officers and instructors were away for the evening. But those who were not and who tried to dissuade their charges from following Rossbach were dealt with quickly. "Gentlemanly" but "firmly and in unmistakable fashion" they were placed under house arrest.

One of them was Major General Hans Tieschowitz von Tieschowa, the school's commandant. Hearing the commotion and shouting in the courtyard, Tieschowitz had rushed out of his quarters to see what was going on. In the corridor he was suddenly stopped by Hans Block and three other young officers. Block announced the new government and the school's role as an honor guard for Ludendorff, then asked stiffly, "Where do you stand, Herr General?"

"I have no information that supports your claims," he replied tersely, "but even if I did, I would adhere to the oath of loyalty I have sworn to the constitutional government of Germany. It is also apparent, however, that I can do nothing to interfere with your plans."

"It is best that you don't," said Block, gesturing toward the SA men who had dashed into the hallway to stand guard. "Please do not attempt to leave this room."

With all potential opponents thus safely locked away, the Infantry School students—Rossbach in the lead—prepared to march out of their barracks in the direction of the Bürgerbräukeller.

Hans Knauth's Third SA Battalion was just reassembling in front of the Arzbergerkeller when Police Inspectors Anton Altmann, Lorenz Reithmeier, and Rudolf Schmäling walked past on their way to the Löwenbräukeller on nearby Stiglmaier Platz.

When the three police officers entered the beerhall auditorium, they found most of the seats already taken or reserved and a crowd of some 1,500 men, most in Oberland, Reichskriegsflagge, or Nazi uniforms. The walls were hung with the blue-and-white bunting of Bavaria, the stage draped with the red-white-and-black flags of imperial Germany. Two brass bands alternated, playing "marches and opera overtures," and the beer seemed to be flowing in torrents.

At the long head table they spotted Ernst Röhm and two of his closest associates, ex-Captain Josef Seydel and Count Karl-Leon du Moulin-Eckart, in apparently urgent conversation with Hermann Esser and Wilhelm Brückner, commander of the Munich SA Regiment. A bit to the side, unnoticed by anyone and looking as stiff as a store-window dummy, stood Heinrich Himmler, a flagstaff clutched in his hand. The bill of his field-gray ski cap seemed to touch the top of his rimless spectacles, and his toothbrush mustache bristled above his small lips.

As Reithmeier and Schmäling surveyed the scene, the beer-hall doors burst open and in marched Knauth's SA battalion. The band played a flourish, shouts of "Heil! Heil!" came from a thousand throats, and two of Knauth's officers strutted forward to plant swastika banners on the stand. Then Röhm mounted the stage slowly to open the meeting and introduce Esser.

"This doesn't look like a 'comradeship evening' to me," Chief Inspector Altmann said, pulling Reithmeier aside. "You and Schmäling stay here. I'm going back to the precinct to put in a call to headquarters."

On his way up Dachauer Strasse he noticed more SA troopers—these armed and in combat dress—apparently heading toward the Oberwiesenfeld and the Infantry and Engineer barracks.

"It's not normal. Something is up or planned," Altmann told one of Captain Fritz Stumpf's assistants, describing the vast number of Nazi storm troopers in the Löwenbräukeller and the contingents on the street.

"Well," the officer said, "the Löwenbräu meeting has a permit and everything else in the city seems quiet. But I'll make a note of it and tell Herr Dr. Frick in case he stops by. He's in charge tonight. Thanks for calling."

Erich Ludendorff pushed his chair slowly away from the dining-room table, rose stiffly, adjusted his smoking jacket—he always felt uncomfortable in civilian clothes—and strode into his study. He was still waiting.

Fifty-five miles to the south, in the picturesque town of Garmisch-Partenkirchen at the foot of the snow-capped Zugspitze, Germany's highest mountain, Wilhelm Völk, thirty-three, the district commander of the Oberland League, studied a plain white envelope that he and other provincial Oberland chiefs had been handed the previous day in Munich by their leader, Dr. Friedrich Weber.

Do not open until 8:30 in the evening, November 8th, the typewritten instructions read.

Völk looked at the pendulum clock on his parlor wall. Well, it was almost time. Reaching for a letter-opener, he slit the envelope. Inside, on red alert paper, was this message:

> Mobilize your unit immediately. Move it at once to Munich by all available trucks to support the National Revolution under the leadership of Kahr, Pöhner, Ludendorff, Hitler!—Heil!

A mud-splattered car with a Nürnberg license plate sputtered uncertainly down Ludwig Strasse toward the center of Munich. The driver was looking for street names. Spotting one that read "Schelling Strasse," he turned right. The car came to a halt across the street from the entrance to No. 39.

Julius Streicher leaped from the car and ran upstairs to the offices of the *Völkischer Beobachter* to find out "at which rally I am supposed to speak." Except for a few secretaries and several subeditors, however, the place seemed deserted. Only a single SA trooper was on duty.

"But where is Herr Hitler or Herr Doktor Rosenberg?" Streicher asked with bewildered impatience and irritation. After all, was it his fault that the drive had taken so long? "I have come all the way from Nürnberg to speak at an important rally. Isn't there anyone here with some authority who knows what is going on?"

"All I know," said the trooper, "is that I was told to send all speakers who might come here to the Bürgerbräukeller. I think that's where all the gentlemen have gone. Do you know how to get there? From here you take streetcar number—"

Streicher rushed out before he could finish.

Konrad Kiessling, of the Oberland League's First Battalion, was late and out of breath as he ran across the narrow footpath connecting the Ludwig Bridge with the Kohlen Insel, the island in the Isar where Munich's new Deutsches Museum of Science and Technology was under construction. Feeling his way through the dark building site, he searched for his unit. The battalion, gathered around a huge truck with trailer, was already assembled in full strength.

Kiessling barely had time to report to his battalion and company commanders, Ludwig Oestreicher and Alfons Weber, before they were ordered to march. With the truck in the lead, its dim, flickering headlights picking the way, Oestreicher's contingent paraded off the island across a side bridge and headed uphill, toward Rosenheimer Strasse.

"Leave the machine guns *on* the trucks!" Josef Berchtold hissed loudly as he stomped around the factory yard on Balan Strasse. "Just take the rifles, check them, then get back on those vehicles. Don't load your weapons or mount bayonets until we get there."

Adolf Lenk clenched the rifle in his hand tightly. The weapon gave him a feeling of strength and power.

"My men are ready," Berchtold said, turning to Hermann Göring. "Are yours?"

Göring, buckling a ceremonial officer's sword to the belt around his raincoat and readjusting the Pour le Mérite dangling from his neck, nodded assent.

The drizzle in the cold night air seemed to muffle the sound of engines being cranked furiously and motors stammering uneasily to life.

"The scouts are back," Walter Baldenius, Göring's adjutant, reported. "The street is clear, the crowd is gone, and there are only about a dozen 'blue' cops left outside the building."

"On the trucks!" Göring commanded. "We're going!"

5

Seemingly lost in thought, Adolf Hitler took another swallow from his beer mug: 8:28 . . .

Chief Inspector Philipp Kiefer, standing in the vestibule near the cloakroom, eyed Hitler and the small knot of men near him suspiciously. He noticed the bulge in the Nazi leader's trouser pocket. What is he doing out here? Kiefer wondered. Why does he keep looking at his watch? Why isn't he listening to Kahr?

In the auditorium, von Kahr was droning on. "The first and foremost task confronting the German people today," he muttered, "is, without question, to regain their freedom. If they do not succeed in this, Germany will lose its place among the ranks of the great nations and slowly but surely disappear."

Hitler glanced at the door toward the main corridor and again at his watch: 8:29. . . . Except for the Iron Cross pinned to it, the cutaway made him look like a waiter taking a beer break.

Outside the arched gateway to the Bürgerbräukeller and the gravel-covered beer garden surrounding it, Patrolman Johann Bruckmeier hunched up his blue greatcoat as protection against the damp cold and tilted back his spike-tipped leather helmet. He was getting sleepy but was still wondering about the two troopers he had seen running back and forth on the street.

Reichswehr soldiers, he thought again. What else could they have been? But why?

He peered up and down dimly lit Rosenheimer Strasse. Suddenly he was startled out of his musings. Convoys of heavy trailer-trucks, one led by an open car with a large steel-helmeted man standing on its running board, were coming from both directions.

Before he could alert other police, the trucks swerved and blocked off the street to all traffic. Dozens of armed troopers jumped off. With bayoneted rifles and tommy guns at the ready, they dashed toward the beerhall, shouting, "Police out of the way! Clear the entrance! Get inside that building! All 'Blue Police' inside!"

Cries of "Hitler! Heil Hitler!" and the roar of more truck engines filled the night as Bruckmeier backed toward the main doorway with the other patrolmen. He caught a glimpse of two machine guns being set up on tripods in the street. Two more, on wheeled carts, were being pulled and carried through the garden toward the beerhall. To his surprise, he spotted Inspector Josef Gerum, wearing the uniform of the Stosstrupp Hitler with swastika armband, lugging and shoving one of them.

Göring, brandishing his sword, jumped from the running board of the car, leaped up the steps through the archway, faced the crowd of storm troopers, and announced hoarsely, "The Berlin government—the Reich government—is deposed. We recognize only the dictatorship of Ludendorff-Kahr-Hitler!" He turned on his heels and, "looking like Wallenstein on the march," strode into the Bürgerbräu.

"They're here!" Ulrich Graf, pistol in hand, called excitedly as he ran ahead of Göring and Josef Berchtold down the long corridor toward the vestibule.

Calmly, Hitler glanced at his watch once more, snapped it shut, and tucked it away: 8:30. Perfect timing! For once, he thought, Göring was punctual. He took one more draught of beer, hurled the glass mug to the floor, and pulled the Browning revolver from his pants pocket.

"What's going on? What are you doing here?" Kiefer, trying to identify himself as the police officer in charge, asked the crush of SA men storming through the narrow corridor from the garden. It was like trying to swim against a tidal wave.

"Out of the way or I'll gun you down," one of the troopers snarled, pushing Kiefer back with his rifle. "If you have any questions, ask Captain Göring. He's coming now."

"There'll be no shooting!" Göring barked. Then, quietly, he turned to Kiefer. "A new government has been named. Police headquarters has been informed. Herr Doktor Frick will be here soon. Keep your men under control, and there'll be no trouble from mine. But do not attempt to leave the building. It is surrounded." Göring strutted on, rushing to catch up with Berchtold and the Stosstrupp.

Kiefer dashed after him but then thought better of it and hurried instead to the kitchen, hoping to phone Ett Strasse headquarters from there. The door was already barred by two ferocious-looking storm troopers. Taking advantage of the confusion in the hallway, he managed to slip past the guards, into the garden, and out onto the street, where more truckloads of SA were arriving and encircling the beer cellar.

Walking as fast as he could, he headed toward the 15th Precinct station, on Weissenburger Platz, several blocks away.

Hitler, agitated, waited nervously in the vestibule as Gerum and other Stosstrupp members maneuvered one of the machine guns into place—just outside the door to the auditorium, its barrel pointing into the hall ready to rake the still unsuspecting audience.

"In national and patriotic circles," von Kahr was saying, "there are some who believe that mere restoration of strong state authority will suffice. But not even the strongest man, empowered with the greatest authority, can save the nation without the energetic support of a nationally and patriotically spirited people."

The Browning clutched in his hand, Hitler gave the signal to yank open the huge doors.

Surrounded by Graf, Rosenberg, and Hess, all brandishing pistols, and with Gerum, Adolf Lenk, and other troopers in the lead, he strode in. Hanfstaengl, holding aloft a Walther revolver, Amann, Aigner, Scheubner-Richter, who peered myopically through his pince-nez, Göring with his sword unsheathed, and more SA men followed closely on their heels. The motley group—some twenty in all—formed a phalanx and began pushing its way through the packed hall.

"Were one to attempt—" Kahr stopped in mid-sentence. Shaken, the little man stared aghast at the mounting tumult and commotion in the rear of the auditorium. The rising pandemonium there rolled like thunder across the hall as Hitler and his men shoved, beat, and kicked their way forward.

"Communists! The Reds! Provocation!" people shouted, not noticing the swastika emblems on the red armbands. "No, look, Hitler! It's Hitler! Heil!"

"*Ruhe!*—Quiet! It is not an action directed against Excellency von Kahr!" Ernst Pöhner screamed to no avail from the head table.

A pistol shot rang out. Chairs and benches overturned. Beer mugs crashed to the floor. The noise became deafening.

In the balcony, Georg Ott and Georg Stumpf rushed to the railing to see what was happening below. The crowd was in a panic. People climbed on tables to get a better look, among them Karl Alexander von Müller and Georg Rauh. Others, notably Johann Wutzelhofer, the minister of agriculture, scrambled to take cover beneath them.

"What's this all about?" asked a police officer, recognizing Gerum in his Nazi uniform.

"You'll find out in a minute," Gerum snapped. "As soon as we get through this mob to the podium."

Some in the crowd tried to escape, only to be pushed back into the hall by the storm troopers streaming in and standing guard around the machine gun. State Police Major Franz Hunglinger, Seisser's adjutant, tried to block the covey of Nazis inching their way forward. Hitler pointed the Browning at Hunglinger's forehead and growled, "Move, Herr Major. I mean it."

On the stage, Eugen Zentz rang his bell wildly in a futile endeavor to restore order, simultaneously trying to calm and reassure von Kahr, Seisser, and Lossow.

Hanfstaengl, towering above Hitler and the others and feeling increasingly uncomfortable in his role as a revolutionary, worried that he might "maim" himself with the "cannon" he was carrying. Spotting Larry Rue and the other American correspondents, he beckoned them to follow.

Hitler had been counting on a quick, dramatic entrance, but it took him and his cohort more than five minutes to jostle, elbow, and rifle-butt their way to the stage. With each step, the din in the auditorium became louder. Meanwhile, more and more storm troopers were rushing in to stand guard at the doorways, along the walls, and in the balcony. Nazi party members, including a number of police detectives who had been sitting incognito in the audience, fished swastika armbands out of their pockets and suddenly displayed pistols and hand grenades.

By the time Hitler reached the foot of the podium, he was drenched in sweat, his ill-cut morning coat rumpled. "Quiet!" he shouted, climbing first onto a chair and then a table. The rumble of thousands of excited voices merely rose. Lifting his revolver high above his head, he fired a shot at the ceiling. The uproar subsided into a murmur. He clambered from the table onto the platform, glared momentarily at the triumvirs, then faced the throng, his face chalk white, his hair matted to his glistening forehead.

"The National Revolution has broken out," he screamed in a shrill, high voice. "Six hundred armed men have this hall covered and surrounded! No one is to leave this room. And if there is not immediate quiet, I shall order another machine gun posted on the balcony."

There was sudden silence.

"I declare the Bavarian government deposed," he shrieked. "The Reich government is deposed. A provisional Reich government is being formed. The police and Reichswehr have joined our banner, the swastika banner, which at this moment is flying above the barracks and police stations of the city."

Shouts of "Heil!" and "Hitler, bravo!" but also jeers of "Mexico!" "South America!" and "Operetta!" echoed through the hall.

Turning to the speechless triumvirs behind him, he said gruffly but for all to hear, "Excellency von Kahr, Excellency von Lossow, Colonel von Seisser—I must ask you to come with me. Everything will be settled in ten minutes. I shall guarantee your safety."

The dumbfounded trio was furious. Yet there was something comical about the situation. There stood this ludicrous-looking ex-corporal, dressed like the concierge of a third-rate hotel, proclaiming the very revolution all three had hoped and worked for. But there was nothing laughable about the pistol he pointed at them, the machine gun in the doorway, or the scores of heavily armed storm troopers surrounding them grimly.

"I have no reason to go anywhere with you," von Kahr sputtered sharply. "We have nothing more to say to each other. You have broken your word of honor not to putsch."

"The revolution can no longer be stopped," Hitler implored. "The time has come to act."

"Has it started in the north?" Lossow asked icily.

Ignoring the question, Hitler flailed wildly with his revolver, and motioned to Lenk, Hess, Graf, and the others to lead the trio out.

"*Komödie spielen*—Put on an act," Lossow mumbled to Seisser and Kahr as they were being marched ignominiously, through the aisle that formed, to the little side room Hess had rented earlier that evening from Korbinian Reindl.

"No talking!" Graf ordered.

A number of the triumvirs' aides—Hunglinger; State Police Colonel Josef Banzer; Lossow's adjutant, Major Hans von Hösslin; and Baron Hubert von Aufsess, the head of one of von Kahr's departments—tried to follow. Rudely, all but Hunglinger were held back by Berchtold's Stosstrupp guards.

As the group reached the side room, Hitler gestured to Hermann Kriebel and Friedrich Weber to wait outside. Then he turned to Scheubner-Richter and whispered, "It is time to get Ludendorff."

Back in the auditorium, the commotion had resumed. People who tried to leave were being shoved brutally back to their seats by the guards.

Editors Fritz Gerlich and Adolf Schiedt sat silently, pale and seemingly lost in bitter thoughts over their beer mugs. It was not the demonstration of confidence they had envisioned for von Kahr.

Zentz, gesticulating wildly, denied indignantly to friends that he had known of the putsch beforehand.

Hanfstaengl, momentarily relieved from his duties, gratefully put the pistol away and tried to explain events to the foreign journalists.

Robert Murphy, insisting on his diplomatic immunity, argued, to no avail, with one of the SA men at the door, demanding to be allowed out.

Georg Stumpf turned to his friend Ott and announced, "I am going to the pissoir." Ott shrugged and watched Stumpf get as far as a balcony exit, where he was turned back by a storm trooper.

Police Chief Karl Mantel, encircled by Georg Rauh, Otto Bernreuther, and others of his aides, was angry. "What do we have informers for in the Hitler movement? Why weren't we told? Now Kahr is going to blame us. If I'd had any idea, I wouldn't have let him talk me out of posting that company of State Police in here."

Near the podium, Prime Minister von Knilling was huddled in conference with Count von Soden and members of his cabinet—Schweyer, Gürtner, and Wutzelhofer, who had come out from under the table.

A few feet away, Police Inspector Matthäus Hoffmann was

engaged in busy, almost chummy conversation with several SA men. Looking around, and noting where the Nazis pointed, Hoffmann scribbled on a piece of paper the names of Jewish businessmen, among them Ludwig Wassermann, a banker.

"I have the feeling," Karl Alexander von Müller said to his friend Robert Riemerschmied, "that we are caught in a trap."

As unrest and grumbling in the huge hall rose, Pöhner mounted the podium. But before he could speak, a storm trooper came up to him. "The Führer wants you in the side room too."

Suddenly Göring, having doffed his rubber coat so that the medals on his chest sparkled, leaped up to the stage. "This is not an assault on Herr von Kahr, the other two gentlemen, the police, or the army, who are already marching out of their barracks with flags waving," he bellowed in a parade-ground voice that brought renewed silence. "It is directed solely against the Berlin government of Jews. It is merely the preliminary step of the national revolution desired by everyone in this auditorium. We have dared this step because we are convinced it will make it easier for the men who lead us to act.

"But until the step is completed, you must all stay seated and follow the orders and instructions of the guards," he commanded. "Long live the new Reich government—Hitler, Ludendorff, Pöhner, Kahr!"

A roar of approval boomed through the hall, and 3,000 voices joined in "Deutschland, Deutschland über Alles."

"Besides, ladies and gentlemen," Göring shouted when the singing ended, "you've all got your beer."

Before going into the side room to join Hitler, Hermann Kriebel slipped into the Bürgerbräukeller's kitchen, motioned to his adjutant Rolf Reiner and to Wilhelm Kolb, and handed Reiner a slip of paper. "Call these numbers," he said, "and give them that message."

Reiner looked at it briefly. "Safe delivery," it read. "Police—Dr. Frick (26880)/Löwenbräukeller—Röhm or Captain Seydel (53568)."

Göring, having restored quiet, came down from the stage and pushed through the crowd in search of Hanfstaengl. Spotting him in conversation with Rue and Knickerbocker, he beckoned him aside.

"Do me a favor, please," Göring said. "This is going to take a while, and I'll be busy for a long time. When you get to a phone, call Carin and tell her I won't be home at all tonight."

Hanfstaengl welcomed the opportunity to talk to Göring after the initial excitement. "Von Lossow worries me," he said. "Did you see the look in his eyes when he walked out with Hitler? I don't trust him. He's an aristocratic general who resents taking orders from a former corporal, no matter what position he gets in the new government. He's going to double-cross us."

Göring chuckled. "Don't worry, Hanfi. We have everything under control." As if to prove it, he turned to his orderly, Julius Schaub, standing a few feet away. "Get a car," he told Schaub, "drive to Freising, and deliver this envelope to Gregor Strasser. He's expecting it." The envelope contained Strasser's orders to move his SA battalion to Munich.

In the vestibule, Heinz Pernet, Ludendorff's stepson, waited impatiently as Johann Aigner helped Scheubner-Richter into his overcoat.

The three rushed through the crowded corridor to a line of hired and private cars waiting on Rosenheimer Strasse. They noticed the trucks blocking the street and the machine guns. Trolleycars, their bells clanging, were backed up behind the barriers. All traffic into and out of downtown Munich had ground to a halt.

"We need an automobile immediately," Aigner told the SA dispatcher.

"Take this one right here," said the trooper, snapping to attention on seeing Scheubner.

"Where to, gentlemen?" Michael Ried, the driver, asked. "Solln—Ludwigshöhe," Pernet ordered. "Heilmann Strasse number five. And step on it."

Hermann Kriebel, emerging from the beerhall kitchen, was surprised and irritated to see Max Neunzert, his "communications officer," just arriving.

"Where have you been all this time?" Kriebel asked, exasperated. "I've been looking for you for over an hour."

"I was here once but went back home to change," Neunzert apologized. "I was almost the only person in uniform. But now, seeing so many others, maybe I should go back and—"

"Stay," Kriebel ordered. "I am going to need you."

Downhill from the Bürgerbräu, where Ludwig Oestreicher's Oberland battalion was helping to block off Rosenheimer Strasse, two men on their way home from work were trying to force their way past the guards.

"No one passes here. Orders of the new government," one of the Oberländers growled, signaling to other troopers, who began kicking the two and beating them with rifle butts.

The men fled, barely noticing the muddy car with the Nuremberg license plates struggling up the steep street.

Julius Streicher showed his party credentials to the guards, was saluted with an outstretched arm, and was waved through.

Breathing hard from the stiff, brisk uphill walk, Philipp Kiefer rushed into the barren precinct station on Weissenburger Platz.

"Call Ett Strasse immediately," he told the desk sergeant.

For several minutes the line was busy. Finally Captain Fritz Stumpf, the duty officer, answered.

"Hitler troops have occupied the Bürgerbräukeller," Kiefer said excitedly. "We're completely outnumbered up here. Most of my men are locked up in the beerhall. What shall I do?"

Stumpf promised to "find someone" and call him back. Kiefer waited impatiently for about ten minutes until the telephone rang. It was Stumpf. "I just managed to get hold of Herr Doktor Frick," he said. "He seems to be in charge tonight and wants to speak to you personally."

The name jarred Kiefer's memory. Briefly, he explained what had happened.

"In view of your description, Herr Chief Inspector," Frick said haughtily, "there is really nothing you can or should do. You say Rosenheimer Strasse is completely blocked off and that there are armed SA men all around? Well, why don't you stay where you are and wait for further instructions. After all, Chief Mantel, the prime minister, the cabinet, and Excellency von Kahr are in the Bürgerbräu. Surely, they'll know what to do—better than you or I. Don't worry. I'll be here, and if you do need additional help, don't hesitate to call again and ask for me."

There was a click on the line.

Interlude III

Three Capitals

Budapest

BUDAPEST, Nov. 8 (AP)—Deputy Ulain was arrested today on a train on which he was proceeding to Munich, Bavaria. He is charged with conspiracy in an attempt to overthrow the government of Count Stefan Bethlen, the Hungarian premier.

The police say they have evidence showing that Ulain was proceeding to Munich on behalf of the members of the Extreme Right in parliament, in an endeavor to obtain the support of Adolf Hitler, leader of the Fascists in Bavaria, for a coup d'état in Hungary and the overthrow of the Bethlen government. In addition to Ulain, ten other politicians have been arrested.

Berlin

After several days of food rioting, plundering, and pogroms against Jewish merchants, Berlin was quiet but tense on Thursday evening, November 8. The city seemed to be under siege, with heavily armed green-uniformed Prussian State Police patrolling the streets.

All day long, bread had been unobtainable and a genuine food shortage was developing. Many bakeries, butcher shops, and groceries had preferred to keep their shutters down rather than run the risk of being looted. Only regular favored customers were sometimes let in at back doors, to sneak out with small parcels— provided they could afford the prices.

There were hints of further unrest, especially among the metalworkers, and that day the police had advertised urgently for 2,500 immediate recruits between the ages of twenty-three and thirty-five and "of absolute loyalty to the Constitution." To complicate matters, after an unusually warm autumn, a sudden cold spell had fallen on the city. The mood was somber.

And yet, in characteristic dogged fashion, life was going on as usual. The Tauentzien-Palast cinema was announcing the premiere of Charlie Chaplin's *The Kid,* co-starring Jackie Coogan and Edna Purviance—"the film which, for months, has enthralled audiences around the world."

Opera lovers were at *Tristan and Isolde* at the Grosse Volksoper, *Tiefland* at the Deutsches Opernhaus, *The Marriage of Figaro* at the Volksbühne, or *Cavalleria Rusticana* at the Staats-Theater. *Caesar and Cleopatra* was playing at the Deutsches Theater, *Joujou* at the Trianon, and Gogol's *The Government Inspector* at the Central. The cabarets were crowded as usual.

Friedrich Ebert was in his apartment in the presidential Residence on Wilhelm Strasse, pondering whether the apparent quiet was a good omen or merely the calm before a new storm. General von Seeckt was quietly at home, as was Reichswehr Minister Otto Gessler.

Only Chancellor Gustav Stresemann was still on the go. The day had been strenuous and trying—spent largely in disputes with various business, economic, and banking experts over his and Finance Minister Hans Luther's plans for a dramatic currency reform, tentatively scheduled to take effect November 15. And it was by no means over. At 10 p.m. he was due at the Continental Hotel for a "working dinner" with one Hjalmar H. G. (for Horace Greeley) Schacht, the prickly young head of the Darmstadt National Bank whom Luther was proposing as "commissioner of national currency." He hoped it would at least be an evening without one of those acerbic midnight cabinet sessions that had become almost routine in recent weeks.

Bavaria—Munich—Adolf Hitler? All that seemed far away. To be sure, no one in Berlin felt quite comfortable about Gustav von Kahr or General Otto von Lossow and their defiance of the Reich government, least of all Seeckt. Moreover, with reports of Hermann Ehrhardt's brigade of radical rightist and Fascist irregulars poised on Bavaria's frontier with Thuringia as a kind of auxiliary border police, the danger of confrontation could not be ruled out. However, intelligence information had indicated that Ehrhardt's ragtag forces were not nearly the menace they had first appeared and would certainly be no match for the Reichswehr, even if they did strike. And the likelihood of their doing that seemed to have diminished with each day since the Reichswehr had moved to restore order and central government control in Thuringia and Saxony.

In fact, matters were actually looking up, as Baron Adolf von Maltzan, the undersecretary in the Foreign Ministry, had been saying that evening to Viscount Edgar Vincent d'Abernon, the British ambassador.

Several hours later Maltzan would be rousing d'Abernon from a deep sleep to announce gravely, "It appears that we are on the brink of civil war."

Rome

Kurt Lüdecke, Hitler's "foreign policy adviser" and self-styled Nazi "ambassador" to Benito Mussolini, was "nervous and restless" when he went to the offices of the *Corriere d'Italia*. Surely, he thought, there must be some news by now. Hadn't the Munich correspondent, Negrelli, cabled yet?

Berlin-born Lüdecke, thirty-three, the silver spoon-fed son of a chemical factory owner, was one of the most opaque and enigmatic figures in Hitler's inner circle. Wheeling and dealing in various business enterprises, among them aircraft sales, had taken him around the world, given him global connections, and made him wealthy. Among his personal friends he not only counted such top Nazis as Röhm, Rosenberg, and Gregor Strasser but leading industrialists such as Henry Ford and Hugo Stinnes. His mistress, Rosita Mapleson, was the Cuban-born widow of the former adjutant to the Duke of Marlborough. He had both Mexican and German citizenship and had spent a postwar year in Mexico, building up a "foreign legion" of German émigré veterans as a guard for President Venustiano Carranza. When Carranza was murdered in 1920, Lüdecke had fled back to Europe.

Outspokenly anti-Semitic, as much at home in Buenos Aires, Lima, Havana, and New York as in Berlin or Munich, Zurich,

Paris, or Rome, he had provided Hitler with moneyed supporters in Germany, Switzerland, France, England, and Italy. He had also contributed a substantial share of his personal fortune to the party, even going so far as to buy the uniforms for an entire platoon of Josef Berchtold's Stosstrupp.

In September 1922 he had made his first trip to Rome to meet Mussolini and explore the possibility of closer cooperation between Il Duce and Hitler. In October 1923, bearing credentials as a correspondent for the *Völkischer Beobachter* and a personal letter of accreditation from Hitler, Lüdecke had traveled south again to prepare the Italian Fascist dictator for the forthcoming "nationalist revolution" in Germany and seek his support in the event of a successful march on Berlin.

But just short of 9 P.M., Negrelli still had not sent any "unusual news." Lüdecke knew that "decisive things were happening—but what, what, what?" The strain "was cruel." He decided to return to his hotel for a while—"but not to sleep."

6

"That will be all for tonight, gentlemen," Major Sigmund von Imhoff said wearily, dismissing the younger State Police officers around him and winding up his special class on riot control. "But if you want to wait just a minute, I'll walk out with you."

Imhoff wanted to let Stumpf know that he was leaving the Ett Strasse building and going home. As he ambled downstairs to the duty officer's room, a detective dashed up to him.

"Have you heard the news, Herr Major?" he announced excitedly. "Hitler and the National Socialists have occupied the Bürgerbräukeller and overthrown the government. They have everybody locked up there."

Incredulous and suspecting it was either a hoax or "all highly exaggerated," Imhoff sauntered into Stumpf's office.

"It's no joke," the captain told him gravely. "I've been getting virtually identical reports for the past half hour or so, the most detailed one from a chief inspector—Kiefer—who slipped out of the building just as the SA barged in. They have all of Rosenheimer Strasse barricaded with large trucks and machine guns, and they're armed to the teeth for combat. One caller said they had even set up a small fieldpiece or mortar down by the Ludwig Bridge.

"But there's something even stranger," Stumpf continued, lowering his voice and showing Imhoff the blotter with the record of incoming calls. "Mantel and just about every high-ranking civilian is in the beerhall, and that fellow Frick—Pöhner's protégé—is supposed to be in charge tonight. But when I finally reached him in his apartment upstairs to tell him about the call from Kiefer, I had the feeling that he wasn't the least surprised. In fact, I'd say he already knew something. It was almost as if he'd expected it. And when he got on the phone with Kiefer, he told him not to do any—"

Stumpf stopped abruptly, looked sharply at Imhoff, then at the door.

There stood Dr. Wilhelm Frick, his prematurely white hair close-cropped in Prussian style, his eyes piercing under dark brows, his sharp features masklike except for a smile that seemed more like a smirk.

"Well, well, Herr Major," he exclaimed with some surprise. "Working late tonight? I didn't expect to see you here at this hour."

"I was teaching a class and just leaving when I heard the news," von Imhoff replied casually. "You know we have a company of State Police on alert in the old cavalry barracks on Morassi Strasse. Don't you think they should be sent up to the Bürgerbräukeller?"

"What? And cause bloodshed?" Frick shot back. "Under no circumstances. That would be very foolish. First of all, they have nothing but carbines, and the reports say the National Socialists are very heavily armed. Besides, they'd be completely outnumbered now. The best thing to do, for the time being—until we find out more—is nothing: wait for instructions. Why, practically everyone is up there in the Bürgerbräu—Colonel von Seisser, General von Lossow, Herr von Kahr, Mantel, the prime minister. We can't just act on our own."

Imhoff agreed that it was now too late to mobilize the company in the cavalry barracks and the unit was too weak, but his suspicions about Frick were mounting. A baron and scion of an old aristocratic family with a tradition of loyal and obedient service, Imhoff was certainly no fan of the floundering republican government in Berlin; like many in the police and military, he was an ardent nationalist and monarchist. But he was even more contemptuous of the Nazis, with their brawling ways and their opportunist sympathizers. The Germany they wanted was not the one he envisioned. He decided to act on his own.

"I think I'll stay around for a while and go to my office," he announced nonchalantly. "I assume you'll be up in your apartment, Herr Doktor Frick?"

Imhoff hurried down the long, bare corridor to his own room and went to work. In quick succession he phoned all available "green police" battalion and company commanders in Munich to place their units on alert. He dispatched company-sized contingents to protect the central telegraph office across the square from the railroad station and the telephone exchange in the main post office at the corner of Maximilian and Diener streets. Repeatedly, but without success, he attempted to reach the beerhall itself, hoping for more information. Then he ordered the captain of the company in the Morassi Strasse barracks to reconnoiter the Bürgerbräukeller but to avoid direct confrontations with the SA.

Frick looked in frequently, trying to conceal his obvious intense curiosity with an air of jocular aloofness. With each "friendly" visit, Imhoff's suspicions rose, and he waited until he had absolute privacy before making his most important call: to Major General Jakob von Danner, Reichswehr city commandant of Munich.

"I'll be there immediately," Danner reassured him, and without stopping to change into uniform he rushed from his home to Ett Strasse. It was a key decision: the start of the counterrevolution.

Baron Michael von Godin, a twenty-six-year-old senior lieutenant in the State Police and acting commander of the First Battalion's Second Company, was looking forward to a quiet evening in his bachelor officer's apartment on Kaulbach Strasse. He was hoping to get to bed early. It had been an uneventful yet tiring day of paperwork and training with his men barracked nearby, right in the Residenz, the palace of Bavaria's erstwhile kings.

There was an unexpected knock on the door. It was Godin's orderly.

"You must come at once to the Residenz," he said. "A Major Imhoff from Ett Strasse called to say that we are on alert."

Godin followed him quickly. It was shortly before 9 P.M.—the beginning of a night and day that were to vault Godin from the obscurity of a police career into the headlines and history books.

The din in the Löwenbräukeller was deafening as Ernst Röhm mounted the podium to open the Reichskriegsflagge's "comradeship evening."

Police Inspectors Rudolf Schmäling and Lorenz Reithmeier noticed that most of the people weren't paying attention to Röhm but were getting increasingly drunk and talking loudly to their table companions.

Stocky and bulging out of a uniform obviously tailored when he cut a more manly figure, Röhm bellowed for quiet. The bullet and shrapnel scars on his cheeks and across his nose were a ruddy pink. Beads of sweat glistened on his round close-shaved head. Conspiracy and arms-running were his stock in trade, but he too knew how to stir up a crowd.

"Tonight," he shouted, "it is exactly five years since the most heinous of all crimes was committed against the German nation. Could there be a more fitting time or occasion to settle scores with Marxism and the November criminals? Comrades, the hour has come for the German people to rise, to demand, to *insist* on their liberation!"

Nearly 2,000 voices broke into thunderous shouts of "Heil!" and "Deutschland! Deutschland!"

Beaming like an impresario, Röhm waited patiently for the tumult to subside. "It was my hope," he rasped, "to have our great Führer Adolf Hitler here tonight to speak to us. Unfortunately, he has other pressing business. But his deputy, Hermann Esser, is here—literally risen from his sickbed."

Laboriously, the muscles in his legs aching with fever, Esser climbed onto the stage. Then, without further ado, he launched into a speech just as rabid and inflammatory as Hitler would have given, ranting against the "international conspiracy of Jewish capital" that was trying to cause "Germany to fall with the help of Bolshevism."

"Just before the war," he began in a sinister voice, almost pianissimo, "the banker Morgan, a Jew, called a secret conference of international capitalists and financiers to discuss how they could systematically and ruthlessly destroy Germany. For them—these Jewish bankers—German industry and finance had become too powerful, a threat. They knew that the German working class, with all its benefits of social welfare, would never revolt to destroy that industrial potential. But a war would do it. Yes, a war! So they decided right then and there, at that conference led by Morgan the Jew, to declare war against us."

It was music to the ears of Heinrich Himmler, Hans Knauth, and Friedrich Mayer, and they hissed and booed, applauded and cheered like a claque as Esser went on, explaining that he had gleaned his wisdom from "an English, yes, an *English* newspaper."

But Röhm, Seydel, Moulin-Eckart, and Brückner weren't even listening. They huddled secretively at the head table below the platform.

Barely noticed by anyone in the auditorium, an SA man ran up and spoke to Seydel and Röhm. They were wanted on the phone. Seydel followed him to the Löwenbräukeller kitchen. Rolf Reiner, at the Bürgerbräu, was on the line and he stammered two words: "Safe delivery." Eagerly, Seydel rushed back to the table and reported.

Röhm leaped up onto the stage, slapped Esser on the shoulder, and whispered into his ear.

His face beaming, Esser turned to the dumbfounded audience.

"I have wonderful news," he cried out, as a trumpet on the bandstand played a fanfare. "According to a telephone call from the Bürgerbräukeller, the Bavarian government has been arrested, the Reich government deposed, and a new national directorate of Hitler and Ludendorff has been declared."

For a fraction of a second there was stunned silence. Then madness. Shouts of "Heil!", "*Hoch!*", and hysterical screaming resounded through the beerhall. Reichswehr soldiers tore the cockades and insignia of the Weimar Republic from their caps and uniforms and stomped on them. Storm troopers embraced each other. Men climbed on tables to shout and dance jigs. Both bands struck up "Deutschland, Deutschland über Alles."

Only Karl Osswald, Munich district leader of Röhm's Reichs-kriegsflagge Society, seemed not to understand. He had arrived late and was standing at the rear of the hall when the tumult broke out. Turning to his friend Theodor Casella, standing guard at the auditorium door, he asked, "What did Esser say? What's happening? Why is everybody yelling?"

"The Nationalist Revolution has been declared," Casella screamed over the noise.

"Oh!" Osswald exclaimed, promptly clambered on a table, shouted "Heil!", and began singing too.

Röhm and Esser, standing side by side, waited for the racket to subside.

Then Röhm announced that everybody—SA, Oberland, and his own RKF troopers—would march in military formation to the Bürgerbräukeller to pay their respects and declare their loyalty to Ludendorff, Hitler, Kahr, and the new government.

As commanders roared orders, the men piled out of the hall and began lining up outside on Stiglmaier Platz and Brienner Strasse. Almost 2,000 in number, they were a small army, though not yet armed. Weapons, however, were soon to come—from the places where Röhm had hidden them: a military depot, the house of a dueling fraternity, and, the biggest cache of all, from a Franciscan monastery. One of the bands, blaring march music and "The Watch on the Rhine," took up position in front of the column. Right behind the tubas, clutching his flagstaff tightly, stood Himmler.

A crowd of onlookers, eager for information, burst into applause and cheers when they learned what had happened. Some of them dashed away to spread the news about town.

Police Inspectors Reithmeier and Schmäling watched for a few minutes, then realized they had better get to headquarters by the fastest means possible. They hurried across Dachauer Strasse to the trolley stop and waited nervously for a streetcar to take them downtown.

Meanwhile, a force smaller than Röhm's, but dressed and armed for battle, was already marching through Kaufinger Strasse, Munich's main shopping street, toward Marienplatz—the officers and cadets of the Infantry School, with Gerhard Rossbach,

Robert Wagner, and Hans Block in the lead. Their swastika banners flying, they were singing at the tops of their lungs.

A few blocks away, on Wurzer Strasse, Edmund Heines had finally assembled his Second SA Battalion in front of the little tavern.

Hans Frank and Kurt Neubauer stood sharply at attention in the front ranks.

Frank was still puzzling out what it was all about. Neubauer knew. He was merely wondering whether his master, Ludendorff, had already arrived at the Bürgerbräukeller and was hoping that Heines would hurry and get the battalion on the move.

Wilhelm Hoegner, having seen Hans Unterleitner off at the station and said good night to Erhard Auer, was walking briskly up Brienner Strasse, past the Wittelsbacher Palais. In the distance, he heard the band of Röhm's contingent and the lusty sounds of the many putschists. Passers-by whom he stopped told him excitedly about the revolution.

I must warn Auer immediately, he thought, and quickly headed in the other direction to walk briskly more than a mile through downtown Munich, to the SPD leader's apartment on Nussbaum Strasse.

At the 19th Infantry Regiment, Chief Warrant Officer Gerhard Böhm continued to give close-order drill to the Herrmann Bund volunteers and eyed Karl Beggel and Hans Oemler's troopers suspiciously. Oemler had been in and out, but still hadn't led his men away. It was getting close to 9 P.M., and a number of men in Böhm's battalion were straggling back from town with vague rumors of events at the Bürgerbräukeller. Böhm listened attentively, and as the story unfolded the Beggel-Oemler puzzle suddenly made sense to him. Now he knew why the SA and Oberländers were in the barracks. Somehow he would have to get them out.

He realized that, of his entire unit, no more than forty soldiers and noncoms were on hand. He alerted them, ordered loaded weapons issued to them, notified the gate guards, and called senior officers at their homes, including Lieutenant Colonel Hugo von Wenz, the regimental commander, who hurried over to the barracks.

Böhm didn't want to use force to drive the Oberländers and SA out. After all, many of them, such as Beggel, were wartime comrades and friends. But if need be, he would. Whatever else was happening in the city, he resolved, there would be no putsch at the 19th Infantry Regiment.

It was a touchy situation and within minutes it became critical. Two events brought it to a head.

Soon after Böhm had mobilized his little force of forty, a heavily loaded truck, covered with a tarpaulin, pulled up on Infanterie Strasse, across the street from the main gate to the barracks. It was filled with rifles, carbines, and machine guns for Oemler and Beggel.

Almost simultaneously, one of the regimental officers, Captain Eduard Dietl, an overt and very outspoken Nazi sympathizer, arrived on the scene. Dietl not only spent his spare time training the SA but earlier that day had been locked in secret conference with Hitler. His mission, though neither Böhm, Oemler, nor Beggel seemed to be aware of it, was obviously to supervise the takeover of the 19th Infantry Regiment barracks and make it safe for the putschists.

With Wenz still on the way, Dietl was the highest ranking officer on the base, and Böhm, innocently enough, reported to him what had been happening. The captain, telling Böhm he would take charge, went into the drill hall, ostensibly to "reason" with the 250 to 300 Oberland and SA troopers but actually to mobilize them. Böhm, meanwhile, was called to the phone inside the headquarters building—apparently on a ruse, for the line was dead when he arrived there. Back outside, on the parade ground, he was relieved to see Wenz arrive.

Just then there were calls of "Weapons, Get them!" and scores of storm troopers rushed out of the drill hall to the barracks gate and the truck parked just outside.

"Stop them! Don't let them back in!" Wenz commanded. Böhm, calling for his little troop of forty men, followed the putschists out of the gate.

"Halt or we'll fire!" he ordered, surrounding the storm troopers and the truck from which rifles were already being handed down. Thirty more SA men—already armed—arrived from a dark side street. But Böhm stood his ground, while Wenz berated Dietl, commanding him to get all the putschists out of the barracks and away from it.

Shouting invective and threatening to "settle scores" later, Oemler and Beggel marched their troops away—unarmed. The weapons on the truck were confiscated and brought inside, and the gate was tightly guarded for the rest of the night.

It was the first instance of the putsch going awry—before it had really gotten under way. The second was about to take place 50 yards away, at the Engineer Battalion barracks. There, Captain Oskar Cantzler had more or less won his dispute with the Oberland League's ascerbic Max von Müller, and Müller had finally agreed to march his 400 troopers inside the drill hall where, Cantzler promised, they would receive their weapons for "training." But as soon as they were assembled there and the arms were being distributed, Müller pulled from his pocket the instructions he had received the previous day from Friedrich Weber. He read out the news: the nationalist revolution and a new Reich government had been declared.

"Under the circumstances, Captain," Müller said defiantly, "I think you will agree there is no further reason why my men cannot take their weapons outside." His orders, he lied, were to lead them to the Bürgerbräu to be reviewed by Ludendorff, "who is also your new commander-in-chief." In fact, his instructions were to take the battalion to the railroad station, to "prevent rich Jewish currency dealers from leaving the city with their loot," and also to occupy the central telephone and telegraph exchanges.

"Not until I find out more about this new government or get specific instructions from the battalion commander or divisional headquarters," Cantzler replied icily but emphatically.

"Well, phone them then," Müller challenged.

Again the two argued loudly. Finally, Cantzler agreed to phone for more information and left the building. But instead of phoning, he alerted the handful of soldiers and NCOs he found in the barracks, ordered the drill-hall doors locked from outside, and posted two machine guns there.

Müller's Oberland troopers were caught in a trap.

Michael Ried drove the heavy gray car at top speed along the banks of the Isar through the southern residential districts of Munich and the genteel upper-crust suburb of Solln, with its villas, mansions, carefully tended private parks, and manicured lawns. As the cabriolet strained up the steep hill to Ludwigshöhe, fog was rolling in and the carbide headlights cut out eerie shadows in the mist. In a cloud of exhaust smoke and road dust, Ried braked to a noisy stop in front of Ludendorff's sumptuous house on Heilmann Strasse. Whatever contempt the arrogant old Prussian general might have for Bavaria, he had certainly chosen one of the loveliest and most expensive spots around Munich in which to "retire."

Aigner jumped out to open the doors, and Pernet and Scheubner-Richter bounded through the gate and across the incline of grass, then slipped inside.

Ludendorff, dressed in a casual smoking jacket, was waiting for them impatiently. Briefly they explained what had already happened. He seemed especially interested in how von Lossow had reacted. But there was really no time to discuss it.

Shouldn't he change into uniform? No, they agreed, that would take too long. Besides, dressed as he was, it would all look more impromptu, less planned.

Pernet helped his stepfather into a loden overcoat and handed him a rather crushed-looking green fedora. Then the three dashed back outside to Ried and Aigner in the waiting car.

In a "wild ride" at "breakneck speeds," Ried drove them to the Bürgerbräukeller.

7

The door to the Bürgerbräukeller's side room slammed shut. Standing guard inside, Rudolf Hess, Adolf Lenk, and Ulrich Graf pointed their pistols menacingly at Kahr, Lossow, Seisser, and Major Hunglinger, who had managed to slip in unnoticed.

"No one leaves this room alive without my permission," Hitler commanded hysterically, flailing about with his Browning revolver.

It was a bizarre scene. Hitler, dripping sweat and visibly trembling, seemed to be in "an ecstatic trance." Yet he looked ludicrously Chaplinesque in his ill-fitting tails and baggy trousers—hardly a figure to impress the three arrogant Bavarian aristocrats he was holding prisoner at gunpoint.

They, on the other hand, were in shock—steeped in emotions that ranged from indignation and outrage to humiliation and abject despondency. Their own conspiratorial plans for a coup d'état against Berlin had been preempted by a fait accompli they felt certain would fail.

Von Lossow, especially, waxed "mournful" that "the patriotic movement in Bavaria, with all the moral pressure it could have exercised on Berlin, had suddenly dissipated—in a puff of theatrical smoke." Seating himself stiffly on the edge of a table, the fifty-five-year-old general fumed inwardly.

The majority of the people will reject a Hitler dictatorship, he thought to himself. Turmoil will follow, the economy will become even more chaotic now. But, worst of all, the French will surely invade us from the west, the Czechs from the east, and Seeckt will order the Reichswehr in from the north and Thuringia. But what could he do, under guard, SA and machine guns just beyond the door, and armed with nothing but a sword?

His thoughts were interrupted abruptly by Hitler's frenetic voice, orating as if he were haranguing a mass rally of thousands instead of an audience of three.

"The Reich government is formed, the Bavarian government deposed," Hitler screeched, gesticulating wildly, revolver still in hand. "Bavaria must be the springboard for the new Reich government!

"Bavaria must have a regent, and that is you," he ranted, looking at von Kahr. "Pöhner is now Bavarian prime minister with dictatorial powers. The Reich government, that will be me. The national army is Ludendorff. Lossow is Reichswehr minister, and Seisser, Reich police minister."

For a second or so he seemed to come out of the spell and notice that Hunglinger was still in the room. "*Raus!*" he snapped, waving the pistol at the State Police major.

"I know the step is difficult for the gentlemen," he continued, lowering his voice a few decibels though still gesticulating with the gun and speaking, almost transfixed, as if the trio were absent. "But the step has to be taken. It has to be made easier for the

gentlemen to act. Each gentleman has to take the place assigned
to him. If he refuses, he loses his right to exist. They must fight
this battle with me, triumph with me, or die with me.

"If things go wrong, there are four bullets left in this pistol:
one each for my three collaborators, should they desert me"—he
pointed the gun at Kahr, Lossow, and Seisser, and then placed it
at his temple—"the last one for me. If I am not triumphant tomorrow morning, I shall be a dead man."

There was total silence in the room as all looked aghast at this
incredible actor. He seemed possessed.

Then von Kahr, not a man with a great reputation for hero-
ism or personal courage, replied with a voice so even and firm it
astonished the others.

"You can do with me what you wish," he said slowly. "You
have the power now. You can hold me captive, you can have me
shot, or you can shoot me here yourself. To die or not to die is
immaterial to me."

It was an expression of both resignation and defiance the likes
of which Hitler had never heard before. He realized he would get
nowhere with the three by using the mesmerizing histrionics that
always seemed to serve so well when he addressed a crowd. He
decided to try a more conciliatory approach.

"Excellency," he said more calmly, to von Kahr, "please forgive me for having caught you by surprise, but you know as well
as I that the need of our people has reached the point where it can
no longer be endured. Further procrastination is no longer possible. That is why I decided on this step today—to enable you and
all honorable Germans to begin the battle against those who are
corrupting and depraving our nation. The criminals of November
1918 must not be allowed to celebrate the fifth anniversary of
their treacherous act of treason with impunity. Tomorrow's dawn
will bring a new Germany, and that is why I implore you to accept the position of Regent of Bavaria. The nationalist revolution
has broken out. There is no turning back."

"But you have broken your word of honor not to putsch,"
Seisser interjected coldly.

"Yes, I have," Hitler replied, again brandishing the Browning.
"Forgive me for that. I had to do it, in the greater interest of the
Fatherland and—"

"But under the circumstances"—von Kahr interrupted what seemed to be the start of a new monologue—"you cannot expect me to collaborate and accept the position of regent. Not when I was taken out of the auditorium under heavy guard. The people in the hall will think that I accepted under duress, and they will have no confidence in me."

Hitler felt stymied. He was becoming more irritated by the minute. Moreover, his throat was parched—a result of having been gassed on the Belgian front in the last month of the war.

"*Masskrug her!*—Bring me a beer!" he commanded, looking at Graf. And, while waiting, he tried a tougher approach again.

"The gentlemen are forbidden to talk to each other!" he barked when he saw von Lossow starting to speak to Kahr.

Angered and disgusted by this behavior, the general bounded from the table edge and stepped toward one of the windows looking out to the Bürgerbräukeller's garden. The storm troopers posted there, apparently thinking he would make a run for it, lowered their rifles and pointed them at him.

Well, he thought, noticing the helmeted and combat-ready SA men peering menacingly through other windows too, we really are surrounded. At least Hitler hadn't been bluffing on that score, so perhaps he had also meant it when he had said that Reichswehr and State Police were on his side and already marching.

Lossow's mood and attitude seemed to be changing. "Where does Ludendorff stand on all this?" he asked.

The question offered Hitler a welcome reprieve. "He has already been notified and will be here any minute," he answered. Then, apologizing once more to Kahr, he went out, Lenk and Hess following obediently behind him.

Outside the room, Hitler summoned Pöhner, Friedrich Weber, and Hermann Kriebel to replace him. Maybe they would be more effective with the triumvirs until Ludendorff arrived. Meanwhile, he decided, he would return to the main hall where he would be in his natural element, working on a crowd that would certainly respond to his call.

"It will succeed," he reassured some of his worried followers standing guard in the vestibule and corridor. "The left bank of the city is being occupied right now."

Hermann Göring's exhortations and his flippant reminder to the audience that, after all, "you've got your beer," had brought only temporary calm. During the fifteen-odd minutes that Hitler had been out of the auditorium, unrest and disgruntlement mounted again, not to mention confusion over what was going on.

Karl Alexander von Müller was talking excitedly with Robert Riemerschmid, Professor Max von Gruber, and other friends and acquaintances who had elbowed and shoved their way through the crowd to him. Von Müller's acute political observations in a monthly magazine, the *Süddeutsche Monatshefte*, and his relationship by marriage to Gottfried Feder, Hitler's chief economic adviser, made him a man whose views were very much in demand. "You don't really think Hitler can carry this thing off, do you, barging in here the way he did?" he was asked. "It's the opportunity Kahr has been looking for," someone in the circle interjected. Von Müller himself, looking at his watch, remarked, "Well, there must be some disagreement. Didn't Hitler say it would all be settled in ten minutes, and then they'd be back?"

At the head table Prime Minister von Knilling and his cabinet members, Mantel and his top aides, and Colonel Josef Banzer were deep in agitated conversation and mutual recriminations. None of them knew what to do, but Franz Schweyer, the minister of interior, his gray goatee quivering with anger and indignation, was extemporizing loudly.

"I knew it," he said. "I knew he'd do this, and I told him he would. 'Herr Hitler,' I said to him when he came to my office a year ago, after Mussolini's march on Rome, 'one of these days you will make a putsch, whatever your intentions, because if you continue your propaganda this way it will lead to an explosion. You can't just go on talking and making the kind of speeches you do without the stream bursting loose of its own accord. You will be faced with the choice of sinking or swimming with it. And you will swim with it. You will have to act.' But he gave me his word of honor. 'Never, as long as I live,' he told me, 'never will I make a putsch.' And see now, what his word of honor means twelve months later.

"Why wasn't he deported in May when he tried it?" Schweyer looked accusingly at Franz Gürtner, the minister of justice. "He's a foreigner, an Austrian citizen, and there would have been every legal basis for a deportation order then, after he caused the troubles at the Oberwiesenfeld."

Gürtner kept silent.

Standing forlorn and chagrined on the stage after Göring's performance, Eugen Zentz had announced that, as far as he was concerned, the meeting was apparently over and everybody ought to go home. But his suggestion was countermanded sharply by SA shouts that the building was surrounded, all exits guarded, and that no one might leave the hall.

And no one could. Inspectors Siegfried Herrmann and Theodor Singer flashed their credentials to Göring and Berchtold but were ordered to stay. Herrmann then tried to help a septuagenarian gentleman out who was having what appeared to be an attack of cardiac collapse or claustrophobia. He was rebuffed again.

Even the press and high-ranking Nazis were locked in, as Hanfstaengl discovered. Having climbed on a chair, and thus towering even higher above the crowd, he was holding an impromptu press conference, translating what had been said and explaining that a new government had been formed which would "restore order and discipline in the country." The correspondents were trying to jot down notes while being jostled by the unruly mass of people. Editor Fritz Gerlich and Wilhelm von Borscht, the mayor of Munich until 1919 and a friend of Hanfstaengl's family, made their way over to the group.

"Can't you help us out of here?" Borscht asked. "We're being kept prisoner."

Hanfstaengl took Borscht to the main door, where Julius Schreck was standing guard with Josef Gerum and the machine-gun squad.

"No one is to go out," Schreck said. "Those are Captain Göring's orders, and only people in uniform can give commands. You are a civilian."

Angered by the officiousness of Göring's SA clerk, Hanfstaengl backed off, went to the serving window, ordered another mug of beer, and had a word with one of the waitresses.

"You can leave through the kitchen," he reported back to Borscht, smiling. The same escape hatch was later to be used by Gerlich, Larry Rue, Hubert Knickerbocker, Lincoln Eyre, Dorothy Thompson, Negrelli, and other journalists, all eager to file their dispatches or, in Gerlich's case, to publish their newspapers.

As the minutes of waiting ticked by with no sign of Hitler and the triumvirs, the mood grew tense. Moreover, Göring and Berchtold's storm troopers were becoming increasingly irascible and bullying some of their captives.

Georg Stumpf, for example, had finally been allowed to go out to the pissoir, but when he returned to the balcony and wanted to open one of the windows up there "because it was getting so warm and smoky," a storm trooper bellowed, "No looking out. Close it!" Defiantly, Stumpf yanked it open, leaned out, and caught a brief glimpse of the armed encampment in the garden and on Rosenheimer Strasse. "Don't you understand German?" the SA man snapped, clicking the safety on the carbine he was carrying and moving toward Stumpf. "Close it. Step back! We're giving the orders in here now." Stumpf pulled back but left the window open.

"What's the point of all this saber-rattling when we are all comrades-in-arms and aiming for the same thing?" Johann Kress, an elderly Munich building contractor and member of one of the "patriotic leagues," asked an SA man he knew.

"If the Führer's orders are not followed," the storm trooper replied, sounding almost as if he were reciting a memorized text, "obedience will be imposed with the force of arms."

"You mean," Kress asked incredulously and indignantly, "that you would actually shoot at other patriotic Fatherland-loving men?"

"That's what the guns are for," the SA man said with a cocky grimness.

Kress pushed back into the crowd. He was "horrified and dismayed." Hitler had just lost another potential supporter. And Kress was not the only one disenchanted by what was happening.

In fact, many in the hall, ultra-conservative and militantly nationalistic as they were, opposed a putsch and the Nazis. And for those with foresight, incensed by the machine gun at the main door, Göring's boorish behavior, and the overbearing manner of the heavily armed guards, it was a hint of the kind of regime Hitler would establish if he came to power.

"If Hitler does not come back in to offer an explanation or do something soon," von Müller remarked to one of his friends, "the audience will turn entirely against him."

But there, suddenly, he was, flanked by Hess and Lenk, making his way to the platform to deliver a speech which Müller later described as "a rhetorical masterpiece that did honor to the greatest of stage performers." The purpose was largely to gain time by telling the impatient audience that the "negotiations" with Kahr, Lossow, and Seisser were taking a bit longer than the ten minutes he had promised. Yet within seconds almost the entire crowd was on his side, virtually giving him its jubilant, frenzied power-of-attorney. As Müller described it, "Never before have I seen the mood of a mass audience change so quickly and dramatically. It was almost as if a sorcerer were casting a magic spell over them."

He began quietly enough, reiterating that his move was not directed against von Kahr, then launched into his oration.

"German nationalist comrades," Hitler intoned, "five years ago today the greatest of all atrocities was committed, plunging our poor, wretched people into boundless misery. Today, after five years, the time has come when that misfortune must end.

"Thus, I propose that the von Knilling cabinet be deposed and a new Bavarian government be established with a regent and a prime minister who has dictatorial powers. As regent, I propose Herr von Kahr, and as prime minister, Herr Pöhner.

"I also declare the government of the November criminals in Berlin deposed. Ebert is declared deposed, Stresemann too. A new German national government will be named today, right here in Bavaria, in Munich. A national German army will be established immediately. I propose that I take over the political leadership of the provisional nationalist government until we have settled scores with the criminals who are bringing Germany to ruin. Excellency Ludendorff is to assume the leadership of the national German army. General Lossow will be the German Reichswehr minister. Colonel Seisser is to be German Reich police minister.

"The duty of the provisional government," he thundered, "will be to rally behind it the whole might of this country and all its provinces, to save the German people, and to march against that den of iniquity, Berlin!"

The applause was tumultuous and the din of acclaim deafening. Hitler waited for it to subside, then, measuring every word, continued in a slow cadence:

"I ask you now where you stand. Outside this hall, in another room, three men—Kahr, Lossow, Seisser—are deliberating and wrestling with their emotions. They are engaged in a bitter inner struggle to reach a decision that depends on you. I ask you now. Can I tell them that you stand behind them, that you are in accord with my proposals, with this solution to the German question?"

An incredible clamor of 3,000 voices shouted "Jawohl!" and "Heil Hitler!"

In the side room, now guarded only by Ulrich Graf, who had discreetly put his pistol back in his coat pocket, the atmosphere had become a bit more convivial—almost chummy. Weber, Kriebel, and Pöhner were trying in a conciliatory fashion—Seisser was later to describe it as "saccharine"—to persuade the triumvirate to collaborate.

Kahr, sitting glumly on the only chair in the room, was still protesting angrily about the indignity to which Hitler had subjected him in the auditorium.

"To march in like that, to interrupt me in the *middle* of my speech, take me prisoner, and escort me out under armed guard like a common criminal—why, it's unheard of, impudent, unforgivable," he spluttered. "I could never cooperate under those circumstances and with someone like that."

Pöhner, seemingly deferential to the stubborn bureaucrat whom he had served so long as the police chief of Munich, tried to mollify him, but with little success.

"And why couldn't he have waited eight or ten days longer?" Kahr continued. "I have already sent trustworthy emissaries to North Germany to win the agreement and support of patriotic forces there. Just another week or so."

Lossow and Seisser, on the other hand, were showing some signs of swinging around. Especially as Weber reminded them calmly and insistently that, after all, "we have been in general agreement on the necessity of this step for months."

"Yes, gentlemen," Kriebel seconded him. "For months, in all our discussions, we have all agreed that steps had to be taken. Tonight we have merely tried to make it easier for you to take them."

Weber lit a cigarette and offered one to Seisser.

"Have you got one for me too?" Lossow asked, sliding off the edge of the table.

At Seisser's insistence, Weber agreed to allow Major Hunglinger back into the room. Indeed, except for von Kahr, still sitting there rocklike and morose, it was beginning to look like a meeting of chiefs-of-staff. There was only one tense moment, when Lossow again whispered to Hunglinger, "Put on an act."

"Please," Weber said sharply. "The gentlemen must not talk to each . . ."

His admonition was almost drowned out by the sound of the ovation in the auditorium.

Surveying the scene, Hitler waited, arms folded, for the roar of approval to ebb. Then he continued.

"You can see," he said, "that what motivates us is neither self-conceit nor self-interest, but only a burning desire to join the battle, in this grave eleventh hour, for our German Fatherland. And we want to create a state based on federal principles in which, at last, our beloved Bavaria will have the position to which it is justly entitled."

Again there was an outcry of approval. Announcing that he would return to his "consultations" with Kahr, Lossow, and Seisser, and "let them know how you feel," Hitler once more reminded the frenzied crowd that the hall was surrounded and that no one could leave. He concluded on a note of hysteria and high drama.

"One last thing I can tell you. Either the German Revolution begins tonight, and the morrow will find in Germany a true nationalist government, or it will find us dead."

He had played like a virtuoso on all the emotional instruments. A regent for Bavaria? There was no such role, but the proposal won over the monarchists and supporters of von Kahr. Federalism? It offered hope to the Bavarian separatists. Ludendorff to head the army? The name was magic. A Reich police minister? There had never been one before, but was there a law-and-order man in the hall who didn't think one was needed? A march on Berlin to throw out the "November criminals"? It sounded like a prayer answered.

The acclaim that followed Hitler out of the auditorium was ear-shattering.

To Karl Alexander von Müller, the histrionics and melodrama were painful. He could not make up his mind whether Hitler was a man consumed, a brilliant showman, or a political Mephisto. But he felt sure of one thing: Kahr, whom he also knew well, would never go along with something like this. Hitler, he told friends at the table, would keep Kahr in custody, and "we will all probably be locked up in here, at least through the morning." He was wrong.

Printshop owners Ferdinand Schreiber and Anton Schmidt looked at each other knowingly. Now, finally, they understood why they had been asked to keep typesetters and pressmen on overtime for "a big poster order" that would be coming through "late."

"I'm going to look for Max Amann and see if he can't get us out of here," Schreiber said to his competitor.

Known to the SA men guarding the doors as "a party printer," Schreiber had no difficulty leaving the hall for the vestibule.

"There'll be a lot of work tonight," said Amann when Schreiber found him. "But you'll have to stay here until everybody is released. It won't take much longer."

Before going triumphantly and confidently back into the little side room, Hitler pulled Hess over to where Göring was standing and handed him a crumpled slip of paper that had been in his pocket for hours.

"Take these men into custody as hostages," he ordered, pointing at the paper. "Keep them in a room upstairs somewhere, under guard, and wait there for further instructions."

Hess looked at the list of scribbled names: Knilling, Schweyer, Gürtner, Wutzelhofer, Berchem, Bernreuther, Zetlmeier. There was also an eighth name but it had been crossed out—that of Josef Banzer.

Göring offered Hess a squad of ten storm troopers "to help," then glanced at the names and suggested adding two more. Police Chief Karl Mantel and Count von Soden, Crown Prince Rupprecht's chef-du-cabinet.

"Did you hear that ovation out in the hall?" Hitler bubbled as he stepped back into the room. "Excellency von Kahr, you will be greeted like a savior; the people out there will carry you on their shoulders when we announce our agreement."

"That is of little importance to me, especially considering the way I was forced out," Kahr grumbled, still hoping, as he insisted later, that somehow the police would come to their rescue.

Their brief exchange was abruptly interrupted by shouts of *"Achtung! Still gestanden!"* and much clicking of bootheels in the hallway outside. The door burst open. It was Ludendorff, stiff and proud as ever, though looking, improbably, not like a field marshal but a pensioner taking his dachshund out for the last walk of the day.

"Gentlemen, I am as surprised by all of this as you are," he announced, deliberately not casting so much as a glance at Hitler—less to avoid compromising him than in apparent irritation at not having been named dictator of Germany himself. "But it appears the step has been taken, and it is a great one for the Fatherland and our patriotic cause," he added stentoriously. "I assume you are with us—all the way."

Not quite, as the next twenty minutes of deliberation and cajoling, especially of Kahr, were to prove. But the atmosphere in the room changed dramatically with Ludendorff's grand entrance, and the old general quickly took charge of the situation.

He turned first to Kahr. "Do not refuse this call to duty. It is the most fateful hour of the German Reich. Do what we all expect of you." But seeing that Kahr was intransigent, Ludendorff left him in the hands of Hitler, Pöhner, and Weber, devoting his attention instead to von Lossow and Seisser, who were standing off to the side.

Both harbored mounting doubts that Ludendorff's "surprise" on entering the room had been genuine, and both were resisting—not because they objected to a coup d'état against a government whose constitution they, as officers, had sworn to uphold. It was their aversion to Hitler, their treatment by the sweaty, pale-faced, hysterical ex-corporal, the timing of the putsch, and their skepticism about the military success of the operation that motivated them to dig in their heels—even in the face of Ludendorff's overwhelming presence.

How soon would it be, they argued, before the French

marched into Aschaffenburg, Bavaria's westernmost city, or Czechoslovakia's President Thomas Masaryk made good on his recent warning not to accept a Fascist dictatorship in Germany and ordered his not inconsequential army through the Bohemian into the Bavarian Woods? And what about the Reichswehr in Thuringia? Who could guarantee that Seeckt would not order that division into combat? And as far as Hermann Ehrhardt's brigade up on the border was concerned, Seisser knew how little they were worth; he had deputized them as auxiliary police. And Ehrhardt, a man with his own consummate political ambitions, was not to be trusted.

These were the arguments of professionals to a man they recognized and respected as their long-time commander. But to Ludendorff they were "tactical," not "strategic," arguments.

Ludendorff had never feared the French. He looked upon the Czechs with the Prussian's traditional contempt for all Slavs, and he believed firmly that "Reichswehr will never fire upon Reichswehr," especially with him in the lead and in command. "Besides," he kept saying, "it is done now. There is no way to go back." Though he, too, seemed to have no clear concept of what going forward would involve.

Moreover, as the discussion dragged on for seemingly endless minutes in two corners of the room, Ludendorff also realized that he would have to appeal to Lossow and Seisser's patriotic emotions and "sense of duty" with more persuasive eloquence.

In the auditorium the continued delay, after Hitler's phenomenally successful performance, was again fomenting unrest, bewilderment, and disgruntlement. "The barometer of opinion," von Müller noted, "is beginning to swing back in the other direction."

Its needle jerked abruptly when Müller's "absentee student," Rudolf Hess—grim-faced, bushy-browed, his dark eyes burning with fanaticism—mounted a chair near the platform, slip of paper in hand. A helmeted SA man stood at his side.

"The gentlemen whose names I am about to read are to go immediately to the main entrance of the hall," he announced sternly.

There was a murmur of confused consternation that turned into indignant protests with the realization that the "gentlemen" were not being summoned to an impromptu cabinet meeting but were about to be arrested.

"Some nationalist salvation this is," someone shouted angrily. "Hitler and his people are swine!"

Nonetheless, the hostages came.

"Prime Minister von Knilling," Hess called out.

"Here," Knilling replied with schoolboy obedience. Red-faced, he rose from his chair.

And so it went with the others. "Interior Minister Schweyer . . . Agricultural Minister Wutzelhofer . . . Ministerial Councilor Josef Zetlmeier . . . Police President Mantel . . . Government Councilor Otto Bernreuther . . . Count von Soden. . . ." Only Justice Minister Gürtner, Zetlmeier, and Lieutenant Colonel Otto von Berchem, Lossow and the Seventh Division's chief-of-staff, failed to answer the call-up. Gürtner tried to hide in the crowd. Von Berchem, having gone to a dinner party that evening, and Zetlmeier, having stayed home, were not in the hall.

As each man dutifully made his way forward, he was taken into custody by one or two SA men and the courteous cordiality ended. The Nazi storm troopers in the foyer were out for "revenge" against the establishment. They shoved and jostled the hostages, especially Wutzelhofer.

"His son got rich speculating with foreign currency," an SA man near the entrance jeered.

"Well, let's find *him* and hang them both," another called out.

"Where's that pig Gürtner?" someone asked.

"He was in the hall earlier," came the reply. "I saw him. He's trying to hide."

Hess dispatched two storm troopers, who swiftly found him.

Georg Rauh, having heard rumors that "Frick will be made police chief," tried to stay close to Mantel and Bernreuther.

"Where do you think you're going?" Göring asked officiously, blocking his path. "*You're* not under arrest. They are."

Rauh persisted and was finally permitted to bring Mantel's coat from the cloakroom. Then he was allowed out of the building. He walked to police headquarters.

Others who wanted to leave were less fortunate. They were truncheoned back into the hall. The situation was becoming so

explosive that Burkhard Büchs, one of the ten remaining municipal patrolmen, feared the Nazis would "start shooting into the
crowd any minute."

Lossow's adjutant, Major Hans von Hösslin, was cornered by
SA men who ordered him to remove the republican cockade from
his garrison cap. "Only General von Lossow gives me orders," he
shot back, escaping their clutches.

One by one, the arrested men were taken upstairs to a private
banquet room not far from Korbinian Reindl's apartment, to wait
until Hitler decided their fate. Two SA men stood guard by the
door; three more, armed with rifles and hand grenades, kept
watch inside. Hess was their supercilious keeper.

Hanfstaengl, having noticed some of the violence and worried
about the impression it might make on the foreign journalists,
rushed upstairs to make sure the hostages were safe and not, as he
feared, being executed on the spot. He bought them all beers,
though he felt miffed when Schweyer indignantly refused to accept one.

In the side room, Ulrich Graf and Adolf Lenk were getting
bored and impatient. Men of simple background and truncated
education, they were somewhat overawed by so much high-ranking
brass and officialdom. They had not expected the revolution to
require so much talking. Moreover, the conversations, at opposite
ends of the room, were being conducted in voices so muted and in
terms so complex that they could barely hear or understand. To
pass the time, Graf inspected and reloaded the Browning, then
handed it back to Hitler, who stuck it wordlessly in his pocket
with barely a nod of thanks.

Kahr was still stonewalling; but Lossow and Seisser appeared
to be weakening under Ludendorff's insistence.

"Well, Lossow," Ludendorff demanded, his voice once more
loud and commandeering, "what do you say?"

There was another moment's pause. Then, with tears in his
eyes, and almost snapping to attention like a raw recruit, Lossow
replied, "Your Excellency's wish is my command."

"So, we're going to do it now, Lossow," Ludendorff beamed.

"I will organize the army as you need it, to win, Excellency,"
he said.

The two clasped hands firmly. Seisser, seeing the little ceremony, stepped up stiffly and offered his hand too. It was apparent
that he had been waiting for a signal from Lossow.

Ludendorff then turned his attention to Kahr, who seemed as
adamant and personally piqued as ever. Pöhner, Weber, Kriebel,
and Hitler had him virtually cornered and were assaulting him
with arguments. Ludendorff, dragging Lossow and Seisser with
him across the room, joined in.

"You cannot deny yourself to the German people in this historic hour," he interjected.

"It won't work, it won't last," Kahr said gloomily. "You
should have waited a while longer. It could have been done in a
week or two."

"But what difference would one or two gentlemen from the
north make?" Ludendorff countered. "If it's going to work in
eight or ten days with their help, it will also work now without
them."

"Besides," Pöhner added, "your name and Excellency Ludendorff's have such a glorious ring and high reputation, and Herr
Hitler has so much ability to influence great masses, there is no
reason at all why it should fail."

Now it was Hitler's turn again. "You cannot renege at this
point," he said defiantly. "You heard how the auditorium thundered when I told people what we were doing and that you would
lead us. Do you really think I can walk back into that hall and tell
all your ardent supporters that it was just a mistake, that there will
be no revolution tonight after all, because Excellency von Kahr
wants to postpone it another week? Is that what you want me to
do?"

These were arguments to which Kahr no longer had rejoin-
ders. He proffered a surprisingly different objection.

"I cannot do it because I am a monarchist," he insisted. "I am
the representative of the throne. To do what you propose, I need
the permission of Crown Prince Rupprecht. He is our king."

"Precisely," Pöhner broke in. "As a royal official all my life, I
feel the same way. But it is our duty to act, because the king
would want us to act were he in this room now. We must undo
the revolution that deposed his father with a new one. As civil
servants, it is our obligation to stand in front of our king and

shield him, not trot along behind him."

"Yes," Hitler added excitedly, recognizing the psychological opening that had eluded him. "It is to right the wrongs that were done to the crown in 1918 that we are acting tonight and imploring you to avenge that crime.

"If you wish, Excellency, I will drive to Berchtesgaden immediately after the meeting to tell His Majesty that our patriotic action, our national revolution tonight, is restitution for the injustice done to his father five years ago."

The idea seemed to appeal to von Kahr.

"All right," he said, agreeing at last—but he would collaborate only as a kind of vicar, a royal governor, on behalf of the crown, not as regent.

Hitler and Ludendorff were elated. It was a double victory.

Neither had ever had much use for Kahr, and both considered him dispensable. They needed only his name and the guarantee that he would not employ his dictatorial powers to thwart them. That von Kahr would collaborate in the *name* of the crown was more than either Hitler or Ludendorff had hoped for.

Agreement having been reached, they all shook hands warmly.

"I, the German people, the nation, are indebted to you, Excellency von Kahr," Hitler gushed. "I will never forget what you have done in this hour, and you will always have my gratitude."

Quickly they drafted the declarations they would make to the assembly.

But just as they were about to leave for the auditorium, von Kahr balked once more, refusing to return to the hall from which Hitler had abducted him so unceremoniously. One of his aides, he said, could read the announcement for him.

Almost shoving the little man, Hitler and Pöhner gave the psychological screw yet another turn. "Excellency, it is you they want out there. You will be cheered and applauded as never before in your life." It would prove one of their few true statements of the evening.

Looking around, Kahr seemed to beam at the thought, adjusted and smoothed his frock coat, and, with the small band of conspirators at his heels, strutted out of the room.

Hitler, glancing at his closest and most loyal supporters waiting in the corridor—Scheubner-Richter, Rosenberg, Amann, Julius Streicher, Gottfried Feder, Göring, Berchtold—gave them a triumphant smile.

It was 9:40 P.M. Slightly more than an hour had passed since the Führer and his storm troopers had barged into the Bürgerbräukeller, surrounded it, and taken the huge audience captive.

The atmosphere in the smoky auditorium was a complex mixture of irritated impatience, glum resignation, indignant outrage, and enthusiastic anticipation—moods all intensified by too much beer.

Karl Alexander von Müller, staring into his mug and still numbed by the vision of von Knilling and the other elected and appointed officials being arrested and removed under guard, was startled out of his musings by the sound of shouting and cries of "Heil!" at the rear of the hall. Climbing up on his chair, he could hardly believe what he was seeing: Hitler, Ludendorff, Kahr, Lossow, Seisser, Pöhner—very obviously unified and in agreement. Now what?

Slowly the group moved forward through the tables. A human aisle formed in front of them and closed the instant they passed. Kahr led the little procession up the steps to the platform. It was too narrow to accommodate them all in a row. Ludendorff stood in the middle, Kahr to his left, Hitler to his right, while the others lined up behind them, almost out of sight.

The silence was tomblike as Kahr, his face an emotionless mask, began to speak.

"In this hour of the Fatherland's greatest need," he said somberly, "I have decided to accept the burden of steering Bavaria's destiny as governor on behalf of the monarchy—"

The ovation that interrupted and swelled up to him was delirious.

"—as governor representing the monarchy smashed by wanton criminal hands five years ago," he continued after the bedlam had quieted. "I do this with a heavy heart and, I hope, for the benefit of our beloved Bavarian homeland and our Great German Fatherland."

Hitler, his pale blue eyes shimmering, a joyful, almost childlike smile on his face, grabbed Kahr's hand and held it long, ritualistically, in what seemed to most people in the auditorium a ceremonial oath. To others, less emotional and impassioned, it seemed like "an agreement between two tax collectors." Some felt Hitler had practically "yanked" Kahr's hand, and one acute observer noted, "My God, what is he doing? Hypnotizing him?"

Hitler stepped forward.

"The thanks we owe Excellency von Kahr cannot be expressed tonight," he said. "But in this moment it is already engraved in the history of the German nation.

"Now I want to explain what has been decided. Herr Pöhner has declared his willingness to share the task of governing Bavaria with Excellency von Kahr. At the same time, I want to announce that the provisional German nationalist government has been formed and that Excellency Ludendorff is the leader and commander-in-chief of the German national army with dictatorial powers—a decision that will remove the stigma of infamy and shame from the brows of German soldiers."

Again there was tumultuous acclaim.

"Further," Hitler went on, "let me tell you that General von Lossow, as Reichswehr minister, has been assigned the task of carrying out the organization of the army, whose mission will be to cleanse Germany of those criminals who five years ago discredited and destroyed us. As Reich police minister, Colonel von Seisser will cooperate in purging Germany of those elements who plunged us into our misfortune.

"And in the coming weeks and months"—his voice rose to a pathos-laden crescendo—"I will fulfill the vow I made to myself five years ago, as a gas-blinded cripple in a hospital here: never to rest or pause until the criminals of November 1918 are crushed, until a Germany of power and greatness, of freedom and glory, has risen out of the wretched rubble that it is today. Amen!

"Long live the Bavarian government of Pöhner and Kahr! *Hoch! Hoch! Hoch!* Long live the German national government! *Hoch! Hoch! Hoch!*"

Ear-shattering screams of "Heil! Heil Hitler!" filled the hall.

And while the fever raged, Hanfstaengl was busily translating for the huddle of correspondents around him.

Now it was Ludendorff's turn. His massive, chiseled face was sinister and somber, as if to say that this was a matter of life and death, more likely death than life. He was every inch the general striving to inspire an army going into a suicidal battle.

"Deeply moved by the momentousness of this occasion, although taken by surprise," he pontificated, "I place myself in the service of the true nationalist government of Germany and will strive to restore to it the old black-white-and-red cockade stripped away by the infamous revolution.

"Everything is at stake. A German who experiences this hour cannot hesitate about giving his all to this cause, both in spirit and with a full German heart. This hour is the turning point of history. But let us look at it in full recognition of the difficulty of the task we face, convinced of and imbued with the gravity of our responsibility.

"Let us go to work, side by side with the entire nation," he continued. "German men, I harbor no doubts about this: if we do this work with a pure heart, God's blessing will be with us. I pray for that blessing, for without God's will, nothing can be done. But I am also convinced that, when God in Heaven sees true German men are there again, He *will* be on our side."

The ovation was milder. God, apparently, was not in such great demand that night.

Then came Lossow. Smiling ironically, he seemed almost casually indifferent and perfunctory. From the back row he expressed the hope that he would succeed in fulfilling the mission assigned him. Seisser seconded the motion, pledging to create a unified national police under the old imperial colors.

Pöhner, his tone nasally arrogant, promised to stand "loyally by Herr von Kahr's side in the fulfillment of his difficult task." After all, he reminded the audience, he and Kahr had always stood and worked together. "His Excellency can depend on me."

Then all six shook hands solemnly, and the notion that the ceremony was not intended seriously hardly entered any one's mind, not even that of von Müller, by far the most perspicacious observer in the hall. To be sure, he regarded what they were saying and proposing—"to try to conquer Berlin and change the course of European politics from Munich"—as madness. But he knew each of the six men on the platform personally—well enough, he thought, to believe that they meant every word they had uttered, no matter how bombastic it sounded. If there was one exception, perhaps it was Lossow. His foxlike face remained enigmatic.

Hitler spoke once more.

"Let us commemorate, in this historic hour, the German Fatherland to which we pledge our loyalty above all else in the world. '*Deutschland, Deutschland über alles.*'"

The 3,000 voices in the hall burst into the national anthem.

Julius Streicher was one of the first to make it through the jubilant, frenzied crowd "to congratulate the members of the new government."

The triumvirs and the conspirators, surrounded by SA and police who, even if they were not Nazis, now believed they were serving "the legitimate government," forced their way back through the throng to the little side room "to get to work" and plan the next step: the march on Berlin.

Taking Göring aside, Hitler told him to select a few "trustworthy" police officers—Hofmann, Glaser, "and perhaps Herrmann"—to conduct a thorough identity check at the exits. "We must be sure there were no Socialist or Bolshevist spies in the hall," he said. "And put a guard on Seisser's deputy, Colonel Banzer. I took his name off the hostage list, but I do not trust him."

Friedrich Weber hunted in the crowd for his father-in-law, publisher Julius Lehmann. He wanted the keys to the Lehmann villa on Holzkirchener Strasse in the fashionable suburb of Grosshesselohe—a comfortable, dignified, and perfectly secluded prison for Knilling and the other hostages. No one would even think of looking there, he mused.

Rosenberg, finding Lenk in the crowd, dispatched him to the *Völkischer Beobachter* with "urgent copy."

Hanfstaengl, seeing the crush at the doors, spirited his journalistic charges out via the kitchen. Spotting him, and thinking he also was going to leave, Göring called out, "Do remember to call Carin, please."

Finally, in the side room, away from the noisy turmoil, the members of the "new government" got busy.

That they were committing high treason—even under duress

or the pretense of "playing a comedy," as Lossow later described it—seemed not to faze any of them at the moment.

In one of his first "official" acts, Hitler named Gottfried Feder as "Reich finance minister." He would preside at "the offices of the provisional government"—a bank that Max Amann was planning to requisition one floor below his own apartment on Kanal Strasse.

Kahr's chief preoccupation, in his talk with Pöhner, was replacing Wutzelhofer as minister of agriculture. Pöhner, on the other hand, seemed primarily interested in having a police chief for Munich, "now that Mantel is, shall we say, detained."

"I assume," Kahr said, "your preference would be Frick. You agree politically, and I recall that you worked well together when you were police president and I was prime minister."

They most certainly had. Pöhner thanked Kahr for "the good suggestion." Looking toward Hermann Kriebel, he asked whether Frick had been notified. Well, yes, but not told that he was the new chief. Kriebel dispatched his "liaison and communications officer," Max Neunzert, to inform Frick "personally" at police headquarters.

Ludendorff, Lossow, and Seisser, meanwhile, busied themselves with problems of military strategy and the army's organization. Kriebel, privy to the talks, offered to serve Ludendorff as "temporary chief-of-staff." "But when things are settled," Kriebel added, "I want nothing more than the command of a battalion or regiment, in keeping with my last active-duty rank."

His first action as "chief-of-staff" was to dispatch a motorcycle courier to Röhm's little army coming up Brienner Strasse. Instead of the Bürgerbräukeller, where they were no longer needed, Röhm should occupy Seventh Division headquarters in the old Bavarian war ministry on Schönfeld Strasse and wait there for Ludendorff's arrival. It would be his command post.

"How should we notify the populace?" asked von Kahr, turning to Hitler. "Should I perhaps hold a public rally tomorrow morning?"

"Why don't you leave that to me, Excellency," Hitler replied swiftly. "After all, propaganda is rather my specialty." Amann and others, he assured Kahr, were already drafting the proclamations for the thousands of posters to be printed. And Streicher would organize scores of mass meetings to be held in the morning.

The crowd in the auditorium was barely thinning, thanks to the "identity controls" being conducted by police, SA, and Berchtold's Stosstrupp members in the hall, the vestibule, and the long narrow corridor leading to the street. In fact, they were blocking the way and requiring each person to show ID cards or passports. It was, so to speak, the new "nationalist order" of a "free" Germany.

Georg Stumpf, Georg Ott, Max von Gruber, Karl Alexander von Müller, Robert Riemerschmid, Julius Lehmann, Eugen Zentz, Johann Kress, Theodor Singer, printers Ferdinand Schreiber and Anton Schmidt, and most of the others were eventually "cleared" as they passed single file, identity documents in hand, through the row of storm troopers and detectives. Some, like Schreiber and Schmidt, who had Nazi connections, were released faster than others.

Banker Ludwig Wassermann was not cleared at all. "*Da kommt das Judenschwein*—There comes the Jewish pig," a storm trooper snarled, spotting Wassermann in the throng. Another one grabbed him and, half shoving, half pulling, hauled him upstairs into Rudolf Hess's care.

Incensed by the arrest, Wassermann's friend and host for the evening, Georg Pschorr, a prominent Munich brewer, sought out Police Inspector Siegfried Herrmann, demanding that he do something to obtain the banker's release.

"There is nothing *I* can do about that," Herrmann replied, shrugging his shoulders and smiling politely. "Why don't you ask Captain Göring or Lieutenant Berchtold over there?"

Pschorr thought better of it and left Wassermann to his fate. He was only the first of scores of Jewish hostages who would end up as prisoners of the Nazis in the Bürgerbräukeller that night.

Outside, on Rosenheimer Strasse, traffic was still blocked off and backed up in both directions, and nearly 1,000 SA and Oberland troopers were milling about.

Down on Ludwig Bridge, another fieldpiece had been added to guard the approaches to the hill.

At the Staats-Theater, the curtain had rung down on the last act of *Fidelio*, Hans Knappertsbusch had retired to his dressing room, and the audience was spilling out onto Max-Josef Platz and Residenz Strasse. Only the last of those who left the opera house noticed the company of green-uniformed State Police double-timing along Residenz Strasse to guard the nearby main post office and central telephone exchange.

At the Schauspielhaus on Maximilian Strasse, Carl Zuckmayer, the hopeful young playwright, was just leaving to join friends in one of the artists' and intellectuals' taverns in Schwabing.

Dietrich Eckart, the Teutonic-Nationalist bard, and photographer Heinrich Hoffmann were quaffing their last beer and playing their last round of tarok in the Schelling Salon.

It was 10 P.M. The temperature had dropped a few more degrees to just about the freezing point, and a light mixture of snow and rain had begun to fall. The sprawling metropolis on the Isar—King Ludwig I's "new Athens"—was, on the whole, still blissfully unaware of the historic events that had just transpired.

As the eyewitnesses to those events began trickling out of the Bürgerbräukeller, breathing in the night air and clearing their lungs of the beery haze they had been inhaling for the past couple of hours, many of them began assembling in columns.

These were the members of the "patriotic leagues"—veterans of the war, the various free corps, the White 1919 counterrevolution, the burgher militias. Young, middle-aged, a few elderly, some of them proudly wore their old uniforms and the medals they had won, others were in Bavarian hunting and highland garb with lederhosen and loden jackets or coats, quite a few in the conservative turn-of-the-century frock coats, stiff high collars, and bowler hats that had remained popular.

They started marching down Rosenheimer Strasse across Ludwig Bridge and into the city, singing and shouting lustily the tidings of the great "nationalist revolution." SA units and Rossbach's Infantry School contingent, on their way to the Bürgerbräu, passed them in the other direction.

Max Neunzert, on his way to Ett Strasse, watched the cheering throng from a seat next to the window as the streetcar he had caught inched and clanged its way slowly forward. He felt foolish now, having gone home to change, and wished he had kept on his uniform. As soon as he was finished at the police station, he decided, he would dash back to his apartment on Mars Strasse and remedy that.

Karl Alexander von Müller and Robert Riemerschmid were walking down the hill from the beerhall together.

"I am surprised you did not offer your services to the new government," Riemerschmid said.

Von Müller reiterated his doubts and his worries about the possibility of French and Czechoslovak intervention.

"And what will you do if, tomorrow morning, they ask you to collaborate?" Riemerschmid persisted.

Von Müller breathed deeply and, lost in grave thought, kept silent for a while. "Well," he said finally, "under those circumstances there is nothing else I can do but cooperate, no matter how fateful one considers this coup or how unpredictable its outcome."

8

Police Inspectors Lorenz Reithmeier and Rudolf Schmäling bounded out of the trolley when it shuddered to a noisy halt at the intersection of Neuhauser and Ett streets. Jostling pedestrians and passers-by they sprinted around the corner to the "night entrance" of police headquarters, jumped into the cage of a paternoster elevator that took them to the third floor, and darted down the corridor to Captain Fritz Stumpf's duty office. He was talking to Wilhelm Frick.

Trying to catch his breath, Reithmeier told them what he had seen and heard at the Löwenbräukeller.

"We know," Stumpf said calmly, offering in exchange the information he had gotten from the Bürgerbräukeller. Then, trying to signal Reithmeier with raised eyebrows, he added, "Dr. Frick here feels that nothing can be done at the moment and that we should wait for further developments."

"Yes," Frick interjected, "really nothing for the time being. But I suggest you stay here for a while, Inspector. I may need your help."

Reithmeier and Schmäling nodded, glanced at each other and ambled out into the hallway, ostensibly on their way to the men's room. "There's something fishy about this," Schmäling said, when he was sure they were out of Frick's hearing. "If he asks about me, make up some excuse. I'm going to the Bürgerbräukeller to find out what has really been happening there."

Striding briskly out of police headquarters, Schmäling turned right to take a shortcut along dimly lit Augustiner Strasse, past the two onion-domed towers of Munich Cathedral. Thus he did not notice Georg Rauh entering the building—just as Rauh, breathing hard from the long walk from Rosenheimer Strasse, did not realize that Ministerial Councilor Josef Zetlmeier happened to be a few paces behind him.

Zetlmeier, a strait-laced civil servant of the old school, and the closest in those days to feeling a commitment to parliamentary democracy, was Interior Minister Schweyer's senior deputy. An acute political observer, he had for almost two years been warning of the potential dangers of the growing Nazi movement and the risks of any kind of collaboration with Hitler. Better, perhaps, than any other official in the Bavarian hierarchy, he knew the extent to which the police had been subverted and won over to the Fascist cause—thanks to Frick and Pöhner. That was why his name had been on Rudolf Hess's list of government officials to be arrested in the Bürgerbräukeller.

But Zetlmeier, not particularly interested in what Kahr had to say, had been at home and blissfully oblivious to his own intended incarceration when the phone rang with the first fragmentary information about the putsch. The informant was his counterpart at the ministry of agriculture, Ministerial Councilor Albrecht Haenlein, Wutzelhofer's ranking deputy.

It sounded preposterous, but Zetlmeier called police headquarters. When he found only Frick in charge there—giving his standard evasive answers and explanations—Zetlmeier sensed there was real trouble indeed. He was galvanized into action. Stopping first at his own offices in the interior ministry, then going to the state parliament building—both dark, empty, and quiet—he rushed to Ett Strasse to find out more from Frick.

"You must have more information than what you told me on the telephone," Zetlmeier insisted.

Smiling enigmatically, Frick shrugged and shook his head.

Still numbed by his encounter with Göring and by Mantel and Bernreuther's ignominious arrest, but unaware of what had happened in the auditorium after that, Rauh hurried upstairs to the senior police officials' apartments on the fourth floor of the Ett Strasse building and knocked at Frick's door. His wife said she did not know where he was.

Rauh thought the explanation oddly inadequate. She must know. But he went first to his own flat—a flight higher, where junior officials lived—to doff his damp coat and freshen up. Just as he was dousing the light to return downstairs, the house phone rang. It was Inspector Reithmeier. Had he heard what had happened? "Not only heard," Rauh replied, "I saw it. I was there."

"Well, Herr Frick is down here, in the duty officer's room, looking for you," Reithmeier said, adding cryptically, almost as an afterthought, "and he would like you to bring the keys to Herr Mantel's suite."

So it was true, Rauh thought, remembering the rumors he had heard in the Bürgerbräukeller.

He was absorbed in thought as he walked down the steps again, past Frick's floor. There he nearly collided with a tall man who was obviously in a hurry—his acquaintance Max Neunzert.

"Do you know where Frick is?" the ex-lieutenant asked excitedly.

"In the duty officer's room, and I'm on my way there now," Rauh answered, even more perplexed at seeing a confidant of both Hitler and Kriebel. What did he want here? Hadn't he seen him in the Bürgerbräu just a while ago?

"But you must agree that it would be pointless to send a small, inadequately equipped company of State Police up there, Herr Zetlmeier," Frick was saying, trying to justify his inaction. "There are supposed to be a thousand storm troopers around—"

He was interrupted by Rauh and Neunzert's abrupt entry. Seeing Zetlmeier, Rauh pulled him aside, reported what had happened, and warned the official that his name too had been on the list of those arrested. Zetlmeier, as uncertain of Rauh's loyalties as he was of the other police officials, and suspecting it was a pretext to get him out of the building, turned instead to hear what Neunzert was telling Frick with so much enthusiasm.

"... and Kahr is governor for the king, Pöhner was named prime minister, and then they all shook hands while the audience roared approval," Neunzert bubbled. "And you, Herr Doktor Frick, I was sent here to tell you that you have been appointed as police president effective immediately."

"But who said that?" asked Frick, feigning incredulity and officious skepticism. "On whose orders? If what you say about Herr Mantel is true, I could not possibly do that. I need written instructions from Herr von Kahr or Pöhner—"

"I have instructions to tell you personally," Neunzert countered, "and should you refuse, you will be ordered."

"Well, under the circumstances," Frick said, "let us say that I am acting chief while Herr Mantel is unable to carry out his duties."

"We have not yet decided where the main revolutionary command post will be," Neunzert added, assuming that Frick's "appointment" was settled. "It may be here, it may be at the division headquarters. You will be notified, probably by me. But now I am going home to change into uniform. I can be reached there by telephone for a while."

After dictating his phone number—"5-4-9-6-3"—to a dumbfounded Reithmeier, Neunzert clicked his heels, saluted, and swerved to leave. Once more he looked at Rauh and Zetlmeier. "We're going to hang a few people tonight," he remarked. Then he was gone.

Zetlmeier, nonplussed and bewildered by what Neunzert had said about Kahr, Lossow, and Seisser's collaboration with Hitler, left a few minutes later for Kahr's headquarters to find out for himself where matters stood. If they were as ominous as he had been told, he hoped there were members of the Bavarian cabinet who were still free to resist a coup d'état by forming an exile government backed by Reichswehr forces commanded from Berlin. Franz Matt, the deputy premier and minister of culture and education, was the man whose name first came to his mind.

As he stalked out of police headquarters into the cold wet night, Zetlmeier heard the sound of raucous singing and the clump of many marching feet on Neuhauser Strasse. He went the back way. The putsch he had dreaded and anticipated for so long was now a grim reality. And the police, he feared, were completely in the putschists' hands.

In the room where Wilhelm Frick presided, it seemed that way indeed. But up on the third floor, in Major von Imhoff's office, events were taking a different turn.

Major General Jakob von Danner had looked improbably unmilitary in his civilian suit and drenched topcoat as he strode into Sigmund von Imhoff's bare office and shook himself like a wet dog. "I can't believe what you're saying. What kind of hoax is this?" he asked repeatedly as von Imhoff spelled out what information he had.

Imhoff was relieved to have the general there at last. It was not merely von Danner's rank but his position as the Reichswehr city commandant of Munich which absolved von Imhoff of decision-making responsibilities. In situations requiring martial law and emergency measures, the army was in charge, not the State Police.

In clipped, precise tones, von Imhoff reported on the steps already taken. He had alerted all State Police units, coordinated with Baron Heinrich von Freyberg, the duty officer at Kahr's headquarters on Maximilian Strasse, and placed the central telephone and telegraph exchanges under guard.

But now what? The two aristocrats looked at each other with a sense of bewilderment. They knew that both Lossow and Seisser, just two days earlier, had left no doubt that collaboration with Hitler and his rabble was out of the question. Officers do not change their minds that quickly. But if they had, what then?

They were discussing possible next steps and studying organization charts to see what forces were at their disposal when Frick sauntered in.

"I wonder how it will all work out," he said casually and walked back out, only to remark at the door, "By the way, the new government—Prime Minister Pöhner—will be coming here. Care to come downstairs?"

Danner and Imhoff mumbled an inaudible reply and bent over their charts.

"I must get out of here," the general said when Frick had left.

"I am going to the city command, where I will have more freedom of movement. Send anyone who comes or calls there."

Von Imhoff assigned Hans Bergen, a young State Police captain, to accompany Danner as a liaison officer. Hurrying down the stairs, the general and Bergen missed another drenched civilian coming up to the third floor on one of the elevators—Lieutenant Colonel Otto von Berchem, Seventh Division chief-of-staff.

"What is happening, what's going on?" he asked agitatedly as he rushed into von Imhoff's room. "I was going home after dinner with friends when I saw SA and Oberland troops marching all over the city. They looked as if they were going to war!"

Von Imhoff tried to calm him and fill him in.

"Why, that is unbelievable. It is preposterous. Outrageous," Berchem interrupted with each successive detail.

The colonel waited long enough for Danner to have reached his office, phoned him from Imhoff's desk, and left.

Captain Karl Wild, deputy commander of the State Police guard detachment at von Kahr's General State Commissariat on Maximilian Strasse, had not been required to accompany Kahr or Seisser to the Bürgerbräu. At ten o'clock, after an ample supper washed down by a number of beers, Wild was relaxing in civilian clothes and house slippers in the parlor of his comfortable ground-floor apartment at the corner of Glück and Amalien streets. He felt like calling it a night when he was startled by loud shouting, singing, and the blaring of a brass band. The noise seemed to be coming from nearby Brienner Strasse. Yanking open the window, he saw uniformed men swinging swastika and red-white-and-black imperial flags.

"What's all the noise?" Wild called out. "Don't you know what time it is? People want to sleep. Oktoberfest ended a month ago."

"The government has been deposed by Hitler!" men shouted lustily. "The Nationalist Revolution has begun!"

Not even bothering to change into his green police uniform, Wild put on shoes, grabbed a coat, rushed out, and ran the half dozen blocks across Odeonsplatz, past the Residenz, to Maximilian Strasse.

"Everything is quiet here," the sentry outside von Kahr's

apartment reported, "but I have heard the same rumor."

Unable to locate any of the senior officers assigned directly to von Kahr's staff—Major Franz Hunglinger, Lieutenant Colonel Wilhelm Muxel, or Major Heinrich Doehla—Wild acted on his own: with unprecedented speed, considering the strictures of military hierarchy and the ingrained habit of waiting for proper orders, and with considerable foresight.

Within fifteen minutes he alerted the company-sized guard detachment, deployed it to surround the entire neo-Gothic building with its innumerable wings and approaches from several streets, and issued strict orders that no one was to enter the Commissariat without his permission.

"Shoot if you must," he told the troopers. Twice during the next three hours they almost had to. But thanks to Wild's prescience, the Commissariat—like the Engineer and Infantry barracks and the telephone and telegraph exchanges—became another key stronghold the putschists did not conquer, though they certainly tried.

The building safely sealed off, Wild went up to Kahr's suite of offices on the third floor to get more information. There he found Baron von Freyberg and Doehla, who had bicycled over from his nearby apartment after getting phone calls from von Imhoff and Freyberg. But they, too, had heard only rumors.

Ernst Röhm's ragtag army of nearly 2,000 SA, Oberland, and Reichskriegsflagge storm troopers was marching noisily up Brienner Strasse. Heinrich Himmler, proudly carrying his banner, was in the vanguard. Röhm's trusted young friend Count Karl-Leon du Moulin-Eckart, straddling a noisy, foul-smelling Viktoria motorcycle, was riding slowly beside the column, trying like a sheep dog to keep the unruly multitude of warriors in line. The band was playing and a crowd of Müncheners, growing larger by the minute as theaters and the opera let out, stood on the sidewalk cheering wildly as news of the "revolution" spread.

In the front ranks with Röhm were his closest aides—Karl Osswald, Josef Seydel, and Hans Streck—the Munich SA Regiment's Wilhelm Brückner, Hans Knauth, and Hermann Esser, who had decided, after all, not to go back home to bed. Not far behind were Himmler's RKF friends Theodor Casella, Martin

Faust, Walther Lembert, Karl Hühnlein, and Ludwig Binz.

Their ostensible destination was the Bürgerbräukeller—albeit with two important intermediate stops along the way: St. Anne's Monastery and the Palatia fraternity house, in both of which there were enough hidden arms to wage a war.

Suddenly another motorcycle came chattering down Brienner Strasse toward the advancing column, its rider wearing a ski cap with the death's-head insignia of Josef Berchtold's Stosstrupp.

Beckoning Röhm off to the side, the cyclist announced, "Orders from Colonel Kriebel and Captain Göring. Only the SA and Oberland are to go to the Bürgerbräukeller. You are supposed to take your men to the war ministry—Seventh Division—and establish the headquarters for Excellency Ludendorff. He and General von Lossow will be there soon."

Röhm hurried forward to catch up and pass the word along. When the column reached Odeonsplatz, it split up in several directions.

"Double-time, march!" Karl Osswald bellowed, and with Himmler still waving the flag, Casella, Faust, Hühnlein, and Binz behind him, his one hundred Reichskriegsflagge troopers jogged across the square, through the Hofgarten, and down Prinzregenten Strasse to Reitmor Strasse and the Palatia fraternity house.

Wilhelm Brückner and Hans Knauth, soon joined by other SA detachments and trucks that had been dispatched from the Bürgerbräukeller, led their battalions past the Residenz and von Danner's city garrison headquarters through the quiet residential Lehel district to St. Anne's.

Röhm, accompanied by Seydel, Streck, and Lembert, with a hundred more Reichskriegsflagge troopers behind them, turned left on Odeonsplatz and, singing loudly, marched down stately Ludwig Strasse, past palaces and government buildings, to the war ministry.

The band from the Löwenbräukeller, not knowing which group to follow, decided to break up and go home.

Andreas Mutz, the sixty-two-year-old caretaker of the Corpshaus Palatia at Reitmor Strasse No. 28, one of the numerous dueling-fraternity houses in Munich, was already in his pajamas when the doorbell rang shrilly. The late summons might have irritated a less kindly man, but Mutz was used to such calls. Student members had keys, but more often than not, one of the boys would forget or lose his and rouse Mutz to get back into the house at night. Struggling into a bathrobe, the old man shuffled to the front door. It was no group of late revelers waiting there.

Osswald and Casella nearly knocked him over as they charged in, Hühnlein, Binz, Himmler, and Faust at their heels, and dozens of other troopers, many of them helmeted, right behind. Taking a key from his pocket, Binz led them downstairs to the basement bowling alley where, three days earlier, he and Hühnlein, assisted by other fraternity brothers who were also members of the Reichskriegsflagge, had stored numerous cases of ammunition, rifles, carbines, a light machine gun, and extra helmets.

Within minutes, Osswald's detachment was armed and ready. His was but the first to be supplied during the next hour from the ample fraternity-house cache. Assembling his men on the street, he marched them off toward Schönfeld Strasse and the war ministry—double-time.

There, Röhm was waiting impatiently.

Father Polycarp, abbot of St. Anne's Monastery and as nonviolent a Franciscan friar as one might find, was shaken out of his meditations by the sound of several truck engines and the voices of a thousand shouting, singing men outside the abbey grounds.

"Aufmachen! Waffen hergeben!" Brückner and Knauth yelled, pounding incessantly on the main door.

The padre, knowing about the huge store of firearms that Röhm had deposited in the crypt of the monastery church "in case the Bolsheviks attack" but suspecting, correctly, that something more sinister was afoot, ran to his office to phone von Kahr's nearby headquarters for help and advice. But before Major Doehla could even tell the flustered monk that "we do not have sufficient forces here," the Nazis had battered down the door.

In about half an hour they had grabbed and loaded onto the trucks—according to the subsequent official tabulation—3,300 infantry rifles with ample ammunition for each. Now properly armed, the Munich SA regiment, bolstered by Oberländers, set off across the river to the Bürgerbräukeller for further assignment.

Thanks to the call he had received from Major von Imhoff, Reichswehr Captain Wilhelm Daser, duty officer at Seventh Division headquarters, knew what to expect when Röhm, Seydel, and Streck, now backed by Osswald's battle-ready detachment, attempted to enter the war ministry. But the forewarning was of little practical use. He had only a small sentry guard at his disposal.

To be sure, those sentries tried to resist and were prepared to fire when Röhm and his men pushed their way into the courtyard of the building where, for nearly five years, he had served on active duty. But Daser cautioned them against bloodshed. The information from Ett Strasse had been fragmentary. He had little choice but to believe Röhm, who announced, "My orders are to form an honor guard for Ludendorff and Lossow, who are due here any moment."

Though doubtful that "this is all legal," Daser bowed to Röhm's arguments and superior force. His reactions and behavior were typical of those of many army and police officers during the confusing early hours of the putsch. Not only were their loyalties divided—the putschists, after all, were their friends, veterans of the war, the White counterrevolution, the free-corps campaigns and men they believed to be true patriots—but the signals they were getting were confusing. If Lossow and Ludendorff were in this together, Daser reasoned, how could he object to Röhm's presence?

Röhm, his advance guard encamped in the war ministry courtyard and corridors, and with reinforcements arriving, established his headquarters in the third-floor anteroom to von Lossow's office. For the remainder of the night it would be the central command post of the putsch.

Daser and his small staff were allowed to carry out their regular duties. Indeed, for the next two hours the captain and his men retained control of the telephone switchboard.

"But I *have* to have an automobile," Max Neunzert pleaded, holding the earpiece of the wall phone in his apartment in one hand, trying to button the jacket of his old lieutenant's uniform with the other. "I cannot just keep going back and forth all night by streetcar or on foot."

He was speaking to Wilhelm Kolb, the Kampfbund's telephone operator in the Bürgerbräukeller's kitchen.

"Yes, to my apartment on Mars Strasse. . . . I was at the police. . . . Because I had to change clothes. . . . That's right. I feel self-conscious in a suit." He was losing patience—with the buttons on his tunic and with Kolb. "Please, just send the car. I will be waiting outside."

It was ten o'clock sharp when Paula Schlier reported back to her job as a stenotypist at the *Völkischer Beobachter*—for night duty at extra pay.

The editorial offices were the scene of an orgy of celebration. Wine and schnapps flowed by the gallon and champagne corks popped as the celebrants toasted one another and the "new patriotic era" that had just begun. Pistols, some still smoking, were strewn on desktops, apparently shot off with blanks in lieu of firecrackers.

Telephones were ringing incessantly, doors slammed as couriers for the Bürgerbräukeller came and went. One of them was Adolf Lenk, with a front-page proclamation to the Jungsturm, summoning Hitler's teenage supporters to a Friday morning meeting and urging parents to send their sons into the ranks of those "fighting for Germany's freedom."

Most of the editors were waiting for Rosenberg to arrive and set the tone for what the morning's extra would say. Only Josef Stolzing-Cerny, a veteran Nazi party member and erstwhile officer in the Austro-Hungarian army, was making an effort to work—as well as he could in his inebriated state. Pacing back and forth in a threadbare uniform, he was trying to dictate an editorial to Paula Schlier.

"'Germany is awakening from a feverish dream,'" he said. "Have you got that? 'From a feverish dream and—' no, make it 'a *wild* feverish dream and a new glorious era is shining through the clouds. The dark night is passing, and a promising new day is dawning. Proudly, the eagle, that symbol of German might and greatness, raises its head and spreads its wings. . . .'

"There will be more, of course, and Rosenberg will have to approve it," Stolzing said, "but meanwhile you can start typing up this much."

Wilhelm Hoegner, oblivious to the icy wind and the snowy

rain that had begun to fall, was short of breath by the time he reached Erhard Auer's apartment on Nussbaum Strasse.

"You are in great danger," he told the Social Democratic leader. "Hitler has staged a putsch. The Nazis are marching all over the city. You must get out of here. The offer still stands. Come to my apartment, at least for the night. They will never think of searching for you there."

Auer agreed, embraced his wife and daughter, looked for a second into one of the bedrooms where an infant grandchild was sleeping, took some papers from the desk in his study, and went toward the door with Hoegner. "If they do come for me," he said, turning once more to his family, "just say you do not know where I am, but I'm probably in Berlin. Be brave." Remembering both the Red and White terror of 1919, he added, "It may be very difficult and unpleasant for you."

The two men hurried out into the cold, wet night and, taking the back streets, walked to Hoegner's apartment on Schelling Strasse, just a block from the *Völkischer Beobachter*, practically under the SA's noses. There could not have been a more secure hiding place.

"Tell me all about it," Philipp Bouhler said excitedly when Ferdinand Schreiber, the printer, phoned him shortly after 10 P.M. Bouhler was at Nazi party headquarters. "You know more than I do. I stayed here in the office all evening."

Schreiber, trying to soothe his foreman and workers with the assurance that it would not be much longer before the copy for the posters arrived, hurried—again by streetcar—across the Isar to the party's shabby headquarters on Cornelius Strasse.

He could have saved himself the 5-billion-mark trip. His competitor, Anton Schmidt, had gone there directly from the Bürgerbräukeller and was telling the Nazi party's assistant business manager all the titillating details.

However, as far as those job orders were concerned, Bouhler shrugged his shoulders apologetically. "I don't have any more information than I had this afternoon." But would the gentlemen please wait a while longer and keep their workers on?

"It may be another hour, two at the most," he reassured Schreiber and Schmidt. "But then, I am certain, you will have the texts and can set type and start your presses. It will be a big job, and profitable."

Schreiber and Schmidt would gladly wait for a profit.

"Let me tell you something, Captain," General von Danner said to Hans Bergen as they walked briskly from Ett Strasse to Danner's headquarters next to the Army Museum on Hofgarten Strasse. "Lossow cuts a sorry figure of a man. He has been meddling in politics and vacillating for months. But the least he could have done in the Bürgerbräu was stand up to that little corporal and tell him flatly, 'No.'"

The young State Police captain looked up, startled. He had never heard a general speak so candidly to a junior officer, let alone so disparagingly, about another general.

What Bergen did not know was that Danner's anger, frustration, and contempt had been simmering for weeks. It was shared by the division's two other major generals, Adolf von Ruith, the infantry commander, and Baron Friedrich Kress von Kressenstein, commander of artillery. They had been arguing and pleading with Lossow since September—ever since he had mutinied, for all practical purposes, against Berlin and von Seeckt by swearing loyalty to the Bavarian constitution and declaring the Seventh Division's unilateral independence from central Reichswehr jurisdiction.

All three were aristocrats, members of the traditional military caste and imbued with the orthodox belief that a German officer must remain unswervingly apolitical. To be sure, their training and code of ethics also prohibited rebellion against their superior, even if he was patently insubordinate to *his* superiors. Moreover, they had been willing to tolerate Lossow's behavior as long as his insubordination could be generously interpreted as "a jurisdictional dispute" with Berlin. But a putsch? Collaboration with freecorps mercenaries, with Hitler, the SA? That was where Danner drew the line, and he knew Kressenstein and Ruith would too.

As he strode grimly down Hofgarten Strasse toward the municipal garrison with the raucous sounds of Röhm's advancing legion just a few blocks away, Bergen occasionally trotting at his side to keep pace, Danner made up his mind. He would oppose "this putsch" by mobilizing "all military means at my disposal"—

with, without, or, if necessary, against Lossow. That would have to be Lossow's decision.

Dashing into the building, he was relieved to discover, first of all, that the putschists had apparently neglected thus far to move against it, and that Ruith and Kressenstein, in the civilian clothes they had been wearing when they were alerted by von Imhoff and von Freyberg, were already there waiting for him. So were other trusted and loyal officers, including his chief-of-staff Lieutenant Colonel Otto von Saur, and Kressenstein's brother Gustav, a retired colonel.

Danner sensed that even seconds counted, for the putschists might attack at any moment. His offices were just a few hundred yards from the war ministry, the Palatia fraternity house, and St. Anne's, and what was happening there could be heard even with the windows closed. They would need a safe command post— with luck, the 19th Infantry Regiment barracks. But first he had to act.

Within fifteen minutes he had alerted the division's subordinate units and garrisons outside the capital—in Augsburg, Landsberg, Eichstätt, Ingolstadt, Regensburg, Nürnberg, and as far north as Bayreuth—instructing the shaken commanders there to march immediately on Munich. Most important, he told each officer he phoned, "Only those orders given by me or in my name are valid, none by General von Lossow, since he has been taken prisoner and may be coerced, against his will, to countermand them or mislead you into taking actions helpful to his captors."

On the whole, von Danner met no resistance or reluctance. The notable exception was the Ingolstadt garrison commander, Lieutenant Colonel Hans-Georg Hofmann, a Nazi and Kampfbund sympathizer, who delayed all night before mobilizing his battalion.

Bavaria's "new prime minister," Ernst Pöhner, was making himself comfortable at Ett Strasse in Mantel's office—to which Georg Rauh had dutifully brought the key.

"Oh, yes, what Herr Neunzert told you is quite correct," said Pöhner, looking at Frick with the straightest and most official expression. "You *are* the new police president, and this is really your office now. It was one of the first matters I discussed with Excellency von Kahr, and it was his suggestion—I would even describe it as his express wish—that you be appointed."

Frick was still feigning surprise and reluctance, especially when he noticed von Imhoff and Colonel Josef Banzer standing in the doorway. He was becoming increasingly suspicious of Imhoff, and about Banzer he already knew. In fact, he was surprised even to see Seisser's second-in-command.

"Ah, the gentlemen have come to congratulate you, Herr Doktor Frick," Pöhner prompted.

Von Imhoff and Banzer were in no mood for pleasantries, least of all Banzer, who had come back to his Ett Strasse command post from the Bürgerbräukeller as the virtual prisoner of one of his own junior officers, State Police Lieutenant Gerhard von Prosch, a Nazi party member.

If loyalties among police and army officers were confused and divided that night, Josef Banzer was one of the important exceptions. Several weeks earlier, in a meeting with other "green police" commanders and ranking officials, he had left no doubt as to how he felt about Hitler's rabble. "Any officer, any member of the State Police," he had said, "who is unwilling to fire on the Nazis when ordered should hand in his resignation right now."

Given the extent to which the police had been subverted by Hitler's followers and sympathizers, some acting as double agents, Banzer's words were soon common knowledge in Nazi circles and he was, more or less, a marked man. His name had originally been on the hostage list Hitler had given Hess, but crossed out as an afterthought by the Führer himself. Feeling confident of Seisser's ultimate collaboration—a grave miscalculation, as events were to demonstrate—Hitler had apparently decided that Banzer's incarceration might be imprudent. But that did not mean he trusted him. He had instructed Göring to assign a "special aide" to the colonel, and Göring had chosen Prosch.

So there stood Banzer with Prosch next to him, in storm troop uniform and helmet.

"What I came down to see you about, Herr Pöhner," Banzer said icily, "is this 'honor guard' who refuses to budge from my side. Am I a prisoner? If not, I assume that you, as prime minister, have the authority to do something about it."

"Can I count on your support, Colonel?" Pöhner asked haughtily.

The question stymied Banzer, and he hesitated for a moment. After all, he had been in the Bürgerbräukeller and had seen the tumultuous, convincing ceremony in which Kahr, Pöhner, Seisser, and Hitler had all pledged allegiance to each other. Was there any reason for him not to recognize Pöhner as the new prime minister and commander-in-chief of the State Police?

"But of course," Banzer finally replied, not knowing whether he was deluding himself, Pöhner, or both.

"There is no need for you to accompany Colonel Banzer if he does not wish your services tonight," Pöhner said, waving Prosch away.

Nudging von Imhoff, Banzer led the way out of the suite, back upstairs to their own offices, where they "felt freer" and where Banzer, not really knowing what to do next, began phoning desperately around the city in search of Seisser, then still at the Bürgerbräu.

Pöhner and Frick, meanwhile, went into "consultation" about methods of "informing the public, especially in the provinces," and "instructing the press." They decided to schedule a press conference for around midnight, then left Ett Strasse together for Kahr's headquarters, where they hoped to discuss "an orderly transfer of power."

Ludwig Hümmert, eighteen, a *Gymnasium* student, was still poring over his homework around 10:30 P.M. when his father, "bubbling with excitement," burst into their apartment on Herzog-Wilhelm Strasse, near the Stachus.

"It is wonderful, marvelous news, my son," he said, barely able to contain himself. "A great new day for Germany. Hitler and Kahr have finally reached agreement. I saw it and heard it all. A new government, a nationalist revolution, and Ludendorff will lead the new army."

Hümmert was less incredulous than dismayed and horrified. His father, who had taken him to some of Hitler's first mass rallies, was not a Nazi but rather an enthusiastic supporter of the "rejuvenation of the Reich" that he thought Hitler's movement heralded. From the outset he had seen in "this remarkable drummer of patriotism" a "German Garibaldi." To the son, an ardent believer in the postwar republic and the parliamentary democracy it was practicing, Hitler had long seemed a demagogue, "a dangerous, potential dictator."

Father and son debated long and acrimoniously that night, though "ours, unfortunately, was not typical of discussions in other Munich homes just then."

At the U.S. Consulate General on Lederer Strasse, Robert Murphy was dictating a coded cable to his friend and most trusted German employee, Paul Drey, a Jew:

> . . . ACCORDING TO HITLER TASK OF THIS GOVERNMENT IS TO MARCH ON BERLIN, WAGE TWELFTH HOUR FIGHT: ASSERTED THAT THE DAWN WOULD SEE EITHER NEW NATIONAL GOVERNMENT OR THE DEATH OF THE SPEAKER.

Murphy had a premonition that the cable might never leave Munich. Turning to his deputy, Albert Halstead, he said, "I know it is a grueling, long drive, especially on a night like this—almost a hundred and forty miles over terrible roads—but it is best that you take a car and go to Stuttgart to transmit a copy of the report through the consulate there. Washington must know what is happening. Paul and I will try to send it from here and keep watch on what is happening. But we must protect ourselves."

Having finally reached their various hotel rooms in the Vier Jahreszeiten and the Bayerischer Hof, Larry Rue, Hubert Knickerbocker, Lincoln Eyre, and Dorothy Thompson locked themselves in to compose their initial dispatches, hurrying to get them cabled or telephoned to the bureaus in Berlin, London, and Paris.

"Adolf Hitler overthrew Premier von Knilling of Bavaria tonight in collusion with Dictator von Kahr," Rue wrote. "Herr Hitler established a national dictatorship with General von Ludendorff as war minister and commander-in-chief of the new national army. . . .

"'We will follow you anywhere,' several hundred in the hall shouted enthusiastically."

And, a few doors down the hall, Eyre was saying, "There was

no bloodshed, even in the districts usually the scene of Fascist battles. . . . But while the proclamation was being read by Hitler himself, the troops outside maintained order with a cordon five men deep, bayonets fixed."

Photographer Heinrich Hoffmann had gone home, after the last game of tarok with Dietrich Eckart, and was in his apartment above the Schelling Strasse studio when the phone rang. It was a friend.

"Haven't you heard the news yet?" his caller asked incredulously, explaining what had happened.

"But that is impossible," Hoffmann exclaimed. "I had tea and cake with Hitler just this afternoon, and he didn't say a word about it."

"But it's true. The SA and Oberland have already occupied key buildings around the city." Hoffmann raced out of his house and across the street to the *Völkischer Beobachter*. There, cars were coming and going and SA stood guard outside. Hurrying back to his studio, he grabbed a camera, plates, and magnesium flashes, hoping to record the great event for posterity.

Senior Lieutenant Michael von Godin called his company of State Police to attention in the inner courtyard of the Residenz.

The green-uniformed troopers, quartered in the wing of the palace that had once housed King Ludwig III's honor guard, listened in silence as Godin reminded them of their oath "to protect the government at all costs." Had any one of them asked Godin which government they were to defend, he would have been embarrassingly at a loss for an answer.

He could only wait for instructions on what to do next. Placing his unit on "combat readiness," which meant they "could go to sleep with their rifles or carbines in their arms," he went to his little office and told his orderly to make some coffee.

Shortly after 10 P.M., Major Hermann Kuprion, the Engineer Battalion commander, arrived at his barracks.

He listened patiently as Captain Cantzler told him of the deadlock with Max von Müller and the 400 Oberland troopers in the drill hall. Kuprion excused himself for a moment, went into

his inner office, and phoned the Seventh Division duty officer—
Wilhelm Daser—at Schönfeld Strasse. Quickly, Daser reported on
the call from Ett Strasse and Röhm's takeover of the war ministry.

"What Herr Cantzler has done is right," Kuprion said, coming out of his office and confronting Müller. "Your men will stay
in that drill hall. And no weapons tonight."

9

In the Bürgerbräukeller's second-floor banquet room,
Prime Minister Eugen von Knilling and the other hostages sat morosely around the table, sipping the beers Hanfstaengl had bought
and speculating about their fate. When Hitler entered to "apologize for the inconvenience" he was causing them and to promise
that they would be treated well, he carefully avoided looking at
Interior Minister Franz Schweyer.

As the guards watched suspiciously and fingered their rifles
nervously, Schweyer rose from his chair, walked straight toward
Hitler, and touched his chest with a finger. "I want to tell you
something, Herr Hitler," he said loudly. "Your promises do not
mean very much. Let me ask whether you remember what you
promised when you were in my office last year? Do you remember what you said then?"

Visibly embarrassed, but without uttering a word, Hitler
backed away from Schweyer's accusing finger, swerved on his
heels, walked toward the door, and beckoned Rudolf Hess to follow him.

"Is everything arranged?" he asked testily. Hess nodded.
"Well, then, what are you waiting for? Take them away. Get
them out of here. I will phone instructions."

Downstairs again, he watched from a discreet distance as the
dignified elderly prisoners were issued their overcoats in the
cloakroom. Jeers and threats of "Hang them now!" greeted them
as they were marched past a line of storm troopers to three open
cars and a truck with twenty SA men waiting out on Rosenheimer
Strasse. Hess climbed in next to Michael Ried, the driver of the
second automobile; publisher Julius Lehmann, reluctant to think
of himself as the captives' "keeper," sat in the first.

"Where to, gentlemen?" Ried asked.

"Just follow the car ahead," Hess replied.

"You have the honor of guarding ex-ministers tonight," Hitler told the troopers on the truck. "Guard them with your lives, for the sake of the nationalist revolution."

Hermann Göring, standing arms akimbo atop the steps to the beer garden, barked a command. Then, with the truck bringing up the rear, a machine gun planted above its cab, the convoy moved slowly up the street toward the wooded suburb of Grosshesselohe and the Lehmann mansion—a comfortable enough prison, to be sure, but, even more important, a secluded and secure one.

Hitler was in an ebullient mood over his apparent success. Everything, he exulted, had gone according to plan, except for the discordant note of his encounter with Schweyer. He circulated around the foyer and hallways of the beerhall to congratulate Göring's SA and Berchtold's Stosstrupp members.

But his mood changed sharply to unbridled anger when news of Karl Beggel's rout at the 19th Infantry Regiment and the detention of Max von Müller's 400 Oberländers at the Engineer Barracks reached him. Those were the first hints of any difficulties, and in a flash of overconfidence he made what was undoubtedly the gravest tactical error of the night. He decided to settle the dispute at the barracks personally, leaving the Bürgerbräu nerve center, where Kahr, Lossow, and Seisser were still talking in the barren side room, in the care of Ludendorff, Kriebel, and Scheubner-Richter.

Screaming hysterically that he would free the troopers "with artillery if need be," he called for the Oberland League's Friedrich Weber and organized an "expeditionary force." With three truckloads of SA behind them, Hitler and Weber headed in two cars for the Oberwiesenfeld area barracks. They were accompanied by Ulrich Graf, Julius Schreck, Walter Baldenius, the Stosstrupp's Ludwig Schmied, and police Inspector Matthäus Hofmann as bodyguards, all brandishing submachine guns and rifles.

But just after crossing Ludwig Bridge, the heavily armed convoy encountered the Infantry School cadets led by Gerhard Rossbach and Edmund Heines's Third SA Battalion, with Ludendorff's manservant, Kurt Neubauer, and Hans Frank, the young law student, in the ranks. They were on their way to the Bürgerbräu.

Ever the propagandist, Hitler decided to stop and deliver a brief speech. Then he ordered a detour to Schönfeld Strasse to congratulate Röhm on his successful conquest of the war ministry. The streets, he noted with satisfaction, were thronged with people cheering whenever they saw a passing swastika or red-white-black banner, and storm troopers appeared very much in control. No State Police or Reichswehr were in evidence—not that he distrusted them at this juncture.

"Radiant with joy," Hitler embraced Röhm and declared that it was "the happiest day of his life." Briefly he addressed the Reichskriegsflagge troopers assembled in the courtyard, declaiming, "A better time is at hand. Let us all work day and night for the glorious goal of saving Germany from its plight and disgrace." Heinrich Himmler, standing among the group, shivered—with emotion and with cold.

After the euphoric meeting with Röhm, Hitler continued to the Engineer Barracks, only to find the gates locked and no visible sign of trouble. His demands—and Weber's—to be allowed in to speak with Cantzler or Kuprion were flatly rejected by the guards.

Had he wanted to, Hitler was certainly backed by a sufficient force to blast his way in as he had threatened. But he didn't really know what was transpiring in the drill hall, and he decided instead to return to the Bürgerbräukeller and ask his "new Reichswehr minister"—Lossow—to intervene.

It was 10:30 P.M. The Bürgerbräukeller's main hall was virtually empty except for a few stragglers. Stosstrupp and SA troopers, quaffing beer and gorging themselves on sausages, had started to bivouac there. The stench of stale beer and acrid smoke hung in the air—the classically depressing scene of a beerhall after a Munich carousal. Overturned chairs and tables were strewn about. Weary waitresses, eager to go home, were gathering the huge empty mugs and making superficial attempts to clean up.

In the side room, the Bavarian triumvirs remained closeted in a "planning session" with Ludendorff, Scheubner-Richter, and Kriebel. But was there anything really left to do or say?

Scheubner-Richter excused himself for "a few minutes." He wanted to phone his wife. "Everything went smoothly—without bloodshed," he announced ecstatically over the phone in the Bürgerbräu kitchen. "But there is a lot of work still to do, so I will not be home tonight."

Ludendorff, meanwhile, was feeling increasingly uncomfortable in his role as "chairman" and "warden." Kahr, he noticed, looked exhausted and emotionally drained. Lossow and Seisser spoke only when spoken to. Perhaps, Ludendorff suggested, "it is time for the gentlemen to go to their respective posts" to instruct their subordinates on the agreements that had been reached and to organize the next steps. As commander-in-chief of the new army, moreover, he saw no cause for spending further time in a beerhall. His place was with the generals and officers who would follow him on the "march to Berlin"—in the war ministry on Schönfeld Strasse. "No doubt you would like to rest at home for an hour or so," he suggested to Lossow. "In the meantime, I shall go to your office and wait for you there."

The three were obviously elated by the proposal. Scheubner-Richter, returning from his phone call, was appalled. "But, Excellency," he pleaded, drawing Ludendorff off to the side, "you cannot just let them leave. Without a guard? Once they are out of this room, we have no means of holding them to their agreements."

"They are officers, and they gave their word," Ludendorff replied sharply. "I forbid you to doubt the word of a German officer. Besides, we cannot keep them locked up in this place all night. They have duties to perform, and they can only carry them out from their proper posts."

Kahr, accompanied by Police Major Franz Hunglinger, was the first to leave—in Seisser's car, since the budget for the Bavarian State Commissariat did not provide for one of his own. Lossow, accompanied by his aide, Major Hans von Hösslin, followed a few minutes later. Seisser waited for Hunglinger to return with the automobile.

By 10:40 P.M., all three were gone.

Hermann Esser, still up and about despite his oft-repeated intention to return to bed, and "reconnoitering the city to test the

mood and atmosphere," was just coming up the hill on Rosenheimer Strasse to the Bürgerbräukeller when he saw Kahr leaving,
followed immediately by Lossow.

In that minute he realized that "all is lost." So did his friend
Hanfstaengl, standing at the door.

"That is pure madness!" Esser stammered. "Who let those
three go? Who is responsible for this stupidity?"

Friedrich Weber, who had returned meanwhile, leaving Hitler to cruise the city with his convoy of storm troopers, shrugged
his shoulders in evident helplessness. "All I know," he said, "is
that Excellency Ludendorff apparently swore the gentlemen to
their word of honor once more. In fact, he even got rather angry
when Scheubner implied they could not be trusted. He also felt
one could not keep an old gentleman like Kahr locked up all night
in the shabby side room of a beer cellar."

Esser and Hanfstaengl were dismayed. "I don't know much
about revolutions," Hanfstaengl said, "but I know enough from
my history books that you don't just let your predecessor go free if
you supplant a government by force. I'm afraid Lundendorff has
muffed it for us, Hermann. We've lost."

Esser nodded in despondent agreement. They went to a serving counter to order another beer for Hanfstaengl. Esser paid,
since Putzi had spent his last billions for the hostages, although he
himself did not dare to take a drink because of the jaundice. They
waited dejectedly for the return of their Führer.

Hitler, his ludicrous cutaway hidden again by the familiar
wrinkled trenchcoat, the holstered Browning on a belt around it,
the rhinoceros whip in hand, came back to the Bürgerbräukeller
in a rather somber mood. Yet it was not so much the triumvirate's
departure that seemed to worry him. At least, if it did, the members of his inner circle failed to notice. Rather, he appeared preoccupied by the lack of revolutionary momentum.

To be sure, both State Police and Reichswehr seemed to be
neutral. In fact, they were not in evidence at all. Moreover, the
war ministry was in Röhm's hands, and Ett Strasse, insofar as he
could ascertain, in Pöhner and Frick's. Platoons of SA and Oberland, all well armed now, were marching through the streets and
being cheered, and reinforcements, he knew, were on the way—
Gregor Strasser from Freising, Wilhelm Völk from Garmisch, and

others from the mountain towns and villages south of Munich.

The hilly right-bank districts of the city, from Max-Josef Bridge in the north, a scant block from Thomas Mann's house, to Wittelsbach Bridge in the south, were in the hands of his storm troopers. That was fine.

But the army and police barracks, the main railroad station, and the central telephone and telegraph exchanges had not been occupied. Nor had key government buildings. In fact, except for SA marchers and lustily singing revelers from the Bürgerbräu, Munich was disturbingly normal.

All that would have to change—very soon, he insisted, shouting orders to Göring, Berchtold, Weber, Amann, Esser, and Streicher. Ett Strasse, the ministries, and Kahr's headquarters would have to be occupied—with "honor guards, naturally"—he commanded, demanding to know why SA and Oberland weren't already on the move but were instead lolling about the Bürgerbräukeller and sleeping under the tables.

He called for more prisoners and hostages, "enemies of the people"—Erhard Auer, rich Jews, currency speculators, the Socialist city councilors, Communists, and Eduard Schmid, the Social Democratic mayor.

The *Münchener Post*—"that cauldron of poisonous, left-treasonous lies"—should be seized, both to silence it and to confiscate its printing facilities as a prize for the *Völkischer Boebachter*. He wanted posters up proclaiming the new government, and summary justice for all those who opposed it. On every street corner. By dawn. "Thousands of placards. Fifty thousand." There were to be mass rallies with the best propaganda speakers—Streicher, Esser—all over the city as soon as it got light and people started going to work.

Strutting back and forth through the Bürgerbräu vestibule, Hitler whipped himself and his followers into a frenzy. "Tomorrow," he screamed frantically, "we shall either be victorious and masters of a united Reich, or we shall be hanging from the lampposts."

His exhortations were interrupted by Kriebel's announcement that Gerhard Rossbach and the Infantry School cadets were assembled outside on Rosenheimer Strasse and wanted to pass in review before Hitler and Ludendorff.

It was an incongruous scene. There on the barely lit street, wet snow coming down more heavily now, their swastika banners flapping in the alpine wind, stood nearly 400 Infantry School officer students, the young elite of the Reichswehr, led by that soldier-of-fortune, Rossbach. Lieutenants Robert Wagner, Hans Block, and Siegfried Mahler, standing stiffly to attention, were in the front row right behind him. Somewhere along their route from Mars Strasse they had recruited the services of a brass band.

"Infantry School reporting to His Excellency General Ludendorff and our Führer Adolf Hitler," Rossbach announced snappily. "Heil! Heil! Heil!"

Bundled into his loden overcoat, with one hand clasped on his fedora to prevent it from blowing away, the warlord beamed. So did the Austrian-born ex-corporal. Together they reviewed the formation as it marched up and down the street a few yards. The band played noisily. Then Hitler delivered another of his little speeches, heralding the great new day that was dawning for Germany.

The student officers were dismissed into the Bürgerbräu to warm up, have some fat sausages with chunks of rye bread, and drink beer. Their great military moment was yet to come.

For Konrad Kiessling of the Oberland League's 1st Battalion, still standing guard near the Bürgerbräukeller, the moment was at hand. Ludwig Oestreicher and Alfons Weber, his battalion and company commanders, shouted orders to assemble.

"We have the honor and duty to protect Excellency von Kahr and the General State Commissariat tonight," Oestreicher announced.

What Kiessling, a police trainee, did not know was that he was a pawn in the putschists' sudden effort to undo the mistake Ludendorff had made in setting Kahr free.

With Alfons Weber shouting orders, the company marched down Rosenheimer Strasse, across the river, and then northward to Maximilian Strasse to occupy Kahr's heaquarters, already tightly sealed by State Police Captain Karl Wild.

Though short-lived and bloodless, it was to be the first serious confrontation of the night between police and putschists. Kiessling remained blissfully unaware of it. Having seen the Infantry School cadets with their Reichswehr uniforms and swastika banners passing in review before Hitler and Ludendorff, he really believed "that the events of the evening were government sanctioned, possibly even government initiated." He thought that the Oberland League had been "officially mobilized as auxiliary police."

"I am sorry it took me so long," Max Neunzert said, apologizing to Hermann Kriebel. "But you told me to change back into uniform. I had to take a streetcar from here to Ett Strasse to inform Herr Frick, and then I wanted to see what was going on at the war ministry and I met Count Moulin-Eckart—you know, Röhm's friend—who gave me a ride on his motorcycle and took me back to Ett Strasse, and from there I caught another streetcar to my apartment and then I called Kolb for a car and—"

"*Schon gut, schon gut,*" Kriebel interrupted, trying not to show his exasperation. "We are still getting reports of some altercation between a Captain Cantzler at the Engineer Barracks and von Müller's Oberland battalion. It seems the Oberländers are locked up in the barracks or something. Herr Hitler already tried to straighten it out, with no success. Now, go to the war ministry, talk to Röhm, and try to find out what is happening. But please don't take so long. I need those troops to occupy the railroad station and the central telegraph office.

"I hope," Kriebel added, almost pushing Neunzert toward the exit of the Bürgerbräukeller, "that this time you told your driver to wait."

Having reviewed the Infantry School students, Ludendorff was getting increasingly impatient. It was eleven o'clock and Hitler was still issuing instructions and commands to his various lieutenants—Göring, Amann, Esser, and, above all, Berchtold. But to the old general, those were "inconsequential matters" of a "political, not a military nature." His place as "commander-in-chief," he felt, was with Röhm at the war ministry.

"I will join you there soon," Hitler promised.

Followed by his servant Neubauer, his stepson Pernet, Kriebel, and Friedrich Weber, Ludendorff paraded grandly out of the beer cellar, past the reveling SA men, to the car that would take him to Schönfeld Strasse. He assumed von Lossow would soon be meeting him there.

Interlude IV

Confusion and Improvisation

"I was, heaven knows, a mere amateur in the business of revolutions," Putzi Hanfstaengl was to write in his memoirs more than three decades later. "My chief claim to fame was as a player of the piano for Hitler. But in those days Hitler must have been even more of an amateur than I was."

And Erich Ludendorff was to say in September 1924, "Hitler misled me. He lied to me. He deceived me terribly. On the eve of his mad putsch, he said the Reichswehr would stand behind us to a man. I allowed myself to believe him. He is nothing but a braggart, an adventurer."

Though written with bitterness, disillusionment, and the wisdom of hindsight, both views explain the situation in Munich around 11 P.M. on November 8, 1923.

It was one of confusion ordained by improvisation.

Hitler, imbued with his passion, his hatreds, and his distorted views of the world, had not only hypnotized the triumvirs into submission, the audience into following him "anywhere," and most of his fellow conspirators into blind obedience, but had mesmerized himself with his fanatical belief in ultimate triumph. In making what he was to describe thirteen years later as "the rashest decision in my life," he had formed no plans for carrying it out, beyond his theatrical performance and show of brute force at the Bürgerbräukeller. Moreover, he had moved with such secrecy that even some of his most loyal followers and closest aides were ignorant of the coup d'état in which they were involved.

To be sure, as he was to say later, "for weeks Munich had been so rife with rumors of a putsch that even the sparrows were chirping the news from the rooftops." But most of his army of storm troopers could not tell the real event from a rehearsal. Many of its "officers" were notified so vaguely, so haphazardly, and on such short notice that organization of their movements was almost entirely left to chance.

The anger, bewilderment, and frustration of some of his faithful followers over this was expressed poignantly in subsequent statements to the police by Karl Beggel and Hans Oemler, the SA and Oberland battalion commanders thwarted at the 19th Infantry Regiment barracks.

As late as 8:30 P.M., when Oemler was still wandering back and forth between the Engineer Barracks, where Max von Müller was arguing with Oskar Cantzler, and the Infantry Barracks, where Chief Warrant Officer Gerhard Böhm was trying to drill the Hermann Bund volunteers and eyeing Beggel suspiciously, he did not know what was happening. He believed his mission was "really to stage a night training exercise on the Oberwiesenfeld" with his Oberländers and Beggel's SA men, "the same exercise that had originally been scheduled for November tenth" and which, he thought, had merely been advanced by two days.

"I am prepared, any time, to swear to that under oath," he told a police detective who interrogated him.

Beggel was in a similar quandary. Told at 6 P.M. to be at the Arzbergerkeller at 7, he sat there with some of his SA men for almost an hour convivially quaffing beer before he received instructions to go to the Infantry Barracks. He was not even in uniform then, and neither were most of the storm troopers under his command.

Thwarted by Böhm's quick thinking, Oemler and Beggel eventually marched their nearly 300 men across town to the Bürgerbräukeller because they had heard that it was "the central command post." They arrived shortly before 11 P.M. and their men dispersed quickly into the beerhall or went across the street to the popular Münchener Kindl cellar. The two were unable to speak to "either Göring or Hitler" because "there was total confusion." No one seemed to be in charge; no one could give them instructions on what to do next. They camped in the Bürgerbräu until morning. As both were to complain later, "The National Socialist leadership had no leadership capabilities."

It was the complaint of many Nazis that night. Yet they marched when and where they were told to march, sometimes aimlessly, lustily singing Dietrich Eckart's "Sturmlied": "Germany, awake! Break your chains in two!" They were men with a cause—right or wrong—and they regarded themselves as soldiers in an army, even if it was a private one, a distinction the majority did not in fact make. And they were also being paid, rather handsomely at that, considering the troubled times. So they marched like soldiers. Orders were orders, especially in a German "army"—even if they seemed to have no purpose or sense of direction.

Disorganization reigned elsewhere at 11 P.M.

Although Ernst Röhm and his Reichskriegsflagge men had successfully occupied Seventh Division Headquarters, they made no attempt to take control of its telephone switchboard for two hours. Thus the duty officer, Captain Wilhelm Daser, was free to communicate with General von Danner, the Infantry and Engineer Barracks, Kahr's office, State Police officials at Ett Strasse, and the division's regimental and battalion commanders outside Munich. The result was that while the putsch was being celebrated in one room of the old war ministry building on Schönfeld Strasse, it was being sabotaged in another.

That Max von Müller's 400 Oberland troopers were locked up in the drill hall of the Engineer Barracks was common knowledge among all the putsch managers as early as 10 P.M., if not earlier. Yet, although takeover of key transportation and communication centers is a prerequisite for any successful revolution, no alternative plan to reassign their task—occupation of the main railroad station and the central telegraph office across from it—was developed until well past midnight, when both places were safely protected by State Police.

Hermann Ehrhardt, the ex-navy commander of Kapp Putsch fame, and his Munich confederate Eberhard Kautter, an ex-navy lieutenant, would have been Hitler's natural confederates. Long before he had adopted the symbol, they had emblazoned the uniforms of their Brigade and Viking League with the swastika. World attention was focused on their force of irregulars, deputized as auxiliary State Police, on Bavaria's northern frontier with the state of Thuringia. Yet, at 11 P.M. no one in the Bürgerbräukeller bothered to find out where Ehrhardt and Kautter's loyalties stood, much less realized that these two right-wing extremist adventurers were conspiring to crush the putsch.

To be sure, dozens of the second-echelon putschists later disclaimed advance knowledge of the coup, in order to evade prosecution for conspiracy to commit treason, presumably hoping to be completely absolved or at least indicted on less serious charges. But many really were ignorant of Hitler's plans, almost to the minute of their execution, and some proclaimed that ignorance to the grave or, if they are alive, do so to the present day.

Hermann Esser, for all practical purposes the "Führer's deputy" in those autumn days of 1923, insisted he was not informed until Hitler came to see him in his apartment the afternoon of the putsch. Heinrich Hoffmann, who had been asked to wait outside, was then one of Hitler's closest friends, yet found out too late to take the photographs that might have enriched history books. Dietrich Eckart, whose "Storm Song" was echoing across Munich and who was regarded as the Nazi party's "house bard," did not find out until Hoffmann called him—around midnight.

Adolf Lenk was instructed at noon, albeit in the vaguest terms. But Wilhelm Briemann and Ludwig Schmied still maintain they had not known why they were ordered to report to the Stosstrupp's favorite hangout, the Torbräu tavern's bowling alley, until Josef Berchtold announced the impending coup and pledged his men to total obedience before marching them to be armed in the factory yard on Balan Strasse.

Hans Frank and Julius Streicher both went to the gallows in Nürnberg, following their conviction for war crimes by the Allied International Tribunal in 1946, still insisting they had not known. Frank at first thought he was going to a "social evening" of Edmund Heines's SA battalion at the Wurzer Hof tavern, and Streicher contended that he would, indeed, have taken that 1:45 express train to Munich, instead of waiting until 4 P.M. to travel more arduously by car, had Max Amann been more explicit on the phone.

An almost conspiratorial secretiveness, even in his relations with intimates and closest collaborators, was Hitler's nature. As Hanfstaengl remarked in his memoirs, "Normally he kept all his various groups of acquaintances isolated from each other in watertight compartments and never told them where he had been or where he was going or took any of them with him." Indeed, Hanfstaengl was one of the few in his entourage who crossed those lines. But on the afternoon of November 8, not even Hanfstaengl had been privy to Hitler's movements, though he was hunting for him desperately all about town to suggest a place where von Knilling and the other hostages could be kept. That Hitler was having separate, neatly compartmentalized meetings with Esser, Ernst Pöhner, Reichswehr Captain Eduard Dietl, and Scheubner-Richter—and was unavailable to any of his other assistants—was known only to Ulrich Graf, his bodyguard, and to accidental observers along the route around town, such as Hoffmann.

The inadequate planning that would lead to frenzied improvisation after eleven o'clock was due also to Hitler's dictatorial nature and the "Führer principle," which he had coerced the founders of the party into accepting in 1920 by threatening to quit as its most effective propagandist and speaker. He had thus made himself the party's absolute ruler. He had launched that evening's events with the aim of destroying the parliamentary democracy he so abhorred, and, in the same spirit, he countenanced no committee or group decision-making in the party. Only one man should give orders—himself. And in his naïveté—and even more his pathological self-esteem, egomania, and zealotry—he assumed that those orders would be carried out. He never checked on or verified their actual implementation.

Ultimately, however, Hitler and his putsch were soon to fall victim to his messianic conviction that the time for revolt against Berlin was ripe, that the people were indeed waiting for it passionately, and that it only needed his announcing it for everyone to fall into line and follow him "anywhere." To what? How? After the first triumph in the Bürgerbräukeller, he himself didn't really know and regarded the question as redundant. The details, he assumed, would be worked out by Ludendorff and Lossow. After all, they were the military experts; that was why he had put them in charge of the army. Had Mussolini a detailed plan for who was to run which government department when he arrived in Rome? Of course not. Being there was the important thing, like declaring the Reich government deposed. He believed in his own declarations, in a sense adumbrating the era of "the medium is the message" with his maxim that propaganda could accomplish anything.

Even if he did not fully trust Lossow, Seisser, and some of the aristocratic generals, colonels, and lieutenant colonels under them, what did it matter? Hitler was convinced that he could bank on the majors, captains, and lieutenants, the sergeants and the corporals, the veterans of the trenches. From them there would be no resistance. They would follow him, and because of that, the generals and colonels also would come along.

This was true to an extent and explains the confusion which reigned that night. Not only were loyalties divided, but because of the stage-managed harmony with the triumvirs on the Bürgerbräu platform, no one in the army, police, or government really knew for hours where matters stood or who was in control. Indeed, even the triumvirate itself, especially Kahr, faced with Hitler's public fait accompli and the enthusiastic frenzy it had created, did not know what to do next. Instead, they hid in their offices, and the longer they remained unavailable and inaccessible to their bewildered aides, the more confusing the situation became.

SA and Oberland storm troopers such as Konrad Kiessling really believed they were a kind of auxiliary police and Reichswehr. And the police, having no other instructions, unable to find superiors who could give them guidance, were inclined to accept them as such. When putschists later claimed that "we were cheered and welcomed by the 'greens'" as they marched about the city, they were telling the truth.

At one point during the night, State Police Colonel Josef Banzer, unable to find or reach Seisser, was asked by a young lieutenant, "Should we regard the Nazis as friends, as enemies, or should we just vacillate for the time being?"

Banzer looked at him long and vacuously, finally replying, "I wish I had the answer to that. I just don't know."

Career police officers and civil servants—especially German ones—are trained and paid not to think for themselves but to carry out instructions from their politically appointed superiors. But who were they at 11 P.M. that night?

The question was particularly baffling at Ett Strasse, where two of the chief conspirators—Pöhner and Frick—were, insofar as anyone could tell, legally in charge as Bavaria's prime minister and Munich's chief of police. Both, moreover, were veteran police officials who commanded the respect, if not always the loyalty, of the underlings now at their beck and call. Whatever doubts there were, who would dare jeopardize his career by countermanding the two if, in the morning, events really did confirm them as premier and chief? Those who doubted decided the best course of action was to play it safe by doing nothing.

Thus, at 11 P.M., with the revolution declared, Munich seemed oddly unrevolutionary, if one discounted the bands of carousing, flag-waving, singing, and marauding storm troopers or the crowds on the street cheering them on.

The putschists now had a force of 2,500 armed men, with at least half again that many converging on the city and expected by morning. But they were mostly marching back and forth, guarding bridges and street corners with little traffic, or trying to sack out under the tables and across chairs in the Bürgerbräukeller.

Except for the contingents Sigmund von Imhoff had dispatched to guard the telephone exchange, the central telegraph office, and the main station, State Police were nowhere in evidence and blue-uniformed city police were patrolling routinely.

As far as anyone could tell, Reichswehr and State Police units were all in their barracks, which seemed silent to the outside world, though behind their walls and gates furious activity was about to begin. So, too, in other cities and towns of Bavaria where troops were being alerted and assembled to board trains and trucks bound for Munich.

Except for military staff cars and couriers rushing through the night, the capital seemed in the hands of the putschists. But it was an illusion.

Ludendorff, who had arrived at the war ministry, was waiting for Lossow. He was to wait in vain, though hours were to pass before doubts began to plague him.

Hitler, still at the Bürgerbräu, seemed almost oblivious to the non-developments. His main preoccupation was the need for more action.

THREE

The Plan Goes Awry

10

Having sent Major Hunglinger back to the Bürgerbräu-keller to pick up Seisser with the only available car, Gustav von Kahr slowly climbed the broad steps to his Maximilian Strasse apartment, absorbed in his disturbing thoughts. Could it be only 10:40 P.M., scarcely more than two hours since Hitler had barged into the beerhall with his SA? It seemed as if an eternity had gone by.

Those two hours had aged the arrogant little "dictator." He was short of breath, in a state of depression, and brooding darkly. The humiliating experience still gnawed at him, but, worse than that, after the hand-shaking ceremony on the platform he was really in a predicament. What should he do now?

He was repelled by the prospect of collaborating with Hitler and Ludendorff in a coup against Berlin that was destined to fail. Why couldn't they have waited another week or two? Yet he had given his word and hand in public. And there was no denying that the pledge had unleashed a furor of approval. To repudiate it would be to commit political suicide. Moreover, unless he was prepared to risk bloodshed in an armed confrontation with "patriotic men"—a thought abhorrent to him—there was no way to renege. The short ride from the Bürgerbräukeller through Hitler's columns of heavily armed storm troopers had convinced him that it was no bluff. In all likelihood, they really had occupied the army and police barracks.

Von Kahr was so preoccupied he barely noticed his daughter waiting for him at the top of the stairs. Absentmindedly he handed her his topcoat, asked her to make some tea, and walked heavily and dejectedly down the hallway to his office, where his aide, Baron Heinrich von Freyberg, and the Ehrhardt Brigade's Eberhard Kautter were waiting.

"At last!" Kautter exclaimed. "What happened, Excellency? We have only heard confused and incomplete reports."

The question seemed to rouse the old man. "It was brigandage—a dastardly, humiliating attack," he said, giving them the details. "I was under duress."

Kautter waited deferentially for Kahr to finish. "You are much too pessimistic, Excellency," he said at last. "All is not lost. Yes, Hitler and Ludendorff acted prematurely and imprudently. But if you move fast, you can take the initiative from them and our cause will still triumph!"

Kautter explained that he had already mobilized the Viking League and all of Ehrhardt's forces around Coburg on the Thuringian border—in Kahr's name.

"With them, you can compel Hitler and Ludendorff to obey your commands instead. But you must issue the following proclamation immediately: Announce that *you* have assumed all dictatorial power in Bavaria as the king's deputy, that the Weimar constitution has been suspended, but also that Bavaria remains loyally pledged to a united Reich. Then declare your continuing battle against Marxism. Hitler and Ludendorff will have no choice but to follow your lead, and patriotic forces in the north will rally to *your* flag."

A hare-brained scheme? Unquestionably. But even if it were not, it was too complex for a mind as plodding as Kahr's. He needed more time to think and—no doubt—to ascertain where von Lossow and von Seisser really stood. Not once during the two hours that they had been closeted in the Bürgerbräu's side room had they had a chance to speak privately.

He retreated to his inner office, hoping one or the other would call soon. Within minutes the phone did ring, but it was a caller Kahr had least expected—Franz Matt.

Franz Matt, the vice-premier and minister of education and culture, was by virtue of his age—sixty-three—the dean of Bavaria's cabinet and a man not only of remarkable energy but of admirable integrity. A leader of the stanchly Catholic and conservative Bavarian People's party, he was also an outspoken political opponent of von Kahr and for years had expressed his disdain of the stocky bureaucrat's machinations.

Kahr's speech in the Bürgerbräukeller had not interested him, so, like three other cabinet members—Heinrich Oswald, the minister of social welfare; Wilhelm Krausneck, the finance minister; and Wilhelm von Meinel, the minister of commerce—he had boycotted it. Instead, he had spent the evening with the Archbishop of Munich, Michael Cardinal Faulhaber, and the Papal Nuncio, Monsignor Eugenio Pacelli. It was in their company that news of the putsch reached him—through Schweyer's assistant, Josef Zetlmeier.

With half the cabinet in the hands of Rudolf Hess, Matt convened an urgent session of the other half in what he hoped was the reasonably safe apartment of a woman friend, Ellen Amann, a member of the state legislature. From there he phoned Kahr at 11 P.M.

"What does Hitler want?" Matt asked, when Kahr had reported on the beerhall scenario.

"To march on Berlin."

"He won't get far. And Pöhner, what are his plans?"

"He intends to form the new government tomorrow morning."

"Well, wish him luck from me," Matt snapped, asking sarcastically whether Pöhner had already fixed a new price ceiling for *Weisswurst*, the fat little veal sausages that Bavarians regard as the most important complement to their morning beer.

"Not yet," Kahr replied in dull-witted naïveté, "and that will be one of his most difficult problems."

This remarkable conversation persuaded Matt that Kahr was either collaborating with the putsch or lacked both the will and the means to crush it. Turning to the others, Matt announced a decision. They would establish a rump government-in-exile in Regensburg, 60 miles north of Munich and far enough from the capital to enjoy the protection of presumably loyal Reichswehr detachments.

Huddling around Frau Amann's dining room table, they also composed a proclamation calling upon all civil servants, police, and army units to remain loyal to the constitutional government and to refuse to obey "the Prussian Ludendorff, who has brought so much misfortune in this night to the Bavarian people."

Then, with a half-dozen reliable aides, the cabinet members bundled up for an immediate journey in their automobiles to the medieval town of Regensburg, the cradle of Bavarian civilization, on the banks of the Danube.

Otto Hermann von Lossow, fifty-five, trim and dignified with his sparse, close-cropped hair, neat gray mustache, and pince-nez, was in appearance the archetypical German general. But his military record was almost the antithesis—an explanation, perhaps, for the contradictions in his behavior on the night of November 8, 1923.

Born in Hof in northern Bavaria where the kingdom's border met those of Thuringia and Bohemia, he had been educated at the war academy in Munich and was a promising general staff officer when, in 1911, he left Germany to serve as a regimental commander in the army of Ottoman Turkey's Sultan Muhammad V. In 1912 he played a key role in Turkey's war against the Balkan alliance of Bulgaria, Serbia, and Greece; then he returned to Munich in 1913 to become chief of the Bavarian Territorial Reserve Army. In 1914, after the outbreak of the war, he was dispatched once more to Turkey as German military plenipotentiary in Constantinople and served there until the 1918 Armistice, rising to the rank of major general.

Many contemporaries described him as a cold-blooded, power-hungry, politically ambitious soldier who had no scruples about disobeying orders when he considered insubordination to be of likely personal advantage. But this picture does not harmonize with his postwar record in Bavaria, first as commandant of the Infantry School, then as commander-in-chief of the Military District and the Seventh Division. In fact, the opposite seems to have been the case.

He was, by nature of his position, the servant of several very different masters and tried to please them all simultaneously—the central Republic government in Berlin, embodied by Reichswehr minister Otto Gessler and General Hans von Seeckt; Bavaria's prime minister, Eugen von Knilling, and Gustav von Kahr; the "Black Reichswehr" represented by the "patriotic fighting leagues"; the free-corps veterans; and Hitler's SA. Politically he had ambitions, to be sure, not the least of which was the establishment of his own nationalist dictatorship. But he was also a chameleon who displayed the political colors dictated by his circumstances—the black-gold-red of the Weimar Republic, the black-white-red of the anti-Republic *condottieri* and Nazis, and the white-blue of monarchist Bavaria.

When he disobeyed orders and ignored the advice of superiors, it was largely because he had been influenced by subordinates, and it seemed to matter little if these represented diametrically opposite political poles. He listened to Hitler and to Ernst Röhm when the captain was his ordnance officer, and he listened to his chief-of-staff, Lieutenant Colonel Otto von Berchem, a stanch opponent of Röhm, Hitler, and the other radical rightists. It was said that Lossow tended to hear whoever was closest to him or spoke loudest at any given moment, and that he agreed with whatever had been the last argument presented. And so it must have been that night.

General and aristocrat that he was, Lossow's initial resistance to Hitler in the Bürgerbräukeller's side room was certainly in character. Whether or not he really did whisper *"Komödie spielen"* to Seisser and Hunglinger, as all three claimed afterward, he was definitely not the kind of man to collaborate with, much less take orders from, a swallow-tailed histrionic ex-corporal brandishing a loaded revolver. But then in came Ludendorff. Was it the old warlord's stature and reputation or awe of rank that triggered Lossow's about-face within minutes after the famous general arrived on the scene? And what persuaded him to change his mind again? Suffice it to say that what Lossow and other witnesses said later, for the record, contradicts much of his given behavior.

Lossow's silence was grim and oppressive as the staff car sped him and his aide, Major Hans von Hösslin, from the beerhall, past marching columns of storm troopers to von Danner's command post on Hofgarten Strasse. Seisser had promised to follow them as soon as Hunglinger was back with the other car. Hösslin, still shocked by the encounter with SA troopers who had wanted to take the cockade from his cap, tried to read Lossow's face as they passed dim street lights, but it was impassive. He dared not speak.

Danner was busy on the telephone, issuing more alert and

mobilization orders to units outside Munich, and Generals Ruith and Kressenstein were in the hallway, preparing to leave for the greater safety of the 19th Infantry Regiment barracks, when Lossow arrived. It was, by his own reckoning, 10:45 P.M. Believing he was still in the Bürgerbräukeller, the generals were as surprised to see him as Hitler, Hanfstaengl, and Esser were to discover that the triumvirs had been released by Ludendorff.

"Excellency, just tell us it was all a bluff," von Danner said hopefully.

"It was an assault," he sputtered, "a base, criminal attack! I was lured into a trap, coerced at pistol point."

If Lossow had not played a "comedy" at the Bürgerbräu, then he was certainly an accomplished actor at this moment. His denunciation of the putschists seemed to mount as Danner, Kressenstein, and Ruith told him of the countermeasures they had already initiated.

He was fulminating so loudly that the other three generals hurried him into Danner's private office, where Colonel Hans von Seisser soon joined them. But what really transpired there? Did Lossow—and, for that matter, Seisser—accede willingly to the others' plans to crush the putsch? Did Lossow approve the decision to issue all orders in Danner's name because his own could be misused by Ludendorff and Hitler; or was it a course of action over which the others gave him no choice because they had, de facto, deprived him of his command?

It was an incongruous scene—Lossow and Seisser, both in uniform, having just been hailed on the stage of the beerhall as Germany's new war and police ministers; the other generals in the civilian suits in which they had rushed from their homes. Their emotions were mixed. All more or less sympathized with the aims of the putschists, if not their methods, regarding them as kindred spirits and comrades-in-arms. They hoped to avoid a confrontation, yet they were already taking the practical steps that could lead to a mini-war on the streets of Munich.

Danner's headquarters, they knew, was unsafe since Lossow's in the war ministry just a few blocks away was already in Röhm's hands. To be sure, they were surprised that Captain Daser, the duty officer there, was still in control of the switchboard and relaying messages back and forth. But it surely would not be long before the putschists were at their door too. Seisser, having heard Hitler's claims at the Bürgerbräu, could give no guarantee for his own headquarters, the police barracks on Türken Strasse. And although Oberländers were still locked up in the drill hall at the Engineer Barracks, that touchy situation could erupt momentarily. Only the 19th Infantry barracks was secure. They agreed to establish their command post there.

The plan of action was vague because the situation was unclear. Nothing could be done until both Reichswehr and State Police reinforcements arrived, and that would take hours. Moreover, no one wanted to undertake anything until it was light. The best step for the moment, they agreed, was to wait.

Lossow, with Hösslin in tow, was driven to the 19th Infantry Regiment barracks, where small straggling patrols of SA and Oberland were still hanging about outside the gate. The others, having no car at their disposal, decided to walk the three miles to the Oberwiesenfeld barracks area, figuring correctly that since they were all in civilian clothes they would not even be noticed.

Seisser, who wanted to reconnoiter the Türken Strasse barracks and check on police units such as Michael von Godin's in the Residenz, promised to pick Kahr up on the way and meet them later.

It was, Lossow noted, shortly after 11 P.M. when they all departed, leaving only a captain, Maximilian Renz, in the otherwise abandoned building.

As the little group of generals and colonels crossed Odeonsplatz and walked up Brienner Strasse, looking very much like ordinary burghers on their way home, Danner turned to Hans Bergen, the police captain accompanying him, and once more gave vent to his anger about Lossow.

"He's spineless, that's what he is. Why didn't he just stand up to Hitler and tell him 'No'? Now Germans may be shooting at Germans soon, patriotic men at patriots. It is all a tragedy."

Gustav von Kahr was still on the telephone with Franz Matt when the State Police officers outside his door were shaken out of their discussion by a nervous, excited gate guard. "Storm troopers—Oberland, I think—at least a company of them outside," he

...st Pöhner, former Police Chief; Hitler's
...ce to become Prime Minister of Bavaria
...r the putsch. (*Copyright, Zeit-*
...chichtliches Bildarchiv, Munich;
...rich Hoffmann)

Wilhelm Frick, senior police official; Reich
Interior Minister from 1933 on; executed as
war criminal after Nuremberg trials.
(*Copyright, Zeitgeschichtliches Bildarchiv,
Munich; Heinrich Hoffmann*)

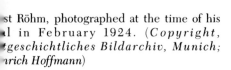

...st Röhm, photographed at the time of his
...l in February 1924. (*Copyright,
...tgeschichtliches Bildarchiv, Munich;
...rich Hoffmann*)

Lieutenant General Otto von Lossow.
(*Copyright, Zeitgeschichtliches Bildarchiv, Munich; Heinrich Hoffmann*)

Hermann Göring, head of the SA, on t
night of the putsch. (*Copyright, Ze
geschichtliches Bildarchiv, Munic
Heinrich Hoffmann*)

Gustav von Kahr. (*Copyright, Zeitgeschichtliches Bildarchiv, Munich; Heinrich
Hoffmann*)

Mayor Eduard Schmid (left, in hat and topcoat) and other city councillors after being taken prisoner by Hitler's Storm Troopers on the morning of November 9, 1923. (*Copyright, Zeitgeschichtliches Bildarchiv, Munich; Heinrich Hoffmann*)

Ernst Röhm (far right), Heinrich Himmler (fourth from left), and members of their organization behind the barbed wire barricades in front of the War Ministry on the morning of November 9, 1923. (*Copyright, Zeitgeschichtliches Bildarchiv, Munich; Heinrich Hoffmann*)

Putschists just before the start of the march on the morning of November 9, 1923. (*Copyright, Zeitgeschichtliches Bildarchiv, Munich; Heinrich Hoffmann*)

Hitler Storm Troopers, autumn 1923. (*Copyright, Zeitgeschichtliches Bildarchiv, Munich; Heinrich Hoffmann*)

Hitler, with Alfred Rosenberg on his right and Dr. Friedrich Weber, head of the Oberland League, on his left, September 1923. *(Copyright, Zeitgeschichtliches Bildarchiv, Munich; Heinrich Hoffmann)*

Adolf Hitler, November 4, 1923. *(Copyright, Zeitgeschichtliches Bildarchiv, Munich; Heinrich Hoffmann)*

From right to left: Dr. Friedrich Weber, Field Marshal Ludendorff, Hermann Göring, and an unidentified Nazi at the dedication of a war memorial in September 1923. (*Copyright, Zeitgeschichtliches Bildarchiv, Munich; Heinrich Hoffmann*)

Left to right: Adolf Hitler, Rudolf Hess, Hermann Kriebel, J. Fobke, and Dr. Friedrich Weber in Landsberg prison, 1924. (*Copyright, Zeitgeschichtliches Bildarchiv, Munich; Heinrich Hoffmann*)

The armored car of the State Police parked in front of the Feldherrnhalle about 9 A.M., November 9, 1923, to cover the flank of loyal army units moving against Röhm's forces. *(Copyright, Zeitgeschichtliches Bildarchiv, Munich; Heinrich Hoffmann)*

First Nazi Party rally in Munich, January 1923. *(Copyright, Zeitgeschichtliches Bildarchiv, Munich; Heinrich Hoffmann)*

Front page of a special section in the news weekly *Die Woche* (No. 46, 1923), showing Hitler, Ludendorff, and von Lossow. (*Copyright, Bayerisches Hauptstaatsarchiv, Munich*)

stammered. "They say they are an honor guard for Excellency von Kahr and are here to relieve us."

Captain Karl Wild rushed downstairs and out to the Maximilian Strasse entrance. Arrayed on the street, bayonets fixed on their rifles, with Konrad Kiessling in the ranks, stood Alfons Weber's 2nd Company of Oberland League's First Battalion.

Weber, a fuzzy-cheeked twenty-two-year-old engineering student who insisted that his men—and also Wild—address him as "Herr Senior Lieutenant," was the eiptome of officious arrogance. "I have orders to take over here. The police are to go home," he snapped, looking contemptuously at Wild, who was still wearing the mufti in which he had dashed from his apartment an hour earlier.

"Whose orders?" Wild shot back, adding that he was in charge of the police guard and had no intention of recalling them or relinquishing his command.

Konrad Kiessling listened with bewilderment as the two men shouted at each other. Wild's warnings that he had given his men orders to fire upon any intruders seemed not to impress Weber, "especially since the captain was not even in uniform." Fortunately, Lieutenant Colonel Wilhelm Muxel of the State Police was, and when he arrived on the scene from inside the building, Weber gave way. Mumbling that "perhaps you haven't been notified yet," he marched his company up Maximilian Street to the river embankment and from there sent a runner to the Bürgerbräukeller for further instructions from Ludwig Oestreicher, his battalion commander.

"*Gut gemacht,*" Muxel told Wild as they watched the Oberland company disappear. "But prepare yourself, Captain. From what I've been overhearing inside, there is a double game being played. I think there will be more trouble before the night is over."

Standing at the corner of Maximilian and Widenmayer streets, waiting for Weber's runner to return from the Bürgerbräukeller, Konrad Kiessling started to have doubts. The tense altercation with Wild and Muxel was his first hint "that all was not as legal" as he had originally thought. His doubts were heightened when Weber announced that there had been "a mixup in the instructions" and that they were to return to the beerhall for a while.

Doubts were also starting to gnaw at Ernst Röhm, entrenched at the war ministry—though not about legality. Where, he wondered, was everybody—especially Lossow, in whose outer office he was pacing back and forth? If, as Hermann Kriebel had told him on the phone, the general had left the Bürgerbräukeller nearly half an hour ago for his Schönfeld Strasse headquarters, he should have arrived.

Shortly before eleven o'clock, Röhm received word that Lossow had gone to Danner's office. He began phoning there—to no avail. The line was busy, and when he was able to get through, there was, strangely, no reply.

Accompanied by Josef Seydel and a platoon of his troopers, Röhm walked the few blocks to the Munich commandant's headquarters—ostensibly to "report to von Lossow, the new Reichswehr minister," but in fact to occupy it, as Danner had expected.

He was too late, by a few minutes, and to his surprise and consternation he found the stately, neo-Baroque building dark and locked. Undaunted, he rang the bell and pounded on the huge door. Finally, a small, barred window in the portal opened. It was Captain Renz.

Lossow? Danner?

"I have no idea where they've gone," Renz lied. "Maybe to the war ministry, maybe to the Nineteenth Infantry Regiment."

Pointing to the Reichskriegsflagge troopers behind him, Röhm demanded to be let in.

"You're outgunned," Renz replied calmly. "I have a machine gun set up in the hallway, right behind this door, and I'll give the order to fire if you make one move to enter this building."

The threat, empty as it was, worked; Röhm retreated toward Schönfeld Strasse. Had something gone wrong or was Renz just being an overeager busybody? And where *was* Lossow? The thoughts gnawed at Röhm as he led his little force through the Hofgarten back to the war ministry, where Ludendorff, Kriebel, Scheubner-Richter, and the Oberland League's Friedrich Weber had now arrived.

"*Ach*, just the man I'm looking for," exclaimed Major Adolf Hühnlein, an avid Nazi party member and active-duty Reichswehr officer on the putschists' side. It was Max Neunzert, being driven up to the war ministry. "I was just on my way to the Engineer Barracks. It seems there is some dispute involving four hundred Oberland troopers. Give me a ride."

Neunzert was none too pleased that someone else was on the same mission Kriebel had assigned to him. What he didn't know, because he had been at home changing clothes, was the extent to which the test of strength between Captain Oskar Cantzler and Oberland's Max von Müller had escalated and that none other than Hitler himself had already tried to intervene. Thus he was even more surprised when they arrived at the Engineer Battalion headquarters to discover ex-General Adolf Aechter, the "military director" of the Oberland League, in Major Hermann Kuprion's office.

"Look here, Major, it is a message signed by General von Lossow personally," Aechter was arguing. "He handed it to me just before he left the Bürgerbräukeller; it says you are to take your battalion off alert. That means, tell Captain Cantzler to let my men out of that drill hall. Now. With their weapons."

Kuprion looked unimpressed. "Anybody's signature could be on that piece of paper you have," he countered, unaware that Lossow had indeed signed it in his rush to escape from the beerhall. "I don't even know General von Lossow's handwriting. Besides, my instructions, since ten thirty this evening, are that the only orders valid tonight are General von Danner's in writing or Excellency von Lossow's *verbal* ones. If you can find Lossow—and I have been trying for almost an hour—and he tells me personally to let the Oberländers go, then of course I will comply."

Neunzert and Hühnlein, unaware of any change of mood on the Seventh Division commander's part, suggested that he was surely at his Schönfeld Strasse headquarters by then, although getting a phone call through was almost impossible. They agreed to drive back and have him call Kuprion with instructions.

But Aechter made a crucial mistake. Hearing that Lossow might have stopped off at the Infantry Barracks before joining Ludendorff at the war ministry, he decided to go up the street to search for him there, only to be promptly and unceremoniously arrested at the gate, apparently on Lossow's instructions. He was the first important putschist to be put on ice that night.

Slowly, a noisy convoy of three cars and a truck picked its way along a muddy road through the dense woods of Grosshesse-lohe and ground to a halt in front of a huge, gingerbreaded, turn-of-the-century house at Holzkirchener Strasse No. 2.

"*Marsch, marsch! Alles aussteigen*—Everybody out!" Rudolf Hess commanded amid the noise of booted feet on the gravel driveway and the clanking of rifle-bearing men moving about in the dark.

"Please regard yourselves as my guests, Excellencies," Julius Lehmann said nervously as the seven hostages were marched under heavy guard into the cavernous hallway of his suburban villa.

Hess didn't see it that way. "Each prisoner must be in a separate room, naturally the more comfortable ones for Herr von Knilling and the other cabinet members," he said. "There is to be no conversation between you, and any attempt to escape will have serious consequences. My men are armed, their weapons loaded, and their orders are to shoot—and there are more than three of them for each one of you. Your fate depends on my instructions from the new Reich government of Hitler and Ludendorff." His dark, deep-set eyes seemed to burn with an inner glow when he mentioned those two names.

Von Knilling, Schweyer, Gürtner, and Wutzelhofer were taken upstairs to bedrooms the Lehmann family had vacated hastily. Police Chief Mantel, his aide, Otto Bernreuther, and Count von Soden were locked into three cold, almost bare guest rooms on the ground floor. The old house had no central heating.

Von Soden, Crown Prince Rupprecht's chef-du-cabinet, caught a glimpse of a machine gun being set up in the vestibule and heard SA men assigned to stand guard outside each hostage's door. Then his lock clicked. Peering through the window, he saw another storm trooper pacing back and forth in the garden outside, his helmet glistening with the mixture of snow and rain still falling.

The young men's faces, he mused, looked indistinguishable from those on the night of the revolution, exactly five years ago, when King Ludwig III had fled the Residenz for Berchtesgaden.

Even the uniforms were similar. Only the red armbands of Kurt Eisner's 1918 followers had been exchanged for those bearing Hitler's swastikas.

SA Sergeant Julius Schaub had that comfortable feeling of a mission accomplished as he steered the heavy, lumbering Selve touring car along the cobblestoned road from Freising back to Munich. He had found Gregor Strasser, Strasser's younger brother Otto, and their battalion of storm troopers from Landshut and Lower Bavaria and delivered Göring's letter, staying just long enough for Strasser to open the envelope and read its contents to the cheering Nazis in his entourage: the news of the nationalist revolution.

"Tell Captain Göring that we will be there as soon as possible, certainly not later than dawn," Strasser said. "We have to organize a few more trucks. I have more men here than I expected. And congratulate our Führer."

Schaub was eager to report back to Göring and to be of "more service to the revolution." But, although it was a distance of only 20 miles or so between Munich and Freising, the driving was excruciatingly slow. The road was slippery, and impenetrable swirls of fog rose frequently from the adjacent Isar River.

"Keep moving that windshield wiper," Schaub told the SA man who had accompanied him.

Suddenly his headlights went out and he was enveloped in total darkness.

"*Verdammt!*" He fought the car to a halt on the narrow, high-crowned, winding road. "Of all stupid God-forsaken places, on a night like this!"

They tinkered unsuccessfully with the lights for half an hour, then gave up. To drive on would be suicidal. It was pitch black, with not a single star visible through the heavy clouds, and the weather and fog were getting worse.

Schaub estimated it was no more than 10 or 12 miles to Munich, but without lights he might just as well be in the wilderness. Even villages such as Garching and Ismaning along the way would do him no good. Farmers were in bed and, even if roused, would be unable to help. There was nothing to do but wait—until another car came along that they could follow, which was hardly likely, or Strasser with his trucks, or until it turned light enough to grope their way along, which might be another eight hours.

At police headquarters on Ett Strasse the telephones seemed to be ringing incessantly, and with each call from precinct stations around the city the reports of SA and Oberland troop movements multiplied.

Major Sigmund von Imhoff and Colonel Josef Banzer tightened controls at the night entrance and, with the forces available to them, took steps to protect the building against attack—a prudent move. Beyond that, they felt helpless. They were waiting for instructions from their chief, Hans von Seisser, and he was nowhere to be found.

"I cannot understand it." Imhoff looked with growing confusion at Banzer. "Where could he possibly be?"

They had tried Danner's headquarters, Godin's command post in the Residenz, the Türken Strasse police barracks, and now—Imhoff was still holding the receiver in his hand—Kahr's offices, where Major Heinrich Doehla had given him a "strangely evasive reply."

Both officers not only sensed they were under surveillance by the Nazi party members and putsch sympathizers among the political and security police officials in the building but were harboring mounting suspicions as to who was on whose side. In that dilemma, Imhoff and Banzer were certainly not alone. In fact, just as they suspected others, their loyalties, too, were being questioned by officers such as Doehla and Muxel, not to mention interior ministry civil servants such as Zetlmeier. Until there was some word from Seisser, Kahr, or Lossow, the only logical, though dismaying, conclusion was that Ernst Pöhner, Wilhelm Frick, and their second-floor Nazi sympathizers actually were the government.

Pöhner and Frick, installed in Mantel's suite, were not only convinced of that fact themselves but were trying to convince others by a dizzying bustle of activity.

Their first "official action" was to schedule a midnight press briefing so that Munich papers would have "proper guidance" in reporting the evening's historic events to their readers. Inspector

Matthäus Hofmann was dispatched to the editorial offices of four of Munich's six dailies to summon their editors-in-chief. The notable exceptions were the Social Democratic *Münchener Post*, marked for "special treatment," and the *Völkischer Beobachter*, whose Alfred Rosenberg obviously needed no instructions on what or how to write. Hofmann, now wearing an old army uniform with both Nazi party and imperial insignia, made it apparent by the pistol on his belt that the nocturnal press conference was a command performance.

Then Pöhner and Frick took steps to establish what they regarded as "revolutionary law and order": they drafted proclamations for two posters that the party's printers would soon run off their presses for the SA to paste up all over Munich. If nothing else, these texts certainly conformed with the views of a man— Pöhner—who had once remarked that too few political assassins were roaming about Bavaria, and of his co-conspirator—Frick— who a scant decade later was to become Nazi Germany's feared minister of interior.

"Open season is hereby declared on the scoundrels responsible for the treason of November 9, 1918," one of the posters read.

> Every German who sees or knows the whereabouts of Friedrich Ebert, Philipp Scheidemann, Oskar Cohn, Paul Levi, Theodor Wolff, Georg Bernhard, and their helpers is herewith informed of his patriotic obligation to deliver the above-named, either dead or alive, into the hands of the new Nationalist Government.

The other placard, declaring summary justice for all "enemies of the people and state," was even more menacing in tone. It announced establishment of a "supreme national tribunal," not only empowered but duty-bound to sentence to death all those found guilty of "opposing the revolution." Sentences were to be executed "within three hours after being imposed." It added that "appeals will not be permitted."

With this copy on the way to the Bürgerbräukeller for Hitler's final approval, Pöhner and Frick left Ett Strasse—much to Banzer and von Imhoff's relief—for what, in retrospect, was perhaps the most peculiar expedition of the entire night: to see Gustav von Kahr.

Pöhner had told Kahr that he would wait to discuss the formation of the new Bavarian government with him until morning.

Did they not trust him and hence hope to draw him more deeply into their coup than the public pledge of collaboration which had been extracted from him in the Bürgerbräukeller? Or, rather, did they believe him to be on their side and, in their eagerness to establish the new regime, really want to discuss "further measures" with him?

In all likelihood, the truth lies somewhere in between. Though Hitler was anathema to Kahr, at best, in his eyes, an effective propagandist to use as a tool, Pöhner—an appeals court judge since his stint as Munich police president—was his political and personal friend and very much a part of the conservative Bavarian establishment. Both career civil servants under the monarchy, Kahr and Pöhner had scratched each other's backs on the way up the ladder, especially in 1920, when Pöhner had paved the way for Kahr to become prime minister.

Thus, Pöhner probably did believe Kahr's word that evening; but also, knowing how easily he vacillated and how susceptible he was to influence, he probably did not trust him to keep that word under pressure from advisers and subordinates such as Barons von Freyberg and von Aufsess, his two key aides. He would need both prodding and propping.

That, apparently, was how Kahr himself saw it when, around 11 P.M., he was told that Pöhner and Frick wished to see him. He stalled for time, hoping that Seisser would arrive or, at least, that there would be some indication of his whereabouts. If Banzer and Imhoff at Ett Strasse were mystified, State Police officers such as Muxel and Doehla and the civil servants at Maximilian Strasse seemed even more dumbfounded by the colonel's inexplicable "disappearance" since Franz Hunglinger had driven back to the Bürgerbräukeller to get him. Somehow, in the excitement and confusion of the first hour after Ludendorff had released the triumvirs, coordination between them had collapsed completely. It was reported that Seisser had been at Danner's headquarters and had gone from there to Türken Strasse.

What worried Kahr, so he said, was that Pöhner and Frick might "induce me to accompany them to police headquarters, to the war ministry, or to some other place where they could involve me in further conferences or discussions, some place where I would again find myself in a difficult situation"; that is, he really wanted to know what Seisser and Lossow had decided.

So he hid in his apartment on the pretext of being busy on the phone with Vice-Premier Franz Matt. Pöhner and Frick stayed in his outer office almost forty-five minutes, until, he felt, "I could not keep them waiting any longer."

At Ett Strasse, meanwhile, Banzer and Imhoff had finally located their commander-in-chief—or rather, he had found them by phoning. Would they please come to the Türken Strasse barracks immediately? Seisser apparently had reservations about being chauffeured around Munich on streets filled with singing and carousing storm troopers. So, for that matter, did Banzer and Imhoff. Stealthily, suspecting that the building was surrounded by putschists, which it soon would be, and that they were being shadowed by Frick's sympathizers, which they were, they left police headquarters by the back entrance for Banzer's staff car and drove hurriedly to Türken Strasse. But if they expected unequivocal instructions and a clear policy statement from Seisser, they were disappointed.

Hans von Seisser, then forty-nine—a man with chiseled aristocratic features, steely eyes, a small trim mustache, but over-large ears—had gained a reputation before and during the war as a brilliant, energetic, and personally ambitious general staff officer. But unlike some of his peers, once the war was over he recognized that career opportunities in the German army would be limited and set out, de facto if not de jure, to create an army of his own— the green-uniformed Bavarian State Police. With nearly 10,000 men, armored and artillery battalions, and even a small air corps of aging Fokkers, it was in all but name a shrunken successor to the old Royal Bavarian Army.

As its founder and chief, Seisser was limited by the dictates of the Versailles Treaty to the rank of colonel, but he received the pay and emoluments of a major general, and it was tacitly agreed by the Bavarian ministry of interior that he exercised a general's authority.

A native Bavarian and Catholic, Seisser harbored a congenital contempt for Ludendorff, the Protestant Prussian; but beyond that he was as implacably reactionary and conservative, as repelled by republicanism, and as skeptical of parliamentary democracy as any of Bavaria's political leaders, the various "patriotic societies," the extremists of the fighting leagues, or Hitler's Nazis. He too would have welcomed a radical change in Berlin. But he was too much a military traditionalist to have given much thought to the means of effecting it, let alone to meddle actively in politics as Lossow had done.

Yet he was a man who thought independently, even if his position as the servant of several masters—Kahr, Interior Minister Schweyer, and, when circumstances dictated, even Lossow—did not always permit him to act that way. Among all the fighting leagues, paramilitary groups, organizations of free-corps veterans, and private armies of mercenaries fanning the flames of political passion and conspiracy in Bavaria in the fall of 1923, it seems that Seisser's sympathies were clearly with ex-navy Commander Hermann Ehrhardt, Eberhard Kautter, and their Viking League. It was Seisser who had legitimized Ehrhardt's "brigade" by deputizing it as a border police force on Bavaria's northern frontiers and supplying it with arms.

His relations with Hitler, on the other hand, had always been cordial and proper but never warm or enthusiastic, and he was too much of a pragmatist to place much hope in a putsch or march on Berlin.

Banzer and Imhoff found Seisser in his Türken Strasse command post, ranting. "It was a second Kapp Putsch, only even more incompetent," Seisser said, alluding to the ultra-rightist Prussian bureaucrat's ludicrous attempt to make himself chancellor of the Reich with the help of Ehrhardt's brigade in March 1920. "It was an outrage, terror. Hitler named me Reich police minister. There is no such post."

But for all his apparent anger, Seisser remained noncommittal and did not give his aides specific instructions to crush the putsch. Instead, he ordered them only to take all steps to "secure and protect" every State Police bastion against attack—measures actually falling short of what Imhoff on his own had already done nearly two hours earlier. Seisser, too, was keeping his powder dry and waiting to see how the wind would blow, in particular from Kahr, who, he said, he would now look up at Maximilian Strasse.

If the building seemed threatened, then he would take Kahr with him to the 19th Infantry barracks, where Danner and Lossow were waiting.

He told Banzer and Imhoff to return to Ett Strasse and supervise operations from there.

But supervise what? The two still had no guidance as to which government they were supposed to be serving or whether to regard Hitler's storm troopers as enemies or friends.

"We thought that you might want to compose a proclamation that we can have printed and distributed throughout the city by morning," Pöhner said.

"Wasn't Herr Hitler supposed to do that?" Kahr replied. "He is the right man for it."

Pöhner nodded agreement.

Of all encounters of the night, Pöhner and Frick's with Kahr was undoubtedly the most wondrous. Having deliberately kept the two waiting, Kahr received them graciously and pleasantly in his official apartment, acting very much the "King's deputy and governor." He appeared, to Pöhner and Frick at least, to be in high spirits. If Hitler's barbarous interruption of his speech continued to anger him, he clearly displayed no signs of it. And if he still harbored doubts about the success of a march on Berlin "before assurances of cooperation from the gentlemen in the north," he was certainly not expressing them around midnight.

To be sure, he demurred that neither Hitler nor Ludendorff's name would mean as much in northern Germany as in Bavaria, largely because of their foreign policy pronouncements in recent weeks and the likely reaction of the Allies. Moreover, he argued that failure to obtain the cooperation of industrial, business, and agricultural leaders in advance had been a grave error. The crucial question in the winter weeks and months ahead would be getting a grip on the economy. But then, he conceded, what was done was done.

An act? A ploy to rid himself of the two as quickly and with as little argument as possible? That would be his explanation later, but if so, neither Pöhner nor Frick realized it.

"Have you notified the district prefects yet, Excellency?" Pöhner wanted to know.

"Not only them but the county administrations too," von Kahr lied, picking up a strip of paper purporting to be a cable announcing that he had assumed the governorship of Bavaria on behalf of Rupprecht.

Pöhner asked for permission to make the text of the cable known to the press, explaining that he had summoned the leading editors for a midnight briefing. In fact, he added, looking at his watch, the gentlemen were probably already waiting, and perhaps he and Frick should leave.

"By all means," Kahr encouraged him, smiling.

"One last question, Excellency," Pöhner said. "I know it has been a long, strenuous night for you, but we must talk about the ministerial appointments and the composition of my cabinet. When may I call on you tomorrow to discuss it?"

"Around nine-thirty in the morning would suit me," Kahr replied, making a note on his desk calendar.

As they left the building to return to Ett Strasse in Pöhner's car, the new "prime minister" and "police chief" did not notice Colonel Seisser's arrival by another entrance.

Erich Ludendorff, his face masklike, sat stiffly on a straight-backed chair in the bare, dimly lit antechamber of Otto von Lossow's office at the old Bavarian war ministry. The erstwhile warlord was simmering with impatience and discomfort there. But breeding and his code of etiquette kept him from entering Lossow's richly carpeted, wood-paneled, lavishly appointed inner sanctum. Without an invitation and during Lossow's absence, he would remain outside.

Sullenly he watched the bustle of revolutionary activity around him. Where was the man? It was nearly midnight, and it had been ten-thirty when Lossow left the beerhall. Doubts were beginning to gnaw at Ludendorff too, but he tried to shut them out and keep his co-conspirators from voicing theirs aloud.

"Nobody knows where he is," Max von Scheubner-Richter said. "Captain Röhm has been phoning everywhere. Don't you think we ought to—"

"Quiet!" Ludendorff interrupted frigidly. "I again forbid you, absolutely, even to suggest that a German officer would not keep his word."

But a Bavarian bureaucrat, Ludendorff began to wonder, a regent for that Vatican-oriented Wittelsbach prince, Rupprecht: could he be trusted to keep his word? Maybe Kahr was exerting pressure on Lossow. Didn't he have to be shoved into the auditorium, complaining all the way about his loss of dignity? Ludendorff had known for years that Lossow was easily manipulated, responsive to anyone with a louder argument. That the pressure might be coming from another general—Jakob von Danner—never even entered Ludendorff's mind. It seemed logical to him that Kahr was talking loudest at the moment. Well, he had a way of dealing with that. They would soon show Kahr who was in command and who wasn't.

Beckoning to Hermann Kriebel and Hitler, who had just arrived from the Bürgerbräukeller, Ludendorff said, "Send word to Rossbach, in my name. He is to take the Infantry School cadets to Maximilian Strasse and occupy it. Immediately."

Lieutenants Robert Wagner, Hans Block, and Siegfried Mahler and the other 400 Infantry School students were drinking beer or trying to catnap in the Bürgerbräu auditorium when their self-appointed leader, Gerhard Rossbach, stormed into the hall.

"*Infanterieschüler, fertig machen und antreten*—Everybody out, assemble on the street!" he ordered.

Within minutes the officer candidates, distinguishable from other Reichswehr troops only by the swastika armbands Rossbach had distributed, were clambering excitedly onto waiting trucks on Rosenheimer Strasse, heavy machine guns and mortars in their midst.

"*Los!*" Rossbach shouted.

The convoy, with a small howitzer bringing up the rear, rolled down the hill, across Ludwig Bridge and toward Maximilian Strasse.

"Kahr must be out of his mind," Fritz Gerlich said, spotting Adolf Schiedt in the second-floor library of the Ett Strasse police headquarters. "Ludendorff's name—I won't even mention Hitler's—is an affront, a provocation to public opinion abroad. The French are going to be marching before the night is over. How could he have stood on that stage and given those two his hand,

Schiedt? If you are going over there, tell him what I think."

Schiedt, who doubled as Kahr's press spokesman, shrugged his shoulders and nodded his head in hapless and helpless bewilderment. Three hours after the Bürgerbräu drama, he still seemed traumatized.

The editors were waiting for Pöhner and Frick. Having been virtually ordered from their offices, they were, by the nature of their trade, curious. But because the interruption was so close to deadline for their first editions, they were also irritated by the delay.

Besides Gerlich of the *Münchner Neueste Nachrichten* and Schiedt of the *Münchener Zeitung,* the two ghost-writers of Kahr's interrupted speech that evening, there were Eugen Mündler of the *München-Augsburger Abendzeitung* and Paul Egenter of the stanchly royalist *Bayerischer Kurier* and *Münchner Tageblatt.*

Since radio as a news medium had barely been conceived and television transmission was just a laboratory experiment, they represented the apogee of opinion-making. But though bourgeois and stanchly conservative, theirs was not the rabble-rousing, intemperate, propagandistic voice of a *Völkischer Beobachter* and certainly not the moderately Marxist message of the Social Democratic *Münchener Post.* They spoke for the establishment. And nationalistic, monarchistic, and reactionary as they were, violence, lawlessness, and revolutionary upheaval were repugnant to them. All were highly skeptical of the evening's developments.

Pöhner's aim in calling them together was to win them over to the putschist cause—with deft and insidious appeals to their patriotic emotions and sense of responsibility but also with barely veiled hints that censorship would follow in case they demurred. The phrase "news management" had not yet been coined, but his briefing was certainly its clever precursor. With Frick standing by his side, he extolled the "noble, virtuous aims" of the men who had formed the "new national government and tonight were anointed to lead us out of the morass created by the perpetrators and profiteers of the 1918 revolution."

The events in the Bürgerbräukeller, he said, were but the beginning of a nationalist wave that would spread, tidelike, from Munich and Bavaria to engulf Prussia, bringing "freedom, prestige, respect, and puissance to a united, rejuvenated Germany." It might be difficult, there might be setbacks, he conceded, and numerous details and technicalities such as the composition of the new government had yet to be worked out. But the signals had been set and the goal would be reached—"provided we all work together and you, of the press, support us." The names of Ludendorff and Hitler did not appeal to all and aroused antipathy among some, Pöhner acknowledged, looking directly at Gerlich. But Kahr's and his own were surely guarantees of integrity and devotion to duty around whom all could rally. Others, he promised, would be named to the new government in the coming days.

Then, politely but emphatically, he became more specific—and menacing.

"As far as the Munich press is concerned," he said, "it has the duty to assist the new German and the new Bavarian government in the pursuit of their national, patriotic goals.

"I hardly need remind you that the foreign press—the British, French, Italian—stands unanimously behind its governments on all issues of national importance, and I hope that you will relegate all partisan political attitudes behind the salient fact that we are all Germans and can regain our freedom only in unity.

"We expect unconditional recognition of the government embodied by Excellency von Kahr and me," Pöhner continued. "The coming days will determine what specific measures both the new Reich and Bavarian governments will take. Even if they seem debatable or not immediately clear to you, we expect you not to comment upon them inimically and to view them in the light in which they are taken—by serious men, determined and committed to help Germany.

"There will be no censorship, but a corollary of press freedom is press responsibility, and I assume you are aware of your responsibilities. *Meine Herren*, are there any questions?"

There certainly were. Egenter of the royalist *Bayerischer Kurier* wanted to know whether Kahr had coordinated with and obtained Rupprecht's permission to pronounce himself "the King's deputy" and governor for the crown.

Pöhner waffled the answer. "I think we can assume that Excellency von Kahr acted in conformity with the Crown Prince's intentions. Herr von Kahr's views correspond so closely with those of His Majesty that his actions were certainly an expression of the Crown Prince's wishes."

"Isn't there a basic contradiction between von Kahr's monarchistic and Hitler's republican-dictatorial aims?" Egenter pressed on.

Well, not really, Pöhner replied. To be sure, in establishing a national dictatorship, Hitler was not going to restore the monarchy. But since the aim of his coup d'état was to avenge the revolution that had toppled the Kaiser and King, it was tantamount to the same thing.

There were rumblings of dissent, and Gerlich had the feeling that Pöhner was losing some of his self-assurance, particularly when it was pointed out that Ludendorff's platform remarks on the new government's foreign policy aims had been rather inflammatory.

"Wouldn't it be prudent to modify some of that so as not to provoke the French?" Gerlich asked.

"Well," Pöhner replied, "if you wish to exercise self-restraint and self-censorship on certain points, that is up to you. I am sure you know best what to do—"

"There is no need," Frick interrupted, to everyone's astonishment. "The French will march anyway, with or without a provocation."

And talking about provocations, Gerlich insisted, what about the detention of Ludwig Wassermann in the Bürgerbräukeller? "That is scandalous. He may be Jewish, but he is a deeply patriotic, nationalistically spirited German man."

"Unfortunately," Pöhner said, with a shrug that struck some as an expression of disdain, others as discomfort, "we can do little about that at the moment."

It was 12:30 A.M., November 9, when the meeting broke up. The editors, by their own admission even more perplexed about the game being played and deeply disturbed about its possible outcome and ramifications, departed for their offices.

Pöhner, leaving Frick in command at Ett Strasse, decided to go home "to catch a few hours' sleep."

As Kurt Lüdecke, Hitler's "emissary" in Rome, was to remark caustically many years later, "History knows no revolutions which have been won between the sheets. This one was no exception."

Captain Karl Wild and Lieutenant Colonel Wilhelm Muxel were standing at the main entrance to Kahr's General State Commissariat on Maximilian Strasse. The captain had just returned from making the rounds of the central telephone and telegraph exchanges to impose a ban on all outgoing cables and long-distance calls. Suddenly they heard the sounds of loud shouting and a commotion near the east wing.

"Now what?" Wild exclaimed as he and the colonel ran up the street.

To their amazement they saw a nearly battalion-sized unit of Reichswehr troopers—the Infantry School cadets—converging on the building, bayonets implanted on their rifles, machine guns posted all around, and fieldpiece poised to fire from across the avenue.

"*Angreifen*—Attack!" they heard Rossbach shouting from a safe distance.

Within seconds some of the cadets had broken through the green-uniformed cordon and were engaged in hand-to-hand scuffling with the astonished State Police.

"*Halt! Nicht Schiessen!*" Muxel shouted, rushing into the melee. "What is this all about?!"

"We have orders from General Ludendorff to relieve the police and take over the guard of the building," Hans Block said, though also ordering his men to fall back a distance.

"There must be some mistake," Muxel said, hoping to bargain for time. He had noticed Siegfried Mahler, a close friend of his son Otto, in the front lines. "You are making a grave mistake," he added, taking the young lieutenant and some of the other cadets aside. Lossow, Seisser, and Kahr, he hinted, had had a falling-out with Ludendorff and Hitler and were opposing the putsch.

Mahler, Block, and Robert Wagner were skeptical. They demanded to speak to Seisser or Kahr.

While Muxel continued to negotiate on the street, Wild hurried inside—on the pretext of looking for Seisser—and called both Ett Strasse and the Türken Strasse barracks for reinforcements. "Send us what you can, including armored cars," he told Sigmund von Imhoff.

The delay was causing tempers to rise outside. Wagner demanded to be taken inside. Muxel agreed. "But if they are not back in ten minutes, we will open fire," Block called out. It was not an empty threat but it was superfluous, for as the three entered the complex with Muxel by one door, Seisser himself came out from another to speak with Rossbach.

It was a brief, acerbic meeting.

"There is no need for you where the State Police are on guard," the colonel said tersely. "March off."

"I cannot, Excellency," Rossbach replied. "I have specific orders from General Ludendorff to take over the guard here, by force if necessary."

"You heard what I said," Seisser retorted, turning his back on the erstwhile free-corps leader. "March your men away immediately or I will give orders to shoot." It was also not an empty threat. Whatever equivocation may have guided his behavior earlier in the night, Seisser had now made up his mind and knew where he stood.

Rossbach, starting to have doubts and perplexed by the stiff resistance from Seisser and the police, dispatched a motorcycle courier back to the Bürgerbräukeller to report the situation to Göring and obtain instructions. Meanwhile, Wagner had come back outside with Muxel and Wild. Kahr and Seisser, he told his comrades, were nowhere to be found. "Somebody is either lying or playing a double game," he said, walking off through the ranks to hunt for Rossbach on the other side of the street.

The situation on that dimly illuminated, tree-lined old boulevard was explosive. A truncated company of State Police—less than 100 men—waited nervously for reinforcements that might not even come. Facing and ringing them at a distance of ten yards—point-blank range—stood 400 Reichswehr officers and candidates with enough hardware to wage a small war. Veterans of the trenches, many of them personal friends, some even brothers and cousins, were poised to shoot at each other. In essence, all believed in the same thing—a reborn, powerful Germany—and a scant two hours before had been told they were also striving for it. Neither side wanted to light the fuse that would lead to a fratricidal massacre, yet any wrong move could touch it off.

As Muxel and Wild continued their efforts to negotiate and compromise, Rossbach waited nervously in the dark beside a clump of bushes for his courier to return. Suddenly the strain was too much for him. "What are you all waiting for?" he screamed hysterically. "What's all the talking about? You know Excellency Ludendorff's orders. Fire now! Stop dilly-dallying!"

The night air was punctuated by the sound of hundreds of rifle bolts being pulled back and the safeties on machine guns being snapped. The cadets moved forward.

And then, just as suddenly, came Rossbach's countermanding order: "Halt. Companies retreat." Wild and Muxel were as bewildered as the young Reichswehr officers.

"New orders from General Ludendorff," Rossbach explained hastily, trying to reassure Block and Mahler there was no truth to the rumors they had heard of a split between the triumvirs and the putschists. "We have been reassigned to guard the railway station. Everybody back to the trucks."

He was not lying, though he did not know that the order, given in Ludendorff's name, had actually come from Friedrich Weber—not because the Oberland chieftain wanted to avoid the bloodbath in the making but because he needed the Infantry School cadets as replacements for his storm troopers, still locked up in the drill hall of the Engineer Barracks.

Even as Rossbach reassembled his force for its seemingly inexplicable retreat, a dark green police staff car was roaring out of a side gate to the Maximilian Strasse complex. In the back sat Seisser and Kahr, on their way to Danner and Lossow's command post at the 19th Infantry Barracks to set in motion the machinery that would turn a night of confusion into a day of bloody decision.

11

Wilhelm Briemann was nursing a stale beer at a table in the Bürgerbräukeller auditorium, only half listening to the conversation of fellow Stosstrupp members who were wolfing down sausages and thick slabs of dark rye bread and drinking from their quart-sized mugs. It was almost midnight. The mood in the hall— empty except for the SA and Oberländers gathered there—was that of a victory won, a job well done. Yet the elite-guard storm troopers with the death's-head symbol on their lapels were getting sleepy, not to mention drunk. After all, besides being the "van-

guard of the German awakening," as Hitler had praised them before leaving to join Ludendorff at the war ministry, they all had
regular trades and most of them had been at their jobs early that
morning.

It was a heterogeneous group seated there with Briemann, the
wiry little book salesman. Among them were twenty-six-year-old
Emil Maurice, handsome and dark-haired, a watchmaker by
training but more often busy as one of Hitler's favorite chauffeurs; Hans Kallenbach, also twenty-six, a mechanic; Josef Gerum,
the thirty-five-year-old police detective who had gone over to the
Nazis after originally being assigned to the party as an undercover
agent; Karl Hutter, a thirty-two-year-old butcher; and two young
freshman students at Munich Technical University, Hans Krüger,
eighteen, and Walter Hewel, nineteen. Their talk, largely idle
rather than of the events they had just helped kindle at gun- and
bayonet-point, was harshly interrupted by their leader, tobacconist Josef Berchtold.

"Everyone from the Stosstrupp outside," he shouted over the
rumble of voices in the hall. "There is work to do."

Gathering their rifles and helmets, buttoning their greatcoats,
and taking last swigs of beer, Briemann and the others scrambled
out of the building to the beer garden. There stood Hermann Göring, like a field marshal surveying his legions.

"I want to congratulate you on what you did tonight," he
trumpeted. "It was a good job. But now I have some others for
you. First, take over that lying red rag, the *Münchener Post.*
Smash it to pieces, for all I care—but don't touch the presses.
They belong to us now. And after that, bring me that Socialist
swine Erhard Auer."

Lugging their machine guns and grenade launchers, Berchtold and more than a hundred of his toughs scurried to the waiting trucks and headed off down the street across the river, into
the center of the city to the offices and printing plant of the Social
Democratic party's daily at Altheimer Strasse No. 19.

For many in Munich that night, it was the start of a wave of
terror, a prelude to the Crystal Night and the Holocaust that was
to engulf Germany fifteen years later. The victims were Socialists,
Communists, Jews, and others perceived to be "enemies of the
people." Many had long been on hit lists, but others were selected

at random from the telephone book because their names "just sounded Jewish," and a few merely happened to be the unfortunate neighbors of Nazis who recognized an opportunity to settle personal scores.

Ferdinand Mürriger, the business manager of the *Münchener Post*, had just dozed off in his fourth-floor apartment in the newspaper building when he was startled by loud yelling and the sound of breaking glass outside. He rushed to his bedroom window and saw the narrow, cobblestoned street below being sealed off by machine-gun squads as dozens of Berchtold's helmeted troopers smashed the paper's ground-floor display cases with their rifle butts. Mürriger scurried downstairs and reached the courtyard just as a group of Nazis was trying to pry open the iron gate.

"*Aufmachen! Schnell!*" Berchtold commanded, pointing his pistol through the staves at Mürriger's face.

Shaken, Mürriger obeyed, and within seconds scores of storm troopers crashed through the portal. Moving from office to office, from floor to floor, they laid waste to everything in sight, overturning desks, file cabinets, bookcases, wardrobes, boxes of type and composing stands. They splintered furniture, doors and newsroom partitions into kindling wood with their bayonets and rifle butts. Jugs of ink were thrown against the walls. Papers, books, manuscripts, letters, advertising, subscription and employee records, pictures and busts of Social Democratic leaders, and the red-black-gold flags of the Republic, all were tossed through the windows to the street below and set ablaze.

While Briemann stood guard with others outside, young Hewel dashed in with the Stosstrupp's swastika flag and hung it triumphantly from the paper's second-floor balcony. Krüger rushed for the garage, hoping to steal the news department's only car. Failing to get it started, he lugged out spare tires instead and loaded them onto one of the trucks. Hutter and some of his men busied themselves carting out all typewriters, while Maurice went to work searching for weapons—though he found none. Gerum and Berchtold broke into Auer's private office and rummaged through it, then smashed his desk and file cabinets, taking with them "for safe keeping at the Bürgerbräu" boxloads of records, papers, and letters, including some from and to President Ebert.

The mob was just about to wreck the pressroom when "police" arrived—in the form of Detectives Thomas Rietzler and Martin Gumbrecht, both wearing swastika armbands.

"Halt!" Rietzler shouted. "Not the presses: on orders of Herr Frick. They belong to the *Völkischer Beobachter.*" Dutifully, the storm troopers stepped back, dropping the crowbars they had found in a tool room.

Those presses were virtually the only pieces of equipment left undamaged by the time Berchtold marched his men off to their next "revolutionary task." One hour of pillage and demolition had left a shambles. Besides the tires, typewriters, and cashboxes containing an estimated 6 trillion paper marks, anything and everything of value—from balls of wrapping twine to newsprint paper —was stolen. Some 320 glass panes had been broken. Almost three weeks were to pass before the damage was sufficiently repaired for the *Post* to resume publication in its own plant.

Müncheners have always been as partisan about their brands of beer as about their preferences between the city's two most luxurious and fashionable hotels. One is the opulently ostentatious Bayerischer Hof, built in 1841 on Promenade Platz adjacent to the Montgelas Palace, official residence of Bavaria's prime ministers. The other is the stately neo-Gothic Vier Jahreszeiten on Maximilian Strasse, diagonally across the street from where Henrik Ibsen lived for fifteen years.

Although the Bayerischer Hof rated then—and now—as the plusher, more gilded of the two, the Vier Jahreszeiten was renowned for the internationally acclaimed culinary artistry of its owner, Alfred Walterspiel, a German chef who had mastered the secrets and intricacies of French haute cuisine with consummate skill.

That was probably the source of its appeal to the French and Belgian officers of the Allied Military Control Commission. Being congenital epicures and appreciably appalled by the monotony and heaviness of Bavarian cooking, they had chosen the Vier Jahreszeiten as their residence when assigned to Munich to investigate Bavarian Reichswehr adherence to the strictures of the Versailles Treaty.

But at 12:30 A.M. on November 9, their choice must have seemed most unfortunate.

The hotel was located one block from the Wurzer Hof tavern, favorite watering spot of Edmund Heines's boisterous Second SA Battalion. Even worse, it was directly in his path as Heines and Hans Frank, loudly singing the "Sturmlied," marched the battalion from the Bürgerbräukeller to the Infantry School on Mars Strasse where Göring had told them to bivouac for the night and await further instructions.

Whether it was Göring's idea to take the Allied officers into "protective custody" or Heines's own, as he later admitted to police, "because I wanted to do something special for the revolution," has remained unknown. Suffice it to say that, as the contingent reached the corner of Maximilian and Wurzer streets, Heines ordered his ragtag army of nearly 300 storm troopers to surround the hotel, then led 20 of his toughest-looking men, including Frank, into the richly carpeted, mahogany-paneled lobby. The last of Herr Walterspiel's well-fed guests were still sitting about on soft leather sofas and easy chairs, chatting over coffee, brandy, and liqueurs.

Followed by six of his armed cohorts, Heines strutted toward the reception desk, pulled his revolver from the holster, and pointed it straight at the flabbergasted night manager, Christian Tauber. "In the name of the revolutionary government," Heines shouted, "take us to the Allied officers' rooms."

The Vier Jahreszeiten, famed also for its wild parties during Fasching, Munich's annual carnival season, had been the scene of many strange events since its construction in 1859, and the staff had a dignified, discreet way of dealing with all manner of pranksters. But these pistols and rifles were real, and this was obviously no joke.

"Under no circumstances," Tauber replied adamantly.

"Yes, you will," Heines snarled, loudly snapping off the safety on his revolver and threatening to arrest not only the manager but the shocked guests in the lobby.

Shrugging helplessly, Tauber gave Heines the room numbers and then was ordered to accompany the posse upstairs to act as translator because he spoke French.

"*Aufmachen! Raus, raus!* Everybody into the corridor!" Heines bellowed, as his troops banged loudly with their weapons on the doors Tauber pointed out to them. Most of the officers had already gone to sleep, blissfully unaware of what had transpired at the Bürgerbräukeller.

"You Boches must be crazy to make so much racket so late at night," a Belgian major named Boychou said indignantly, opening his door a crack.

"Translate," Heines ordered Tauber. "Tell him he is under the arrest and custody of the new Reich government of Hitler and Ludendorff."

Dutifully, the manager explained what had happened. With each word Boychou's eyes widened in astonishment. "You really are crazy," he sputtered in French, "but you are also armed and I am not. I am at your disposal. Do with me what you wish. Shoot me if you want. But remember that I am a Belgian officer and think of the consequences."

A French colonel named Wild was not quite as compliant. Bolting his door when he heard the noise in the corridor, he shouted back at Frank and Heines that he was armed and would resist any attempt to enter his room. He meant it.

Wild's defiance turned Heines "livid with rage." He had "to teach the hated *Franzose* a lesson" and show him "who gives the orders and who does not in the newly born Germany." An ex-lieutenant, he regarded himself "as a soldier of the new Reich government that night." With his revolver pointed at the door, Heines signaled to one of his troopers, who smashed through the thin paneling with his rifle butt, leaving a jagged, splintered hole. Beyond it, grim-faced, stood the pajama-clad colonel, service pistol in hand. For a paralyzing fraction of a second the Frenchman and Heines faced each other with their fingers on the triggers.

Then Tauber, screaming "Don't shoot!", stepped between them. In a torrent of French he implored the colonel not to resist. Seeing Heines, Frank, and the other troopers with their rifles now pointed straight at him too, Wild agreed and unlocked what remained of the door. One of the SA men bounded in, shattered the room phone with his rifle stock, and ripped it off the wall.

Heines ordered Wild and Boychou to get dressed, intending to take them as hostages back to the Bürgerbräukeller, but again

Tauber intervened, suggesting that the officers would not leave the hotel if asked not to. The proposal seemed to mellow Heines. He posted a guard in front of each officer's door, then proudly led the rest of his men out of the hotel. Assembling the battalion outside, he marched it to the Infantry School, where they camped until called back to the Bürgerbräu by Göring at 3 A.M.

The guards in front of the Allied officers' doors remained until, so Tauber noticed, they were silently withdrawn on orders from a courier around 4 A.M.

Erhard Auer's wife, Sophie, a strong-willed, courageous woman of fifty-five, had reacted with composure when Wilhelm Hoegner whisked her husband away to safety at 10 P.M. Having experienced the 1918 revolution, Kurt Eisner's murder, an assassination attempt on her husband, the violent Soviet republic, and the even more violent Red and White terror, she was accustomed to politically ordained danger and was prepared for it now.

In the spacious fourth-floor apartment at Nussbaum Strasse No. 10 were her three daughters, Agnes, eighteen, Sophie Fengler, twenty-four, Emilie Luber, twenty-one; Sophie's two-year-old baby girl; and Emilie's husband, Dr. Karl Luber. The newly married couple and Sophie, all still living there, had gone to bed around midnight.

But Frau Auer and Agnes had remained up, in anticipation of the adversity they were certain would come. There was an eerie, ominous silence in the parlor, accentuated by the constant ticking of a regulator clock on the wall. Neither of them spoke much. They were steeped in thoughts of impending troubles.

Around 12:30 A.M. they heard the noise of motors outside. Looking out, Frau Auer saw a truck with armed men in uniform and two passenger cars on the street below: Berchtold, Kallenbach, Maurice, and other members of the Stosstrupp. She assumed "the visitors were for us," and since she "wanted everything to happen as calmly as possible," sent Agnes downstairs to open up for them.

What happened then was told most poignantly by Frau Auer herself in her subsequent deposition to police. "My daughter took the lift down, but the intruders had already entered the building foyer and I heard them shout, 'Stop that lift or we will cut the cables.' When my daughter arrived downstairs, she asked whether the gentlemen were coming to Auer's. They said yes. Fifteen to twenty stormed upstairs and I could hear the command, 'Be ready to fire.'

"One of the first ones to enter the apartment was a tall, dark-haired man [Maurice] who pointed a pistol at my face and asked, 'Where is your husband?' When I explained that he had gone away, I was asked when he had been here last and where he might be. I said I did not know.

"'Now we are the rulers and the government,' he said. 'If you won't tell us where your husband is but we find him anyway, you are done for.' Just then my daughter Emilie Luber and her husband came out of their bedroom, and as the man said this to me, he gave me such a hard shove to the breast that I stumbled backward through their open door and would have fallen on the floor had I not been able to catch myself on their bed. Then he locked me into their room. I was kept prisoner there for a few minutes until another man, I think it was Berchtold, opened up again.

"Although the other men in the apartment—in all about fifteen—behaved rather decently, especially Herr Berchtold himself, the dark-haired one was very gruff.

"When [Maurice] went into the room of my daughter Sophie Fengler, she asked him not to make too much noise so as not to wake her baby, but he said that was not his concern. He asked her where the child's father was and whether she had any weapons. He wanted her to open a sideboard in that room to which the lock happened to be broken. So he took his rifle and smashed the doors with the stock, to satisfy himself, apparently, that there were only dishes inside it. With the rifle he also knocked a brass tray from the sideboard to the floor. Then he went through her wardrobe, threw out the clothes and laundry, and trampled on them. He tore off the bedding and smashed with his rifle butt into a suitcase containing more dishes. When my daughter asked him not to do this, he said, 'Keep your mouth shut.'

"I went out to Herr Berchtold to complain and he told the man to stop that. Smashing into the suitcase, he had broken two glass trays and a butter dish. In my daughter Agnes's room he turned the chaise longue over.

"In my husband's study there is a safe. [Maurice] asked Berchtold whether it should be opened, too. 'Yes, if there are keys to it,' Berchtold replied. Since I had the keys in my possession, I opened the safe at his insistence. He rummaged through it and cleaned it out and gave some of the papers to Berchtold. Among them were copies of letters to President Ebert. Berchtold said these would be confiscated. The same was true of documents about their National Socialist party. When I said that the school diplomas and report cards of my daughters in the safe were hardly of interest to them, the tall dark man shouted, 'Shut up,' and again gave me a shove so that I stumbled back but was caught from falling by my son-in-law, Dr. Luber.

"The tall dark man kept insisting there must be weapons to be found. I explained that other than a revolver in my husband's night stand and an old pistol, both his personal property, there were no arms in the apartment. Both of these were confiscated."

The storm troopers then ransacked Auer's library, overturning the bookcases, and rummaged through his desk and took a petty cashbox with them. They demanded to search the attic in the building, though, curiously, not the basement laundry room and storage area.

Furious because they had not found Auer, Berchtold and his men settled for second best—they took Luber prisoner instead.

"Get dressed," Maurice commanded, "and take your identity papers along. You'll do until we find your father-in-law. You are coming with us."

He was marched to the waiting truck at gunpoint and driven to the Bürgerbräukeller, where he was locked into the same upstairs room with Ludwig Wassermann, the Jewish banker, and other hostages.

The Stosstrupp's visit to the Auer apartment was not the only one that night or the following morning. Squads of Nazis seem to have chosen it as a special target for demonstrations as they marched by shouting and threatening soon to "hang the Marxist women by their hair." The second "night visitors" were a gang of a dozen toughs led by one Ernst Hübner.

A bank clerk, Hübner was a platoon leader of the Oberland League who had either not received his "mobilization" orders the afternoon of November 8, had ignored them, or had failed to understand their significance. For while Hitler was declaring the nationalist revolution in the Bürgerbräukeller, Hübner, wearing a uniform tunic but civilian trousers, was merrily quaffing beer in the Donisl beerhall on Wein Strasse, across the street from Munich City Hall.

Around 11 P.M., news of the Bürgerbräu events drifted in to this oldest of the city's beer cellars, in the form of witnesses eager to spread the word and quench their thirst with another stein or two. Joyous and inebriated, Hübner stormed out on the street toward Marienplatz, just in time to meet some of his Oberland friends—members of Ludwig Oestreicher's battalion—marching by. Their mission, they told him, was to "search for Jews and other enemies of the people" who might try to thwart the "great patriotic upheaval."

Hübner was not only delighted to join them but, identifying himself as an Oberland "officer," took over their command. With some ten to fifteen men at his heels, he headed down Neuhauser Strasse, stopping first at the popular café of the Fürstenhof Hotel. Armed with little more than bravado, the squad barged in, shouting, *"Alle Juden raus!* All Jews on the street!" When none of the patrons responded, the manager explained patiently that apparently there were no Jews in the café. Disappointed but undaunted, Hübner led his contingent farther down the street to the Spatenbräu Restaurant to repeat the performance, but it too had no Jewish customers that evening.

From there they marched in the direction of the railroad station, stopping off at the venerable Excelsior Hotel on Schützen Strasse, where surely "there must be Jews." With a swastika armband now embellishing his uniform tunic, Hübner strutted grandly into the lobby and up to the reception desk, announcing to the startled concierge that he and his followers were there to arrest all Jews.

"We don't have any tonight," the clerk said.

Hübner didn't believe him and demanded to see the register. The names were all "good German ones."

Now what? Hübner was tiring of the game. After all, they could not walk around Munich all night searching haphazardly for Jews in restaurants, cafés, and hotels.

"Forget the Jews," someone in the group suggested. "Let's get Auer."

It seemed a great idea, and off they went to nearby Nussbaum Strasse. Thus it was that, approximately a half hour after the Stosstrupp's departure and Luber's arrest, Ernst Hübner and his band of vigilantes arrived.

Frau Auer and her daughters were trying to pick up the pieces of the shambles left by Berchtold's men. Hearing the commotion on the street below, she looked out and then again sent Agnes downstairs. Once more the apartment was rudely ransacked and searched by a dozen Nazis, though, as she noted later, "Hübner at least had the decency to apologize for his intrusion and for the 'outrageous wreckage' that had been left by the earlier intruders."

But where was her husband? he wanted to know. Had he left by car? Yes, she lied.

"The dog, the scoundrel!" one of Hübner's entourage snarled. "I'll bet he's escaped across the border to Württemberg. But I swear, we will find him. You Social Democrats had your turn. Now we are at the wheel at last, and we'll stay in power—forever." Looking intensely at Frau Auer, he added, "Surely you must remember me? I have been in this apartment before, in 1919. We almost nabbed him then, but he got away. This time he won't be so lucky."

Sophie Auer remembered only too well, and also the fact that the man had then been a Communist and member of the Red Army. It was not uncommon apostasy among Hitler's early followers, who swayed with the political wind from extreme Left to extreme Right, depending largely on who offered them more pay as mercenaries.

Hübner, seeing no point in staying longer if Auer had fled, had just assembled his men to leave the building when he noticed the enticing name on the door of the apartment across the hall: Löwenthal. That one must be Jewish, he mused, ringing the bell and pounding on Max Löwenthal's door.

But the bachelor businessman, scion of one of Munich's oldest Jewish families, was not at home. Indeed, he had fled shortly after Auer's own departure, wisely anticipating that a search for his prominent political neighbor was imminent and that the Nazis would attempt to arrest him too.

So it was Löwenthal's terror-stricken housekeeper, forty-six-year-old Emilie Heller, who finally opened the door. "He is not here and I do not know where he has gone," she stammered.

Hübner and his men pushed her aside and surged into the apartment, searching all rooms without success and remarking caustically about Löwenthal's impressive art collection, which they attributed to his "profiteering." But it was also apparent that "the Jewish swine had been warned" and was not at home. Frustrated by his "lack of success," Hübner ordered the posse out of the apartment and back downstairs. Just as they were about to leave the building, he noticed another "promising" name on a ground-floor apartment door: Lövenstein.

"*Jüdisch?*" Hübner asked arrogantly when Bernhard Lövenstein's shaken wife, Margaretha, finally opened to the Nazis' incessant ringing and pounding.

"Yes, but it is—" she replied, unable to finish as the gang marched in.

"We are here to arrest your husband in the name of the new Reich government," he announced. "Where is he?"

Lövenstein, pajama-clad and struggling into a robe, was right there. But this time Hübner had made a grave mistake. Bernhard Lövenstein, conservative, prominent, and well-to-do, was not only a very active member of one of Bavaria's "patriotic societies" but a veteran of the Einwohnerwehr, the 1919 anti-Communist "burgher militia."

Like the detention of Ludwig Wassermann in the Bürgerbräukeller, the raid on Lövenstein's apartment was called one of several cases of "mistaken identity" that night. More than that, however, it was symptomatic of the pathologically distorted thinking among Hitler's fanatically racist followers—then and in the years to come—as well as tragically expressive of the attitudes and naïveté about the Hitler movement among the majority of German Jews.

The Nazi movement's hysterical anti-Semitism, deeply rooted in Bavaria, to be sure, had been fomented by the "Jewishness"—both real and imagined—of Eisner's 1918 revolution and the Red terror of 1919. Articulated by Hitler, it was based on the nonsensical contention that the quintessential cause of Germany's postwar misery and plight was an "internationalist-Jewish-Bolshevist-capitalist plot," whatever that was supposed to be.

German Jews, on the other hand, regarded themselves as Germans first and Jews second—a logical attitude, given their history in the many little duchies, principalities, and mini-kingdoms that had been forged into modern Germany under Prussian hegemony in 1871, but one that also explains their bewilderment and ultimate tragedy under Nazism.

Politically, they were as diverse as non-Jews. Some were Communists, quite a large proportion were Social Democrats or Independent Socialists, the majority inclined toward a middle-of-the-road liberalism, but many were monarchists who pined, like many non-Jews, for the return of a Kaiser or, in Bavaria, a king. And not a few were militantly conservative, incorrigibly reactionary, and shrilly chauvinistic. That they happened to be Jewish was, to most of them, regardless of their political views, coincidental. That the platforms of Gustav von Kahr, Erich Ludendorff, Ernst Pöhner, and Adolf Hitler were harshly and quintessentially anti-Semitic was to Jewish rightists more a source of irritation than concern—at least in the early 1920s.

Few men in Munich, for example, were more stridently jingoistic than Nikolaus Cossmann, the Jewish-born albeit later-converted publisher of the *Münchner Neueste Nachrichten* and editor of the ultra-right-wing *Süddeutsche Monatshefte*. Only recently he had said, "Hitler is all right with me as long as he continues to imbue the German workingman with nationalism and patriotism." He was equaled in his bellicosity only by Kahr's spokesman, Adolf Schiedt of the *Münchener Zeitung*.

Fortunately for him that night, Bernhard Lövenstein was cut from similar political cloth. When he produced his credentials as a "patriotic combatant" and veteran of the Einwohnerwehr, Ernst Hübner apologized for the intrusion and immediately ordered his squad of vigilantes out of the apartment.

Still bent upon finding *some* Jews to arrest—or molest—for the "glory of the revolution," Hübner and his followers set off for the nearby Bavaria Ring district, where their ravaging was directed next at a master tailor, named Max Ambrunn, at No. 5 Uhland Strasse. Ambrunn's misfortune was that he always kept a rubber billy club in his apartment. That night he did not have an opportunity to use it, being rudely roused from deep sleep around two o'clock. Instead, when the gang found the club after ransacking his home, it served as "evidence of possession of weapons," and as the pretext for his detention. He was ordered to dress, then marched out under guard to wait almost an hour or so in the bitter, wet cold on a street corner, ostensibly to be taken to the Bürgerbräukeller or strung up on a lamppost. But Hübner, acting on his own and without any instructions from the putschists' command post, "did not really know what to do with him" and finally let the tailor go free.

Shaken by the experience and incredulous that he had not been murdered as threatened, Ambrunn returned to his apartment to discover that the marauders had stolen his gold pocketwatch, an American silver dollar, and 1 trillion paper Reichsmarks.

Two other Jewish businessmen in the neighborhood—Salomon Herz at Rückert Strasse No. 6 and Emil Crailsheimer of No. 7 Bavaria Ring—reported similar experiences of nocturnal raids, searches, and petty thievery at the hands of Hübner's team.

Ernst Hübner's gang was only one of many engaged in spreading terror that night. Some raided indiscriminately, others selected their victims specifically to settle long-standing grudges.

Abisch Grünspann, owner of the tobacco shop at Pariser Strasse No. 2, just a few blocks from the Bürgerbräukeller, was fast asleep in his apartment behind the store when he heard loud shouting on the street and the sound of smashing glass. Startled, he rushed down the corridor toward the shop, falling prone when a shot was fired at him and lodged in his bedroom wall.

Running into his little store, he saw two steel-helmeted men with swastika armbands swinging their rifles wildly like clubs as they shattered window and door panes, then bayonetted the frames into splinters.

"*Du Saujude*—you Jewish pig—we'll be coming to get you soon!" one of them screamed, on seeing Grünspann. "If not tonight, then tomorrow at dawn." The shopfront a shambles, they dashed up the street.

Grünspann did not recognize them and said he had never seen the two before, but he did not rule out the "likelihood" that they were "some of the swastika-wearing neighborhood teenagers who often hang out around my store."

Salomon Scheer, twenty-nine, his wife Berta, twenty-seven, and her brother Eduard Kohn, thirty-five, knew exactly who was leading the posse of five SA troopers that barged into their third-floor apartment at Franziskaner Strasse No. 19 near the Bürger-bräukeller: Friedrich and Anton Engl, twenty nine and twenty four, the sons of a neighbor a floor below, and both members of the Munich SA Regiment in which the elder Engl commanded a company.

Three months earlier, the Scheers' live-in maid, Susanne Koller, nineteen, had allegedly been sexually molested and beaten by the Engl brothers, who subsequently were tried and convicted of assault and battery largely on testimony by the Scheer family, especially Kohn, and sentenced to fourteen days in jail. Now, as "masters of the reborn Germany," they were out for revenge.

At 12:30 A.M., Scheer and his wife were already asleep. Kohn, a partner in their ground-floor dry-goods store and a bachelor with a small cold-water flat on nearby Weissenburger Strasse, had used their apartment to take a bath and was just getting dressed to go home.

Suddenly the doorbell rang loudly and jarringly. Kohn heard shouts in the hallway.

"Open up in the name of the new government. *Wo ist das Kommunisten-schwein Kohn?* Open up immediately in the name of the law or we will use force!" Friedrich Engl bellowed.

Kohn recognized the familiar voice and through the frosted glass of the front door saw a gang of uniformed storm troopers. Dressed in nothing but his underwear, he ran through the kitchen to the terrace facing the courtyard, climbed over the railing, and gingerly lowered himself to the balcony on the second floor. His heart pounding with fright, he heard the apartment door being bashed open with rifle stocks and the Engl brothers' troopers charging in.

"We want Kohn!" they shouted, banging open various doors as they stomped down the corridor toward the Scheers' bedroom.

The terrified young couple, startled out of their sleep and trapped, scrambled underneath their bedstead to hide but were dragged out bodily and then stood up against the wall at bayonet point.

"Where is that swine?" the elder Engl raged. When Scheer,

trembling, and his wife, weeping hysterically, said that they did not know, one of the troopers fired several shots into the bedroom wardrobe and then yanked open its door, apparently expecting Kohn's body to come tumbling out. Infuriated at seeing only clothes and laundry inside it, they ransacked the apartment, rifle-butted and bayonetted every piece of furniture in sight, and made a superficial search of the courtyard with flashlights from the Scheer apartment's balcony as Kohn pinned himself against the wall on the terrace beneath them. Then, after looting some silver-ware and jewelry, the Nazi troopers disappeared—back to the Bürgerbräukeller.

Kohn, certain they would have lynched him, waited, nearly freezing, on the downstairs balcony for almost fifteen minutes be-fore calling out to his brother-in-law to let him know where he was hiding. After Scheer had dropped him the rest of his clothes, Kohn lowered himself to the ground floor and escaped to spend the night with friends.

But for Saly and Berta Scheer, the night of terror and vandal-ism was by no means over. An hour later, the younger Engl broth-er was back with another posse of storm troopers. Again they rummaged through and vandalized the apartment, and this time Anton Engl told Scheer, "If Kohn is not here by morning, we will take you."

The warning was enough for the Scheers. Throwing a few clothes into a suitcase, they left their home, walked quickly, fur-tively, by back streets to the Ostbahnhof, Munich's East Side Sta-tion, and waited there for the first train in the direction of the Austrian border and Vienna, where Kohn and Berta Scheer's par-ents lived.

Their decision to flee was prudent, for the storm troopers' threat had not been an empty one. An hour or so after the second raid, the gang returned a third time. Enraged at finding the apartment abandoned, except for the Scheers' new maid, nine-teen-year-old Elisabeth Jordan, cowering with fright in her room, they rampaged again, then vented their anger on Scheer and Kohn's store by shattering its show windows with their weapons.

Otto Fischbuch, a sergeant of the blue-uniformed city police, heard the noise on his way from the 15th Precinct station at Weissenburger Platz, but he was too far away and too slow on his feet. The storm troopers vanished into the dark, shadowy streets of Munich's East End.

The Engl brothers were engaged in a personal vendetta, like many others that night, and Ernst Hübner was a self-appointed vigilante spreading terror on his own. In a sense they were but coincidental confederates of gangs under specific orders to take hostages and spread fear. These, by comparison, carried out their dreadful "assignments" with grim methodicalness—especially those dispatched at Hitler and Göring's behest by the Oberland League's Ludwig Oestreicher.

The storm troopers of Alfons Weber's Oberland company were given only a short break at the Bürgerbräukeller after returning from their unsuccessful attempt to capture Kahr's headquarters. Then Oestreicher ordered them out again—in small armed patrols—to make arrests and, almost as important, extort foreign currency wherever possible in the plush Bogenhausen area, a district of villas and mansions where Munich's most affluent burghers, Jewish and non-Jewish, lived.

Konrad Kiessling, by now skeptical but still willing to obey the orders of what he regarded as the "rightful new government," joined one of the teams and stood guard outside a Jewish businessman's house on Ismaninger Strasse while his cohorts entered through a ground-floor window, held the man at bay with their pistols, and robbed him of his "foreign riches"—a Czechoslovak 100-crown note.

Theodor Roth, son of an ultra-rightist former Bavarian minister of justice, using a car he captured at gunpoint—one of many "requisitioned" in similar fashion by putschists—led another of the patrols. He had been assigned the job because Oestreicher believed him to be especially familiar with "conditions in Bogenhausen." To the putschists' subsequent embarrassment, he wasn't. Hostages were selected according to the "Jewish sound of their names" from the phone book and by the mail boxes on their garden gates and front doors. There were some gross "mistakes."

In all, some fifty-eight prisoners were taken to the Bürgerbräu, where they filled the room in which Wassermann and Luber were waiting. Among them were several septuagenarians and some men whose wives and daughters had insisted on being taken along. Young Roth's father, Christian, searched a number of them personally "for weapons and money." A few were brutally beaten and others threatened with execution—until Göring, passing through the room, put a stop to that emphatically with the announcement, "We do not have the right or authority to execute—yet."

Those SA and Oberland troopers not needed to take hostages, patrol the streets, or guard the Isar River bridges were instructed to find quarters for the night—in Bogenhausen mansions.

Franz von Stuck's at No. 4 Prinzregenten Strasse was among the houses chosen. At least they had taste: Stuck was one of Munich's most famous painters and the pacesetter of art nouveau in the city, and his house, built in 1898, was renowned for the wild, scandalous parties its owners gave. It was early morning when Stuck was rudely awakened by the doorbell and the raucous shouting of Alfons Weber with forty of his Oberländers in tow. On orders of the "new government," Weber announced, Stuck would have to take the troopers in for the rest of the night. Peering into the muzzles of their rifles and carbines, the renowned artist shrugged, showed them to his salon and studio, and went back to bed. He was accustomed to late callers.

Prince Alfons von Bayern, a nephew of the late king Ludwig III, was not. When Weber rang his bell, across the street from the Stuck villa, the aristocrat demurred. But when Weber pulled a pistol and announced that he represented the "new government of Excellency von Kahr," the prince decided resistance was pointless. Within a few minutes Weber had another forty of his men, including Kiessling, tucked away for the night.

And so it went in others of the "great houses" along Munich's most elegant residential avenue.

At the Bürgerbräukeller, Wilhelm Briemann, Emil Maurice, Hans Kallenbach, Josef Gerum, and other members of the Stosstrupp were again sitting around the table, drinking beer and talking about the night's deeds, when Josef Berchtold, their indefatigable leader, came in.

"You had better get some sleep," he commanded. "In a few hours there will be much more work for us to do."

Interlude V

Impact and Reaction

Berlin

Reich Chancellor Gustav Stresemann leaned back in his chair in the private dining room of the Continental Hotel and studied the man across the table from him. In his stiff high collar and with his hair parted in the center as if drawn by a ruler, Dr. Hjalmar H. G. Schacht was rather odd-looking. Prim, meticulous, he appeared every inch the bookkeeper-accountant, except that he smoked incessantly so that his face seemed constantly veiled by blue-gray haze. And those middle names of his—Horace Greeley! How very un-German, Stresemann thought. But there was no question the man was a financial wizard.

Schacht's and Finance Minister Hans Luther's proposals for a currency reform had appealed to Stresemann immediately. To be sure, it was a scheme tantamount to monetary sleight of hand— issuing *Rentenmarks,* "mortgage" marks, backed by a "mortgage" on the nation's gold supplies, to be backed, in turn, by a "mortgage" on all Germany's assets and land. It really meant nothing, just "a cover for the new money," but it would give people confidence in the currency, and confidence was the only thing that could save the country from the deepening whirlpool of runaway inflation. All Schacht wanted was an office with a telephone to implement it. Even a storeroom for cleaning supplies in the finance ministry would do, he had said. Which was what he got.

It was 11:30 P.M., and the chancellor and his designated "commissioner for the national currency" had finished dessert when one of Stresemann's aides rushed in, apologized for the interruption, then bent down to whisper, "There are press reports of a putsch in Munich. The Bavarians are intending to march on Berlin."

Stresemann's face paled to chalk white. "I am calling an emergency cabinet session immediately," he said. "Has President Ebert been notified? Seeckt? Phone them at once and get everyone to my office."

This is the end, he thought, as his car sped him back through the cold night, thick with fog, to the Reich Chancellery on Wilhelm Strasse. In Saxony the prime minister, Erich Zeigner, had formed a "popular front" government with the Communists to create a Red state that threatened secession. In the Rhineland and the Palatinate, French-supported separatist movements and revolts were bursting out like mushrooms in the forest. And now, the obstinate Bavarians! It seemed the whole edifice of the German Reich was creaking and splitting at its joints. Would it collapse by morning? What could shore it up? Unfortunately, only the army, the Reichswehr, and von Seeckt. Could there be a man whom Stresemann disliked and distrusted more?

By midnight the courtyard at Wilhelm Strasse was in pandemonium as Ebert and Stresemann's ministers arrived, most of them still trying to rub the first hour's sleep out of their eyes. Through the fog, the headlights of their automobiles cast broad pools of eerie light onto the damp cobblestone pavement. Car doors slammed. Enshrouded figures hurried into the half-lit building and climbed wearily up the broad staircase to the cabinet chamber.

The information was scant and fragmentary, consisting largely of short, often conflicting, press reports. Attempts to telephone Munich had proved futile; no calls seemed to be getting into or out of Bavaria. Worst of all, Edgar Haniel von Haimhausen, the Reich's "ambassador" in Bavaria, had not been located. He had gone to a Munich dinner party, but no one seemed to know where.

"Is everyone here?" asked Friedrich Ebert, the stout erstwhile saddlemaker and bartender who had been, for the past five years, the crisis-shaken German Republic's first president.

Aides and undersecretaries scurried about making cursory

head counts. "We are only waiting for General—" one of them said.

Just then the door burst open. Instinctively, everyone stepped back to form a little aisle as General Hans von Steeckt made his dramatic entrance. Tall, steel-muscled, and trim in his close-fitting gray uniform, despite his fifty-seven years, he seemed entirely the soldier. His even-tempered, close-mouthed coldness had given him the nickname of "the Sphinx." Did he ever display emotion? Yes, on the way from his home to the Reich Chancellery he had remarked sardonically to his adjutant, "Well, it appears I have been relieved of my command by Ludendorff and Lossow. It's their army now."

But compared to the politicians in the room, the Reichswehr chief seemed a paragon of calm and decisive composure, enigmatic and unspeaking as ever. What they could not know was that behind the expressionless face, he was both elated and busily scheming. This was the moment he had anticipated for months. Ebert and Stresemann, that "compromiser with the French," had no choice. Either the government would flee ignominiously, as it had done during the Kapp Putsch of 1920, or they would have to centralize power in him, make him military dictator. A fortuitous development indeed, thanks to those fools in Munich.

The gray-haired general was the focus of attention. But his grim face seemed to deflect the glances like a shield. Rubbing his slim hands against the cold, he nodded barely perceptible greetings to all, settled on a chair, crossed his arms, and, sitting ruler-straight, stared speechlessly at the assembly of cabinet members and senior civil servants. The monocle in his left eye—there was widespread speculation in Berlin about whether he slept with it—reflected the lights in the room. The other eye, pale blue but penetrating, was expressionless. He listened as Ebert and Stresemann read out the sketchy reports from Munich.

"Herr General," Ebert finally asked, "tell us please where the Reichswehr stands. Does the Reichswehr obey the laws and the government or the mutineers?"

"The Reichswehr, Herr President," Seeckt replied coldly, peering through the monocle, "stands behind me. It obeys me." It was the predictable answer of the man who had once said that if there was to be a putsch, "I will do the putsching."

But given the circumstances of Lossow's apparent collaboration and the turmoil elsewhere in Germany, someone in the circle interjected, was there not a danger of civil war?

"The Reichswehr will not shoot at Reichswehr," the general retorted.

Stresemann, in a state of high agitation during the meeting, suggested a private conference in his study with Ebert, Seeckt, and Otto Gessler, the defense minister, a Bavarian who had served as mayor of Regensburg and then Nürnberg, before and during the war. Gessler had telephoned his successor in Nürnberg, and the news was bleak: Reichswehr units there were mobilizing to go to Munich and had apparently fallen in with Hitler and Ludendorff. The information, of course, was incorrect; those were the contingents Major General Jakob von Danner had alerted. But it was alarming news.

On the strength of it, and largely at Gessler's prodding, the three politicians, democrats all, though ranging from moderate internationalist Left to moderate nationalist Right in their persuasions, reached a heavy-hearted decision. Ebert would transfer his constitutional authority as the nation's commander-in-chief to the general. Effective immediately, Seeckt would be given executive jurisdiction over all of Germany, with dictatorial power to enforce it.

The formal investiture, hastily composed at Stresemann's desk and conforming with Article 48 of the Weimar constitution, was signed by Ebert and endorsed by Stresemann and Gessler. No dictator in history, before or since, has ever been installed so quickly, easily, legally, and peacefully—with just the stroke of a pen—by men to whom dictatorship was abhorrent.

After asking Prussia's prime minister, Otto Braun, to mobilize his State Police to guard the government district and help protect Berlin against the anticipated Nazi and Bavarian invasion, Ebert, Stresemann, and the others drafted a determined, poignantly worded proclamation. It left no doubt about the resolve and steadfastness of the government of Germany's five-year-old Republic— the "November criminals," as Hitler had called them. It read:

> In these critical times of external and domestic need, deceived forces have set out to destroy the German Reich. An armed horde has overthrown the government in Munich . . . and arrogated the right to form a Reich government around General Ludendorff, as

the alleged supreme commander of the German army, and Herr Hitler, who only recently acquired German citizenship, as the man entrusted with determining Germany's fate.

It is self-evident that . . . those who support this movement are traitors. . . . Instead of aiding those who are fighting for Germany, our brethren in the Rhineland and the Ruhr, they are plunging Germany into misfortune, jeopardizing the food supply, provoking invasion from foreign enemies, and destroying all hope for economic recovery.

The most recent financial measures of the Reich government have resulted in a pronounced improvement of the exchange rate of the mark on foreign bourses. All this will be lost if the mad beginning made in Munich succeeds. . . .

. . . All measures for the reestablishment of order have already been initiated and taken and will be rigorously enforced.

It was signed by Ebert and Stresemann, and immediately sent for printing in hundreds of thousands of copies. This time the German government was determined to make a stand.

Rome

Kurt Lüdecke, Hitler's emissary in the Italian capital and hopeful liaison to Benito Mussolini, was waiting out the night fitfully in his hotel room. Tense, almost sick with waiting, he could not have slept even if he had wanted to.

Finally, "unable to endure it for a moment longer," he dressed and rushed again to the editorial offices of *Corriere d'Italia*. A friendly editor "who was especially interested in Munich because of our work together" told him nothing new of importance had been reported, either by the agencies or by their correspondent, Negrelli, in the Bavarian capital. But he advised Lüdecke to wait with him. Some new telegrams, he explained, had just arrived and were being read.

As they were talking, another editor stormed into the room waving a cabled dispatch and shouting its message: *"Colpo d'estato a Monaco!* Coup d'état in Munich!"

Though the telegram gave no real details, Lüdecke was drunk with joy and excitement. It had worked! They had done it! He was torn between wanting to stay for more information as it came in or taking the next available train to Munich to find out for

himself and—presumably—get in on the action: Hitler's emula-
tion of Il Duce, the march to Berlin. He resolved to leave at once
for Munich.

Returning to his hotel, he found reporters waiting; he had
become a celebrity. It seemed the entire Italian press wanted to
interview him. Who was this Adolfo Heedler? Did he believe in
the same things as Mussolini? And as new dictator of the Reich,
what would be his attitude toward Italy, especially on the disputed territory of Trentino and Alto Adige, the southern part of Ty-
rol with its predominantly German-speaking population.

Lüdecke went to see Virginio Gayda, then the influential editor of the *Messagero,* and gave him a "jubilant interview" on
condition that it would not be published until there was confirmation that the march on Berlin was really well under way. Then he
went back to his hotel to pack.

New York

It was 8:30 P.M. in Gotham—six hours behind Munich and the
continent—and the city was vibrant as ever, especially in mid-
town Manhattan, where the theaters, movie houses, auditoriums,
and concert halls were filled.

At Carnegie Hall there was the discreet applause of anticipation as a young Dutchman—Wilhelm van Hoogstraten—mounted
the podium to conduct the New York Philharmonic in César
Franck's Symphony in D. Only thirty-nine years old, Hoogstraten
had been causing a sensation that season, his first, and so had his
German wife, pianist Elly Ney, who, the evening before, had giv-
en a recital at Aeolian Hall which left the *New York Times* gush-
ing about the "storm and violence" of her style. At Broadway and
42nd Street a long queue shivered in the wind and near-freezing
weather outside the Cameo Theater, waiting to get in for a double
feature that was the talk of the town: *David Copperfield,* billed as
a "superb and faithful picturization of Charles Dickens' world-
loved novel," and Harold Lloyd in *A Sailor-Made Man.*

Nearby, at Town Hall, Israel Zangwill, the British-born Jewish author and playwright, was delivering a lecture. The enter-
tainment there, if it could be called that, was of a more provocative nature. Zangwill was scandalizing his listeners with his

outspokenness about America's "decay."

Brandishing a thin finger at the standing-room-only crowd, he fulminated about prohibition, the abomination of tipping, the rubbish he had seen strewn all about Central Park, the Ku Klux Klan, and U.S. immigration laws, under which "Jesus Christ Himself could no longer get into the country because He would have to admit at Ellis Island that He had once been convicted of a felony." Ultimately he came around to American foreign policy and the administration of President Calvin Coolidge.

"America got into the war too late," he said, "held up a vision of peace, but then sneaked away to indulge in an orgy of oblivion ever since, trying to forget and to shirk its responsibilities. . . .

"There is very little of honor, dignity, or justice in this country today," he concluded. "You are inconsequential, you act without thinking, and you think without acting."

As many in the crowded hall roared their approval, and far many more jeered and booed with anger, the reporters who had been assigned to cover the lecture were exhilarated. They figured Zangwill's remarks were so outrageously controversial they were sure to get the lead front-page spot, at least in the earliest editions.

Undoubtedly, they would have, had it not been for the cables coming into New York editorial offices just as Zangwill was speaking. An even better story was in the making.

The dispatches were fragmentary, sketchy, sometimes garbled and rather confused, especially when, unlike the *Herald*'s Lincoln Eyre's, they were based on second- and third-hand information relayed from the papers' bureaus in Berlin instead of Munich.

Names were misspelled and titles juxtaposed or, in several cases, invented. Thus, on the assumption that any German general had to be an aristocrat, a "von" was added to Ludendorff. It became "Otto" instead of Gustav von Kahr. The *New York Tribune* promoted Hitler to the rank of lieutenant, *The World* demoted him to "Ludendorff's aide," and the *Daily News*, which regarded the sensational divorce trial of one C. D. Stokes as worthy of equal billing, spelled him with two t's.

Moreover, Americans having been singularly preoccupied with the devil image of the Kaiser during the war, and rather hysterical in years since about rumors of his or Crown Prince Friedrich Wilhelm's possible return from exile in Holland, there was an inclination by many editors to misread the news about the Bürgerbräukeller as an imperial gambit.

But regardless of how truncated, patchy, inconsistent, and incomplete the reports coming in from wire services and correspondents, every managing editor in New York recognized instantly the significance of the story and the need to play it for each sensational word. All over the city there was a mad search for pictures of the principals—photographs or artists' drawings, it made no difference. Neither did the price. And, amazingly, they turned up: Hitler, Ludendorff, Kahr, Seeckt, Bavarian Crown Prince Rupprecht and his bride, Princess Antoinette of Luxembourg. Even little-known Premier Eugen von Knilling. Front pages—already budgeted for such stories as the Zangwill lecture and the Stokes divorce—had to be hastily remade. *The New York Times,* the *Tribune,* and the *World,* using the largest typefaces available in their composing rooms, announced the news two and three lines deep, all across their eight columns.

Thus New Yorkers, leaving theaters, concerts, and movies late, were confronted with these early edition headlines:

**BAVARIA IN REVOLT,
PROCLAIMS LUDENDORFF DICTATOR;**

**MONARCHIST FORCES REPORTED
MARCHING ON BERLIN;**

**CAPITAL CRIES TREASON AND MASSES
TROOPS FOR DEFENSE**

—New York Times

**LUDENDORFF LEADS ROYALIST ARMY
AGAINST BERLIN;**

BAVARIAN CAPITAL SEIZED; FRANCE THREATENS WAR

—New York Tribune

**BAVARIAN GOVERNMENT OVERTHROWN
IN REVOLUTION; LUDENDORFF AND HITLER RULE;
MINISTERS ARE ARRESTED; VON SEECKT BERLIN
DICTATOR DESPITE PARIS WARNING**

—New York World

What undoubtedly frightened and worried American readers most that night, just three days short of the fifth anniversary of the 1918 Armistice, was the fear, exacerbated by French threats, that developments in Munich might throw Europe—and the world—again into war. For, as stories from Paris often running parallel to those from Munich and Berlin made clear, the French had already announced that their response to the establishment of either military or monarchist rule in Germany would be armed intervention.

As Laurence Hills, chief of the *Herald*'s Paris bureau, reported:

> No military dictatorship in Germany; no restoration of a monarchy, whether it be a Hohenzollern or Wittelsbach monarchy—that is the fiat of the Allies as Republican Germany hangs in the balance. The whole collective force of the Allies is to be thrown into the scales against the German Nationalists and in favor of Chancellor Stresemann and the Socialists.
>
> . . . France, acting individually but apparently as a preliminary to an allied move to the same effect, has instructed its Ambassador at Berlin to inform everyone interested, including Chancellor Stresemann, that it will not tolerate a military dictatorship, as . . . such an action . . . would lead to a repudiation of the Treaty of Versailles and the beginning of a war of revenge.

Though this news was blazoned not only in New York but Paris and London, it apparently never reached President Ebert, Chancellor Stresemann, or General von Seeckt in Berlin that night.

Chicago

In November 1923, Chicago was the veritable capital of the isolationist mood that had gripped America after the Great War. Few other large American cities were as inward looking, as preoccupied with their local problems, of which Chicago certainly had an inordinate share, or as parochial in their attitudes.

Against that background, the *Chicago Daily Tribune*'s claim to be the "world's greatest newspaper" evoked derision not only from its foes but even from its friends. Yet in its coverage of foreign affairs, the paper was in many respects remarkable. Its publisher, Colonel Robert McCormick, had provided the paper with a foreign staff second to none in American journalism. For example, by hiring Larry Rue in 1919, McCormick had taken the pioneering step of assigning a reporter who was also a trained aviator to cover Europe. By "flying for news," as Rue described it, he had a mobility no other correspondent could match and gave the paper's coverage of continental affairs an immediacy none could equal. But Rue was only the centerpiece of the team. Indeed, on November 8, 1923, besides Rue in Munich, the *Chicago Tribune* had no less than three other correspondents reporting from Germany: John Clayton in Berlin, Vincent Sheehan from the troubled Ruhr, and Paul Williams from Frankfurt.

Around 7:30 P.M. Chicago time their combined efforts began trickling into the editorial offices—by cable, transatlantic phone, and even wireless radio. Bolstered by reactions from the paper's bureaus in Paris and London, the reports galvanized the staff. Local stories that might have made the lead were quickly shunted into secondary spots and nearly two full pages opened up for Rue's dramatic, sensationally colorful eyewitness account of the events in the Bürgerbräukeller and Clayton's up-to-the-last-minute report of Stresemann and Ebert's midnight cabinet session.

Within a few hours, as the paper's first editions hit the streets, Chicagoans were greeted with a huge eight-column two-inch-high banner headline that had them grabbing the paper out of newsboys' hands:

"ON TO BERLIN!" ROYALIST CRY

Berlin

It was 2 A.M. when the meeting at the Reich Chancellery adjourned.

With a nod from Stresemann, Baron Adolf von Maltzan, the foreign ministry's undersecretary, went to the telephone. There was no avoiding it. The Allies would have to be notified of the decisions reached. With trepidation, Maltzan asked to be connected with the residence of the British ambassador, Lord d'Abernon. They had conversed only hours before, when Maltzan was waxing optimistic. Now the British diplomat, roused from deep sleep and barely able to fathom the news he was being given, was even more pessimistic than the German.

Yes, he agreed sadly, Germany did indeed appear to be on the brink of civil war, with unforeseeable, but surely dire, consequences for the rest of Europe, the world.

That prospect also nagged at General Hans von Seeckt. Throughout most of the meeting he had hardly uttered a word. But his mind was reeling.

Now, at last, he had the power he had sought so long—commander-in-chief, dictator, executive authority. And the Socialist president of the republic himself had handed it to him, with the broad consent of the entire cabinet. Von Seeckt yearned for power. He thought of himself as a man born to rule and for almost his entire life had acted like one. Here at last was his opportunity to change the course of history—in fact, to reverse it—to undo the republican system, with the hapless, floundering parliamentary democracy that he abominated, and replace it with a government that would restore the glory of the Reich.

But he hesitated. The risks in pursuit of his own ambition seemed too great in that moment, and the traditional Prussian sense of apolitical duty, ingrained since birth and instilled throughout his military career, prevailed. Thus the most sinister man on the postwar German stage, "the Great Unknown Factor," as he was frequently called, decided then and there to do no more than save the new German state, the republic that was so repugnant to him, from demise.

Von Seeckt issued instructions to quarantine Bavaria for the time being by cutting all nonmilitary telephone and telegraph communication. He ordered all rail traffic between Bavaria and the rest of the Reich halted, with trains either stopped or sent back at the frontiers. He placed a general staff officer, Lieutenant Colonel Joachim von Stülpnagel, in charge of operations and mobilization of units for a possible invasion and told him to try to establish contact with loyal Reichswehr officers, whoever they might be, in Munich. He did not expect Otto von Lossow to be one of them.

Then, since there was nothing else he could do until morning,

Germany's new military dictator left the Reich Chancellery as stonily as he had arrived, announcing to all that he was going home to bed.

Had von Seeckt stayed up and awake for another forty-five minutes or so, he might have been privy to a most remarkable Morse code message being transmitted repeatedly from Munich "to all German wireless stations" like a plaintive cry in the dark:

> GENERAL STATE COMMISSIONER VON KAHR, GENERAL VON LOSSOW, COLONEL VON SEISSER REJECT HITLER PUTSCH. STATEMENTS EXTORTED FROM THEM IN BÜRGERBRÄUKELLER UNDER FORCE OF ARMS ARE INVALID. BEWARE POSSIBLE MISUSE OF ABOVE NAMES. SIGNED VON KAHR, VON LOSSOW, VON SEISSER.

12

The wet snow was falling harder, though still not sticking to the cobblestones, as the dark green State Police staff car picked its way along deserted Dachauer Strasse toward the military bases near the Oberwiesenfeld. Inside, huddled against the damp cold, sat Colonel Hans von Seisser, Gustav von Kahr, and Majors Franz Hunglinger and Heinrich Doehla. Seisser had chosen the opportune moment during the confrontation with Gerhard Rossbach and the Infantry School cadets to arrange their departure from Maximilian Strasse.

Slowly, the car approached the main gate of the 19th Infantry Regiment barracks. Its weak headlights illuminated the heavily armed sentries and the machine guns which Lieutenant Colonel Hugo von Wenz had ordered Chief Warrant Officer Gerhard Böhm to set up there.

"The gentlemen are expecting you in the signal section hut," one of the guards said, saluting snappily as the iron gate was opened warily to let the car pass.

Though the barracks was now protected like a fortress and virtually all SA and Oberländers, except a few stragglers, seemed to have retreated from its perimeter, General von Danner had thought it prudent to establish the night's command post as far inside the complex as possible, away from the more exposed main buildings facing the street.

Inside the low single-story wooden structure, Danner, Otto von Lossow, Generals Ruith and Kressenstein, and a bevy of their staff officers, almost all in the civilian clothes they had been wearing when alerted, were waiting impatiently for Kahr and Seisser. They had been there nearly two hours since leaving Danner's office at Munich city garrison. Insofar as communications with either Maximilian Strasse or police headquarters had been possible at all, they were erratic and confusing. The long delay had again nurtured doubts about who was loyal to whom. Could it be that Seisser and Kahr were collaborating with the putsch after all? If not, where were they and what were they doing? It was a night of indecision. As Kahr had told Doehla when asked why he had not just ordered Pöhner and Frick's arrest while the two were in his office, "One must not play one's good cards too soon, Herr Major."

"At last!" Lossow exclaimed, when Kahr and Seisser entered the dim, spartan hut. For the first time since Hitler's dramatic entrance at the Bürgerbräukeller, the Bavarian triumvirs were together without being under Nazi guard or surveillance. If they still toyed with thoughts of collaboration with Hitler and Ludendorff, or if there were recriminations among the trio as they met again, none of it was recorded for posterity.

Indeed, if von Kahr is to be believed, "not another word" about collaboration was uttered. "Our minds," he said later, "were like one, and the three of us had but two thoughts: how could we rescue the situation for the best interests of the State and could reinforcements be brought in that would lead to a bloodless resolution of the catastrophe?"

To be sure, not all those standing about saw von Kahr in as firm and determined a posture as he was later to paint himself. According to some, he sat hunched and brooding on a bare bench for more than an hour; according to others, he occasionally was close to tears as he spoke dejectedly and incoherently about "the glorious opportunity for the Fatherland that had been lost" by Hitler's impatience and imprudence.

Be all that as it may, the others in the room displayed determination. For the time being, they knew, their situation was desperate. With the Infantry School on the putschists' side, they were clearly outnumbered. Only one of the 19th Infantry Regiment's battalions was actually stationed in Munich. The others, like the rest of the Seventh Division's units, were garrisoned elsewhere in Bavaria and would have to be brought in by train and truck. The Engineer Battalion was of little use in any kind of combat, the thought of which was repugnant to all anyway. Thus, the only meaningful and effective forces immediately available were the 1,000 Munich-based troopers of Seisser's State Police. But they were clearly no match for the 2,500 SA, Oberland, and Reichs-kriegsflagge irregulars already estimated to be roaming the city, with more undoubtedly streaming in.

There was, moreover, a reluctance to undertake anything during the night, especially since no one knew what other Nazi strongholds there were besides the Bürgerbräukeller and the war ministry on Schönfeld Strasse. Thus, the triumvirs agreed, they would have to wait until morning, by which time—so they hoped—the reinforcements of Seventh Division and State Police contingents ordered by Danner and Seisser would have arrived.

But to accelerate and organize the convergence on Munich, General Ruith was dispatched to supervise personally mobilization of the army units in Augsburg and Kempten. General Kressen-stein, the divisional artillery commander, set off to take command of the contingents that had been ordered by telephone from Re-gensburg.

No one in the room knew that Franz Matt, the vice-premier and cultural minister, was already on his way to Regensburg with the remaining members of Bavaria's cabinet to establish a rump "government-in-exile."

With the two generals on their way, the triumvirs huddled in a corner of the room to seek solutions to their other problems.

One such problem was certainly Ludendorff, whose emissar-ies had been telephoning persistently, both from the Bürgerbräu-keller and Schönfeld Strasse, in search of Lossow and Seisser. The defensive tactic developed, no doubt with a sense of embarrass-ment, was evasion. They were simply not available. Callers were told that Lossow and Seisser either were on their way to the war ministry or en route between the Infantry and Engineer Barracks. The phones were either incessantly busy or were not answered; often, Ludendorff and Hitler's plenipotentiaries were informed to "hold the line because Excellency is on another call." Then, after a while, the connection would be cut. And those who came in person were invited into the command post and then politely but firmly placed under house arrest.

That, for example, was the misfortune of ex-Major Alexander Siry and SA Sergeant Julius Schreck. Though a sympathizer and an acquaintance of Ernst Röhm and Hermann Kriebel, Siry had not been actively involved in the putsch; the first he heard of it was after a dinner engagement that evening. But, enthusiastic about the news, he had gone to the Bürgerbräukeller around midnight to congratulate the principals and, for the first time, met Hitler. He was "impressed" by the Nazi Führer and offered his services to the "national revolution." They were not needed until around 1 A.M., when it was becoming apparent to both Hitler and Göring, though not yet to Ludendorff, that something was amiss. Where were Lossow, Seisser, and Kahr? Repeated efforts to reach and locate them had been to no avail. Would Siry try to find them? He certainly would. Göring provided him with one of the cars that had been confiscated or rented and sent Schreck along to accompany the major.

On the whole, the mission was "peaceful and exploratory," though Schreck did load the car up with "five submachine guns, fifteen to twenty hand grenades, and a case of .38-caliber ammunition." First they went to Munich city garrison, which was dark and where they were refused admission by Captain Maximilian Renz. Their next stop was the war ministry. Siry wanted to congratulate Kriebel and Röhm and also get a situation report. The situation, as Kriebel explained it, was rather puzzling.

Lossow and Seisser, he was sure, were at the 19th Infantry barracks. But their presence there was being either denied or veiled, and their expected arrival at Schönfeld Strasse had been postponed from hour to hour on one unconvincing pretext after another.

"I refuse to believe," Kriebel said despondently, "that generals, officers, or Herr von Kahr would repudiate the word of honor I personally heard and saw them give. But something stinks."

Siry set out to ascertain what. First, he stopped by his apartment to change into his old uniform as a Reichswehr staff officer; then, with Schreck still in tow and the arsenal stashed visibly in the car, he headed for the barracks. Despite the regalia of his uniform, replete with medals and the insignia of his rank, he was barred at the gate—until Major Hans Schönharl, an old friend and commander of the regiment's 1st Battalion, appeared.

"Look, you're placing me in an awkward position," Schönharl said, using the familiar second-person *du.* "I have orders to defend the barracks."

"But against whom?" Siry asked incredulously. "Isn't the Reichswehr allied with the new national government that was declared?"

"The word I've gotten, Siry, is that Kahr, Lossow, and Seisser are repudiating Hitler's putsch. If you want my advice, as a friend, get out of here now and take that car and the SA fellow with you."

It was advice Siry refused to heed. He insisted on being taken to the triumvirs.

As Siry was being escorted to the communications shed, his driver and Julius Schreck were unceremoniously arrested on the parade ground and marched off under guard to another building. For Schreck, the "revolution" was over.

For Siry, the denouement came within fifteen minutes. He was led into the room where Kahr, Lossow, and Seisser were assembled with their staffs. Kahr, so Siry noted, was seated on a low "canapé-like bench, and were I a painter who had been commissioned to portray a guilty conscience, I would have chosen him as a model."

"Excellency," Siry said with a salute, snapping to attention and first addressing Lossow, "I have come here on Hitler and Kriebel's behalf to ascertain what position you and your troops are taking."

The general peered warily through his pince-nez at the major but said nothing. His silence persuaded Siry that "something really was wrong."

"Excellency," he reiterated, "may I please ask for a reply?"

"You may not," Lossow snapped, wheeling away.

Siry now turned his attention to Kahr, sitting there silently. "Am I correct in assuming that this is the national government here of which you, Herr von Kahr, are a leader?" he asked.

"There can be no further discussion or consideration of that," von Kahr said sharply. "Whatever assurances were made are null and void because they were extorted at gunpoint."

Siry, who had not been privy to the beerhall drama, was as much astounded by the remark as he was suddenly deeply concerned about the course events might take. "But then Ludendorff and Hitler and the other gentlemen who believe they are serving the new national government should at least be informed," he urged.

"No, you are staying here," Lossow interrupted adamantly, apparently fearing that Siry was a spy and had seen or heard too much about the preparations being made to defend the barracks. Lossow led Seisser and Kahr into another room.

Confused and astonished, Siry stood there speechless for a while, appalled at the shooting and bloodshed which he foresaw. Then, following the triumvirs, he again approached Kahr. "The other gentlemen have no inkling that you no longer consider yourself bound to your word," Siry implored. "Allow me to use what influence I have to initiate negotiations to call the whole thing off."

"If you had seen the affair with the pistol," Kahr replied, "you would be speaking differently."

Again Siry was left standing by himself, but after a few more minutes he made another attempt. He asked one of the staff officers to take him in to Lossow. "Excellency," he insisted, "they must be notified. Or do you really want to assume the responsibility for patriotic German men shooting at each other?"

"There will be no negotiations with rebels, Herr Major," Lossow retorted, adding that Siry was not to leave the barracks. To make sure, he ordered him placed under detention in another building, where Siry discovered the Oberland League's Max von Müller and Adolf Aechter, who had been transferred from the Engineer Barracks.

Their keeper, at least for a while, was Senior Lieutenant Max Braun, a 19th Infantry Regiment company commander who not only made no secret of his contempt for Nazis and mutineers but also disclaimed Hitler's assumption that all junior officers would rally to his cause.

"It's outrageous what happened here earlier this evening," he told Siry. "They wanted to take the barracks by storm and tried to disarm us. If I have a chance, I'll shoot those dogs down with a laughing face."

"Well, don't forget that those people you describe as dogs are as patriotically German as you," Siry said.

It was almost 3 A.M. when the latch on Siry's door was shut—from the outside.

For all the apparent resoluteness that Kahr, Lossow, and Seisser were now displaying in matters military and in their determination to extricate themselves from the putsch, their political decisions and actions remained rather slow in coming.

To be sure, while Siry had been waiting for them in one room of the shed, they had been in another, drafting the terse wireless message of their repudiation. It was first transmitted at 2:55 A.M., more than four hours after they had left the Bürgerbräukeller, a delay that cannot be simply explained by shock or lack of coordination.

The drafting of a proclamation to Munich's—and Bavaria's—confused populace took even longer. Von Kahr was master of neither the written nor the spoken word.

"How does this sound?" he asked Lossow and Seisser, after several hapless starts and struggles with the language.

"Deceit and breach of promise on the part of dishonorable men turned what was to have been a demonstration for Germany's national reawakening into a repulsive act of terror. The declarations extracted from me, General von Lossow, and Colonel von Seisser at the point of a pistol are null and void. Had this senseless and aimless attempt at overthrow succeeded, it would have plunged Germany, and Bavaria with it, into the abyss.

"This act of treason has run aground on the loyalty and conscientiousness of the Reichswehr and State Police. Thanks to their support, executive power now rests again in my hands. The guilty will be ruthlessly prosecuted and punished, and I hereby declare the National Socialist German Workers' party, the Oberland League, and the Reichskriegsflagge Society disbanded and prohibited."

It was not exactly an inspiring call to rally around the legitimate government, and one of Kahr's subordinates tactfully suggested the addition of "some stirring phrase about Your Excellency's future course."

Wrinkling his brow, the weary little state commissioner sat down once more to write.

"Here," he finally said, reading out an appendage:

"Undeterred by ignorance or perfidy, I will pursue my German goal—the restoration of inner freedom for our Fatherland."

Well, it would have to do. Kahr's handwritten text was given to one of the 19th Infantry Regiment's clerks to be typed and then rushed to Ett Strasse with instructions to have it printed and distributed throughout the city. But in fact many hours passed before Kahr's stilted, apologetic renunciation of the putsch was actually pasted on Munich's *Litfass-säulen*, the outdoor advertising pillars at nearly every street corner. The first placard did not go up until shortly before noon. By then it was largely redundant. Worse, however, it contradicted the thousands of posters proclaiming the "revolution" and the triumvirs' collaboration greeting Müncheners wherever they looked. These had been drafted during the night by Hermann Esser and others among Hitler's skillful propagandists, hastily printed at the shops cooperating with the Nazis, and then distributed en masse by Göring's SA and Josef Berchtold's Stosstrupp.

Though the triumvirs seemed to have reached agreement regarding the putsch and their course of action, they were still keeping it a well-guarded secret, especially from three men whom they would need to enforce their decisions—Colonel Josef Banzer and Major Sigmund von Imhoff at Ett Strasse, and Lieutenant Colonel Karl Schnitzlein, Banzer's deputy and commander of the State Police Third Battalion at the Türken Strasse barracks, the largest contingent of "green police" in the city.

To be sure, Hans von Seisser had met with all three at the Türken Strasse barracks earlier that night, but he had given them no guidelines to follow and had hedged his replies to their questions.

Around 3 A.M., Schnitzlein's patience wore out. His troops had been on alert for hours. His company and platoon commanders—Senior Lieutenant Michael von Godin among them—had been called from their bachelor quarters and homes and were at their posts. But for what? Alert against whom? Who was the government? Repeated calls to Banzer, Imhoff, and Seisser had brought him no satisfactory answers. His men were getting restless, especially as rumors about the night's events had filtered into the barracks.

"*Es wird mir jetzt zu dumm*—This is stupid. I've had enough!" Schnitzlein blurted to his adjutant, Lieutenant Emmanuel von Kiliani. "Take my car to Ett Strasse and find out what is going on and what the devil we are supposed to do. Whose side are we on?"

For Kiliani, as for many others in those confusing pre-dawn hours, it was an odd reconnaissance mission without immediate results.

Sigmund von Imhoff and Josef Banzer were staring at each other bleary-eyed, trying to keep awake with much coffee and tea, when the phone rang. It was Captain Karl Wild.

"Are you free to talk?" Wild asked warily. "Well, I have top-priority instructions for you from Excellency von Kahr and Colonel von Seisser personally."

Banzer, startled, sat up straight. Instructions, any kind, were what he had wanted for hours.

"You are to arrest Herr Pöhner and Frick as soon and as discreetly as possible and place them under detention until further word," Wild said.

It was not the clarifying word for which Imhoff and Banzer had been waiting, but it was an order they did not have to be given twice. And to their total astonishment, the first catch—Frick—virtually walked into their arms only a second or so after Wild had hung up.

"What was that all about?" Munich's "new" police chief asked flippantly, sauntering into their third-floor office after having taken a short nap. "Did you ever locate or talk to Colonel Seisser?"

"No," Banzer replied, trying to stall as Imhoff moved casually toward the door to turn the key and lock it.

Banzer's presence in the building was making Frick edgy. "You really ought to go home now and catch some sleep, Colonel." Frick suggested. "Everything is quiet in the city, and there will be much work to do in the morning."

"Well, Herr Frick," Banzer said calmly, "I do have one more

thing to do and also some information for you. You are under arrest."

"On whose orders?" the bewildered Nazi official asked, almost laughing until he heard the click of the lock behind him.

"The government's," Banzer answered.

"But which government, Colonel?" Frick demanded angrily.

"Excellency von Kahr's. I am arresting you on the orders and in the name of the General State Commissioner."

Frick was beside himself. How could the man with whom he had been exchanging pleasantries just a few hours before suddenly turn on him? Did that mean Kahr had renounced the coup?

Banzer and Imhoff merely shrugged and smiled politely. "I do not know, Herr Frick," the colonel said honestly. "All I can tell you is that I have instructions from him to take you into custody."

Imhoff phoned for two other officers in the building to take Frick away and keep him locked up, under surveillance, in a nearby room—one without a telephone.

"If there are any calls for Herr Frick or if anyone should come looking for him," the major told the switchboard operator and the guards at the building entrances, "just tell them he was with me a little while ago, that no one knows where he is now, and that others have been searching for him too."

Then Banzer and Imhoff planned their next action: Pöhner's apprehension, which they guessed would not be as swift and easy. Bavaria's "new" prime minister had gone home after his meeting with the press, and it was to be expected that his apartment and the street around it would be well guarded by SA. Two amply armed platoons of State Police were dispatched to carry out the raid.

Imhoff had just completed the arrangements for that undertaking when Wild called again, asking him to go to the Infantry Barracks for a conference.

"Perhaps," Banzer said hopefully, "you will get a clearer picture of how matters actually stand while you are there."

Lieutenant Kiliani and Sigmund von Imhoff nearly collided in the stairwell as the major was leaving.

"Colonel Schnitzlein sent me," the young officer said, breathless from running up the steps. "He wants to know—"

"I have no time now," Imhoff interrupted him sharply, hurrying down for the car that was waiting for him. "Colonel Banzer is up there. Speak to him."

But Banzer was also in no mood to talk to his deputy's adjutant, especially not when the lieutenant bluntly asked the question to which, in fact, he did not yet have an unequivocal reply himself: "Whose side are we on?"

"I don't know," Banzer replied with apparent irritation. "But stay around and make yourself useful by answering the telephone."

Kiliani did—until shortly after 4 A.M., when Imhoff returned with the information everyone in the State Police had been waiting hours to hear.

"You can tell Colonel Schnitzlein that Kahr, Lossow, and Seisser are resolved to oppose Hitler's putsch," Imhoff reported. "The plan calls for waiting until Reichswehr and our reinforcements arrive from outside—in the course of the morning. Then steps will be taken to regain control."

History is not only the product of man's actions but also of his inactions, and Gustav von Kahr was a master of the latter, especially in the early hours of November 9, when his greatest failure was in literally not stopping the press. As a result, long after the triumvirs had taken steps to crush the putsch, most of Munich's daily newspapers were still blazoning the details of its success. The "mishap," if it was one, was to compound immeasurably the confusion in the city, already programmed by the Nazis' own high-gear propaganda effort and the triumvirs' lack of one.

This would not have happened had Kahr acted promptly on the advice of his own press spokesman, the *Münchener Zeitung*'s Adolf Schiedt. Schiedt had left Pöhner's Ett Strasse press briefing early to rush, first to Maximilian Strasse and then to the Infantry Barracks, in search of Kahr. When he learned from the trio that they were renouncing the coup, Schiedt urged Kahr to use his emergency powers to ban publication of the morning editions of all Munich papers.

"Otherwise," he warned, "they will be reporting only what happened in the Bürgerbräukeller."

Schiedt's proposal was accepted in principle, though not in

practice. It was given such low priority in the turmoil of improvisation which reigned in the little communications shed that Schiedt was unable to act on it for hours.

Indeed, it was not until shortly before 4 A.M. that he was allowed to use one of the few telephones in the command post to call his own publisher, Hans Buchner, the chairman of Munich's association of editors and publishers.

"You must stop the presses," Schiedt told him, "and notify as many of the others as you can. Tell them anything, even that publication is a capital crime."

Buchner agreed to do what he could, but except for his own midday paper, still in production, it was too late, especially for Fritz Gerlich's *Münchner Neueste Nachrichten*, by far the largest-circulation daily in the city.

Gerlich was fast asleep when the phone at his bedside rang shrilly. It was Buchner.

"*Herr Kollege*," Buchner said, using the familiar form of address among German journalists, "this will come as a shock, I know, and it may not do you any good, but Excellency von Kahr has just issued an edict to stop printing and distributing, on pain of death."

Gerlich was not only dubious but adamant that it could not be done. "By now," he said, peering at the clock on his nighttable, "I have at least thirty thousand copies already out and being delivered. There's no way to stop the run. But why? What is it all about?"

"I don't know," Buchner said in all honesty. "I'm only passing on the instructions I was given."

Fritz Gerlich was not only baffled but infuriated by the news. It must be Pöhner's doing, he thought, an insolent violation of his promise that there would be no censorship under the new regime. Late as it was, he decided to call him.

"Herr Prime Minister," Gerlich shouted into the phone, "what is the meaning of this? Three hours ago you stood there in front of us and pledged there would be no controls, no restraints on freedom of the press. And now this! In the middle of the night, in the middle of my press run and distribution. I demand an explanation."

But there was none. Pöhner was even more mystified than the

sputtering Gerlich. "I am sure there must be some mistake," he said, trying to shake off the drugging effect of the first hours of sleep. "I haven't issued any such instructions, and I am absolutely certain Excellency von Kahr hasn't either. Why would he? It must be a hoax of some kind, but if you can find out more from Buchner, please call me back."

As Pöhner waited for the return call, doubts and worries began to plague him. They turned into alarm when Gerlich telephoned again some twenty minutes later.

"All I can tell you is what I told you before," the editor said. "According to Buchner, Herr von Kahr's office has issued an edict under his emergency powers act to suspend publication of all papers. Violators face execution. I couldn't comply even if I wanted to. It is just too late. Goodnight, Herr Pöhner, I am going back to sleep."

Sleep was now the last thing on Ernst Pöhner's mind. What was this all about? Could somebody be playing a double cross? He had to reach Frick. Perhaps he would know more.

Pöhner waited impatiently for an operator to connect him with Ett Strasse.

"Herr Frick?" said the police sergeant at the switchboard. "I can try again, but I just don't know where he is. Quite a number of people have been phoning for him, but he doesn't seem to be anywhere in the building. Not in his apartment, not in his office, not in Major von Imhoff's nor Colonel Banzer's, though apparently he was with them about an hour ago. Do you wish to leave a message for him?"

Odd, Pöhner thought, deciding to get dressed.

His bewilderment was heightened when the doorbell rang. It was Max von Scheubner-Richter, looking tired, morose, and dejected.

"You must come with me immediately to the war ministry," he said. "There is something very wrong. Hitler and Ludendorff are beside themselves. Neither Lossow nor Seisser has made an appearance there all night, and we cannot locate them anywhere. Kahr seems to have disappeared too. It is all very ominous. Come, I have a car waiting downstairs."

"If anyone calls for me," Pöhner said to his wife, struggling into his coat, "I will be at Schönfeld Strasse for a while."

As they sped away in Scheubner-Richter's car, the convoy of State Police trucks approached the apartment house.

"Pöhner is not at home," Sigmund von Imhoff reported to Banzer. "His wife says he has gone to the war ministry."

That, the major and the colonel knew, was a putschist bastion far too well defended for their forces to penetrate. Some other way would have to be found to arrest Ernst Pöhner.

13

Startled by the noise, Erwin Aubele sat up straight in bed. Aubele, the caretaker and building superintendent of the Bavarian Agricultural Credit Bank at No. 29 Kanal Strasse, had failed to hear the incessant ringing of his apartment bell. But the knocking and pounding on his door, the shouts of *"Aufmachen! Schnell!"* had roused him out of deep sleep.

"Who could that be?" he said angrily, shaking his wife by the shoulder. "My God, it's the middle of the night."

Struggling into his bathrobe, he padded barefoot to the bedroom window, parted the curtains, and peered down on two large automobiles and a knot of uniformed, helmeted men, some with rifles, in the street below. He groped for his slippers and the light switch. It looked like police or soldiers down there, and he was frightened.

From the stairwell outside his apartment he could hear someone shouting officiously: "Open up at once, Herr Aubele! In the name of the new Reich government!" The voice sounded oddly familiar.

Aubele shuffled down the corridor, cautiously hooked the chain lock of his front door as precaution, then pulled it open. Through the crack he saw, of all people, his stocky neighbor, Max Amann. The Nazi party's business manager, Hitler's wartime platoon sergeant, had once been employed as a junior executive by the state-owned "farm development bank" on Kanal Strasse. He still had an apartment in the building.

Among the men and women in Amann's entourage were Hermann Esser and Gottfried Feder, Julius Streicher and Helmut

Klotz from Nürnberg, Amann's assistant Philipp Bouhler, with two pretty young secretaries from the party's Cornelius Strasse headquarters, and a man who seemed to be omnipresent that night, Police Inspector Matthäus Hofmann. Members of Josef Berchtold's Stosstrupp, brandishing carbines and submachine guns menacingly, stood guard behind the group.

"This building has been requisitioned by the new national government," Amann announced grimly. "I want you to open the offices and the main conference room. Don't cause us any trouble, and don't try to do anything funny, Aubele, or there will be corpses here tonight."

Trembling as the guns were leveled at them, Aubele and his wife obediently led the group down two flights of stairs to the bank's second-floor offices, turned on lights, and watched open-mouthed as cards with the names of various members of the "provisional government"—"Dr. Feder," "H. Esser," "J. Streicher," "Speakers"—were tacked up on the doors. Two storm troopers stood guard in front of each suite.

"See, I told you there would be plenty of typewriters here and no need to bring any from Cornelius Strasse," Amann said knowingly as he turned to Bouhler. "Why don't you put your girls in here and let them wait until we're ready."

Dutifully, the two typists—Elsa Gisler and Anna Schürz, both twenty-two—scooted behind the desks assigned them. They tried to look alert, though they had been at work since 8 A.M. the previous morning.

"Esser and Klotz will be preparing the texts for the posters," Amann added. "But you can call the printers now, and have them come here. The copy should be ready in an hour or so."

While Esser and Klotz busied themselves with their propaganda proclamations, Feder settled behind the desk of one of the bank's officers and assumed his duties as "provisional finance minister." His first task was to draft a proclamation "to prevent a panic or a mass flight of capital abroad," once Müncheners awoke to the realities of the putsch in the morning.

"Until further notice," it read, "all banks and other credit institutions are hereby deprived of their private business character and placed under state supervision. Any changes in or transfers of accounts will be prosecuted."

The relationship between Feder and Hitler was a special one. Few men had been as influential in Hitler's life as this construction engineer turned-amateur economist. Regarded by many in Munich as an "economic and fiscal genius," Feder's 1919 lectures on the mysteries of capital, the stock exchange, and "breaking the bondage of interest slavery" had provided Hitler with "the most essential premises" for reorganizing the little German Workers party both had joined. Now, Feder reasoned, the association with Hitler was at last bearing fruit.

He looked once more at the announcement which an SA courier was waiting to rush to the offices of the *Völkischer Beobachter*. How should he sign it? After a moment's hesitation, he scribbled beneath the text: "The Finance Committee—Gottfried Feder." That sounded official. Watching the storm trooper leave, he pondered his own future. Too bad about those stocks in the bank, he thought, realizing he had just signed the edict that would prevent him from picking them up on Monday. But then, as the new government's finance minister, he no longer needed them. He sauntered across the hall to see how Esser, Streicher and Klotz were doing.

While Streicher was thinking out the harangues he was to deliver on Munich's main squares in the morning, Esser was drafting a long "proclamation to the German people." Its strident, ranting tone revealed how he and Hitler thought with almost one mind and why they rated almost equal as propagandists.

"The revolution of the November criminals is ended today," Esser read aloud to test its effect. "The regime of economic racketeers and political swindlers has been broken, and a German national government has been declared.

"Five years have passed since the day when howling, miserable deserters and escaped convicts stabbed the heroic German people in the back. As a pretext for their deed they promised the gullible peace, freedom, beauty, and dignity. . . . And what became of that? Today our unfortunate nation stands broken at the brink of its own grave. . . . Hunger and need are rampant among our hardworking people. . . . The portals to wealth are open only to the economic speculators, profiteers, and political frauds who alone monopolize the leadership of the state and the government. . . . Unscrupulous criminals have given away territory after territory of our Fatherland so that today 17 million Germans have been torn from us, dishonored and enslaved by foreign rule.

"And in the hour of the German Reich's death throes the instigators of all this misery preach to us of the need to maintain peace and order; a former brothel-keeper who has usurped the title of a Reich President besmirches the honor of the German People and the German Republic.

"Germany," Esser continued, "can expect no help from men such as these, and it is in recognition of that fact that the regime of the November criminals in Berlin has been declared deposed and a new provisional national government proclaimed."

How should it be signed? He deliberated a moment with the others, then placed the names of Ludendorff, Hitler, Lossow, and Seisser at the bottom. Now it was ready for the printers.

For Hermann Esser, the proclamation was the end of a long night's work. He had already done more than he had promised Hitler. He was flushed with fever, his limbs ached, and his head throbbed. More than that, he had been disillusioned and despondent for hours—ever since he had seen Ludendorff allow the triumvirs to leave the Bürgerbräukeller. From that moment he had considered the coup finished, the putsch a failure. The spate of bad news and ominous signs that had been reported in the meantime merely strengthened him in his conclusion that "all is lost."

Yes, of course, he would also take a copy of the proclamation to the *Völkischer Beobachter,* where Alfred Rosenberg was waiting to have it set in type for the front page. But after that, he resolved, he would return home to the bed he should never have left.

As he went out of the bank building on Kanal Strasse, he noticed the two secretaries, obviously as exhausted as he, slumped asleep at their desks.

"Where is that Major Siry who was sent over to the Nineteenth Regiment?" Ludendorff asked, looking at Hitler, Hermann Kriebel, and the other putsch leaders assembled in von Lossow's anteroom at the war ministry. "He has been gone well over an hour and has not reported back."

Hitler and Kriebel nodded helpless agreement and looked to Röhm, Scheubner-Richter, and the Oberland League's Friedrich

Weber for plausible answers and support. The mood in the drab room was funereal, vacillating between bafflement, despondency, boredom, and spurts of frenzied but largely artificial activity. Without Lossow, without Seisser, there seemed no purpose in being there. The mystery of their whereabouts and their failure to come around as they had promised was deepening.

Siry was not the only emissary who had simply disappeared. But Ludendorff, still refusing to countenance so much as a suggestion that the two might have reneged, exhorted Röhm to continue calling and dispatch more intermediaries.

"Excellency, there is something wrong, something that we are not being told about," Scheubner-Richter said at one point.

"But what?" Ludendorff insisted. "What could·they want? All three stood there and gave their word and their hand in honor, before several thousand witnesses. I just cannot conceive of their acting differently now."

No one seemed to have an answer to that, least of all Hitler.

Yet if the leaders were dejected and puzzled, few of their followers, such as Ludendorff's stepson Heinz Pernet, Josef Seydel, Hans Streck, Ulrich Graf, or Karl Osswald, displayed much awareness of it. Even less so the "troops"—Heinrich Himmler, Theodor Casella, Martin Faust, young Count Moulin-Eckart, the Stosstrupp's Ludwig Schmied, who had been assigned to accompany Hitler for the night, and the several hundred other members of the Reichskriegsflagge, SA, and Oberland who were encamped at the Schönfeld Strasse complex. They did what "soldiers" usually do after having been told to hurry up; they waited. And to a man they believed themselves to be soldiers in the new army. When not setting up barbed-wire barricades and machine guns around the war ministry or doing guard duty in the windy courtyard, they tried to keep warm or slept in the corridors and various offices.

Captain Wilhelm Daser, the Seventh Division duty officer, had finally been "relieved" and arrested when Röhm realized he was playing both sides of the street. The putschists had taken over control of the switchboard at 1 A.M. But despite the captain's incarceration in his own office, and the removal of the small Reichswehr contingent that had guarded the building, few of Röhm's men seemed cognizant of the fact that they and the Reichswehr were no longer "revolutionary comrades-in-arms."

While the war ministry served as the nerve center and command post of the putsch, there was at first a flurry of traffic in its hallways and offices: visitors offering congratulations or seeking jobs, favors, and recognition, and a few registering their protests with the men they believed to be the new rulers of Germany.

Even Robert Murphy, the U.S. consul general, had stopped by—not to congratulate, but demanding indignantly to see Hitler because he had been denied permission at the central telegraph office to send his coded cable to Washington.

"That is correct, Mr. Murphy," Hitler replied, "mildly" but officiously. "Under the circumstances, I am sure you understand, there is temporary censorship."

Murphy's protest, of course, was largely a formality. On the other hand, neither Murphy nor Hitler seemed to know that the ban on outgoing telegrams had been imposed by the State Police on instructions from Gustav von Kahr.

But as the night wore on, even callers such as Murphy became fewer, and the frustration among the leaders grew. It was in this mood of desperation that Kriebel went into the war ministry's switchboard room, where Max Neunzert had busied himself trying to locate Lossow and Seisser, and asked the ex-lieutenant to scout the city.

"Find out what is going on at the railroad station and the central telegraph office," Kriebel told him, "and also see if there are any signs of leftist counterrevolutionary action. You will have to go on foot—there doesn't seem to be an automobile available at the moment. But Herr Neunzert, please, do not stay out all night. Come back soon. I may need you for other assignments."

Proud to be of such "important assistance," Neunzert, the Iron Cross 2nd Class and Bavaria's Cross of Merit sparkling on his uniform tunic, hurried out of the war ministry and bent his head against the sudden gust of wind and wet snow that hit him at the corner of Schönfeld and Ludwig Strasse.

Fog enveloped the Selve touring car stopped on the narrow cobblestone road between Freising and Munich, and icy blasts whipped at its canvas top and the oilcloth side curtains. Julius Schaub, shivering with cold, was slumped behind the wheel, trying to catch a few winks but too angry over being stuck there to sleep.

"Hey," the SA man next to him shouted, nudging Schaub roughly. "Listen! I think I hear something coming. Sounds like a car."

Startled, Schaub sat up, peering through the wet windshield. Amid the swirls of fog outside, he saw the dim, barely recognizable headlights of an approaching automobile. Clambering out of the Selve, he stood squarely in the middle of the road and flailed his arms. *"Halt! Kontrolle!"*

The big Reichswehr staff car came to a sudden stop as the driver noticed Schaub gesticulating wildly. It was an ironic meeting. Outside stood a key courier of the Nazi putschists; in the staff car were men on a vital mission to crush the putsch—Major General Friedrich Kress von Kressenstein and his adjutant, Captain Hermann von Hanneken. Yet neither Schaub nor Kressenstein was aware of the other's role. Noticing the general inside, Schaub sprang to attention, saluted, and was about to ask for assistance when Kressenstein explained his "urgent mission." "I have orders from General von Lossow to assume the command in Regensburg," he said.

"Oh, I am sorry, Herr General." Schaub saluted once more and let the officers drive on. Disappointed, he returned to his frustrating vigil. "Surely someone else will come along before morning," he said to his companion. "But I'll bet Captain Göring is fuming. If there were only a way to notify him."

Telephones were ringing, typewriters clattering, and doors slamming at the *Völkischer Beobachter* on Schelling Strasse. The mood was exuberant, close to delirium, and the noise deafening as editors, SA storm troopers, various party officials, and a constant parade of passing well-wishers, all of them getting progressively drunk on the ceaseless flow of champagne, hailed each other and shouted mutual congratulations.

But Paula Schlier, who had been at work since early evening, was close to exhaustion from taking dictation and typing all night. The pandemonium made matters worse. When she finally had a chance to take a few minutes' break, she surveyed the crowd and felt repelled by their mindless reveling. The ease with which they spoke of "revolution" and the "march on Berlin" troubled her deeply. How naïve, how ridiculous to think that Germany's fate could be changed with simple pronouncements from the stage of a beerhall. Didn't all these people realize that they would have to send an armed force north across the border, against other Germans, against people of different political persuasion? And that could only mean war—civil war. She sensed that tragedy and bloodshed were in the air.

Paula Schlier's moment of rest and reflection was brief. The first edition was not even finished. Proof still had to be read on Josef Stolzing's pompously verbose editorial, already running well over a column in length. No doubt he would want to make changes—he usually did—and add even more bombastically turgid prose. God, the man was a bore. And she had also heard that there was still a gaping space on the first page, being held open for some kind of "proclamation to the German people." Yet it was already past 3 A.M.

"*Endlich!*—At last!" Rosenberg exclaimed when he saw Hermann Esser come in. "Is that it?"

Esser nodded wearily.

"Well, it's about time," Rosenberg snapped, barely glancing at the text before handing it to Paula Schlier to type up for the composing room.

"*Bitte, machen Sie schnell,*" he said tersely, turning on his heels toward his own room.

Esser studied the frenetic scene briefly before walking downstairs, back out into the frigid cold. He stood there for a moment, observing the confusing jumble of storm troopers, messengers, and chauffeurs; then he crossed the street and went up Schelling Strasse a few yards to Heinrich Hoffmann's studio.

"You're crazy to be out on a night like this, with your jaundice," Hoffmann said, looking at his young friend's sallow complexion and yellowed, bloodshot eyes.

Esser merely shook his head. "*Alles ist aus!*" he said sadly. "It's all over. Ludendorff let Kahr, Lossow, and Seisser go. Just like that. And the three are already preparing to announce publicly that they joined Hitler under duress. The rumors are all over the city. The green police are moving out in force, and the Reichswehr will too. And some of our best Oberland troops are locked up in one of the barracks. It's finished. I thought you should know. We're just going through the motions. But you're right; I really should not be out. I can barely stand. I promised Adolf to help—I've done what I can. I'll go home now and get into bed."

Anton Schmidt, the printer, studied the bank and apartment house on Kanal Strasse skeptically. He had called Bouhler several hours ago at Cornelius Strasse, and this was where he had been told to go. Amann would be here; Bouhler too.

"Is this the headquarters of the new government?" he asked one of the grim-looking SA troopers standing outside.

"Right, *mein Herr!* You will find everybody on the second and third floors. But you will need indentification to get through the guards."

Schmidt climbed the stairs heavily. He was not accustomed to late nights, and the long wait was starting to take its toll.

"Halt!" said a stern-faced storm trooper standing spread-legged on the third-floor landing, a rifle gripped in front of his chest. "Your papers, please. Are you here on official business?"

Schmidt was frisked for weapons, then ushered toward a frosted-glass door.

"One has to be careful," the SA man called after him. "One never knows what Red provocateurs and Jewish spies may be around."

Entering the office area, where a bevy of men, some in uniform, were scurrying back and forth importantly with pieces of paper in their hands, Schmidt was surprised to find that he was by no means the first to arrive. His two competitors for Nazi party business, Ferdinand Schreiber and Hans Stiegeler, were already waiting in the reception area.

"You, too?" he said, trying to be jocular. "How long have you been waiting?"

Schreiber, in no mood for banter, pulled out his pocketwatch, snapped it open, and studied the dial. "Too long."

"Ah, but it may be worth it," Stiegeler interjected. "I heard Bouhler and Amann saying something about handbills or posters with a press run of twenty thousand each. Can you imagine?"

"Well, it had better be something like that," Schmidt grumbled. "Keeping my people on overtime this long is costing me a fortune."

Schreiber and Stiegeler nodded in agreement, and the three made themselves as comfortable as they could on the straight-backed settees in the bank's reception room. From down the hall they could hear the voices of Amann, Bouhler, Streicher, Kotz. Typewriters were going, telephones ringing. But their wait, they soon realized, was by no means over.

In fact, it was nearly four o'clock when Bouhler and Amann appeared, beckoning Schreiber to one side. By then it had been almost twelve hours since the three printshop owners had first received the cryptic phone calls asking them to keep typesetters and pressmen on for a "late night" job.

"We will need five thousand of these," Bouhler said to Schreiber. "About one thousand will be distributed in Munich, the rest are for other parts of the state."

Schreiber looked at the typewritten copy—a proclamation to the people of Bavaria announcing the revolution and the new government—with the name of "Dr. v. Kahr" at the bottom.

"Are you sure this has been approved?" he asked, noting that it did not have a police stamp on it. "I've already had trouble with Ett Strasse, and I don't want any more."

"Everything is perfectly in order, Herr Schreiber," Amann assured him. "Can you have them ready by nine o'clock? We will send people to get them. But it must not be later than that."

"You know you can always count on me," Schreiber said, putting on his overcoat. "But I hope my friends here do not have to wait much longer."

In fact, they didn't. A few minutes later Bouhler reappeared with the copy for handbills announcing that Hitler and other Nazi party leaders would be holding ten mass meetings all over Munich later that day.

"*Meine Herren,*" he announced, beaming, "of these we will need fifty thousand from each of you. Can you do them by nine o'clock?"

Stiegeler and Schmidt looked at each other incredulously, then nodded with some hesitation.

"I must apologize for it being so late and your having waited so long," Bouhler added. "But I think you understand that the delay was caused by the circumstances of this historic night and the events that have taken place. The size of this order is a token of the party's and the new government's appreciation."

Suddenly wide awake, the two men took the texts and hurried out of the building to their shops.

Max Neunzert was alarmed and dismayed by what he saw at the railroad station and the central telegraph office. Both were being guarded not by Oberland troopers, as Kriebel had believed, but by green-uniformed State Police. It was an ominous sign. Kriebel would have to be told.

But Neunzert was also freezing and "soaked to the skin" from his reconnaissance mission. He decided "to go home to change into civilian clothes again and warm up a bit." From there he phoned the war ministry to tell Kriebel the bad news.

"Yes, yes," Neunzert said, holding the receiver in one hand, trying to button his shirt with the other. "I will come back as soon as possible. I just want to stop off on the way to see my father-in-law, who also wants a report on the situation."

Adolf Hühnlein, a Seventh Division general staff major and organizer of the Black Reichswehr, felt diffident about the mission on which Ludendorff had sent him from the war ministry. So many emissaries had been dispatched, and none had returned. Would he be the next? Well, at least there was the consolation that he was on his way to neutral if not friendly territory: the Infantry School.

"I am sorry to have to wake you up," he said, as he was let into the quarters of Colonel Ludwig Leupold, the school's deputy commander. "But Excellency Ludendorff wishes to speak to you urgently—at Schönfeld Strasse."

Leupold was sympathetic to the putschists' cause, and his favorable attitude toward Hitler and Ludendorff had done much to encourage the school's officer candidates to be enthusiastic about following Gerhard Rossbach that night. But like so many other officers of his persuasion, he was torn between his code of duty and obedience to superiors, in this case Otto von Lossow, and his admiration for and loyalty to Germany's greatest war hero, Ludendorff. When the cadets and student officers assigned to him had marched out of the school, and then back in after their debacle at Maximilian Strasse, and finally back out to the Bürgerbräukeller around 3 A.M., Leupold had done little to dissuade them, maintaining a neutral position—and also a safe one, considering the students' determination.

What was it that Ludendorff wanted?

"Information," Hühnlein insisted. "A clarification of the situation. Come, I have a car waiting outside."

The mood at Schönfeld Strasse was gloomy when Ernst Pöhner arrived with Scheubner-Richter shortly before 5 A.M. Ludendorff, sitting grim and silent in the corner of the room, looked like a stone statue. Hitler was off to the side with Röhm and Weber, threatening histrionically, "We will all hang ourselves if we don't succeed," but he was still convinced of success. To be sure, by now he too was certain that Lossow had jumped ship; only Ludendorff could not bring himself to accept the fact. But Hitler had not given up hope in Kahr and Seisser. Moreover, various scouts he had sent out had reported back full of optimism about the mood in the city. The public, he felt sure, was on his side; but it would have to be mobilized.

"Once the will of the masses is known," he was ranting as Pöhner and Scheubner-Richter came in, "no one will dare to resist. It will be like a storm flood, and both the army and the police will be swept along with it. More propaganda, nothing but propaganda. That will turn the trick."

But to launch that propaganda effort he would need a base, a safe haven from which to operate. It could not be the Bürgerbräukeller on the largely residential right bank of the Isar in Munich's East End, nor could it be the war ministry, located in a stately no-man's-land of palaces, government buildings, and libraries between the city's thriving commercial hub and the arty, intellectual quarter of Schwabing. He wanted a base in the center, near Marienplatz and City Hall. Could there be a better place than police headquarters at Ett Strasse? And for that he needed Pöhner.

"Herr Prime Minister." He gestured dramatically, seeing him. "We have given you this power, now use it. Use your authority. We must seize the initiative now, or others will. Take a battalion of Oberland that I am putting at your disposal, lead it to police headquarters, and occupy it at dawn. Then our patrols will set off through the city calling 'Flags Out!' and you will see the enthusiasm that will be generated."

Dutifully, Pöhner set off to do his Führer's bidding—but not in the manner Hitler had prescribed. The suggestion of leading an army of roughneck Oberland League irregulars through the streets of Munich struck this scheming civil servant as ludicrous, if not repugnant. Moreover, unaware of Frick's arrest or the extent to which Josef Banzer and Sigmund von Imhoff had already established their authority, he was convinced that his personal influence and stature as Munich's erstwhile police president would suffice. These were, after all, "his" men in that building. Surely they would listen to him.

Accompanied only by Adolf Hühnlein, who had just delivered Colonel Leupold and whom he was planning to install anyway as Banzer's "replacement," Pöhner left to "capture" the Ett Strasse headquarters.

"Finally!" Julius Schaub shouted, as he heard the rumble of trucks in the distance on the road behind him. Lifting the side curtain, he peered back and saw the faint pinpoints of approaching headlights through the fog. "Let's crank up so they won't have to wait and we can fall right in with the convoy," he said, certain that the trucks were carrying Gregor Strasser's SA battalion.

Laboriously, the engine sputtered to life just as the first truck pulled up behind the Selve.

"You mean you've been sitting here all night?" Strasser asked incredulously, then laughed. "Well, follow me. We'll lead you into Munich. You must be frozen stiff."

The truck had just swung out in front of the car and was about to drive on when there was the sound of loud wailing horns behind them. Looking back, Schaub saw spotlights and an approaching convoy of much faster trucks being led by a dark green automobile—State Police. The commander's vehicle passed, then swerved to a sharp stop in front of Strasser's truck, blocking the road. Police Lieutenant Georg Höfler jumped out and walked toward the SA vehicles.

"You!" Strasser exclaimed, using the familiar second-person

du. "Where are you coming from?"

"Landshut, like you," Höfler replied. He was Gregor and Otto Strasser's brother-in-law, the husband of their sister Olga, and he was deputy commander of the company of "green police" in the Isar Valley city that had been Bavaria's first capital.

"But where are you headed?" Strasser asked.

"The same place I think you're going, Gregor. To Munich."

"Are you for or against us?"

"I don't know yet," Höfler answered candidly. He explained that he had merely been sent in response to Seisser's call for reinforcements. "We will get our orders in Munich."

"So will we," Strasser said.

For a moment Strasser, a blond giant of a man, and Höfler, smaller but with a chiseled face that revealed his innate decisiveness, stood there looking at each other in the glare of the carbide lamps of the trucks. The fog from the river was thinning but the snowflakes, still wet, were getting thicker.

"Well, we'll see later in the day," Strasser said philosophically and reached out his hand.

Georg Höfler grasped it firmly. "I wish you luck, Gregor," he added, as he walked toward his staff car. On his shouted signal, the police vehicles sped on toward Munich.

Strasser climbed back into the cab of the rented truck. "*Los!*" he said gruffly. "Let's get moving. The Führer and Göring are waiting for us."

Colonel Banzer and Major von Imhoff were still listening to the report of the officers who had led the platoon to capture Pöhner when their office door flew open.

"Where is Herr Frick?" Pöhner asked. "I've called several times and no one seems to know. The guard downstairs said I should ask you."

Banzer and Imhoff barely trusted their eyes. What luck.

"I don't know either, Herr Pöhner," Banzer lied, and smiled. "But I do know that I have to arrest you. Now. You too, Herr Hühnlein."

Pöhner, open-mouthed, stared through his pince-nez. He felt as if he had been "hit by a club."

"Arrest me? You don't say! May I ask on whose orders, please, by what right?"

"Excellency von Kahr's," Banzer replied.

"Von Kahr? Personally?"

"Yes, Herr Pöhner, personally, on charges of treason and attempting to overthrow the state."

Pöhner was still shaking his head incredulously as he was led away to an empty office, not far from the one where Wilhelm Frick had been under lock and key for three hours.

Max Neunzert was knotting his tie when the telephone rang in his apartment.

"*Mein Gott,* Max, are you *still* there?" It was Ernst Röhm.

"Yes, but I'm just about to leave," Neunzert replied. "I had to change. I was soaked and my uniform looked terrible."

Röhm was breathing heavily, and it was apparent that his patience was running thin.

"You must get back here at once," he said emphatically. "Hitler wants you immediately, for an important assignment."

"I will be there right away," Neunzert implored, "but I must look in on my father-in-law first. He wants to know—"

There was a click on the line.

Colonel Leupold was getting irritated. First to be called out of bed like that, and now to be kept waiting. He studied the scene: Röhm's troopers, a few SA and Oberländers too, sleeping fitfully in the corridors, their weapons in their hands.

"Excellency Ludendorff and Herr Hitler would like to see you now," Hermann Kriebel said, apologizing for the delay. He led Leupold into a small office where the warlord and the Führer were waiting alone.

"What's the matter with Lossow?" Ludendorff asked sternly. "Where is he? I have been waiting for him here since eleven o'clock—nearly seven hours. My telephone calls are not answered, my messengers do not come back. What is going on, Colonel?"

"He is not coming, Excellency," Leupold replied. "But I thought you knew that."

Ludendorff looked stunned as Leupold explained that he had been informed as early as 1 A.M. that Lossow, Kahr, and Seisser were reneging because they had been forced to make their declarations under duress.

"I went to see Lossow personally between two and three

o'clock," Leupold continued. "He is at the Nineteenth, in the communications shack with the others. And he confirmed that decision personally. Moreover, he has called up reinforcements. They are prepared to use force to restore order, Excellency."

"I cannot believe that," Ludendorff said. "I just cannot believe it."

"It's treason, it is a double-cross!" Hitler screamed, as Leupold gave his report.

"But Herr Hitler," Leupold interrupted him, "it was an extorted agreement, extorted at pistol point. I have heard that from other eyewitnesses myself. Under the circumstances—"

"A coup against the state is not an afternoon tea," Hitler shot back, "and I do not have all of my people under control every minute. But I apologized to all three of them and they accepted my apologies."

"Yes," Ludendorff added, "the gentlemen knew what was at stake, and our plans were not new to them."

"But they would never have agreed to them except under pressure," Leupold argued.

The discussion was at an impasse.

Would Leupold go back to Lossow and pass on Ludendorff's views, especially that the "patriotic movement is crushed, finished," unless there could be a compromise?

"I will do whatever you wish, Excellency," Leupold said. "But I think there is no hope of changing von Lossow's resolve. Moreover, no matter what their feelings or sympathies, the troops will obey him. As they should. I will come back with a message if Lossow has one for you. But I doubt that he will."

Ludendorff and Hitler glared at each other as the colonel left. What now?

For Hitler the decision was not long in coming. "I am prepared to die for my cause. Lossow may have more cannons than we, but if he destroys my work he has no right to exist," he thundered. "We will go on as planned. And if it fails, I will always have one last bullet in my pistol for myself."

Theatrically, he announced his decision to retreat to the city's right bank, to the Bürgerbräu, and plan the next moves from there. He would just stop off at his Thiersch Strasse apartment to get out of the swallow-tail coat and change into more sensible clothes. Those who wished, who believed in him, should then come to the beerhall and join him there.

They did, in short succession: Kriebel, Scheubner-Richter, Weber, and, within a half hour after Hitler's departure, Ludendorff too. Huddled in his loden coat, the felt hat placed squarely on his massive head, he ordered Röhm to hold the war ministry at all costs.

As Josef Seydel escorted him to the car that was waiting in the courtyard, Ludendorff gave vent to the bitterness that had been simmering beneath his stoic exterior for hours. "Did you ever think," he asked rhetorically, "that a German general would break his word that way? Never again can I put on the uniform that Lossow also wears."

"Yes, Hitler wanted you urgently," Ernst Röhm said, as Max Neunzert came panting into the Schönfeld Strasse command post at 6:30 A.M. "But he left just a few minutes ago for the Bürgerbräukeller. You will have to find him there. As I understood it, he wants you to travel out of town on a most important assignment. To Berchtesgaden, I believe."

14

Dawn came sluggishly to Munich on the morning of November 9, 1923. Slate-gray clouds blanketed the city, spasmodically disgorging more cold wet snow, and a damp, biting chill hung in the air.

Except for the SA guards on patrol around the Bürgerbräukeller, Rosenheimer Strasse seemed almost deserted. But in the beerhall the barometer pointed to doomsday, though the more than 1,000 unshaved, unwashed storm troopers encamped in and around the smoke-filled main auditorium were not yet aware of it. To be sure, the elation and excitement of the previous night had evaporated, but largely through fatigue. The truth that the putsch had failed was known to only a few, if any, of the more perspicacious rank and file.

Unwashed, unshaven, clutching their weapons in their hands and arms, most were sleeping under or slumped over tables, on chairs they had shoved together as makeshift cots, or on the bare floor. A few were eating a spartan breakfast of dark bread, cheese, wurst, and ersatz coffee. Some, as is the wont of Bavarians, who consider it food, not a beverage, were starting the day with yet another stein of beer.

There were the members of Josef Berchtold's Stosstrupp and most of the Infantry School cadets who had marched back to the Bürgerbräu with Gerhard Rossbach, Hans Block, Siegfried Mahler, and Robert Wagner. There was most of Hans Knauth's Third SA Battalion and Karl Beggel's truncated First Battalion. There was the Oberland League's Hans Oemler with most of his men, who had been routed at the 19th Infantry Regiment, and there were also most of Max von Müller's Oberländers, who had finally been released from the Engineer Barracks drill hall, though without weapons and without Müller or General Adolf Aechter—both of whom were being held under lock and key with Alexander Siry, Julius Schreck, and the various other emissaries at the Infantry Barracks. There was also the Munich SA Regiment's commander, Wilhelm Brückner, and his adjutant, Heinrich Bennecke, who lived nearby on Orleans Platz and was anxious "to get home for an hour or so to wash up and have some breakfast."

And there was Hermann Göring, periodically strutting about to "inspect" his ragtag army and pump up spirits but wondering, primarily, "whether Carin is feeling better" and whether Hanfstaengl had ever phoned her after leaving the Bürgerbräu to go home and sleep. He was also wondering what had happened to Julius Schaub and to his car.

That mystery was soon to be solved, for just a few blocks away, Schaub and Gregor Strasser's convoy of trucks was rumbling along noisily on Ismaninger Strasse toward the Bürgerbräukeller. Noticing the peaceful street and Müncheners starting to go to work as on every other morning, the driver of the lead vehicle turned to Strasser and mumbled, "This is not much of a revolution, is it?"

Strasser, too, thought it strange but merely replied, "We shall see."

Other reinforcements were also starting to arrive or were on their way.

Hans Frank was crossing Ludwig Bridge along with most of

Edmund Heines's second SA Battalion. They had spent five aimless hours camping at the Infantry School after the misadventure with the Allied officers at the Vier Jahreszeiten Hotel.

Ludwig Oestreicher had just dispatched couriers to rouse Alfons Weber's Oberländers bivouacked in the Stuck Villa and other Prinzregenten Strasse mansions in order to send those men out on patrols of the city and to set up more bridgeheads on the Isar.

Three trucks were wheezing slowly up Rosenheimer Strasse with some seventy of Wilhelm Völk's Oberländers from Garmisch-Partenkirchen.

Meanwhile, over on Jahn Strasse, in the schoolyard across from his father's piano-making shop, Jungsturm leader Adolf Lenk, tired from "such a short and exciting night," was reviewing about 100 of his teenage followers and getting ready to parade them to the beerhall.

In all, there would soon be a force of 3,000 men.

Among those encamped in the beerhall, nerves seemed to have rubbed raw, especially in Berchtold's Stosstrupp. Hostages, still being taken and brought in at dawn, were the first to suffer the consequences. One of them was Engelbert Wallner, a young schoolteacher and active Social Democrat who a few weeks earlier had been in a coffeehouse altercation with the SA. He was arrested and brought to the Bürgerbräu around seven o'clock and kicked and bludgeoned unconscious by some of the troopers there. Several of them objected to the maltreatment. One was the Stosstrupp's Karl Hauenstein.

"Leave the man alone and just lock him up," he protested.

"Keep out of this or I'll put you up against the wall for target practice," snarled Heinrich von Knobloch, a Stosstrupp platoon leader and one of Berchtold's most vicious toughs. Knobloch had already drawn his pistol and would probably have made good on the threat had Berchtold not stepped between them.

Little if any of this reached the second floor, where Hitler, Ludendorff, and the other leaders, deep shadows under their eyes, the stubby bristly growth of a day's beard on their faces, had closeted themselves in a private dining room not far from Korbinian Reindl's office and just a few feet away from where most of the hostages were being kept. For the moment, at least, the putschists had no interest in their prisoners. They had other worries and were arguing bitterly with each other. The group, which included Kriebel, Weber, and Scheubner-Richter, had been enlarged by Julius Streicher and Max Amann, who had rushed over from Kanal Strasse, and by Göring.

Ludendorff, stony-faced and frightening in his anger, stared glumly at a glass of red wine his stepson Heinz Pernet had brought him. Hitler, shaken by the sense of failure, was still trying to whip up everyone's zeal, but his theatrics were not having the usual effect.

The corporal and the field marshal were blaming each other. Hitler was remonstrating with Ludendorff for having trusted the triumvirs and let them go, while the general, having heard the full story of what had happened from Colonel Leupold, was reproaching the Nazi for his impetuousness in having affronted Lossow, Seisser, and Kahr with his drawn pistol and armed troopers.

Both had known from the outset that the cooperation of the army and police was a prerequisite to success, but now they faced the dilemma of either calling the entire thing off or risking bloodshed and armed confrontation with Lossow and Seisser's forces. One alternative was as unacceptable as the other.

Was there a third possibility? That question was to preoccupy the leaders for the rest of the morning, and many hare-brained plans were proffered; but meanwhile Hitler, ever the improviser, had some schemes that he moved to implement immediately.

As always, he banked on propaganda, which he felt would turn the tide back in their favor, provided his sense of Munich's mood was correct. To a large extent it was. But too shaken to harangue any crowd himself, he turned to Streicher. "Speak at every street corner and mobilize the masses," he exhorted the stocky Jew-baiter from Nürnberg. "Will you do it?" He looked at Streicher intently.

"I will," Streicher vowed, thus winning Hitler's gratitude forever.

"All right. Streicher is henceforth responsible for the entire propaganda organization." And what about all those posters and proclamations?

Amann and Göring promised to get things moving at once, sending out teams of SA to fetch them from the printers and paste them up.

Hitler realized he would also need money. The troops had to be paid if they were expected to remain loyal, and the coffers were empty. But he knew where money could be obtained quickly, in vast amounts and fresh off the presses: at two banknote shops—Parcus Brothers on Promenade Platz and E. Mühlthaler & Co. on Dachauer Strasse—where inflation marks by the quadrillions were being printed every day. And he also knew two SA battalion commanders ideally suited for a fiscal operation of this nature: Karl Beggel and Hans Knauth, both bank clerks by vocation.

"Ask them to come up here," he told Göring.

Finally he decided on another move in those early morning hours: risky, and certain to embitter Ludendorff even more, but one which, given the precarious situation, even that staunch enemy of Bavaria's Catholic Wittelsbach family would have to accept. Hitler intended to appeal to the "king," Crown Prince Rupprecht, to intercede as a mediator. It was a trump card, considering the strong monarchist emotions in Bavaria, and though he too was no friend of the monarchy, Hitler was prepared to play it in desperation. He knew that Kahr was totally loyal to the crown and would do whatever Rupprecht ordered. He also knew that the crown prince was highly sympathetic to the nationalist movement and the "patriotic leagues," especially Oberland, and would try to prevent any confrontation that might lead to their destruction. Besides, was not one of the aims of the putsch to "right the wrongs" done the crown and the late King Ludwig III by Kurt Eisner and the "November criminals"? Surely Rupprecht would honor that.

It was for this delicate mission that Hitler wanted Max Josef Neunzert. In theory, the choice was an excellent one. Neunzert, thirty-one, had belonged to Hitler's party since May 1920 and was one of his most devoted followers. He also happened to be a close personal friend of Ernst Röhm and a member of the Reichskriegsflagge Society. More important, however, he was a drinking and hunting pal of Rupprecht, part of his coterie of ex-officers from Bavaria's highlands. They were friends as much as a commoner and the pretender to an abolished throne could be. But as it turned out, the selection was disastrous.

Having indeed stopped off to chat with his father-in-law, who was visiting Munich and spending the night at the Bavarian Automobile Touring Club, Neunzert reported back to Röhm at the war ministry a few minutes after Hitler had left for the Bürgerbräukeller. So he followed his Führer by streetcar, of which only a few were running at that early hour.

It was 7:30 A.M. when he finally arrived at the beerhall, tired from the long night, to be sure, but looking noticeably fresher and crisper than the other putsch leaders.

"Ah, Herr Neunzert." Hitler was relieved to see him, but also worried about the likely impact of his words on Ludendorff, who was sitting right there, staring at his wineglass. "I have a most urgent assignment for you. Please take one of the automobiles downstairs and have yourself driven as quickly as possible to Berchtesgaden, to His Majesty, the King. Implore him, in my name, to mediate between us and Herr von Kahr, who has declared himself his governor and representative. There is imminent danger of patriotic nationalists shooting at each other. I want you to explain to him exactly what took place here yesterday evening and what has happened during the night. Impress upon him the great threat of impending misfortune and the likelihood of a national disaster. But hurry, please, for every minute counts."

Neunzert glanced fleetingly at Ludendorff and Scheubner-Richter, who had listened in total but obviously disapproving silence.

"I shall go immediately, Herr Hitler," he promised. "You can count on me."

Neunzert hurried in his own inimitable way. Discovering that there was neither a rented, requisitioned, stolen, nor party-owned car available to him just then on Rosenheimer Strasse, he walked doggedly through the falling snow to Orleans Platz and the East Side Station to wait for the next train to Berchtesgaden. It was the 8:35 express. The five-hour rail journey brought Neunzert to the picturesque mountain town near the Austrian frontier at 1:30 P.M.—nearly an hour after the onset of the bloody catastrophe he had been dispatched to prevent.

Shortly before eight o'clock, Karl Beggel and Hans Knauth of the First and Third SA battalions assembled "thirty-two of our best and most trustworthy men" on the street in front of the Bürgerbräu and ordered them to climb aboard two waiting trucks. Beggel and Knauth had selected their team well, for among the men were a number of other "monetary experts," bank employees like themselves.

"*Los!*" Beggel commanded, and the trucks rumbled down Rosenheimer Strasse, across Ludwig Bridge, through the Isar Gate, and into the center of Munich toward the printshop of Parcus Brothers near the opulent Bayerischer Hof Hotel.

There a German Reichsbank official was just taking inventory of the night's press run of "small bills"—50-billion-mark notes, each worth about 8 U.S. cents at that day's exchange rate, and all crisply new. There were larger denominations, too: in all, exactly 14 quadrillion marks, or roughly $22,200. The money was neatly stacked in piles.

"It is all confiscated in the name of the new national government," Beggel announced importantly, handing the startled official and the printshop manager a requisition order and receipt with the scrawled signature of "A. Hitler."

There were no protests from anyone—either because the Parcus staff believed, like many in Munich that morning, in the legitimacy of the "new government" or because the presence of the thirty-two armed SA toughs made resistance useless.

"How much did you say there was?" Beggel asked, then dutifully filled in the amount on the receipt, making everything "legal." He told his troopers to start loading. Groaning under the weight, they carried the loot out in boxes to one of the trucks.

"I'll take half the detachment with the money back to the Bürgerbräu," Beggel said, turning to Knauth. "You go on to the other plant."

The group split, and Knauth directed his vehicle—a beer truck "borrowed" from an Ingolstadt brewery—to the firm of E. Mühlthaler & Co. at No. 15 Dachauer Strasse.

There the night's press run was also just being counted, but "some objections" were raised by the printers, who apparently were "leftist-oriented."

"I have direct orders from the new government," Knauth said officiously, "and I also have sixteen armed men here who will enforce those orders." Yet his threats and bravado were not having the desired effect.

"This piece of paper means nothing to me. I cannot just hand over money without authorization from the police," Ludwig Eil-hauer, the plant manager, insisted, pointing out, however, that there was a blue-uniformed city patrolman assigned as a guard in the courtyard.

"Take me to him," Knauth said.

It worked like a charm. Knauth identified himself as a "representative of the new government" to Patrolman Ludwig Schrenck and invited him to come along to the Bürgerbräukeller to make sure that "everything is proper and legal."

"Well, under those circumstances, Herr Eilhauer," said Schrenck, "I see no reason to delay."

It was, surely, one of history's few bank heists carried out under police surveillance.

The haul was not quite as lucrative—"only" 12.6 quadrillion marks, or exactly $20,000. Knauth filled in the amount on the blank receipt that had been signed by Hitler and told his men to start loading.

"Are you coming along?" he asked Schrenck. The policeman hopped aboard, and the beer truck drove off in the direction of Rosenheimer Strasse and the Bürgerbräukeller. There, Knauth asked Schrenck to wait and supervise the "transfer" to Heinz Pernet.

"May I have a receipt from you that I have delivered it?" Knauth asked Ludendorff's stepson, after the crates had been neatly stacked on the bandstand in the main auditorium.

Meticulously, Pernet wrote one out.

"You see," Knauth said to Schrenck. "I told you everything is perfectly legal."

And the money? By midmorning wads of it were being doled out—2 trillion marks, or about $3.17 for each man—to the assembled SA and Oberland troopers. It was their pay for the night's services.

Of Hitler's enthusiastic followers, the Fiehler brothers—Werner, thirty-four, Otto, thirty-two, and Karl, twenty-eight—were among the most ardent. All three were in the SA: Werner and Karl in the Stosstrupp, Otto as deputy commander of the 9th Company in Hans Knauth's Third Battalion.

For all of them the morning of November 9 was a busy one,

but it started earliest for Otto when Göring ordered him out to paste up a stack of Ernst Pöhner and Wilhelm Frick's placards announcing the establishment of a summary "state tribunal" and threatening death "within three hours after the verdict" to all "enemies of the people."

Accompanied by six men "selected at random from my company," Fiehler set out for what fanatic Nazis regarded as "enemy territory"—the largely working-class and "pro-Socialist" district of Giesing.

His was one of many such teams dispatched from the Bürgerbräukeller that morning to spread the word of "Germany's awakening." But it was the misfortune of Police Inspector Otto Freiesleben and one Johann Canis, official catechist at Giesing's Holy Cross Church, to run into Fiehler's group just before eight o'clock, in the underpass beneath the railroad tracks near the corner of Pilgersheimer and Untere-Weiden Strasse.

It was a most remarkable encounter for all concerned. Freiesleben was on his way to duty at the 18th Precinct station nearby, and Canis was walking toward the parish school to teach his first religion class of the day. The two men had been casual acquaintances for many years and often met this way in the morning.

"Have you heard the latest, Herr Inspector?" Canis asked with a note of indignation to his voice. "Our government has been overthrown."

"Yes, it is terrible news," Freiesleben replied. "I first heard about it two hours ago—at the railroad station. I had to take my wife there to catch a train. Have any of the names of the new regime been announced?"

"Oh, it's all right here in the paper," said the teacher, pulling a folded copy of the *Bayerischer Kurier* from his overcoat pocket. The two sauntered into the underpass to escape the snow and the wind.

"Why, it's incredible, just incredible," the inspector mumbled, shaking his head in amazement as he read.

"Worse than that, Herr Freiesleben, worse than that," Canis said loudly—much too loudly. "It is just like the putsch in 1918. That one came from the Left; this time it is from the Right. But the principle is the same, and it is very unfortunate, for it will hurt the patriotic movement. It is just like five years—"

"Hey, you, hold your tongue! Keep your mouth shut!" Otto Fiehler interrupted him. The two had not noticed Fiehler's squad of helmeted, rifle-bearing SA come into the underpass to paste up one of the posters on the wall.

"I wasn't talking to you but with this gentleman here," Canis shot back, gesturing to Freiesleben. "Moreover, I assume I can still express my opinions."

"You are under arrest!" Fiehler shouted, grabbing Canis roughly by the coat collar and motioning to his storm troopers. "Your remarks are a provocation to the new government."

"How dare you treat me this way!" Canis retorted. "Take your hands off me! But if you think my conversation with this gentleman was a provocation to your new government, then all right, arrest me."

Freiesleben no longer doubted that they would. He tried to defuse the situation.

"I don't quite understand how you can regard this conversation between Catechist Canis and me as a provocation," he interjected calmly, "especially since he is at least as patriotic and nationally minded as you. I have known him for three years. Besides, I think you should know that he is a clergyman and you would be making a serious mistake in arresting him."

"And who are you?" Fiehler demanded arrogantly.

Freiesleben identified himself as a detective inspector and produced his papers.

"If you are a clergyman, you can go," the SA man said to Canis. Then he vented his anger on Freiesleben. "You call yourself a police inspector, yet you support this man who utters provocations against our government! Now I declare *you* under arrest. We have overthrown this rotten government that has let us all starve for five years. We don't need a Catholic government any more."

"Well, you don't have to get so worked up about it," the detective replied, "and you cannot blame me. Moreover, I think you should know that you have no legal right to arrest me."

For Fiehler, now literally frothing at the mouth, that was the epitome of "provocation." "The police have nothing more to say!" he shrieked. "All power is now in our hands. We have overthrown the government." Trembling with anger, he turned to his patrol and bellowed, "Take this man away!"

Guarded by four of Fiehler's troopers, Freiesleben was marched more than a mile to the Bürgerbräukeller's "prison."

"Keep an eye on him," one of the SA men said. "I am going to report him to the leadership."

After he had been gone for about ten minutes, Freiesleben's patience began to wear thin.

"Look, I'm supposed to be on duty at my precinct station," he said angrily to another of his guards. "Either let me go or find out what you are meant to do with me."

Another of the guards made his way through the crowd of SA and Oberländers in the vestibule. He too did not return. After another wait, the other two drifted away, leaving the police officer standing there alone. By then he was more baffled and amused than angry and went in search of the "leadership" himself.

"Upstairs in one of the dining rooms," he was told, and made his way to the second floor; there he found a sentry posted in front of the inner sanctum where Hitler and Ludendorff and the others were conferring.

"If this is the new government," he said, "I have a complaint to register."

"No one is allowed in this room," the guard said officiously.

Freiesleben identified himself as a police officer, which at least had some effect. The sentry offered to inquire inside but was back within minutes.

"I am sorry, Herr Inspector," he reported. "You cannot register your complaint now. The gentlemen do not wish to be disturbed and are accepting no appointments."

Shrugging, Freiesleben walked downstairs and out of the beerhall—to work.

The demoralizing impression that "something is wrong" was starting to penetrate even the walls of the Bürgerbräukeller, and Hitler and Göring soon realized how urgent the need was to prevent its spread.

Göring dispatched Wilhelm Brückner to "round up some music"—a band. Maybe that would help. But more energetic steps were also needed. The discerning among the putschists' rank and file, such as Oberland's Konrad Kiessling and Hans Oemler, had been harboring doubts for hours. The more gullible and fanatical were starting to get the word from various callers and messengers to the Rosenheimer Strasse command post. Measures would have to be taken to isolate the troops from any information that might cause defections.

One such bearer of gloomy tidings was a Lieutenant Spoida from the Infantry School, who visited the Bürgerbräukeller around eight o'clock looking for friends, among them Manfred Müller, a young senior lieutenant. "Look," he told Müller, "I think you ought to know you are making a mistake. You are on the wrong side. I've just come from Lossow personally, and Colonel Leupold was there. Lossow is not going along with Hitler and Ludendorff. In fact, he has called for reinforcements and will take all measures to crush this rebellion. It seems Lossow and Kahr were pressured into going along at gunpoint. You have been lied to."

Müller not only believed him but was "livid with anger over this fraud." He went looking for Gerhard Rossbach. "I'm quitting and going home," he told the erstwhile free-corps leader. "But I'm also going to tell some of the others in my company what is going on."

"No, you're not," Rossbach said gruffly, barring Müller's way into the main auditorium where the officer candidates and students were bivouacked with hundreds of storm troopers. "Get out of here if you want; that's your privilege. But you are not speaking to any of the men."

Müller, Spoida, and a couple of other defectors left the beer-hall and returned to the Infantry School to report their repudiation of the putsch to Leupold and General Tieschowitz. For them, the "nationalist revolution" was over. For others, such as Hans Block, Siegfried Mahler, and Robert Wagner, the worst was yet to come.

Block, too, had begun to doubt, especially after the debacle at Kahr's headquarters on Maximilian Strasse. Several times during the long night as the battalion of officer students had marched purposelessly through the city from one inane assignment to the next, he had confronted Rossbach and asked him to "put the cards on the table." But each time Rossbach had reassured him that "everything is in order, trust me."

In the morning Block challenged him again with the rumors that were spreading.

"Lieutenant Block," Rossbach said testily and with mock indignation, "I have given you my word of honor several times that everything is all right. That should be enough. I will give it to you again." But even Rossbach questioned whether his persistent lying and reassurance would suffice to hold the cadets in line. He asked Hitler to intervene personally—with a speech.

The harangue the Nazi leader delivered in the main auditorium to his own troops and the student officers was one of the most effective of his early career. "It is your patriotic duty to follow His Excellency General Ludendorff wherever he leads you," he declaimed. "Those who doubt, those who question, are free now to leave this room!"

He paused dramatically. No one left.

"Now," he continued, "I will call upon each of you to swear an oath of loyalty and obedience to the leader of Germany's new national army, to Ludendorff, the man who will guide us to renewed greatness!"

And swear they did in that foul-smelling beerhall.

Shortly after this desperate ceremony, Putzi Hanfstaengl—having had a reasonable night's sleep, a solid breakfast, and looking refreshed—returned to the Bürgerbräukeller from his Schwabing apartment.

He was surprised by the appearance of Ludendorff, dressed in the same jacket in which Scheubner-Richter had delivered him nearly twelve hours before. Hitler still had the Browning in a holster belted around his trenchcoat. Had they really been up all night? They certainly looked it. The air in the second-floor room, much to the discomfort of Hitler, a nonsmoker, was filled with cigar and cigarette fumes.

On his arrival, Hanfstaengl had noticed the piles of marks that Beggel and Knauth had confiscated. He eyed the money longingly, needing some desperately—his "hospitality" the previous evening had left him without a pfennig in his pocket.

He was even more surprised by the band that Brückner had found. The musicians had demanded first breakfast and payment

in advance, neither of which they had been given. Instead, Brückner had ordered them onto the platform to play. There they were,
"tootling away without any life to the music, even making a hash
of Hitler's favorite *Badenweiler* march."

Slowly Hanfstaengl began to piece together the story of what
had happened during the night. It was what he had feared. Now
what? Plans were being batted back and forth, but the leaders
were undecided as to what to do next.

"The most important thing is the mood of the public," Hitler
said, turning to Hanfstaengl. "Please go out and look around—
keep me informed about the general feeling and the atmosphere
in the city."

Interlude VI

A *Tissue of Disconnected Accidents*

At 7:45 A.M., a messenger arrived at Ett Strasse and rushed up to the offices where Colonel Josef Banzer and Major Sigmund von Imhoff, both exhausted from the long, tense night, were in conference with Friedrich Tenner, a high-ranking civil servant in the Bavarian ministry of interior and the State Police, who was now in charge.

In the courier's hand was the proclamation from Gustav von Kahr condemning the putsch and announcing his ban on the Nazi party, the Oberland League, and the Reichskriegsflagge. It was written in ink and closed with Kahr's name, but it did not have his personal signature, familiar to Tenner and the two police officers. The three could not know that Kahr had indeed composed it hours earlier, with the assistance of the *Münchener Zeitung's* Adolf Schiedt.

They had good cause to be skeptical about its authenticity. Several hours earlier, Helmut Klotz, one of Julius Streicher's aides from Nürnberg, had been in to see Imhoff, Banzer, and Police Inspector Siegfried Herrmann, asking for a police approval stamp on the text of a poster proclaiming the revolution and purportedly signed by Kahr. Recognizing the penciled signature as a forgery, the police officers had refused permission to have it printed and distributed. They did not know that Klotz, Philipp Bouhler, and Max Amann had given another copy of the text to printshop owner Ferdinand Schreiber at Kanal Strasse anyway, or that it would soon be pasted up by squads of SA all over Munich. Now, quite logically, they suspected the new proclamation as another fake.

Thus began one of the disconnected accidents of the morning

that wove the tissue of history.

Tenner spent almost half an hour on the phone before ascertaining that the text was genuine. As usual, the few lines to the communications shed at the 19th Infantry Barracks were busy. Meanwhile, Imhoff called the printing plant of Knorr & Hirth, publishers of the *Münchner Neueste Nachrichten,* to arrange for 1,000 posters with the proclamation. He asked the foreman, Georg Gross, to come over and pick up the copy, emphasizing that speedy printing and distribution of the placards was a matter of top priority.

Gross arrived as requested, but when he saw the copy he was to set in type he was skeptical. All the news he had read that morning was in his own paper, and it had spread the story of the successful putsch and Kahr's cooperation over its entire front page. The text Tenner was showing him said the opposite. But Tenner assured him it was correct—he had just spoken to von Kahr personally.

Forty-five minutes later, Gross returned with a proof of the placard to have it checked for corrections. He then went back to the plant on nearby Sendlinger Strasse, a five-minute walk, and ordered the form locked up and the press started.

When, at 9 A.M., the posters had not been delivered, Tenner phoned Gross. He was told he could have eighty or ninety advance copies immediately by messenger. A half hour elapsed before the messenger arrived, explaining that the police building had been suddenly surrounded by Nazi storm troopers, that Kaufinger Strasse was filled with them, and that he had been forced to take a circuitous detour to reach Ett Strasse.

The events on the street, the messenger's delay, and some questions from one of his pressmen started serious doubts gnawing at foreman Gross. In 1919 he had once been forced to flee for his life from Munich because a revolutionary tribunal wanted to put him on trial for printing a proclamation not to its liking. He no longer trusted anyone. It was 10 A.M.; some 500 posters had come off the press. Gross decided not to print any more and called Tenner to announce his decision.

"I have just been looking out my window to the street," he said, "and if you will look out of yours, I think you'll agree that the political situation is currently too uncertain. I don't want to take the risk entailed in printing the wrong thing."

"If you refuse," Tenner replied, "we will send police over to the plant to force you to print."

The threat was enough, apparently, to start the press again, but it was close to 11 A.M. before the finished posters were delivered to Ett Strasse. Which was not to say, however, that they were even then distributed. Some twenty blue-uniformed municipal police, armed with carbines, were detailed to paste up Kahr's repudiatory proclamation, but the truck assigned to them would not start. A vehicle had to be borrowed from the State Police. Thus, it was almost noon before any of the posters explaining the new situation were visible, and then only in those sections of the city left of the Isar River where the Nazis and putschists were not in control.

Similar mishaps also prevented speedy distribution of the proclamation by Vice-Premier Franz Matt and the rump cabinet which had fled to Regensburg during the night.

Welfare Minister Heinrich Oswald had not made the journey with Matt but had remained in his Munich apartment to maintain telephone contact with the others. Early in the morning he had gotten in touch with the Hartl & Pierling Company to run off 1,000 copies of Matt's proclamation.

Later he called Ett Strasse with instructions to pick up the posters from the printers and distribute them, so Detective Inspector Rudolf Schmäling, who had returned to duty that morning, accompanied by Inspector Fritz Neeb, went to the plant. The posters were ready and waiting, neatly bundled on a table, but the manager refused to turn them over.

"I have strict instructions from Minister Oswald's office," he said, "not to release these to anyone who does not have a written authorization from the ministry."

Almost two hours of frantic telephoning followed. Oswald could not be reached, either in his office or at his home or in any other government ministry. Nor was his deputy available. Calls went back and forth between the printshop, police headquarters, and the welfare ministry, with the manager listening in on an extension line.

The phone conversations finally convinced him that the two police officers did have legitimate authority to pick up the placards, but it was 10:45 before he agreed to release them, and then only on condition that Schmäling and Neeb sign a receipt freeing him of any blame or responsibility.

Thus Franz Matt's appeal to the people of Bavaria to resist the putsch, drafted nearly twelve hours earlier, was finally delivered to Ett Strasse at eleven o'clock. Distribution began, but haphazardly, as was the case with Kahr's proclamation.

The extent to which the delay in distribution of both announcements really influenced the mood and events in Munich the morning of November 9 remains a matter of speculation. But there can be no question that Müncheners would have reacted differently had it not been for another "disconnected accident" which contributed immeasurably to the reigning confusion: Adolf Schiedt's failure to stop the publication of the morning newspapers. His own *Münchener Zeitung* was a midday paper, for which typesetting normally did not start until 6 A.M. and which usually did not appear on the streets until around 10.

Thus, as people went to work that morning, they bought the *Münchner Neueste Nachrichten* and the *Bayerischer Kurier*, not to mention the Nazis' own *Völkischer Beobachter*—all of which announced the putsch and the new government in banner headlines with the biggest typefaces available.

Hitler himself could not have arranged for a propaganda effort more to his advantage, and the impact was immense, as the case of foreman Gross at the Knorr & Hirth printing plant demonstrated. It was even greater on some of the putschists, especially those who had begun to have doubts, such as Konrad Kiessling.

When, around 8 A.M., Kiessling's platoon was called out of the Stuck Villa to patrol along the Isar and secure the bridges, he stepped out of the ranks on the way to buy the *Neueste Nachrichten*, paying the vendor 10 billion marks. Avidly he read the details of the events in the Bürgerbräukeller.

"It was the first time I got a clear picture," he said later, "and I was elated. Now I no longer questioned that I might be doing something illegal. As we passed a detachment of State Police at Maximilian Bridge, they cheered us in a most friendly fashion and we exchanged shouted greetings."

The early edition of the *Neueste Nachrichten* had a similar effect on Heinrich Bennecke, Wilhelm Brückner's adjutant. Having gotten Brückner's permission to leave the Bürgerbräukeller to go home for "an hour or so to wash up and have a proper breakfast," he too bought a copy of the paper and read the colorful report of what had transpired in the beerhall.

"The contents of the paper," he explained, "merely reinforced my belief that the new national government which had been declared was legitimate and that I was acting legally in its service."

And so it was for tens of thousands of Müncheners that morning. That Kahr had changed his mind, that he had called the putsch an "act of treason" whose perpetrators he intended to "prosecute and punish ruthlessly," was not known to the people of Munich until Schiedt's *Münchener Zeitung* began appearing on the streets after ten o'clock and the police started pasting up proclamations after eleven. By then the signals had been set and the switches thrown for a collision course.

FOUR

The Plan Revised

15

The 640,000 inhabitants of Munich awakened on the dismal morning of November 9, 1923, to find their world dramatically changed.

Those who had not yet heard of the night's events—and they were by far the majority—were rudely confronted with the news at almost every corner of the city: by the headlines on the papers being sold and the proclamations the SA had posted on hundreds of advertising pillars and walls; by the swastikas and red-white-and black imperial flags flying from many house fronts; by the squads of storm troopers marching noisily through the streets and the platoons of green-uniformed State Police grimly guarding the railroad station, the central telegraph office, the main telephone exchange, and key government buildings; by the barbed-wire barriers Ernst Röhm had hastily ordered at his war ministry command post on the corner of Schönfeld and Ludwig Strasse; and by the machine-gun nests and howitzer emplacements at the bridges across the Isar River.

Though only a few shots had been fired, the loudest of which undoubtedly was Hitler's into the ceiling of the Bürgerbräukeller, there was the tense foreboding of war in the air—civil war.

And yet in many respects the city was quite normal, almost impervious to the unfolding drama, thick-skinned in a stolid Bavarian way—like the lederhosen and the loden coats that were the popular local garb. As usual, streetcars clattered and clanged their way through the narrow, cobblestoned streets and along the broad majestic avenues and boulevards that King Ludwig I had planned to give his capital sophistication. Cars, trucks, horse-drawn wagons, pushcarts, and bicycles created a jumble of traffic. On the Viktualienmarkt, the vegetable stands and butcher stalls were open for business. Even the bearded, pipe-smoking early imbibers were at their customary tables in the cavernous ground-floor *Schwemme*, the "trough" of the famous Hofbräuhaus, quaffing their quart-sized steins of beer.

At 8 A.M. many people were already at work, including Professor Ferdinand Sauerbruch, who had completed his first operation at the University Hospital. And those not yet at work were on their way.

Dr. Hans Ehard, the assistant prosecutor, was so engrossed reading about the putsch as the trolley he was riding passed the corner of Schönfeld Strasse that he did not even notice the barricades erected there by Heinrich Himmler, Count Moulin-Eckart, Theodor Casella, and other members of the Reichskriegsflagge.

But Ehard was soon confronted with the realities of the revolution. As he got off at Karlsplatz, the Stachus, and walked across the square to his office in the Palace of Justice, he was taken aback by the sight of two sentries "in shabby-looking uniforms" standing in front of the building, bayonets implanted on their rifles.

"What are you doing here?" he asked.

"We are guarding the justice ministry against counterrevolutionaries," they replied.

Ehard could barely control his laughter. The whole thing was more amusing than menacing, he thought—until he got inside. There, on the ground floor, some colleagues from the ministry of justice and the prosecuting staff were gathered around a huge poster "threatening immediate execution to all enemies of the people and revolution." The others were debating heatedly what to do about it.

"Just tear it down," Ehard suggested.

"But, *Herr Kollege*," they explained, "we cannot do that without permission from the minister."

"Well, ask him," Ehard said innocently.

"You mean you haven't heard?" one of the officials asked

incredulously. "Herr Gürtner was taken prisoner last night in the Bürgerbräu, along with Prime Minister von Knilling, Interior Minister Schweyer, and Herr Wutzelhofer. No one knows where they are being kept."

The news came as a shock to Ehard. Perhaps, he thought, this putsch was not a joke after all. Anger swelled in him. Swiftly he tore the placard down, crumpled it up, tipped his hat to his dumbfounded colleagues, climbed the stairs to his office, and reported to his boss, Ludwig Stenglein.

For Hans Ehard it was the beginning of a very long day.

Dr. Wilhelm Hoegner, too, did not learn the details of the putsch until he had bought a copy of the *Neueste Nachrichten* after leaving his Schelling Strasse apartment. He had advised Erhard Auer to stay there for a while—"until we have a clearer picture of what is going on." That there were no copies of the *Münchener Post* was in no way unusual, since it was a midday and afternoon paper, and the first edition was not due for another few hours.

Hoegner went to his office in the courthouse in the Au district, but it was immediately apparent to him that work "in the normal sense" would be impossible that day. The night's events were all his fellow prosecutors could talk about.

Moreover, Hoegner's chief, Johann Appelmann, was concerned for his safety. "You are an excellent jurist," Appelmann explained, "and you would have a promising career ahead of you if you didn't dabble in the wrong politics. This morning your politics are so wrong that I think you are running a personal risk in being here. May I suggest that you take the day off."

It was a prudent suggestion, for only an hour or so after Hoegner had departed, the Nazis came around to arrest him too. His association with Auer and the Social Democratic party was not as unknown to them as Hoegner had thought.

For young Ludwig Hümmert, the morning had a personally disconcerting tone. The family argument, after his father had returned so full of enthusiasm from the Bürgerbräukeller, had been long and it still gnawed at him. To him the Nazi putsch seemed no different from the Communist one of 1919, after Eisner's assassination. Why couldn't his father see through this Herr Hitler and his demagoguery?

Hümmert decided to make a personal display of his political sympathies and convictions. Putting on his overcoat to go to school, he hesitated a moment and then went back into his room. There he took a little black-red-and-gold emblem off his dresser— the pin of the pro-Weimar "Republican Reichsbund" which he had joined—and stuck it on his lapel.

Defiantly, he walked out of the apartment house on Herzogspital Strasse, but he did not get far.

"Hey, look, there's one of those swine," a group of SA standing on the corner jeered. "See the dirty colors on his coat? Hey, *Sozi!* The flag as of today is black, red, and *white*. Take that thing off fast!"

They were surrounding Hümmert. But he slipped out of their clutches, ran back into the house, and bolted the door. He would not go to school after all.

Hostility permeated the air that morning for everyone in Munich known to be Hitler's enemies, among whom Father Rupert Mayer of St. Michael's Church on Neuhauser Strasse was notorious.

Square-jawed Father Mayer was a born fighter, and insofar as a man of God could, he had fought—as a chaplain and medical corpsman during the war, from which he returned with a wooden leg. He was also a staunch German and Bavarian patriot.

He was not a clergyman who dabbled in politics gladly, but God and country were the two poles of his life, and when he regarded either as threatened he felt compelled to speak out. The first time he spoke was against communism at a meeting of the embryonic Nazi party in late 1919. Hitler had followed him on the platform, and at first the priest was impressed by the ex-corporal. But it did not take him long to recognize the agitator for what he really was.

The initial break between them had come after one of Hitler's earliest mass meetings in the Hofbräuhaus. Asked his opinion of the Nazi leader by the enthusiastic audience, the hot-blooded padre mounted the stage and said flatly, "Herr Hitler is an excellent public speaker, but he is none too careful of the truth." He had to flee the beerhall.

While Hitler agitated, Father Mayer became increasingly active in the "patriotic movement" but always kept his distance from the Nazis, in particular when he recognized the strident anti-Catholicism of Hitler's message.

Early in 1923, at a mass rally in the Bürgerbräukeller, the ex-corporal and the ex-chaplain moved onto a collision course. "I am going to tell you quite clearly," the Reverend Mayer said from the platform as Hitler glowered at him, "a German Catholic can never be a National Socialist." He was shouted down and out of the hall by the assembly of Hitler's mesmerized followers, who, after that, passed up no opportunity to agitate against the priest.

Having read mass as usual on the morning of November 9, Father Mayer went out on Neuhauser Strasse to test the mood of the city he loved. Never before in his life, he was to recall years later, had he encountered "so many hostile glances" on the streets.

The historian who not only witnesses but becomes a part of history ought, by rights, to regard himself as especially fortunate. Yet Karl Alexander von Müller was brooding.

He had gone to the university as usual to deliver his regular schedule of lectures. But the atmosphere among the students and his fellow professors, most of them ultra-conservative nationalists like himself, was an unreal one of such high elation, almost a frenzy of patriotic ardor, that any normal teaching program was out of the question. Munich's academic community was virtually unanimous in its support of the putsch.

In that sense, von Müller was no exception, though, unlike many of the others, he was no admirer of either Hitler or Ludendorff. But the doubts and concerns over the consequences that had gnawed at him the previous evening when he left the Bürgerbräukeller continued to plague him. They mounted sharply as rumors began spreading that the triumvirs had repudiated the coup and were intending to crush it with armed force.

It was as though von Müller were seeing a rerun of the scenes in Munich five years earlier. He recalled the words in his mind at the time: "a world in transformation." This time the change was even more radical, and there seemed to be nothing he or anyone else could do except watch helplessly.

Whatever thoughts may have troubled Thomas Mann that morning he kept to himself. It was all too unpleasant, too repugnant for this aesthete, and he followed his usual unwavering routine: breakfast with Katja, then off to his study and his desk by nine o'clock.

Like many great writers, he was meticulous about keeping a diary in which he recorded his moods, thoughts, and experiences. Yet he made no entries for November 8 and 9, 1923. Why? Some say he loved Munich too much and was too pained that morning by what he regarded as an "aberration." He did not want to set his emotions down on paper.

To Carl Zuckmayer, the young playwright working at the Schauspielhaus, the streets of Munich seemed like the stage for a drama written by a sorcerer. In his months of living in the Bavarian capital and on his periodic visits there he had stood at the rear of many of Hitler's rallies and mass meetings, not to cheer but to watch, both fascinated and repelled. As a man of the theater, he recognized in the Nazi leader "a real professional."

Zuckmayer was drawn by "Hitler's ability to put masses into a trance like the medicine man of some barbarian tribe." Now he was seeing the first fruit of the seeds of hatred and violence, envy and frustration, which Hitler had sown.

And yet, as he made his way to the theater on Maximilian Strasse past von Kahr's tightly guarded headquarters, he was also struck by the feeling that to many Müncheners it was just "*noch oa Gaudi*," another of the shows these Bavarians loved. Be it the annual Oktoberfest, *Fasching* and Mardi Gras, or a coup d'état and revolution, they wanted action for its own sake; the spectacle was what counted. And with the police, the storm troopers, the knots of discussing people on every street corner, the Nazi banners flying, that was certainly what they were getting this morning.

Heinrich Hoffmann looked with irritation at the leaden sky from his studio window and watched the wet snow falling. It was no day for photographing, he knew, cursing his bad luck. But he also knew he would have to get out there, for history was being made. Besides, the illustrated weeklies and journals such as *Die Woche* would be demanding pictures.

He loaded as many plates of film into his case as it would hold, mounted an old bicycle, and pedaled down Ludwig Strasse, stopping first at the corner of Schönfeld Strasse and the war ministry to snap a shot of Heinrich Himmler, flag in hand, and other members of Röhm's contingent. They were standing grimly and defiantly behind the rolls of concertina wire and the barriers they had erected.

From there Hoffmann cycled quickly toward Marienplatz, arriving to see the famous central square in front of Munich's neo-Gothic City Hall filled with a crowd of many thousands that brought traffic, including streetcars, to a standstill. All eyes seemed glued on a bare-headed, bald little man, standing on the back seat of an open car, several helmeted, rifle-bearing storm troopers around him as guards. It was Julius Streicher, haranguing the multitude with a rasping tirade against Jews, Communists, Socialists, Ebert, Stresemann, and that "den of iniquity in Berlin."

Elbowing his way through the press of humanity, Hoffmann reached the base of the Mariensäule, a Baroque column with the figure of the Madonna atop. There he climbed halfway up and took what he later regarded, justifiably, as one of his most important historical pictures.

Hang the weather, he thought. The city was literally bursting with dramatic events to record for posterity.

Paula Schlier was exhausted when she returned to work at the *Völkischer Beobachter* at 9 A.M. She had stayed until 6 o'clock and gone home only to catch a short nap, wash up, and have some breakfast. She could barely keep her eyes open as she operated the central switchboard at the party paper, its red, green, and yellow lights blinking constantly.

The place was in pandemonium, the mood a mixture of defiant hope set against the gloom. Calls with anxious questions were streaming in incessantly. "What has happened?" "Is it true Kahr has reneged?" "Where is Hitler?" "Where is our savior?" "A traitor? Oh, no, it is Kahr who is the traitor!" "Kahr and Lossow are just putting on an act to calm the French—they're really still all for the march on Berlin." Callers by the scores, by the hundreds, still believed that the putsch was a success and that the SA would march any minute. Wives called looking for their husbands, mothers for their sons, all convinced of the rightness of the cause.

The offices were crowded with foreign correspondents—Italian, British, French, Danish, and American. Putzi Hanfstaengl was trying to assuage and calm them. Larry Rue and Lincoln Eyre besieged him with questions and demands for interviews with Hitler and Ludendorff.

"If you can't get us in to see them," Rue insisted, "then who the hell can? You're supposed to be the press chief."

"Besides," Eyre interjected, "where is your revolution this morning? Where are Kahr and Lossow? What's with this so-called new government and march on Berlin?"

"Well," Hanfstaengl said with his permanent smile, trying to cover up his own worries, "a few personal differences have arisen between some of the leaders, and they are settling them now. I think I can get you an interview in an hour or so."

The turmoil of downtown Munich did not reach Obermenzing. That sedate suburb of tree-lined streets and expensive new houses on the city's northwestern edge was so quiet and peaceful it might have been in another world. But Carin Göring, tossing and turning in her bed, was not quiet or peaceful. Was it the fever she was still running, or a kind of intuition?

Hanfstaengl had phoned during the night, reported on the events in the Bürgerbräu, and told her that Göring—"*mein lieber guter Hermann,*" as she always called him—would not be home.

Carin Göring had taken that news with equanimity, not to mention pride in her husband's achievements. But now she had a premonition that the "national awakening for which my dear, good Hermann had worked so long and arduously" was headed for disaster.

Count Josef Maria Soden, Crown Prince Rupprecht's chef-du-cabinet, awoke with a start to the knock on his "cell" door in the villa of Julius Lehmann in Grosshesselohe. "*Herrein!*" he called instinctively, not quite certain where he was or how he had gotten there. He fumbled for his watch—8:30 A.M. It was barely light outside. Then he remembered. He had been taken prisoner. Through the window he saw the helmeted SA men patrolling in the garden.

"Your breakfast, Excellency," said one of Lehmann's daughters, entering the frigid little ground-floor guestroom with a cup of steaming hot coffee and some wurst and cheese sandwiches on dark rye bread. "We were not quite prepared for so many visitors," she apologized.

Through the door she had left ajar, Soden saw another storm trooper standing guard in the hallway and eyeing him suspiciously. It was so cold, Soden decided to stay under the quilt and breakfast in bed. But as he sipped the coffee and munched his food, his mind began clicking. Someone had to be notified of their whereabouts, especially the king. But how?

Similar thoughts were racing through Justice Minister Franz Gürtner's head in his room upstairs. After the light breakfast, he called for his "host." "I do not know what your role in all of this is, Herr Lehmann," Gürtner said indignantly, "but I want to know why I am being kept prisoner here and on whose orders. I would like to transmit an open letter to von Kahr. Can you arrange it?"

That, Lehmann explained, would be up to the "lieutenant in charge"—Rudolf Hess—who, indeed, soon gave his approval, provided the message contained neither the names of the other six high-ranking prisoners nor any clue as to where they were being kept.

The letter left no doubt that Gürtner at least believed von Kahr and Hitler were conspirators together.

> Your Excellency,
> I have the honor to inform you that yesterday evening I and other gentlemen were brought to a house outside the city and that we are being detained here under strictest solitary confinement. I should like to ask your Excellency whether this action has your consent. If so, I beg to know the reasons for my detention. If not, I should like to ask your Excellency for a speedy clarification and decision.

Hess studied the note carefully. There seemed no harm in it. He called for his driver, Michael Ried, who together with the other SA guards had spent the night encamped on the sofas and the floor in the Lehmann family's huge parlor.

"Take this to Captain Göring in the Bürgerbräukeller," Hess said. "It should be transmitted to Excellency von Kahr. You and the car may be needed for other things there. We have two more cars here, but telephone if you think it is going to take long."

Saluting snappily, Ried put the letter into his tunic pocket and left the secluded suburban house where half of Bavaria's cabinet, Munich's police chief and his aide, and Count Soden were being held prisoner. He was, indeed, needed for "other things" at the Bürgerbräukeller.

The acrid odor of stale cigar and cigarette smoke filled the communications shed of the 19th Infantry Regiment. The triumvirs were drained with fatigue, in particular Gustav von Kahr, whose bullish head kept nodding deeper toward his chest, only to jerk up, startled, whenever the telephone rang.

For hours it had been largely a matter of waiting—for reinforcements to arrive, for scouts to return with a clearer picture. From a tactical military viewpoint, the situation in the city was not as bleak at daybreak as it may have seemed to Kahr, Lossow, and Seisser during the night. With the exception of the war ministry and the Infantry School, all military installations, vital government buildings, and communications and transportation centers remained in their hands. Putschist control was limited largely to the Bürgerbräukeller and the right-bank districts.

But in their self-imposed isolation at the Infantry Barracks, the three were oblivious to the public mood in the city, inflamed by Hitler's propaganda efforts. Moreover, they were also isolated from the rest of Germany and Berlin. That President Ebert had named Hans von Seeckt military dictator and commander-in-chief during the night, that all rail traffic and telecommunications to and from Bavaria had been cut off—those were developments the triumvirs were not to learn for many more hours.

Since 2:55 A.M., wireless messages confirming the trio's repudiation of the putsch had been transmitted periodically to all radio receiving stations in the country. The last one, at 5:30, had announced that the Reichswehr and State Police were in control of the situation and that the city was quiet. Oddly, none of these calls had been heard in Berlin.

Indeed, it was not until 7:30 that Captain von Hanneken, General Kressenstein's adjutant, managed to place a call from Regensburg to Berlin to apprise Seeckt's chief of operations, Lieutenant Colonel Joachim von Stülpnagel, of the situation in Munich and to reassure him that Lossow had enough forces at his disposal to put down the coup without outside help.

By then, too, Lossow and Jakob von Danner were finally ready to act. At 7:40, orders left the little communications shack to recapture the war ministry. Von Danner was in command of the operation, and he had both Reichswehr and State Police reinforcements at his disposal to do the job. The plan called for encircling the building and demanding that Röhm disarm his troops and surrender. Force was to be used only if Röhm refused and resisted.

But armies move slowly by nature, even more so when their heart is not in their work. Von Danner's was no exception. Besides the predictable delays of mobilization that result when orders must be channeled through lower-echelon chains of command, there was resistance from those officers who were open sympathizers or supporters of the Nazis, and hesitation from those repelled by the possibility that they might have to "fire on men who are really our comrades-in-arms."

Captain Eduard Dietl, for example, a radical spokesman for Hitler, declared categorically in those morning hours that he would "never shoot at Ludendorff." On the other hand, there were men such as Senior Lieutenant Max Braun, who had taken Alexander Siry into custody during the night and locked him up. He was as emphatically opposed to the Hitlerites as Dietl was for them, and announced categorically that he would "open fire on anyone who resists me, no matter who he is." For most of the company and battalion commanders being lined up to carry out the operation, it was a crisis of conscience. Even those who were not overt sympathizers with the putschist cause were torn between loyalty to their friends on the rebel side and their sense of soldierly duty to obey orders. For some, the crisis was unmanageable. One of these was Lieutenant Emil Werner, commander of a company of reservists, most of them Munich University students. "I cannot order my men to shoot at their brothers and friends," he told Major Hans Schönharl, asking that he be relieved of his command and that his company be disbanded. The request was granted.

The debates and discussions were prolonged, heated, and agonizing. Though the order had been given at 7:40 A.M., four more hours were to pass before the mixed force of Reichswehr and State Police—some 1,600 men in all, backed by armored cars and light artillery—moved out of the Oberwiesenfeld area and the Türken Strasse barracks toward Ernst Röhm's command post at the war ministry.

Almost as many hours passed before Colonel Hans von Seisser's green-uniformed State Police were out with any appreciable force, and then it was largely to guard a few major buildings and streets and the Isar bridges against further incursions by SA and Oberland to the left bank and into the center of the city. As late as 11 A.M., City Hall, Ett Strasse, the central telegraph, the main telephone exchange, the railroad station, all of downtown Munich, and even Kahr's abandoned headquarters were still there for the putschists' taking—if Hitler, Ludendorff, Kriebel, and Göring had wanted to use a little force and run the risk of an armed confrontation, for they were still clearly numerically superior and had the greater firepower. But confrontation was neither Hitler's nor Ludendorff's plan—at least not yet.

Mixed emotions and divided sympathies also hampered Seisser to some extent, until his Munich battalion was bolstered by reinforcements from other cities and towns.

In its sense of duty and personal commitment to him, its founder, the State Police was a much more cohesive and politically reliable force than Lossow's Seventh Division. Nor had it been as widely subverted and infiltrated by Nazi agents as had Munich's municipal police. To be sure, there were overt Hitler sympathizers such as Lieutenant Gerhard von Prosch and covert ones such as Captain Rudolf Schraut. But the majority of officers thought like Josef Banzer, Wilhelm Muxel, Sigmund von Imhoff, Franz Hunglinger, and Karl Wild—politically far right, yes, but opposed to the fanaticism of the disorderly Nazi mob and to a coup d'état. At worst, those among them who wavered were like Lieutenant Colonel Karl Schnitzlein or Lieutenant Georg Höfler from Landshut, both of whom felt honor-bound to carry out orders. All they really wanted were orders to obey and a clear reading on whether to regard the putschists as friends or foes.

Since those orders had been so slow in coming, there naturally was confusion, which culminated in scenes of State Police detachments and contingents of storm troopers cheering each other when they met on patrols during those morning hours. Appreciably, the confusion was intensified for officers such as Höfler, who not only had a friend—Heinrich Himmler—but relatives—the Strasser brothers—on the other side.

Höfler was still waiting for orders after he had arrived with his men in Munich and gotten them fed and bivouacked at the Türken Strasse police barracks. At 10 A.M. he finally received instructions to take two of his platoons and a machine-gun squad to Ludwig Bridge, beneath the Bürgerbräukeller, and guard it. But even those orders were ambiguous.

Yes, guard the bridge, he was told. "But if there are any patrols of National Socialists already there when you arrive, just position your men next to them. Should any detachments of National Socialists approach and want to cross, ask them politely to take a different route. All other traffic can pass. Bloodshed must be avoided."

Had Gregor Strasser then again asked Höfler, "Are you for or against us?" his brother-in-law would still have been justified in replying, "I don't know yet."

For Senior Lieutenant Michael von Godin, there was no conflict of loyalty to duty or to family and friends—which was not to say, however, that he was any the less confused. Throughout the night there had been contradictory rumors about the events in the Bürgerbräukeller, but superior officers whom he had called for clarification "did not really know what was going on."

At 8 A.M., he called the roll and assembled his company of State Police in the richly decorated Kaiserhof, the main courtyard of the Residenz, ordering them to stack the rifles with which they had slept all night into pyramids and "to stay close to them."

More precise information of the previous evening's events in the Bürgerbräukeller did reach him as the morning wore on, and also the news that Hitler's forces were camped at the beerhall and that Röhm's occupied the nearby war ministry. But it was a quiet morning, with no orders to move.

At one point, getting bored, Baron von Godin went in search of Lieutenant Colonel Wilhelm Muxel, whose office was close to his own in the State Police command post within the Residenz. "What are we supposed to do, *Herr Oberstleutnant?*" he asked. "My men are getting restless."

"I am not quite certain myself," Muxel replied. "Stay on duty, I suppose. And wait."

16

The ex-corporal and the general stared glumly at each other as their co-conspirators looked on with chagrin and embarrassment. Sheer fatigue was beginning to tell. The arguments and debates of the last few hours had frayed nerves and worn tempers thin. To Hermann Kriebel it was obvious; "the situation is hopeless." He pleaded for an orderly retreat—perhaps to Rosenheim, 35 miles to the southwest, from where a new beginning could be made. Simultaneously he wanted to prepare defenses along the river and around the beerhall to cover the withdrawal. But Hitler and Ludendorff would not even hear of it: the warlord because he "did not want the national revolution to bog down ignominiously in the mud of country roads"; the ex-corporal because he still believed in the power of propaganda and felt he could turn events in his favor by mobilizing the masses of Munich.

To do so, he needed a real base. He could not work from the Bürgerbräukeller or by holding impromptu rallies on street corners. The police station was still his goal. But what had happened to Ernst Pöhner? More than three hours had passed since he had dispatched the "prime minister" to Ett Strasse, and there had been no word from him except that a contingent of Oberländers had been rebuffed by the State Police guarding the doors. If Oberland could not do the job, Hitler reasoned, he had a unit that could: Josef Berchtold's Stosstrupp.

"*Los, los, los!*" the tobacconist commanded. "Everybody out. *Macht schnell!*"

Ludwig Schmied and Wilhelm Briemann, Hans Kallenbach

and Heinrich von Knobloch, Emil Maurice and Josef Gerum, Hans Krüger and Walter Hewel, Karl and Werner Fiehler, and a hundred other men wearing the death's-head insignia scrambled from their tables and makeshift cots to assemble on Rosenheimer Strasse.

It was 9 A.M. and Patrolman Karl Spreng's misfortune to be on the street at the time. Spreng had reported to duty punctually at the 17th Precinct station that morning and been told by the desk sergeant of an order from headquarters to remove and destroy all posters with forged signatures by Gustav von Kahr and all proclamations declaring the establishment of a state tribunal.

He was walking his beat near the Bürgerbräukeller when he spotted two of the placards freshly pasted to an advertising pillar on a pedestrian island at the corner of Rosenheimer and Stein Strasse. Patrolman Christian Kreppel was standing in the intersection, directing traffic as usual.

"*Guten Morgen Kollege Kreppel,*" Spreng said cheerily. "Can you give me a hand? See those posters over there? There is an order from Ett Strasse to take that stuff down."

Kreppel knew nothing of that but was willing to help. Together, the two blue-uniformed police began tearing away at the hastily attached signs, unaware that they were being watched by members of the Stosstrupp assembling just a few yards away.

"Herr Berchtold, look!" Johann Wegelin stammered. "Look at those two up there on the corner. Aren't they taking down our proclamations?"

"Get them!" Berchtold commanded, and fifty of his troopers rushed to the intersection, surrounding Spreng and Kreppel.

"You are under arrest for damaging the property of the new government," Berchtold announced. The two were disarmed, led as prisoners back to the Bürgerbräukeller, and turned over to Hermann Göring.

"Now, let's go, men," Berchtold repeated.

Three platoons of the Stosstrupp, a couple of machine guns in their midst, double-timed down Rosenheimer Strasse toward the police building.

"You want to know what this new government will do?" Julius Streicher screeched to the multitude gathered around him on

Marienplatz. "I will tell you what it is going to do. It will hang the Jewish profiteers from the lampposts. It will close the stock exchanges, those dirty Jewish dens of exploitation, and it will nationalize the banks!"

Thousands of voices roared their approval.

"The new government will also give you bread," Streicher continued. "Adolf Hitler, our great leader, has already put behind bars those men who have robbed and plundered us. Minister Schweyer is already in the very same bleak cell in Stadelheim Prison where he once put Adolf Hitler. It is a sign that the time of shame is over, that the time of freedom has begun. In the future, there will be only two parties in Germany. You have your choice between them. One is the party of the poor, the hungry, the people; the other that of the usurers. The party of Christian Germans against that of the Jewish bloodsuckers. To which do you want to belong? Those who side with the Jews should go; those who want to be Germans should come: to us. The flag of black-red-and-gold will no longer exist, and those who wear its colors of shame will be shot. Those who refuse to cooperate will be hanged, and those who join us shall look forward to a glorious German future."

A deafening crescendo of "Heil Hitler, Heil Ludendorff, Heil Pöhner!" echoed across the square, and the crowd burst into an ear-shattering rendition of "Deutschland, Deutschland über Alles."

"Look at that mob on Marienplatz," Josef Berchtold shouted to Hans Kallenbach, his machine-gun chief, as they trotted down the Tal right past Berchtold's own tobacco shop, closed for business that morning. "We'll never get through there. Let's try the back way."

Following him, the Stosstrupp swung left through the Viktualienmarkt and past the stalls of startled market women, up the Rosental, along Färbergraben, and past the scene of its nocturnal triumph—the devastated *Münchener Post* with its scores of broken windows, like gouged-out eyes, and the piles of broken furniture and burned books still on the street.

"Halt!" Berchtold barked, as they reached the corner of Kaufinger and Ett Strasse.

Trained as commandos, the platoons spread out to guard the

approaches to the police building from several directions. Squads barged into the shops of the houses adjacent to it, hoping to find passageways through courtyards and back doors by which they could infiltrate, and Kallenbach set up the .50-caliber gun facing the main entrance.

"Shut your windows and don't look out!" Berchtold bellowed to the curious surveying the scene on Munich's main shopping street. "What are you all gawking at?" Then, with young Walter Hewel at his side, he marched up to the main door, demanding admission and surrender.

"We will return your fire," said the State Police captain commanding the guard. He slammed the heavy oak door in Berchtold's face.

Now what should he do? Berchtold was a man who covered his tracks by never doing anything without a *Befehl*—an order. His orders from Göring had not included instructions on what to do in case of resistance. He was baffled by the attitude of the police. Should he try to take the building by storm? Josef Gerum, the police inspector in his ranks, advised against it. Gerum knew every corridor and cranny of the huge structure: the Stosstrupp had too few men to take it by force.

Telling his platoon leaders to stay in position, Berchtold went looking for a telephone to call Göring at the Bürgerbräu.

"Just come back here," the SA leader ordered. "There has been a change of plans."

To the bafflement of his men, the astonishment of the beleaguered police in the building, and the derisive surprise of the crowd of sensation-seekers on Kaufinger Strasse, Berchtold reassembled the company, told Kallenbach to pack up the machine gun again, and marched the Stosstrupp back to the Bürgerbräukeller by the circuitous way it had come. The "Siege of Ett Strasse" had lasted some fifteen minutes.

Göring's plans had indeed changed—in accordance with Hitler's demands for more propaganda. To carry them out he called upon his trusted courier, Julius Schaub.

Schaub had not had much rest after returning to the Bürgerbräukeller in the wake of Gregor Strasser's convoy. In fact, he had been sent right back out again on another mission: to rustle up food supplies for the growing army of storm troopers encamped in the beerhall.

Korbinian Reindl's stock had run out during the night, nor did he seem disposed to feeding the revolutionary horde without pay. Even in a revolution everything has its price, and in a German one everything has to be "properly in order." Those putschists who lived near enough, such as Wilhelm Brückner's adjutant, Heinrich Bennecke, had gone home for breakfast. Others, if they had the money, sauntered across the street to the Münchener Kindl cellar or the nearby Hofbräukeller on Wienerplatz. But the majority were broke and they were getting hungry. All armies march on their stomachs, and this ragtag one of Fascist desperadoes was no exception.

Schaub's assignment had been to procure bread, sausages, and cheese from the shops in Munich's East End—"by requisition on orders of the revolutionary government" wherever possible, and, if that was too troublesome, by paying with some of the marks Hans Knauth and Karl Beggel had conveniently brought in.

Shortly before 9:30 A.M. he had returned, mission amply accomplished, to find Göring again waiting for him impatiently.

"I want you to go to City Hall as quickly as possible and make sure that the black-white-and-red flag and our swastika banners are raised there," the SA commander said. "It should be no problem, but take some protection with you."

Obediently Schaub singled out another storm trooper to accompany him and hurried—this time by streetcar—to Marienplatz and the Rathaus.

True to his promise, Putzi Hanfstaengl had arranged the interview with Hitler and Ludendorff for his retinue of American correspondents.

Larry Rue found the scene at the Bürgerbräukeller "reminiscent of the early days of a war. Rations and equipment were being issued, small youths were drilling in the garden and various courtyards. Recruits were being enlisted. The utmost optimism and enthusiasm prevailed. Rows of lorries were drawn up which moved off at intervals with troops, munitions, or supplies. All thought that the movement was a success."

That, precisely, was the impression Hitler, Ludendorff, and

the others were trying to convey. They were studying maps of the city and various papers when the correspondents were led in.

Hitler received the group courteously, "but was obviously overwrought and dead tired." The *New York Times*'s correspondent noted that the Nazi Führer who was purporting to be Germany's new dictator "scarcely seemed to fill the part—this little man in an old waterproof coat with a revolver at his hip, unshaven and with disordered hair, and so hoarse that he could scarcely speak."

Ludendorff, too, was "extremely friendly," but "seemed anxious and preoccupied as he talked with Hitler and some other political advisers."

"My government," he told the correspondents, "is eager to have the approval of the United States and of England." He began discoursing on the "future glory of the new Germany" that the "nationalist revolution" portended.

The reporters listened patiently, but were less interested in Ludendorff's declamations than in whether he had practical solutions to their problems. Since midnight, they complained, they had been unable to place long-distance calls out of Munich or send cables to their offices in Berlin, Paris, London, and the United States. Moreover, the city being in a state of siege, they were having trouble moving about.

Magnanimously, Ludendorff offered "passes" that would permit freedom of movement and also promised to arrange for communications with Berlin. But like many promises of the past twenty-four hours, it was an empty one, which neither Ludendorff nor anyone else at the Bürgerbräukeller would be able to keep.

Josef Berchtold and the Stosstrupp were weary from their hurried march to Ett Strasse and back to the Bürgerbräukeller. They were hoping for a break. But Göring, who had been waiting with mounting irritation for the unit's return, had other plans. Hitler had been adamant about getting those flags out on the Rathaus, and he doubted Schaub's ability to do the job alone, without a "little persuasive help." Moreover, Hitler wanted more prominent hostages than the Jewish businessmen and other odd victims of the various nocturnal raids and vendettas who were still locked up in the beerhall. He wanted Bürgermeister Eduard

Schmid, Munich's Social Democratic mayor since 1919, and members of the city council.

"But only the Socialists and Communists," Göring cautioned Berchtold. "And, of course, don't forget the Jewish swine, whatever parties they may belong to."

At least it was an assignment that made some sense, the tobacconist thought. Barking orders frantically, he hurried Heinrich von Knobloch's platoon back out on Rosenheimer Strasse to a couple of waiting trucks. The contingent included some of Berchtold's most trusted followers: Emil Maurice, Wilhelm Briemann, Walter Hewel, Hans Krüger, and the Fiehler brothers—fifty men in all.

"*Los!*" Berchtold shouted from an open touring car, and the convoy, machine guns mounted on the trucks, rolled down the hill toward the center of the city.

Though Julius Streicher had left for other spots to deliver his diatribes, his harangue of the masses had made an indelible imprint on downtown Munich. When Julius Schaub, followed by the rifle-toting SA man, hopped off a streetcar on Marienplatz, the city's main square was still in pandemonium and a crowd of thousands was shouting insults and lewd invectives at the mayor and councilors meeting in emergency session behind the elaborate facade of the town hall.

"*Die Fahnen raus! Schwarz-weiss-rot!*" the multitude chanted hysterically. "Hang out the old flags! Black-white-red!"

Forcing his way through the unruly mob, Schaub strutted into the building and up the stairs to one of the committee rooms where Schmid was conferring with senior councilors. He yanked open the heavy oak door and left it ajar so that all could see the armed storm trooper standing guard.

"The shameful days of black-red-gold are over," Schaub trumpeted at the startled city fathers. "I bring you orders from my commander, Captain Göring, to raise the black-white-red banner immediately."

Eduard Schmid, sixty-two, was not a man quickly frightened or easily intimidated. Neither was Albert Nussbaum, the ranking Social Democratic councilor. Both eyed the unshaven young Nazi, wearing the rumpled uniform in which he had spent the night on the highway, more with amusement than with contempt or anger.

"You say you have orders for us from Captain Göring," the mayor bellowed back, his magnificent handlebar mustache quivering with defiance and indignation, his massive round face turning scarlet. "Who is this Captain Göring? I have never heard of him. But anyway, tell him we shall have to look about first to see if there are any flags in those colors still around."

"And should we happen to find one," Nussbaum interjected, "we have no authority to raise it. That requires the approval of the entire city council, not just the committee of elders meeting this morning. There would have to be a debate and, of course, a vote would have to be taken."

Schaub, unaccustomed to having Göring's instructions questioned or challenged by anyone, was fuming. "I will report your impudence to Captain Göring," he declared officiously. "I shall be back, and then you will see who gives the orders in the new Germany."

It was not an empty threat. Rushing angrily out of the building and onto the square, where the crowd had grown larger, noisier, and more insistent in its demands to raise the old imperial colors, Schaub was surprised to find Berchtold and the Stosstrupp arriving.

"They refuse? What do you mean?" Berchtold asked. "No one refuses us any longer, least of all those Jewish and Socialist swine. Knobloch—get going! Take your men and help Schaub carry out Captain Göring's orders."

Reinforced by a dozen of the Stosstrupp, their rifles, carbines, and tommy guns at the ready, Schaub and Knobloch pushed back into the building through the swelling rabble on the square.

Just at that moment, too, Helmut Klotz, the Nazi propagandist from Nürnberg, arrived on the scene. Hearing what had happened, he clambered atop the cab of one of the trucks, ordered the Stosstrupp's Karl Hauenstein to fire a couple of bursts into the air with his submachine gun to "get people to listen," and began haranguing the mob once more in the style his friend Streicher had taught him.

"Today, five years after it was hauled down and trampled in shame," Klotz shrieked hysterically, "our black-white-red flag has been restored to honor and glory. But the mayor and the council, I hear, refuse to display it."

Jeers and shouts of "Hang the pigs!" thundered across Marienplatz. Like a tidal wave, the horde surged forward, storming into the Rathaus on the heels of Schaub, Knobloch, and the Stosstrupp. Within minutes swastika and black-white-red imperial flags were flying from the balconies beneath the town hall's famous carillon tower and along its rich facade. Marienplatz seemed to burst out with the colors of the old Reich and the Nazi movement. A deafening roar of approval erupted from the square, and the multitude lustily began singing the "Deutschland Lied."

Others of the rabble, shouting, "Get the dirty swine! Beat them to death!" followed the Stosstrupp to the door of the ornate council chamber. Rifles cocked, pistols drawn, Schaub, Knobloch, and twelve of the helmeted storm troopers barged in. The others stood guard outside holding back the mob in the corridors.

"Anyone who attempts to flee will be shot without warning!" Knobloch announced.

"All Marxists and Jews stand up!" Schaub commanded.

Defiantly, the council members all remained seated.

"What is your definition of 'Marxist'? Whom do you mean by that?" Deputy Mayor Hans Küffner, a stanch conservative, asked.

"I am not here to quibble or argue," Schaub snapped. "All Social Democrats, Independent Socialists, and Communists are under arrest by orders of the provisional government."

Everybody remained seated.

"Get them! I know who they are," Schaub said, pointing to the mayor, Nussbaum, and seven others.

Grabbing Schmid by the jacket collar, one of the troopers pulled the mayor up from his chair and slammed the old man viciously against a wall. Werner Fiehler brought his rifle barrel down on the side of Nussbaum's head, grabbed him by the arms, and yanked him up.

"Now, are there any more?" Schaub asked, when the nine men were arrayed against a wall. "These men will be tried by a summary tribunal and shot within twenty-four hours. You won't be bothered by them again."

Deputy Mayor Küffner, shaken and white with rage, shook his head.

"Then you will please excuse the interruption of your meeting, Excellency."

Schaub saluted, turned on his heels, and nodded to Knobloch.

The prisoners were allowed their hats and coats. Then they were marched out through the jeering crowd in the corridors and stairwells and forced to run the gauntlet of the mob outside.

"Lynch them! Beat their heads in! Hang the swine!" came the shouts, as Schmid and the councilors were shoved and jostled along. They were spat upon, screamed at by hysterical women and teenagers, kicked and punched before Berchtold, barking commands, hustled them onto one of the trucks.

Watching the scene, photographer Heinrich Hoffmann captured it for posterity on his plates of film.

It was eleven o'clock. As they had every other day for years, the forty-three chimes in the ornate tower of the Rathaus began ringing; the brightly painted figures of its carillon started their mechanical-doll movements. One of the city's great tourist attractions, the figures depict jousting knights at the wedding of Bavaria's Duke William V to Renate of Lorraine, followed by the "Dance of the Coopers" to commemorate the end of the terrible Black Plague that had decimated the population of Munich in 1515. But that morning there were no tourists on Marienplatz.

Honking, the Stosstrupp trucks with their storm troopers and frightened hostages picked their way slowly through the crowd, then up the Tal, and returned to the Bürgerbräukeller.

News that the State Police was starting to guard the Isar bridges, and apparently encircling the Bürgerbräu, had been reported to Hitler and the other leaders shortly after Lieutenant Georg Höfler's detachment was posted at the Ludwig Bridge.

Ludendorff sent Ulrich Graf and Göring out to reconnoiter. What they discovered was worrisome. State Police were squared off against SA and Oberland troopers all along the riverfront, from Max-Josef Bridge, near Thomas Mann's house, in the north, to as far south as the Wittelsbach Bridge.

It was a potentially explosive if confusing situation for both sides. The police still did not know what their role really was, and many of them regarded the putschists as comrades-in-arms.

"*Herr Kamerad*, you have no idea what kind of a predicament I am in," said Police Major Rudolf von Kramer, when Göring inspected the detachment from Edmund Heines's Second SA Battalion guarding Cornelius Bridge. "Just night before last my people and I protected one of your meetings, and afterward your men and mine drank and talked like friends. Now I am standing here and may receive orders to fire." The officer had tears in his eyes.

Göring did not. "My instructions from Excellency Ludendorff," he said coldly, "are to tell you that the first dead or wounded in our ranks will mean the death of the hostages we are holding."

"Well," Kramer said, "I suggest we reach an agreement. There will be shooting only if one side or the other attempts to advance over the bridge."

"Yes," Göring agreed, "but the instant one of my men falls, I will give orders to execute all the hostages we have."

"How about this?" the police officer proposed. "If I receive orders to advance further, I will tell your commander on the other side in plenty of time so that he can pull back."

"All right, that's an agreement," Göring lied, having no intention of pulling back. Then he left to convey similar threats at other bridges. The conversation convinced him and Graf that the police undoubtedly had, or soon would have, orders to use force.

Hitler, looking more harried by the moment, watched in grim silence as Schaub and Knobloch marched their prisoners into the beerhall, frisked them, and lined them up in the vestibule near the cloakroom.

"We have a few juicy ones," Berchtold announced proudly. "Bürgermeister Schmid and Albert Nussbaum."

The Führer seemed uninterested and turned on his heels.

"Do you think this is right?" Nussbaum asked quietly, when he noticed Bavaria's former justice minister, Christian Roth, among the group of people in the foyer. "Do you approve of this, Herr Minister? Is this your concept of justice and law and order?"

Roth shrugged his shoulders and walked away.

The prisoners were just being led off when Ludendorff passed by. "Who are those people?" the general asked.

"City councilors," Berchtold replied with an air of pride.

"*Ach, so!*" Ludendorff remarked with disdain but also apparent disinterest as he, too, walked off to return to his council of war in the private dining room.

Mayor Schmid and the councilors were locked up with the other hostages.

For the putschists, the pressing question was what they should do next.

"Try again," Göring had suggested at one point, seconding Kriebel's proposal to retreat to Rosenheim and launch a counter-offensive from there. The city, nestled at the foot of the Alps, was not only his birthplace but a militant stronghold of the "patriotic" movement. They already had enough weapons and enough men, he argued, and he knew that in the highlands they would find willing reinforcements.

But it would also be a signal for open civil war, and thus anathema to Hitler and Ludendorff, both of whom remained implacably opposed to the idea.

What then?

Hitler was still banking on Max Neunzert's mission to Berchtesgaden to seek Crown Prince Rupprecht's mediation. But here it was past eleven o'clock—more than three hours after he had dispatched Neunzert to "the King"—and there had been not so much as a word of his arrival, to say nothing of a call from the mountain palace. Why was it taking so long?

Meanwhile, however, another idea had been germinating in that smoke-filled second-floor dining room, this time in Ludendorff's mind: a demonstration march of some kind into the city to galvanize the populace and convince Lossow and Kahr that they were swimming against the current of public opinion. It was a proposal uncharacteristic of the stiff-backed Prussian, propaganda and drumming up the masses being the ex-corporal's specialty. But the idea had its merits, and the longer it was bandied about, the more it seemed to promise success.

As the morning wore on, matters somehow came to look less hopeless than in the first dreary light of dawn. There were so many encouraging signs: the crowd on Marienplatz, for example, the banners flying there and the singing multitudes. Hermann Esser, who had risen from his sickbed and scouted the city, had reported wild enthusiasm on the streets. Similar versions had come from Hans Frank, Streicher, Klotz, and the SA's Wilhelm Brückner, who had gone for a leisurely and customary coffee break in his favorite café at Gärtner Platz. Various "recruiting offices" had been established by the SA, and all were registering lively business in "volunteers for the new national army."

Wouldn't such a propaganda march help crystallize and bolster the mood, which was clearly on the putschists' side? Though Hitler, the master propagandist, was oddly lukewarm to the idea, it had begun to gain support among the other collaborators, in particular Kriebel and Scheubner-Richter. And their arguments seemed to make sense.

For one thing, such a demonstration would bolster the spirits of their own rank-and-file followers, stimulate them, give them a sense of momentum. Simultaneously it would prevent defections due to doubt while disciplining the more radical and militant among them who were getting bored lolling about the Bürgerbräukeller or being sent out on seemingly senseless patrols of the river embankment and Munich's East End.

Furthermore, it would be a show of power to the populace. Scheubner-Richter, who fancied himself a strategist of revolution, reminded the others how five years earlier Kurt Eisner had turned a similar demonstration into action. Munich, they knew, was a seething cauldron. What it needed was a catalyst.

Moreover, a march such as they envisioned, with flags flying and a band playing, would force the triumvirs' hand. Kahr, Lossow, and Seisser would have to react—either by taking a position with the putschists or against the masses of people. Of course there might be an armed confrontation, but with Ludendorff, the great war hero, in the lead, the risk seemed to everyone in the room, especially Ludendorff himself, a small one. The odds, they reasoned, were very much in their favor for turning events around once more.

And finally, as Ludendorff put it, "We cannot just sit around here all day and wait—for what?"

The more the idea took shape, the more Hitler seemed opposed to it. The great improviser wanted to wait—for the word from Neunzert and Rupprecht that would not be forthcoming. The genius of propaganda, now despondent and fatigued, suddenly despaired of its effectiveness. He who a scant twelve hours earlier had wanted to call for an artillery barrage against the Engineer Barracks to free Max von Müller's battalion of Oberländers now had no stomach for the confrontation, the violence, and the bloodshed that he sensed would come. But he was overruled, in part by events over which he no longer had control.

Shortly before eleven-thirty, Göring and Ulrich Graf returned to report what they had seen at the Isar bridges. Concurrently, word reached the Bürgerbräukeller that Reichswehr and State Police had left the barracks, in two powerful detachments backed by armor, to surround the war ministry and force Ernst Röhm's surrender.

For Ludendorff it was a question of now or never, of acting before being acted upon. To remain in the Bürgerbräukeller and wait to be encircled seemed as nonsensical to him as trying to defend the beerhall or escaping pellmell to Rosenheim. Neither retreat nor beleaguerment were in his military textbook. Thoughts of Tannenberg, Verdun, the Marne raced through his mind.

His face grim, the general looked around the room.

"*Wir marschieren!*" he said icily, in a tone that left no further margin for discussion or opposition. "We shall march!"

17

Ernst Röhm, his small eyes bloodshot, the scars of his war wounds glistening pink against the shadow of a day's beard on his puffy cheeks, stared morosely at his companions. Assembled in the austere anteroom to General von Lossow's war ministry office were Josef Seydel, Karl Osswald, Count Moulin-Eckart, Theodor Casella, Martin Faust, Walther Lembert, Heinrich Himmler, and a few other loyal friends and followers.

Almost six hours had passed since Ernst Pöhner and Adolf Hühnlein had been dispatched to police headquarters; more than five since Hitler, Ludendorff, Kriebel, and the others had left to return to the Bürgerbräukeller. There had not been another word from them. In his command post, Röhm felt "alone, abandoned, and perplexed by developments."

Even worse, however, reports had just reached him that General von Danner, under orders from Lossow, had dispatched nearly four battalions of Reichswehr and State Police, backed by mortar and artillery batteries and eight armored cars, to dislodge him and his 400 men from the Schönfeld Strasse complex.

For Röhm it posed a quandary. His last orders from Ludendorff, whom he regarded as commander-in-chief, had been to "hold the building." Yet, as an officer still listed on the active Reichswehr rolls, he considered Lossow his direct commanding officer.

"I just refuse to believe this is happening," he said to his friends. "Why hasn't Lossow sent me appropriate orders or at least made some attempt to communicate during the night?"

For Röhm, a political schemer as well as a professional soldier, it was an uncomfortable situation. Which of the two—Lossow or Ludendorff—should he obey? He hedged his decision.

"We shall not surrender and we shall defend the building," he announced. "But we shall not fire upon the Reichswehr unless fired upon, and then only if I give the order."

Within minutes, the sprawling war ministry structure was converted to a fortress. The Reichskriegsflagge troopers camping in its corridors rushed into the offices and courtyards to set up sniper and machine-gun nests. They did not have long to wait.

It was a strange scene. Ludwig Strasse was crowded with civilian spectators—the sympathetic and the curious, many of them just passers-by who had stopped to watch. Rifle and machine-gun barrels bristled from every window of the huge building. At the corner of Schönfeld Strasse, protected by chevaux-de-frise and coils of barbed wire, stood Himmler, Röhm, Seydel, and a small patrol, occasionally singing patriotic songs such as "Deutschland Hoch in Ehren."

Then, from all directions one could hear the approaching rumble of the armored cars and occasional salvos of blank rifle and machine-gun fire. As Jakob von Danner's small army encircled the ministry, the crowd scattered in panic. Röhm and his aides watched as the Reichswehr and State Police troops took up positions from a safe distance—in side streets and on the roofs and upper stories of surrounding palaces and houses. They had mortars, small fieldpieces, and heavy machine guns: a grim-looking force indeed, and one obviously prepared for a long siege if need be.

Munich was starting to resemble the battleground for a genuine civil war. But when it became apparent that it would probably first be a war of nerves, more a *sitz* than a *blitzkrieg*, the throng of onlookers came streaming back.

Moreover, emissaries and self-appointed mediators began appearing at Schönfeld Strasse to persuade Röhm to capitulate: Lieutenant Colonel Franz von Hörauf, Röhm's former regimental commander, and Lieutenant Colonel Hans Georg Hofmann, the Reichswehr commandant in Ingolstadt, both staunch backers of Hitler, and, most important, recently retired Major General Franz von Epp, Lossow's predecessor as Seventh Division commander.

Epp was certainly the most honest broker in Röhm's eyes. In 1919, it had been Epp's free corps of White soldiers that brought counterrevolutionary terror to Munich and crushed Bavaria's short-lived Soviet Republic. As recently as the spring of 1923 he had been Röhm's commanding officer at the Seventh Division, and it was under his aegis that the "Black Reichswehr" of irregulars—the "patriotic leagues"—had been created and the vast stores of illegal arms and ammunition stashed away. Epp was not only every bit as much a militant nationalist as Röhm and Ludendorff, but also an ardent supporter of Hitler and the Nazi party. In fact, his personal donation of 60,000 Reichsmarks in early 1921—then a sizable fortune—had enabled Hitler to buy the failing *Völkischer Beobachter*, an obscure ultra-rightist weekly, and turn it into the party's official daily.

"It is hopeless," Epp said, explaining that Kahr, Lossow, and Seisser had repudiated the putsch and were determined to suppress it with armed force. "You are in a beleaguered bastion here, totally outnumbered and outgunned. Give up, Röhm; there is no point in further resistance."

Epp's advice was seconded by Hörauf and Hofmann. They were standing near the corner of Schönfeld and Ludwig Strasse, behind the barricades and within earshot of Himmler. A Reichswehr soldier with a white flag of truce had accompanied Hofmann and Hörauf.

But Röhm refused to listen to these men who had been his military mentors and comrades-in-arms and whom he regarded as his political friends. "I cannot do it," he explained wearily. "I have orders from Excellency Ludendorff personally to hold this position, and will retreat from it only at his command. He left here this morning relying on me, and I cannot violate that trust."

"But what more do you want, Röhm?" asked Hofmann, stressing that he had come to the building at Lossow's behest. "Everything we've struggled for has already been achieved. There is a new government in Berlin—von Seeckt has been named commander-in-chief with full dictatorial powers. There is even talk that Admiral Tirpitz may be named Reich president. Wasn't that our goal, man?"

Röhm remained skeptical, but the three continued to urge him. Danner, they said, would guarantee an orderly, peaceful withdrawal from the building with all military honors.

"It is a very difficult decision to make," Röhm insisted. "I must have some time to think about it. I have been in here all night, and since Ludendorff left early this morning have had no information as to what is going on outside."

"Look," Hofmann said. "Why don't you go and talk to Danner? He has set up a command post at the Police Barracks on Türken Strasse."

"Could I get an assurance that nothing will happen here, to my people, if I leave?" Röhm asked.

Hofmann and Epp assured him that Danner would certainly hold off the attack if Röhm were to come and negotiate.

It was 11:45 A.M. when the feisty putschist captain finally agreed to a two-hour "cease-fire."

Hofmann promised to hurry to the Bürgerbräukeller to see Ludendorff and obtain his consent for an honorable surrender. Epp led Röhm across Ludwig Strasse to Reichswehr Lieutenant Colonel Hugo von Pflügel, the "field commander" of the operation, to arrange the "truce."

Then, leaving Karl Osswald in charge at the war ministry, Röhm—accompanied by Seydel, Moulin-Eckart, and Epp—walked the two short blocks to meet Danner at the Türken Strasse barracks.

In the Kaiserhof of the Residenz, Senior Lieutenant Michael von Godin, increasingly bored with the morning's waiting game, noticed that his company of State Police was becoming restless too. To keep them occupied—an old military ploy—he decided to have the men check their weapons, then put them through some close-order drill.

Lieutenant Colonel Wilhelm Muxel, Godin's battalion commander, watching the useless exercise, beckoned him over.

"You may have more to do soon," Muxel said calmly. "The Reichswehr and some of our companies have surrounded the war ministry, and there is also a report that the Hitlerites are grouping at the Bürgerbräukeller, apparently in some kind of march on the city. Be prepared for real trouble, Godin."

Jakob von Danner, surrounded by his staff officers, glanced contemptuously at the swarthy Röhm, standing there in the rumpled uniform in which he had spent the night.

"Excellency von Lossow wants his office and his headquarters back," Danner said coldly.

"But, Herr General," Röhm stammered, "I am not stopping him. On the contrary, my orders from Excellency Ludendorff, since last night, have been to hold the war ministry in readiness for General von Lossow and to provide him an honor guard when he arrives. We have all been waiting for him for many hours."

"Clear the building," von Danner said curtly. "Get your people out of there now, or they will be forced out by mine, and if any blood flows in the process, you, Captain, will be held personally responsible."

"But I have orders from General Ludendorff to hold the building," Röhm protested. "He is the commander of the new national army. As a soldier, I cannot leave my post unless General Ludendorff releases me from my duties and gives me—"

"*Hauptmann* Röhm," Danner interrupted him sharply, "you are still an officer on active duty in the Reichswehr and a subordinate of the Seventh Division commander. It is his orders you must obey, not General Ludendorff's. The commander-in-chief of the German national army is General Hans von Seeckt, not Erich Ludendorff. Ludendorff has no authority to give you any kind of orders, and you have no right or obligation to obey him. Get your men out!"

Röhm's rotund face was chalk white. His scarred cheeks twitched with anger and humiliation. But he was not a man who gave up easily.

He implored Danner to let him send another courier to the

Bürgerbräukeller to ask Ludendorff to "rescind his orders and relieve me of my duty."

Danner refused. But even if the request had been honored, it
was too late. Not only had Ludendorff already left the Bürgerbräukeller, but the bloodshed all had sought to avoid had already
taken place.

Senior Lieutenant Max Braun, commander of the 19th Infantry Regiment's 2nd Company, was a man true to his word. That
morning he had threatened to return the fire of "anyone who
shoots at me or my unit." He and his company carried out the
threat only minutes after Röhm, Seydel, Moulin-Eckart, and Epp
had left the Schönfeld Strasse complex to confer with Danner.
The result was that the putschists had their initial martyrs: Martin
Faust, twenty-two, and Theodor Casella, twenty-three.

How that brief lethal gunfight began remains as much a mystery as who actually fired the two rifle shots that unleashed it. But
those shots came from within the war ministry and wounded two
Reichswehr soldiers posted near a wall behind the building—on
Kaulbach Strasse.

"Nicht schiessen!" Karl Osswald and Casella screamed, rushing to where they thought they had heard the retorts—"Don't
shoot!"

But it was too late. Osswald and Casella dived for cover as
erratic gunfire erupted and one of Braun's machine-gun emplacements sprayed the building's central courtyard from a nearby
rooftop.

Faust, standing there, was killed almost instantly. Casella was
mortally wounded as he rushed out to try to pull Faust to safety.
Hysterically, Himmler, Lembert, and several others ran into the
courtyard to drag the two men back.

The shooting stopped as quickly and spontaneously as it had
begun, but what many in Munich had regarded as a "comic-opera
putsch" was suddenly a deadly serious matter.

Shaken by the bloody episode, Himmler, Lembert, and Osswald rushed their fallen comrades across Schönfeld Strasse to the
Josephinum Hospital. Faust was pronounced dead on arrival. Casella died of his massive wounds an hour later.

18

It was high noon.

Jungsturm leader Adolf Lenk looked solemnly at Hitler as the two stood on the steps of the Bürgerbräukeller watching the hundreds of marchers assembling on Rosenheimer Strasse. The wet snow had stopped falling for a while. Instead, cold gusts of wind stung their faces.

"You appear so preoccupied, Lenk," Hitler said. "What are you thinking about?"

"Frau Ebertin," the twenty-year-old head of the Nazi youth league replied.

Hitler winced as he remembered the prediction of Elsbeth Ebertin, a well-known astrologer and fortuneteller.

It had been the previous March, a Sunday morning. Lenk was in Hitler's dingy little Thiersch Strasse apartment to discuss plans for a forthcoming youth rally. The doorbell had rung, and soon Hitler's landlady, Frau Dachs, had knocked on the door of the Führer's room.

"Herr Hitler," she had said, "that strange woman is here again and refuses to go away. She absolutely insists on speaking to you."

"What woman?" Lenk had asked. "Did she give her name?"

"Ebertin," the landlady had replied.

"She is very famous," Lenk had explained. "She's an astrologer. The whole city is talking about her. You really should let her in."

"What have women and stars got to do with me?" Hitler had protested, but on Lenk's insistence he finally relented.

"I have worked out your horoscope, Herr Hitler," Elsbeth Ebertin had said, after being shown into the room. "It says that a man born on April 20, 1889—your birthday—is destined to sacrifice himself for the German nation and play a leading role in future struggles. But he can expose himself to personal danger and touch off a possibly uncontrollable crisis in November. For your own good, do nothing drastic or violent in that month, for I see nothing then but blood, blood, and more blood."

Eight months earlier, Adolf Hitler had laughed derisively and dismissed the episode. So, for that matter, had Lenk. But now, as the two stood on the steps of the beer garden watching the preparations for the march, the wintry gale of that bleak November morning whipping at them, both were suddenly haunted by her prediction.

"What should I do, Lenk?" the Nazi Führer asked with a tremor in his voice. Ever since Ludendorff had insisted on the demonstration, Hitler had worried that they would meet armed resistance from the police and army.

"I think you should give the word for everyone to unload their guns before we start to march into the city," the young man suggested. "At least that way, if blood is spilled, it will not be our fault."

Remarkably, Hitler followed Lenk's advice. He walked up and down the street along the columns forming there and ordered the various commanders of SA and Oberland units to tell their men to unload their weapons, belt up their hand grenades, sheath their bayonets, and hide the dum-dum bullets which quite a few were carrying.

What he did not do, however, was make certain that his orders were actually carried out.

The ragtag army assembling on Rosenheimer Strasse numbered more than 2,000 men. Some counted almost 3,000.

The three battalions of Wilhelm Brückner's Munich SA Regiment were there almost in full strength: Karl Beggel's First, Edmund Heines's Second, and Hans Knauth's Third. Ready to march were such loyal followers as Kurt Neubauer, and Hans Frank. The companies not represented were busy guarding various Isar bridges.

There was Gregor Strasser's battalion from Landshut.

The Oberland League was represented by Ludwig Oestreicher's battalion, with Konrad Kiessling and Alfons Weber in the ranks; Max von Müller's 400 men; Hans Oemler's detachment; and Wilhelm Völk's from Garmisch-Partenkirchen.

Gerhard Rossbach was lining up the Infantry School cadets and Josef Berchtold the Stosstrupp.

All had been paid—2 trillion marks each, in crisp 50-billion-mark notes from the Parcus and Mühlthaler printing plants.

The leaders were all there too: Ludendorff and his stepson Pernet, Scheubner-Richter with his faithful servant Johann

Aigner, Oberland's Friedrich Weber, Hermann Kriebel, ex-Major Hans Streck, Alfred Rosenberg, Julius Streicher, Helmut Klotz, and, of course, Göring, Hitler, and his ever-present bodyguard Ulrich Graf.

It was a huge cast of political desperadoes and fanatics: extremists, demagogues, free-booters, military adventurers, rabidly anti-Semitic bigots, haters, opportunists, and hundreds upon hundreds of the simply gullible, all somehow convinced of the righteousness of their cause.

A few were conspicuously absent.

Hermann Esser had gone back into the city to test the mood once more, as he had done earlier that morning.

Putzi Hanfstaengl, on the other hand, feeling that the "situation seemed hopeless," had more or less abandoned his journalistic charges to hurry home to his apartment on Gentz Strasse and "prepare for a getaway."

Photographer Heinrich Hoffmann, having taken pictures all over the city, including the Bürgerbräukeller, had run out of film plates just when Ludendorff had announced stentoriously, *"Wir marschieren!"* Could there have been a more inappropriate moment? Hoffmann had swung onto his bicycle to pedal furiously back to his Schelling Strasse studio, hoping that he would need "no more than one hour" for the trip back and forth.

Rudolf Hess, blissfully unaware of the night's developments, was still guarding the Bavarian cabinet and his other high-ranking hostages at the Lehmann villa in Grosshesselohe.

Max Neunzert, alas, unknown to Hitler, who had sent him on that crucial mission of mediation, was still sitting on the train chugging slowly through the snow-capped Bavarian Alps toward Berchtesgaden and Crown Prince Rupprecht.

And except for a couple of SA trumpeters, there was no music. Hungry, unpaid, and disgruntled, the band which Brückner had organized earlier that morning had gone home.

Hermann Göring, his rubber coat belted tautly around his paunch, the Pour le Mérite sparkling from beneath his double chin, the steel helmet with its swastika emblem tilted back rakishly, strutted officiously among the troops lining up on Rosenheimer Strasse.

"Berchtold!" he bellowed. "Get the prisoners—Schmid, Nuss-baum, the other councilors. I want them at the rear of the col-umn, and if there is any trouble, shoot them."

The burgomaster and the others were brought out of the beer-hall. Guarded by Wilhelm Briemann, Heinrich von Knobloch, Emil Maurice, and other Stosstrupp members, they were lined up on the street.

"But they're not worth a bullet," Berchtold announced loudly. "When I give the signal, just bash in their skulls with your rifle stocks. Don't waste ammunition."

It was not an empty threat, and it would no doubt have been carried out had Hitler himself not intervened. "Take that pack back inside the Bürgerbräu and lock them up," the Führer said sharply, when Göring reported that he intended to take the hos-tages along. "I don't want any martyrs."

Ruffled at being humiliated in front of so many of his men, but obedient, the SA commander ordered Berchtold to take May-or Schmid and the councilors back inside the beerhall to rejoin the dozens of Jewish prisoners still being held. A half-dozen Stoss-trupp members, including Julius Schaub, were hurriedly assigned to stay behind and guard the hostages. Most of the others were sent ahead to act as skirmishers and protect the mainstream of marchers.

The chimes on the tower of the Müller-Volksbad, Munich's art nouveau swimming pool at the foot of Rosenheimer Berg, had just struck noon when the column—twelve marchers abreast—was finally ready to move off.

It was a bewildering sight, made all the stranger by the fact that trolleycars and normal morning traffic moved right past it.

In the vanguard were four flag bearers, their swastika and black-white-red banners snapping in the wind. They were fol-lowed by Adolf Lenk and Kurt Neubauer, Ludendorff's servant. Behind the two came more flag carriers, then the leadership. Hit-ler was in the middle, his slouch hat in his hand, the collar of his trenchcoat turned up against the cold, the holstered Browning belted around his waist. To his left, ramrod-straight and looking martial despite the battered green felt hat and loose loden coat, was Ludendorff. To the Führer's right, peering nearsightedly through his pince-nez, was Scheubner-Richter. "Matters look ugly," he said to Rosenberg, walking beside him. Then he turned to Hitler and predicted darkly, "This may be our last walk together."

Arrayed in the front row with them were Ulrich Graf, Hermann Kriebel, Friedrich Weber, Julius Streicher, Göring, and Wilhelm Brückner, who had come back from his "morning coffee break" at the Gärtner Platz Café just in time to join the march.

Immediately behind came the second string, Heinz Pernet, Hans Streck, Johann Aigner, Gottfried Feder, and Brückner's adjutant, Heinrich Bennecke.

Behind the leaders were the Stosstrupp, the SA battalions, the Infantry School, and the Oberländers—all armed to the teeth, most of them, unknown to Hitler, with their weapons loaded, bayonets mounted, and even safety catches off. There were several squads carrying machine guns on tripods, ready for action, and about halfway along the column a truck full of rifle-brandishing storm troopers, a belted machine gun mounted on the roof of its cab.

At the very rear, barely noticed by anyone, was a small Opel automobile, painted a dazzling yellow. A Red Cross flag fluttered from a staff on the driver's side. At the wheel sat Michael Ried and in the seat next to him, as a trusty guard, the Stosstrupp's Ludwig Schmied. In the back was young Dr. Walter Schultze, the Munich SA Regiment's "staff physician."

On Ludendorff's shouted command to Lenk and Neubauer, the column began moving down Rosenheimer Strasse toward Ludwig Bridge, where Lieutenant Georg Höfler and his small detachment of State Police from Landshut were standing guard.

The marchers broke into a dissonant rendition of Dietrich Eckart's "Sturmlied."

Georg Höfler and his platoon—two squads with carbines, one with submachine guns—had been guarding the eastern end of Ludwig Bridge since around 11 A.M. He had followed his orders precisely.

Discovering a strong detachment of Oberland storm troopers there on arrival, he had posted his men chummily right beside them. When a platoon of sixty SA, flags waving, rifles slung over their shoulders, had marched down the hill and attempted to cross, Höfler had "politely" asked them to take a "different route." And they did. There had been "five or six more" such detachments which, instead of turning back or going by some other bridge, had posted themselves a bit off to the side along with the Oberländers. Under instructions not to halt or disrupt "normal" traffic, Höfler had allowed cars, trucks, and trolleys to pass—blissfully unaware that two of the trucks were the Stosstrupp convoy with Mayor Eduard Schmid and the city councilors aboard as prisoners.

All in all it had been uneventful duty. Yet, for the hour or so that he had been guarding the bridge, Höfler and his men still did not really know whose side they were on. In a sense, most of the Oberländers and SA clustered there did not know either. They had hailed Höfler and his detachment on arrival, treated them as comrades-in-arms. That the putsch had gone awry, that Kahr, Lossow, and Seisser had repudiated their pledges of the night, was a secret that had been closely kept from the rank and file of storm troopers, and even Höfler knew only vaguely of the changed alignment.

"Are you for or against Kahr?" the young lieutenant from Landshut had asked.

"For him, of course," the Oberländers had replied, astonished at the question. No doubt Höfler would have received the same reply from his brother-in-law, Gregor Strasser, busily regrouping his men just two blocks up the hill for the "propaganda march" into the city.

But Georg Höfler did know his orders: not to allow any closed or armed formations to pass his bridgehead and cross the Isar into downtown Munich.

It was almost twelve-fifteen by the clock on the Volksbad tower when he first heard the raucous singing of the marchers and spotted the column coming down the hill where Rosenheimer Strasse makes a bend toward the bridge. It seemed an entire army was converging on him.

"Form a line! *Schnell!*" he commanded. "They must not pass!"

Höfler's men, some thirty in all, dashed to form a human chain across the bridge, their carbines and tommy guns at port. Arms outstretched against the approaching tidal wave, Höfler stood a few paces ahead of his platoon.

"*Halt!*" he called out sharply, stepping ahead toward Lenk, Neubauer, and the leaders.

"Keep going," Göring commanded. "Move ahead slowly."

"If you refuse to halt," Höfler shouted, "I will have to use firearms." Simultaneously he turned his head back to his men and commanded, "Load with live ammo."

"Don't shoot at your comrades!" Göring bellowed.

Suddenly there was a trumpet signal, and before Höfler realized what was happening, Berchtold's Stosstrupp, shouting "Charge the police!" broke ranks and bore down on the detachment with fixed bayonets and rifles pointed.

Within seconds the thin police line had been broken and pushed aside from the roadway. They were bludgeoned bloody with rifle stocks and pistol butts, stabbed with bayonets, and had their teeth knocked out by Berchtold's brawlers. They were beaten, slapped, spat upon, their helmets and caps tossed over the railing into the river. Their uniforms were ripped and weapons yanked out of their hands.

"You are all dogs, swine, traitors to the Fatherland," Hans Kallenbach snarled at the patrolmen. "We ought to stand you all up against a wall and machine-gun you for resisting us."

Höfler was shoved and jostled into the middle of the advancing column, from which he soon managed to escape to report what had happened to his superiors. But most of his men, hands above their heads like prisoners of war, were marched at gun and bayonet point back up the hill to the Bürgerbräukeller. Kallenbach, Hans Schön, Karl Fiehler, and Wilhelm Briemann were among those assigned by Göring and Berchtold as their keepers.

Doggedly, and apparently oblivious to the melee at the bridge, Hitler and Ludendorff led their singing and "Heil"-shouting followers on. The route they had chosen went down wide Zweibrücken Strasse, lined with enthusiastic spectators, many of whom waved swastika banners and cheered frenetically, through the medieval Isartor Gate, up the Tal, past Berchtold's shop, toward Marienplatz.

As the ragtag army of putschists continued toward the center, many of the bystanders joined the ranks of the marching column—some out of genuine enthusiasm, some simply overawed at seeing "the great Ludendorff" and Hitler in the vanguard, others out of sheer curiosity and hunger for action.

If it had indeed been Hitler's intention to "propagandize the masses" and "test the atmosphere and mood of the city" by marching, he was getting enough of an enthusiastic earful from the sidelines to spur him on. His spirits rose again as he saw the frenzied response on the streets. Perhaps all was not lost after all.

Marienplatz was tumultuous. Swastika and black-white-red imperial flags fluttered from the balconies of the Rathaus. Though more than an hour had passed since the arrest of the city councilors, and the last propaganda speakers had left the scene, the old square still bubbled with excited humanity—thousands of people, discussing, arguing, gossiping. It was as if there were a vast festival in the city. Traffic was almost halted, with the streetcar tracks and the roadway virtually blocked. Drivers trying to get through tooted their horns and trolley bells clanged insistently, all to no avail. The noise was deafening.

Karl Alexander von Müller was standing with friends at the corner of Marienplatz and Kaufinger Strasse, observing the scene and debating the news of Kahr's repudiation of the putsch, the first rumors of which had reached him shortly before noon. The reports were contradictory. According to one, Kahr, Lossow, and Seisser were planning to move with massive armed force against the putschists; according to another, Hitler and Ludendorff were assembling out-of-town reinforcements at the Bürgerbräukeller for a full-scale military attack on the city.

A few yards off, Larry Rue and Lincoln Eyre were working their way slowly through the crowd, trying to pick up bits of conversation and collecting local color. They were wondering what ever had happened to Hanfstaengl after the brief meeting with Hitler and Ludendorff.

Robert Murphy, the U.S. consul general, and his translator-aide, Paul Drey, were also pushing their way through the throng. They had spent most of the morning at the U.S. mission on nearby Lederer Strasse trying to make sense of conflicting reports. Unable to communicate by phone or cable with the embassy in Berlin, having tried futilely to locate von Kahr or Prime Minister von Knilling, Murphy felt stymied. He decided to make his way toward the war ministry on Schönfeld Strasse, where he had last seen Hitler and Ludendorff.

Carl Zuckmayer, the young playwright, on his lunch hour downtown, was amazed at the pandemonium on Marienplatz. Mixing with the teeming multitude, he felt that most were there not so much out of any political conviction for or against as merely for the excitement. The city was charged with electricity. Yet the mood of Müncheners seemed less revolutionary than inquisitive. It was a kind of "second Oktoberfest," and they did not want to miss it.

Father Rupert Mayer, moving awkwardly on his stiff wooden leg, sensed none of that. He had experienced Eisner's 1918 revolution first hand, not to mention the 1919 Soviet Republic, the Red terror, the White counterrevolution, and the terror from the Right. To him the cold air and leaden sky, from which snow had again begun to fall in large wet flakes, presaged catastrophe. It looked and sounded ominously familiar to this fighting man of God.

Heinrich Hoffmann was pedaling his bicycle furiously against the gusts of wind on stately Ludwig Strasse. His overcoat was soaked through. He had barely noticed the armored car parked menacingly in the middle of Odeonsplatz near the Feldherrnhalle or Lieutenant Max Demmelmeyer's company of State Police guarding the approaches to the square.

Even the Reichswehr battalions with their mortars and machine guns facing the war ministry at the corner of Schönfeld Strasse had not really registered. The chevaux-de-frise and the barbed-wire barricades were still up and the same forlorn troopers continued to stand guard behind them. That the day's first blood had already been spilled there was something Hoffmann could not know. He glanced quickly at the standardbearer—a young man with a little toothbrush mustache, rimless glasses, the bill of his cap down over them—who seemed to be shivering in the gale: Himmler. But Hoffmann already had that picture. His mind was on just one thing: to reach his studio and get more plates of film.

He turned left into Schelling Strasse and, without looking up, bicycled intently right past the offices of the *Völkischer Beobachter*.

Inside that building, Paula Schlier was still working the switchboard feverishly. Alone at the job now, bleary-eyed from lack of sleep, she could not keep up with the incoming calls, most of them from mothers, wives, fiancées, and sisters of Nazi storm troopers.

Where is my husband? Where is my son? Have they started to march north yet? I have heard music on the streets—does that mean they are moving against the enemy?

To each question Paula Schlier could only say, "I don't know. We have had no news here for hours."

Indeed, virtually the last visitor from the Bürgerbräu command post had been Putzi Hanfstaengl, now locked into his apartment and wondering whether he should skip across the border to Austria.

Suddenly the phone rang. He was startled. Who would know that he was here? Should he answer? With relief he heard the voice of his sister, Erna, an early admirer and promoter of Hitler.

"They're marching," she said, bubbling with excitement. "Ferdinand Sauerbruch just phoned me. He saw them."

"Marching where?" Hanfstaengl asked, a bit baffled by the apparent turn in events. "To Berlin?"

"No, no, not yet," Erna explained. "Through the Tal toward Marienplatz. Hitler, Ludendorff, everybody. There are thousands, and they are being cheered along the way. That is what Sauerbruch said."

Hanfstaengl's hopes soared. Perhaps all was not lost. Hitler's plan was apparently to whip up a huge following of people, mass support against which von Kahr could do nothing. Estimating, wrongly, that after Marienplatz the demonstration would probably go down Kaufinger and Neuhauser streets toward Karlsplatz, the Stachus, Putzi abandoned his plans to flee, dashed out of the apartment, and hurried toward the center of Munich hoping to meet his comrades.

The vast crowd on Marienplatz burst forth with a thunderous cadence of "Heil! Heil! Heil! Ludendorff! Hitler!" as the faces of the two men became visible. Spontaneously the multitude began singing "Deutschland, Deutschland über Alles!"

Karl Alexander von Müller turned from his circle of friends to watch. Soon the vanguard of the column was almost within arm's reach of him. The moment left an indelible impression on the professor. Though von Müller had never had much use for Ludendorff's Prussian ways and views, he could not escape feelings of both patriotic exhilaration and despair.

There, he thought, is the great field marshal of the war, one of the most ingenious and imaginative generals in Germany's history, the architect and victor of so many battles. There he is in a wrinkled civilian coat, that shabby, soft felt hat, leading not an army but a desolate, pathetic-looking revolutionary rabble. For what von Müller saw in the ranks behind Ludendorff and Hitler, pressed in by the mass of people on the square, was not so much a proud marching column as a gang of thugs in helmets, military caps, and odd scraps of ill-fitting uniforms. It was the mob personified.

Von Müller and many others on the square expected the column to head straight—along Kaufinger Strasse—toward the Stachus, or perhaps to halt for a rally in front of the Rathaus, and then to swing back to the Bürgerbräukeller. So, for that matter, did most of the other putschist leaders. But Ludendorff suddenly had other plans. Shouting over the din to his trusted servant Neubauer and to Adolf Lenk, he told them to turn right at the City Hall. The demonstrators began marching up Wein Strasse—toward Theatiner Strasse, the Feldherrnhalle, Odeonsplatz, and in the general northward direction of the beleaguered Ernst Röhm at the war ministry.

If Ludendorff wants to march this way, Hermann Kriebel said to himself, naturally we'll go this way too.

Ludendorff had not planned it that way. In fact, he had not planned anything at all, and Hitler was too preoccupied "assessing the mood" to pay attention.

"There are times in life," Ludendorff was to say later, "when one acts without really knowing why. I won the Battle of Tannenberg. When I ask myself how and why, I cannot really say. The explanations are in the history books where I have tried to rationalize my decisions. Perhaps what I wanted to do that noon was to go and fetch Röhm, bring him back."

It was a fateful decision.

Lieutenant Max Demmelmeyer was short of breath and highly agitated as he stormed into the State Police command post in the Residenz and ran up to Senior Lieutenant Michael von Godin.

"Godin, quick," he said frantically. "Where is Muxel? There is a huge demonstration of Hitler people in uniform on Marienplatz. They've broken through Höfler's cordon at the Ludwigsbrücke and it seems they're coming this way. I've heard there are thousands of them, and they're armed."

Demmelmeyer's company, posted on Odeonsplatz, had been assigned to provide flank protection for General von Danner's offensive against the war ministry.

The two young officers hurried to their battalion commander, Lieutenant Colonel Wilhelm Muxel. They found him on the telephone, listening with visible alarm to the details of the debacle at the Ludwig Bridge.

"Demmelmeyer says they're on Marienplatz now, apparently headed this way," Godin reported. "They're probably planning to move on Schönfeld Strasse. What should we do?"

Muxel placed a hasty call to Colonel Hans von Seisser, still entrenched with Lossow and Kahr at the 19th Infantry Regiment barracks.

"Von Seisser's instructions are to stop them," Muxel said gravely, hanging up the phone. "Our orders are to protect Odeonsplatz and all points north—at all costs. The demonstrators must not reach the square, Godin. Get your company ready to back up Demmelmeyer's—with all means at your disposal."

The orders were clear. Godin assembled his 130 troopers in the Kaiserhof and told them to load their rifles and carbines and to fix bayonets. Then he waited for a few more minutes.

As the column of marchers headed up Wein Strasse, hundreds of the cheering and curious bystanders from Marienplatz followed and joined the demonstration, among them Karl Alexander von Müller, Carl Zuckmayer, and Father Mayer.

Barely noticed by anyone, the yellow Opel bringing up the rear fell behind, and by a circuitous route, Michael Ried drove to the corner of Residenz and Maximilian Strasse, parking the car on Max-Josef Platz in front of the State Opera House. There, he, Ludwig Schmied, and Dr. Schultze waited, the Red Cross banner on the car now hanging limp and wet in the falling snow.

"Godin! *Raus!*" Muxel shouted. "*Schnell, schnell!* The Nazis are coming!"

19

"Disperse as planned," Godin commanded, as his green-uniformed, helmeted company stormed out of the Imperial Gate of the palace.

His tactics called for sealing off all streets that led into Odeonsplatz with the exception of Ludwig Strasse, already well protected by Reichswehr and other police. Sergeant Friedrich Fink's 1st platoon posted itself as a thin cordon across Residenz Strasse at its narrowest point—between the Imperial Gate and the entrance to the Konditorei Rottenhöfer, one of Munich's finest cafés and confectionaries. One platoon closed off Brienner Strasse, another access from the Hofgarten. Godin, leading the 3rd platoon himself, dashed in front of the Feldherrnhalle, the memorial to Bavaria's military heroes and a replica of Michelangelo's Florentine Loggia dei Lanzi, to help Demmelmeyer seal off Theatiner Strasse, where, in the distance, they could see the putschist column approaching.

Access to the square was closed.

The armored car parked there for the past hour had turned its turret, the cannon pointing southward. A police machine-gun team lugged its weapon up the steps of the Feldherrnhalle and mounted it on a tripod equidistant between the two huge bronze lions there, ready to fire at either Residenz or Theatiner streets, which converge just a few yards beyond.

The marchers were surprised to spot the heavy police guard ahead as they reached the corner of Theatiner and Perusa streets. After Höffler's detachment at the Ludwig Bridge, so the Oberland League's Friedrich Weber explained later, "we had not expected to encounter additional State Police."

"To the right, to the right!" Ludendorff commanded. "We shall go around them."

Lenk, Neubauer, and the flag carriers in the lead turned right into Perusa Strasse.

Neubauer fell back a few steps to confer with the general as they walked along. "Where to now, Excellency?" he asked.

"To the left! Turn into Residenz Strasse!" Ludendorff ordered, as they reached the intersection at the Opera House where the yellow Opel was waiting. Dr. Schultze bounded out of the car and joined the front ranks to march right behind Hitler and Göring.

Residenz Strasse is still fairly wide at this point, but it soon narrows as it curves gently past the palace of Bavaria's kings. Here too the sidewalks were mobbed with the curious and the sympathetic. Demonstrators and crowd burst forth with a raucous rendition of "Die Wacht am Rhein" as they continued defiantly up the street.

Was it in the spirit of comradeship, as some claimed later, and to give each other heart? Or was it, perhaps, the brawling tactic of forming a phalanx, a human wedge? Either way, Hitler, Scheubner-Richter, and others in the front ranks suddenly linked arms. In his left hand the Nazi leader carried his Browning. Twelve abreast, in some cases sixteen, the marchers now filled almost the entire roadway and carried many of the bystanders with them like a flash flood rushing down a narrow ravine.

Farther ahead, where Residenz Strasse narrows to barely more than alley width between the palace and the private houses across from it, they could see another green-uniformed police line—Fink's platoon. Hitler and Göring figured it would be as easy to crash as Höfler's at the Ludwig Bridge.

The noise of the singing and cheering and the thousands of marching feet in the canyonlike street was deafening. If Fink did shout *"Halt!"* many times, as his men claimed subsequently, chances are it was heard no more than Ulrich Graf's repeated cry: "Don't shoot! Excellency Ludendorff is coming. Don't shoot!"

Within seconds the mob coming up the street had overwhelmed Fink's first line, trying to defend itself with truncheons, carbine stocks, and rifles held at port. The police were pushed along toward the Feldherrnhalle by the onrushing marchers, all of them screaming, shouting, or singing at the tops of their lungs.

Demmelmeyer had run through the vaulted Feldherrnhalle at

hearing the commotion in Residenz Strasse. "Godin! Godin!" he yelled, gesticulating wildly. "Quick—help! They're over here! Reinforcements! They're breaking through!"

"Second Company, double-time!" Godin shrieked. "Doubletime!" A carbine held high, he led his men running around the monument from its Theatiner Strasse side to meet a virtual tidal wave of demonstrators in hand-to-hand combat. As members of the Stosstrupp charged forward with bayonets fixed, Godin's police tried to parry the thrusts with rifles and carbines held at port, with flailing truncheons, and by swinging their guns as clubs.

Suddenly a shot rang out. It killed Sergeant Fink.

Who fired the shot has never been clarified. Scores of witnesses were later questioned—marchers, police, Reichswehr soldiers watching from a distance, bystanders, and residents surveying the scene from nearby buildings. Each told a different story.

Godin and the police insisted afterward that it came from the demonstrators' ranks. Some claimed it was Hitler himself, others that Julius Streicher was to blame. The Nazis accused the police. Adolf Lenk insists to this day that "we were simply overpowered and taken completely by surprise," that the first shot fired came from "the police line," and that it was the one which killed his friend Kurt Neubauer, walking next to him, by blowing half his head away. In fact, Lenk has maintained that "if Neubauer and I hadn't changed places just a few minutes earlier when he stepped back to talk to Ludendorff at the corner of Perusa Strasse, that bullet would have hit me."

Dr. Kurt Stordeur, a spectator, was certain the first shooting "came from the police side."

Gertrud Rommel, a retired schoolteacher standing on Odeonsplatz in front of the Feldherrnhalle among the crowd that had suddenly gathered there, swore that she saw a kneeling policeman firing from the sidewalk close to her.

Anton Reithinger, a student who had followed the crowd and the demonstrators up Residenz Strasse, was certain—"from the sound"—that the "first shot came from Odeonsplatz," and that when it rang out, "the marchers still had their rifles slung over their shoulders."

The Stosstrupp's Hans Krüger made the same claim, saying

that his unit did not shoot back "until after the police first fired on us."

Yet his platoon mate and friend, Walter Hewel, carrying the Stosstrupp banner, testified that he was marching next to Heinrich von Knobloch "when a shot rang out immediately to my right, but I could not see who [in the Nazi ranks] it was who fired."

It could also have been accidental—the discharge of a policeman or demonstrator's rifle as they grappled and struggled with each other in hand-to-hand fighting at the head of the column.

There were witnesses, too, who said that the first shot came from neither side but, instead, from the roof or a high window of the ornate Preysing Palais, which adjoins the back side of the Feldherrnhalle. A sniper? A provocateur? A Reichswehr lieutenant and sergeant, watching from the far corner of Odeonsplatz, said later they both heard a retort and saw the smoke of gunpowder from a window just below the roof of the Preysing Palais. Godin, to this day, has never ruled out that possibility. In fact, he later sent one of his men into the building to investigate. Empty shell casings and powder burns were discovered on a number of windowsills.

What really happened at that moment at the Feldherrnhalle at 12:45 P.M. on November 9, 1923, remains a mystery. But not its consequences.

Was it that first shot? A second? Perhaps even a third unheard over the deafening noise? No one could say. But suddenly a bullet zinged past Godin's left ear and smashed sickeningly into the forehead of a police corporal—Nikolaus Hollweg—standing right behind the lieutenant. Hollweg was killed instantly.

There was a split second or two of shock. Deathly silence. Then Residenz Strasse erupted in a wild firefight as Godin's and Demmelmeyer's men, without so much as a command, began shooting back.

Scheubner-Richter, his arm linked with Hitler's, was one of the first to be hit, struck in the heart by a bullet that killed him immediately. As he fell, he pulled Hitler down with him, so hard that the Führer dislocated his shoulder and screamed out with pain. Ulrich Graf, trying to protect his leader, took eleven bullets in the chest, stomach, arms, and thighs before falling on top of the two. Ludendorff instinctively hit the pavement; Göring too, but not before being hit in the thigh and groin. Lenk, horrified by the sight of Neubauer, tried to pull himself and his dead friend to safety behind one of the lions guarding the main gate of the Residenz.

All along the street, bystanders fled into doorways, pressed themselves against the walls of buildings, and hid in archways. The marchers—most of them with vivid memories of front-line battle—hit the ground, piling on top of each other, sometimes in a mass of humanity a yard high. Those on top used their comrades' bodies as protection and as bastions from which to fire.

The Stosstrupp machine guns could be heard sputtering, and volley after volley of pistol, rifle, and carbine fire—whatever was available.

A full-scale gunfight, it lasted a scant minute. But when it was over, Residenz Strasse and Odeonsplatz were a shambles of blood, lacerated chunks of human flesh, and twisting, writhing, wailing, screaming men. Only those toward the front of the marching column really knew what had happened. The hundreds upon hundreds toward the rear, having heard the gunfire, scrambled away in panic, rushing to doff their uniforms as they hurried through open stores, banks, and building entrances.

On the battlefield, fourteen putschists lay dead or mortally wounded. Among them were Scheubner-Richter; Neubauer; Oskar Körner, a toyshop owner who had been donating half of his profits to the Nazi cause; and Dr. Theodor von der Pfordten, a fifty-year-old Bavarian high court judge and Nazi sympathizer, who was carrying a draft of a constitution for the new "Nationalist Republic" in his coat pocket.

Dead and dying, too, were four state policemen, including Fink, Hollweg, and Captain Rudolf Schraut.

Scores more were seriously injured. Some twenty-three were soon rushed to the university hospital, where Dr. Ferdinand Sauerbruch headed a team of surgeons that worked feverishly through the rest of the afternoon and night to save their lives.

The bloodshed would have been even greater had the majority of Godin's men not fired at the ground, causing largely ricochet and splinter injuries.

Most of the wounded, no matter how critically, did not wait

long for help. Instead, they made their escape to avoid falling into police hands—especially the leaders.

Hitler was the first. When the firing stopped, Max Kronauer, a veteran party member, pulled him from under Scheubner-Richter's body and helped him struggle painfully to his feet. Hair falling into his chalk-white face, he was in agony. In horror he shrank back from the carnage, seeking the Residenz wall for safety. Dr. Schultze hurried toward him and led him through the fleeing, panic-stricken mob toward the yellow Opel on Max-Josef Platz, where a stunned Michael Ried and Ludwig Schmied were waiting, the engine of the car still running. On the way they came upon a ten-year-old boy, an innocent spectator—Gottfried Mayr—lying at the curb and bleeding profusely from a bullet wound in his upper arm. At Hitler's suggestion, Schultze and a cousin-in-law, a Munich student, took the youth along to the car and hastily gave him first aid.

Hermann Göring, bleeding and in excruciating pain from his thigh wound, crawled slowly along the store fronts on Residenz Strasse, helped by Wilhelm Brückner and two young SA men. He was carried into the Jewish-owned Ballin Furniture Company, where the owner's sympathetic wife, Ilse, and her sister dragged him to the back and dressed his wounds. At his pleading, they called Carin and then helped arrange for his removal to the private clinic of one Dr. von Ach.

Alfred Rosenberg, who had served as cover for a wildly firing SA trooper while cowering prone on the pavement, crawled to the side and crept backward on his belly, finally finding sanctuary near Lenk behind the little lions. Both were smeared with the blood of their dead and dying co-conspirators but unhurt. Keeping close to the wall of the Residenz, stepping over the dead and wounded, they slunk toward Max-Josef Platz just a few paces behind Hitler and Schultze, then joined the fleeing crowd. Lenk rushed home to his parents' piano-making shop on Jahn Strasse, where, as he recalled, "my mother was horrified by my appearance." Rosenberg, shocked, wandered aimlessly about the turbulent streets of Munich and met with others in various cafés that afternoon.

Oberland's Friedrich Weber, weeping hysterically, fled down Residenz Strasse but was arrested later in the day. Hermann Kriebel managed to escape—for a while—to Austria. Hans Frank and some of Edmund Heines's storm troopers dashed for safety among astonished customers in the retail store of the Eiles Coffee Roasting Company, hid their uniforms in the back, and mingled with the crowd. Josef Berchtold, Emil Maurice, Knobloch, Krüger, Hewel, and a score of other members of the Stosstrupp, some with flesh wounds, sought sanctuary in shops and passageways on their hasty retreat back to the Bürgerbräukeller. One of them, Adalbert Stollwerck, finding himself encircled by police near the Hofbräuhaus, left his rifle in the courtyard entrance of the Weinhaus Schneider, a tavern, borrowed a civilian jacket from the innkeeper, and "hurried home" in disguise.

The Oberländers of Ludwig Oestreicher, Max von Müller, and Hans Oemler scattered in all directions, hoping to get out of town. Many of them did. Konrad Kiessling, on the other hand, wanted nothing more than to report as soon as possible to his job as a police trainee, "in order to save my career."

Wild rumors had spread instantly through the mass of putschists and marchers who were too far back to see what was going on but close enough to hear the gunfire and see the panic. Ludendorff had been reported dead. Hitler, too.

Well, not quite. But where was Ludendorff?

The gunsmoke had not yet lifted and the cries of the wounded and dying still pierced the cold noon air when the old warrior struggled to his feet. Battered felt hat in hand, he brushed off his coat and stepped over Johann Aigner, lying stunned but unhurt near the body of his master, Scheubner. As straight-backed as ever, he walked on—right through Godin's men, themselves shocked by the carnage—into Odeonsplatz. Behind him, his nose bleeding, his old Reichswehr uniform covered with the mud of the street, came Hans Streck.

It was a macabre sight, witnessed by many of the curious who had assembled just beyond the Feldherrnhalle, among them Carl Zuckmayer and Robert Murphy.

Ludendorff continued on, apparently headed right across the square, his eyes fixed on Ludwig Strasse and the war ministry. He did not notice Lieutenant Max Demmelmeyer standing in his path.

"Excellency," the young police officer said, "I have to take you into custody."

"If those are your orders, Lieutenant, I will follow you," Ludendorff said stiffly.

He was led inside the Residenz to Lieutenant Colonel Muxel. There he waited, along with some twenty other arrested putschists, until his first interrogation later that afternoon by an assistant prosecutor from the Munich district attorney's office, Dr. Hans Ehard.

Muxel, embarrassed and chagrined by the sight of the great hero in his soiled coat, offered to inform Ludendorff's family that he was safe.

"Do not call me 'Excellency,'" the general shot back gruffly. "From now on I am simply 'Herr Ludendorff.' The German officer lost his honor today. I am ashamed to have ever been a German officer. You are all revolting. I want to vomit before you. As long as you and others like you wear that uniform, I will never put mine on again."

20

Father Rupert Mayer limped hurriedly to Odeonsplatz as soon as he heard of the shooting. He knew many of the marchers personally, and though he had broken with them politically, wanted to give them the solace of religion.

Grimly he walked among the many dead and wounded and through the crimson puddles of blood where police were already strewing sawdust.

He offered last rites to the dying and words of comfort to the injured. But one by one, as he approached the Nazis and Oberländers lying there, they turned away their heads or snarled at him.

"Get away, you popish jackal!" said one storm trooper as the priest bent down to him. In the war they had been at the front together, as servants of God, Kaiser, and King.

Heinrich Hoffmann, new plates of film in his huge bag, pedaled furiously down Ludwig Strasse toward the center of Munich, expecting to find the demonstrators at Marienplatz, or perhaps the Stachus. He stopped abruptly as he saw the gruesome scene at the Feldherrnhalle.

The wounded were being carried away to waiting ambulances. After the brief volley of gunfire that had scattered them, the pigeons had flocked back to Odeonsplatz. Some sat on the corpses laid out there.

Sickened and horrified by the sight, but also disappointed that he had missed "a historic picture," Hoffmann bicycled back to his Schelling Strasse studio, where to his surprise he found Hermann Esser, Max Amann, and Dietrich Eckart, the Nazi party bard, waiting for him in an open car.

"Quick!" Esser said. "We must get out of here, out of Munich, out of the country."

"Second Company, fall in!" von Godin commanded in a subdued voice.

The green-uniformed troopers assembled on the square, their bayonets sheathed but their weapons still hot. Impassively, Godin surveyed the scene and thought about his dead and wounded. Fink and Hollweg had been among his most trusted men.

"Forward, march!" he ordered. The 2nd Company of the Bavarian State Police's First Battalion, the sound of their boots echoing across Odeonsplatz, headed back to their quarters inside the royal palace.

Godin made sure his men got fed, then secluded himself in his cubicle-like office to write his formal report. For the next twenty-two years he would be a marked man, hounded by the Nazis.

Karl Alexander von Müller, following the jubilant crowd as far as Marienplatz, had turned back quickly when he heard the first gunfire, instinctively aware of what was happening. He had hurried home by streetcar, noting that, even as close to the scene of the battle as the Isar Gate, life seemed to be resuming its "normal course."

His wife was waiting for him in a state of high disquiet. Gottfried Feder, their brother-in-law, had telephoned from downtown, almost incoherent in his agitation. She had asked him to come over.

That instant the doorbell rang. It was Feder, shaking with fear and emotion. "I was walking in the second row, right behind Rosenberg," he sputtered in explanation. "I had no military experience, and when the first shots came, I just kept right on going while everybody around me hit the ground.

"It was terrible, horrifying. I just kept on, somehow, past the Feldherrnhalle, throught the police lines. Then I ran into Theatiner Strasse, but they started shooting that way, too. I hid in an entrance of the Preysing Palais there, then in the office of a lawyer I know.

"That's where I phoned." Turning to his sister-in-law, he said, "You must help me, Irma. Please. They will be looking for me. I have to get to Austria!"

Finally calming down, the "Reich finance minister" prepared his escape across the border—like many of his comrades that afternoon.

Putzi Hanfstaengl was half walking, half running in the direction of Brienner Strasse, still hoping to join the march and demonstration. He was just past the Pinakothek, Munich's great art museum, when he saw a mass of people flooding down Arcis Strasse—right toward him. He recognized an SA man in a state of collapse, being helped along by others.

"What happened?" Hanfstaengl asked, seeing the smears of blood on his comrades.

"My God, Herr Hanfstaengl, it's too terrible," the storm trooper wailed. "It's the end of Germany! They opened fire on us at the Feldherrnhalle. It was pure suicide. They're all killed. Everybody's dead—Ludendorff, Hitler."

Shocked at the news, Hanfstaengl dashed back toward his Gentz Strasse apartment to prepare for his escape.

As he hurried along, an open car came toward him and screeched to a stop. In it sat Esser, Amann, Eckart, and Hoffmann.

Hanfstaengl got in, and the group headed back to Hoffmann's studio to prepare their plans for a getaway.

"There is only one thing to do," Hanfstaengl suggested. "We

must get out of Munich immediately—over the border to Salzburg or Innsbrück—and see what we can reorganize from there."

The five bade each other farewell and went their separate ways—Putzi to his apartment to pack, then, with the help of sympathizers, to Rosenheim, and from there across the frontier.

"The last place it would have occurred to me to go," he was to write many years later, "was my home in Uffing, where I would surely be sought and arrested."

"Where to now, gentlemen?" Michael Ried asked, after Dr. Schultze's cousin and Gottfried Mayr, the injured boy, had gotten out of the car at the Isar Gate.

No one in the automobile, least of all Hitler, really knew. His plan to return to the Bürgerbräukeller had been thwarted by the police detachments now in control of all the bridges. They had even been shot at by the "greens" at various intersections, and were driving aimlessly southward along the Isar River.

"Just keep going for a while," Hitler said, then lapsed into brooding silence.

Ludwig Schmied and Schultze studied him carefully. His face was ashen and depressed, and he was in obvious pain.

They were some 10 miles outside the city, on the bumpy, winding cobblestone road that follows the Isar upstream, when Hitler announced abruptly that he must have been shot in the arm, though there was no sign of blood or a wound. Schultze told Ried to park the car in the woods. After helping Hitler out of the trenchcoat, jacket, two sweaters, shirt, and tie he had put on during the night, the doctor examined him. The left shoulder was seriously dislocated, but that was all. Since Schultze had no way of setting it without help, he fashioned a makeshift sling from a handkerchief. Then they drove on.

Schmied and the SA doctor suggested that they try to flee to Austria, but Hitler would not hear of it. They were on the road to Garmisch-Partenkirchen and had just passed through the village of Spatzenhausen, on their way toward Murnau and the Staffel Lake, some 40 miles south of Munich, when Hitler remembered that the Hanfstaengls had a house in Uffing, just a few miles away. Putzi's wife, Helene, he recalled, had gone there with little Egon the previous day. That was the place to stay until he could decide what to do.

He told Ried to stop and let him out. Accompanied by the doctor, he set off on foot for the Hanfstaengl house. Helene let them in without comment and provided a bedroom for him. It was well into the afternoon.

Michael Ried and Ludwig Schmied drove back toward Munich.

Ernst Röhm was still negotiating with General von Danner at the Türken Strasse barracks when the first reports of the Feldherrnhalle shooting—and the rumors of Ludendorff's death—reached him. The assembled officers, putschists and opponents alike, were stunned. Von Danner sank into a morose silence.

"I must return to my men," Röhm declared.

Without giving Danner a decision or waiting for the general's, Röhm—accompanied by General von Epp, Josef Seydel, and Count Moulin-Eckart—hurried back the two blocks to the war ministry, where he was told of Martin Faust and Theodor Casella's deaths. Faust's body was lying in the hallway.

Heinrich Himmler, among others there, was so incensed by developments that he urged Röhm to make a stand. But the captain wanted no more bloodshed. Above all, he knew he was outnumbered and outgunned. They were still deliberating when a captain arrived from Danner's command post with the conditions for capitulation.

The Reichskriegsflagge troopers would have to hand over their weapons to the State Police. After that, they would be allowed to leave the war ministry honorably, in formation, as free men. Röhm was to surrender to the Reichswehr and face possible court-martial for mutiny.

A scant few minutes had passed when yet another courier arrived with a handwritten message. *Captain Röhm must decide immediately!* it read. It was signed by Otto von Lossow.

Röhm was in a quandary. How much longer could he bargain for time? While Epp was beseeching him to surrender, Osswald, Seydel, Moulin-Eckart, Himmler, and others wanted to fight. With Ludendorff dead, they argued, what difference did it make? They wanted a battle for life or death, for revenge. More bloodshed? Yes, Röhm's aides demanded unanimously.

The deliberations were interrupted by the arrival of Lieutenant Colonel Hofmann, the Ingolstadt commandant. Ludendorff was not dead, not even wounded, he told the assembled putschists. And as for holding the war ministry: well, he had rescinded his orders. Röhm was "free to make a military decision."

"We accept the conditions," Röhm announced, turning to Osswald. "Assemble the men in the courtyard for an orderly and honorable surrender."

It was 1:30 P.M.

Senior Lieutenant Max Braun's Reichswehr company streamed into the complex, followed by other 19th Infantry and Engineer Battalion units and police.

The putschists, standing at attention, were stripped of their weapons, their helmets, and a host of other equipment they had taken from the war ministry supply rooms.

Röhm, under guard, was led to a waiting staff car to be taken first to von Danner, then to Stadelheim Prison. Seydel and Moulin-Eckart volunteered to accompany him.

"You can take your men out the back door," Braun told Osswald and Lembert.

"But that is not the honor promised us," Lembert protested. "We have a dead man. He was your comrade too. At least show him some respect."

"That's not my affair," Braun said. "I have my orders."

Placing Martin Faust's body on a stretcher, the Reichskriegsflagge troopers marched out the back gate. Some 400 men strong, with a defiant Heinrich Himmler still clutching the flag, they set off for a two-mile procession through seething, turbulent downtown Munich to the home of Faust's parents on Gollier Strasse, in the city's West End. Hundreds joined them. It was their last act of defiance.

Lembert rang the bell as the battalion stood silently on the street. Then they placed the dead storm trooper on the doorstep and dispersed.

For Ernst Röhm and his Reichskriegsflagge, for Friedrich Weber's Oberland League, and for Hitler's SA, the putsch that was to herald "Germany's rebirth and reawakening" was over.

Hearing the news at the 19th Infantry Regiment barracks, where they were still entrenched in the communications shed, Gustav von Kahr, Otto von Lossow, and Hans von Seisser looked at each other with what seemed to witnesses a sense of relief. A message was drafted to report the news to Berlin—to President Ebert, Chancellor Stresemann, and Germany's newly appointed military dictator, General Hans von Seeckt. Lossow made plans to return to his freed headquarters, Seisser to go to the Türken Strasse barracks, and von Kahr to his official apartment on Maximilian Strasse, where he hoped to get some sleep.

But the triumvirs were soon to be disabused of the notion that Munich was now at peace. The city was a cauldron of opposition, which that afternoon was just starting to build up a head of explosive political steam. It was to last for days—days during which Munich was under rigid martial law. In a sense, the worst was yet to come.

The traitors, in the eyes of tens of thousands of Müncheners, were not Hitler and Ludendorff but Kahr, Lossow, and Seisser. Wasn't it they—the agitators on hundreds of street corners were soon to ask—who had broken their pledges to the Führer, who had made a mockery of the handshake they had given him on the stage of the Bürgerbräukeller? And the multitudes screamed back, "Yes!"

Nor was the putsch over for its most direct victims—the hostages in the Bürgerbräukeller and the prisoners being held in the Lehmann villa in Grosshesselohe. Indeed, for many of them the hours of real terror were just beginning.

21

Julius Schaub could not believe his eyes as the first members of the Stosstrupp straggled back to the Bürgerbräukeller— Knobloch, Emil Maurice, Walter Hewel, and then, finally, Berchtold—their uniforms covered with dirt, some without weapons, and a number bleeding. They looked as if they were returning from a war, and in a sense they were.

"Where are the councilors?" Berchtold shouted. "Load them on that truck over there. We have to get out of here fast!"

Mayor Schmid and the city councilors were hustled aboard an open truck, and a score of Berchtold's troopers scrambled aboard. Berchtold and Knobloch jumped into an open car and led the way

up Rosenheimer Strasse, toward the villages of Perlach, Otto-
brunn, and Höhenkirchen.

Left behind were Wilhelm Briemann and a few others to
guard the captured members of Georg Höfler's police platoon and
the Jewish hostages.

Slowly, many shocked, dazed, and wounded marchers converged on the beerhall. Gregor Strasser assembled his storm troopers from Landshut and left Munich hurriedly, on foot. Oberländers, too, dashed away in waiting trucks and cars, most of the
men taking their weapons with them.

It was later estimated by police that during the first hour after the Odeonsplatz shooting at least 1,000 putschists made their
getaway.

What remained at the Bürgerbräukeller, when several companies of State Police surrounded and captured it without a fight
around 2 P.M., was a largely deserted command post, manned by
a small detachment of stunned and demoralized mutineers for
whom the world seemed to have come to an end. Their company
and battalion leaders had disappeared—most of them in the direction of Rosenheim and the Austrian frontier. Those who had
stayed behind were disarmed quickly; the police collected no less
than four truckloads of weapons—rifles, carbines, machine guns,
mortars, and boxes upon boxes of ammunition and hand grenades.

The captured policemen and the Jewish hostages were freed.

For Munich's mayor and the seven councilmen, the hasty retreat from the beerhall was the start of a harrowing hours-long
ordeal, later to be described by Albert Nussbaum.

"While standing on the truck, to which a trailer with much
ammunition was attached, we were guarded by twenty armed
men," Nussbaum reported. "I tried to start a conversation with
one of them, but before we had exchanged more than two or
three words, one of the others—an officer with a revolver—pointed his pistol at both of us and said, 'One more word and I'll shoot
you both down.'

"We had no idea where they intended to take us, but after
leaving the city I noticed we were going through Perlacher Forest
and assumed the destination was Rosenheim, where, so I over-
heard the guards saying, they had six cannons which they intend-

ed to bring to Munich for an artillery barrage.

"After a while, the convoy stopped in a woods and we were ordered to get down from the truck. The Bürgermeister turned to me and said, 'At this point I wouldn't give a pfennig for our lives. I think it is over for us.' As we were led further into the forest, with Berchtold and Maurice in the lead and some others guarding us from behind, I had the sinking feeling that Herr Schmid was right. We walked about forty to fifty meters, then Berchtold stopped. 'I have to make an unpleasant announcement to you,' he said. And in that minute I lost all hope."

But Berchtold's "announcement" was not what Nussbaum had feared.

Instead of declaring that he was about to execute them, the Stosstrupp leader explained that he and some of the others intended to return to the city "to get money and reconnoiter the situation." To do so, they would need civilian clothes.

Schmid, Nussbaum, and several of the other hostages were unceremoniously relieved of their hats, coats, and jackets; some had to give up their trousers. Then they were marched back to the truck and again prodded aboard. Berchtold, Maurice, and two others drove off in the car—not to be seen again for many weeks—leaving Heinrich von Knobloch and Julius Schaub in charge.

The strange odyssey continued with the mayor and the others standing on the open truck in freezing weather. In Höhenkirchen, Knobloch ordered a halt at a village inn. Some of the weapons and ammunition were unloaded, defenses established, and the prisoners ordered inside and told to sit at a corner table.

"Anyone who makes so much as a move to leave," Knobloch threatened, "will be shot on the spot."

Patiently the prisoners awaited what they thought was certain death. But in fact their terrifying experience was soon to end happily—on a note as ludicrous as it was revealing of the putschists' mood and the Germany of the times.

From the moment they had left the Bürgerbräukeller, they had been followed at a safe distance in another car by a municipal employee who had been dispatched to search for them. A half hour after the Stosstrupp had barricaded itself in the Höhenkirchen inn, the man drove up and announced himself to Knobloch.

It being Friday afternoon and payday, he explained, the burgomaster and the councilors were needed urgently at the Rathaus
to sign that week's payroll for Munich's many unemployed. Without their signatures, payment could not be made and thousands of
people on the dole would go hungry.

"Are you prepared to accept responsibility for that?" he
asked, staring at von Knobloch officiously.

Knobloch certainly was not.

It was a ruse, and it worked perfectly. Without further ado,
except to extract a promise from them that they would not reveal
where the remnants of the Stosstrupp were hiding, Knobloch told
his hostages they were free to leave. They did so in a hurry. While
Schmid and the oldest of the city fathers rode back to Munich in
the car, Nussbaum and the others took the first train from Höhenkirchen. By 5:30 P.M. all were back in the Rathaus on teeming
Marienplatz, chilled, shaken, but, on the whole, hale and hearty.

For Prime Minister von Knilling and Rudolf Hess's other prisoners, in particular Interior Minister Franz Schweyer and Agricultural Minister Johann Wutzelhofer, freedom did not come so
quickly or easily.

Publisher Julius Lehmann's villa in the isolated, secluded suburb of Grosshesselohe resembled a bristling fortress preparing for
siege. One machine gun in the garden pointed down the road,
ready to strafe any and all who might approach. Another in the
entry hall faced out the front door. Menacing muzzles of rifles
and carbines pointed from various windows here and there. Two
helmeted SA men, bayonets fixed to their rifles, potato-masher
grenades dangling from their belts, patrolled the surrounding
park. Periodically a team would leave on a brief reconnaissance
mission through the woods. The truck that had brought them and
two remaining vehicles, one a touring car owned and driven there
by a rental-car operator named Otto Lippacher, had been hidden
behind the house.

The seven prominent prisoners—Knilling, Schweyer, Wutzelhofer, Justice Minister Franz Gürtner, Police Chief Karl Mantel,
his aide Otto Bernreuther, and Crown Prince Rupprecht's chef-
du-cabinet, Count Josef von Soden—had been served a "simple
but ample" lunch. Shortly after three o'clock, they had the feeling

that the atmosphere was becoming a bit more convivial, for they were released from their solitary confinement. Explaining that he wanted to "clear the ground floor," Rudolf Hess asked Soden, Mantel, and Bernreuther to go upstairs, where they could join the four cabinet members. But it was a short-lived illusion, for in fact the mood "had suddenly become ugly, ominous and tense."

Reports of the shooting at the Feldherrnhalle, rumors of the death of Hitler and Ludendorff, even of Friedrich Weber—Lehmann's son-in-law—had reached Hess and his men by telephone and through a group of fleeing Oberländers who had stopped by the house. There was pandemonium on the ground floor as the storm troopers set up more machine guns and prepared for the siege by State Police that they expected momentarily. Thirsting for revenge, they were determined to put up a fight.

Appalled and confused, Lehmann rushed upstairs to the prisoners. "You are my guests," he stammered apologetically, "and I promise to do everything I can to protect and make you comfortable. But I can guarantee nothing any longer. The guards are demanding reprisals. I am not sure their lieutenant can keep them under control."

The hostages could hear the SA troopers downstairs arguing loudly and heatedly with Hess.

"Our leader has fallen," some of them shouted. "His blood has to be avenged. There's enough royal blood up there, and enough trees around to string them up. An eye for an eye!"

"But we still need them as hostages," Hess insisted coldly, trying to calm the rabble. He had other plans—at least for Schweyer and Wutzelhofer, who seemed to have roused the greatest ire among the Nazis.

Holing up in the Lehmann villa, he reasoned, would be futile. Sooner or later the hideout would be discovered. And if not, they would all run out of food and supplies anyway. "I decided to take Schweyer and Wutzelhofer into the mountains somewhere," he was to testify later. "I hoped to hide them in some hut or keep them as hostages among our retreating troopers as long as possible—in a ski hut or cow herd's shack, high up."

For ransom? As bargaining chips? The question was never answered.

As for the other prisoners, Hess told his men to procrastinate as long as possible—until after dark, at least. If police or army forces arrived, they were to demand "written instructions from Hitler or Göring" on what to do before releasing the five. But, he instructed, if by evening the house was still undiscovered, they were simply to retreat to the hills in small groups—without the hostages.

"No bloodshed, no executions, no reprisals," Hess insisted. "Not unless we have authorization from the leadership. Just leave them here and get out."

The proposal was met with disgruntled mumbling. But fortunately for the prisoners, the storm troopers had enough discipline to obey orders.

Guarded by two other SA men selected "because they looked the most trustworthy and reliable," Hess marched Wutzelhofer and Schweyer out of the house to Lippacher's big touring car.

One of the guards, Johann Niederreiter, carried a parcel and placed it on the back seat next to Wutzelhofer. It contained 20 trillion Reichsmarks in 50-billion-mark notes—part of the morning's loot from Karl Beggel's raid. Hess had obtained the money from a passing squad of retreating Oberländers, "to buy the supplies I would need for keeping the ministers in a ski hut."

It was 4:10 P.M. and almost dusk. The heavy car was cranked to life and roared down the driveway toward the same cobble-stoned road that Hitler and Dr. Schultze had taken some two hours earlier. Lippacher headed in the direction of the mountain town of Bad Tölz, where Hess hoped to meet the local Oberland leader, a veterinarian named Dr. Seitz, who was to guide him to a secluded hut in the craggy Alps.

For Wutzelhofer and Schweyer it was the start of an agonizing, terrifying journey, exacerbated by Hess's sadism.

Periodically—at least four times on the 22-mile trip through the snowy landscape—he ordered Lippacher to stop the car in dense woods and park so that the headlights shone into them. Then he and Niederreiter left to explore, as if searching for a convenient spot to hang or shoot the two.

"It was uphill and downhill and through one dark, eerie grove after another," as Schweyer was to say later. "Each time they disappeared for long minutes, obviously hunting for a place to do us in, Wutzelhofer and I were certain the end was imminent."

When they finally reached the outskirts of Bad Tölz and halted in front of Seitz's house, it was almost six o'clock. Hess disappeared inside, leaving his prisoners no less terrified in the car. Seitz, already providing sanctuary for a group of fleeing Oberländers, assigned Hess a guide who was supposed to know a well-hidden shed high on a steep, rocky slope above the nearby town of Lenggries.

Off they drove again, but as heavy swirls of fog surrounded them, Lippacher repeatedly lost his way on the winding, snow-covered mountain roads, most of them little more than wide cow paths. To Schweyer, nearly freezing in the back seat and growing more apprehensive by the moment, it seemed "that we were driving in circles."

"The guide and I," Hess was to explain later, "decided there was just too much snow to reach the hut without climbing equipment, especially with the two elderly ministers.

"But he said he knew of a villa in the vicinity which might be suitable for at least one night's stay, perhaps even longer."

Back they drove, Lippacher cursing the weather and picking his way slowly through foggy, barren alpine countryside, at last parking the car on the outskirts of Bad Tölz. The house was near, the guide explained, and he and Hess got out to hunt for it on foot. They left the automobile in a densely wooded area with Wutzelhofer, Schweyer, the SA guards, and the packet of money.

By this time Schweyer's nerves were frayed to breaking. The fanatical Hess, with his haunting, deep-set eyes, had not been a man to inspire confidence in the prisoners, but at least they knew he was an officer and, presumably, a gentleman. By comparison, the two swarthy, gruff-looking storm troopers—Niederreiter was later to admit to eight previous convictions for larceny and assault—seemed the very incarnation of violence.

Nearly an hour passed. It was bitter cold, and the deathlike silence in the car, the interminable waiting, became unbearable. Suddenly Schweyer began sobbing hysterically. "For God's sake," he cried, "just tell us what you intend to do with us. Why are we waiting here?"

Wutzelhofer, a rugged highland farmer, tried to calm him. So, surprisingly, did Niederreiter.

"Herr Minister, just relax," he whispered, barely audibly, ap-

parently unsure himself of his even grimmer and more surly-look-
ing companion. "Nothing will happen to you, I'll guarantee that.
But please be quiet and keep calm. In two days at the latest you
will be back in Munich, safe."

Schweyer was somewhat reassured, but remained skeptical,
especially as the waiting dragged on—almost another half hour.
Hess, it seemed, had simply disappeared, and the storm troopers,
too, were getting edgy. Suddenly they left the car to confer in
private. Schweyer and Wutzelhofer could not hear their debate.

"Let's go," Niederreiter said as they returned.

"Go where?" Lippacher asked.

"Back to Munich. By way of Holzkirchen."

Mystified, Lippacher started the vehicle and drove, as fast as
conditions allowed, back to the city.

"Was this supposed to be just an excursion into the country?"
Schweyer asked indignantly, having regained composure.

"Please, quiet," Niederreiter said, pressing his hand on the
interior minister's knee as if to signal him.

When they had reached a residential section of Munich, Niederreiter suddenly asked Lippacher to pull over and stop the car.
To Schweyer's and Wutzelhofer's total surprise, he and the other
guard got out.

"Take the gentlemen where they want to go," Niederreiter
said, and, saluting, disappeared with his companion down a dark
street.

It was almost 9 P.M. For Interior Minister Schweyer and Agricultural Minister Wutzelhofer the terrifying experience was
over—almost twenty-four hours after Rudolf Hess had mounted
the podium in the Bürgerbräukeller auditorium to read out their
names from the slip of paper Hitler had handed him.

Freedom came at just about the same time for Prime Minister
von Knilling, Gürtner, Mantel, Bernreuther, and Count von Soden.

For nearly three hours they were left alone after Wutzelhofer
and Schweyer's abduction by Hess; but around 7 P.M. Julius Lehmann came up to them with the tentative news that "your release
may be at hand soon." One by one or in small groups, the more
than twenty SA guards at the house had simply disappeared.

When Lehmann was sure the last of them was gone, he phoned Munich police headquarters at Ett Strasse to reveal the whereabouts of the missing cabinet members and officials, and within an hour they too were safely back in the city. Count von Soden in particular wondered why he had been taken prisoner in the first place.

When he asked Gustav von Kahr that question several days later, the stocky, stubborn little Bavarian triumvir shrugged his shoulders and said he did not know. "But I can guess," Kahr added slyly. "Among certain people, it seems, you have a reputation for being an emissary of the Vatican."

And Rudolf Hess?

He returned to the wooded spot where he had left the car only minutes after Lippacher had driven off, puzzled to find everyone gone. He spent several more hours searching for them in Bad Tölz and then, dejected, feeling he had "failed the Führer," asked Seitz, the veterinarian, to put him up.

The next morning, stranded and afraid of arrest, he finally managed to contact his fiancée, Ilse Pröhl, who dutifully bicycled to the little mountain town to rescue him. Taking turns riding the bike, they walked and rode through the foothills and forests on isolated roads and trails back to Munich.

Hess hid with friends for a few days and then left the city for the mountains again, hoping to reach Salzburg by hiking across the frontier. He returned once more when Ilse became ill, and six months later he surrendered voluntarily to stand trial.

When news of the shooting reached her in their house in Obermenzing, Carin Göring bolted from bed, her fever suddenly gone. Stuffing only the barest necessities and money into her purse, she rushed by taxi to the private clinic of Dr. von Ach to see her "dear good Hermann," then barely conscious. She arranged for their immediate escape.

"It was terrifying," she was to write her mother in Sweden several days later. "From Munich we were driven by car to Garmisch. Hermann was almost delirious and the wound, still with the first bandage, was dirty and bleeding and in danger of becoming infected. We spent two days in the villa of friends, but it became known that he was there. People started gathering outside the house and calling for him. We thought it best to leave and drive to Austria."

They were stopped at the frontier by State Police on the evening of November 11. The border authorities phoned Munich, asking what to do. But before the answer came to "arrest him immediately," Göring and Carin had left the border post at Griessen, pledging their "word of honor" not to flee the country. They returned to Garmisch, where he entered a private hospital. His passport had been taken at the border and State Police were assigned to guard and keep an eye on him. Within hours, however, he had disappeared mysteriously.

"A miracle," Carin was to write from Innsbrück. "We were helped. Hermann was carried outside—he could not walk so much as a step—placed in a car in his night-shirt and covered with furs and blankets. Within two hours he was supplied with a false passport and we were brought across the border. . . .

"Mama, do not believe that Hitler's cause is lost, that it has been given up. Oh, no, on the contrary, our energy is greater than ever before. He will triumph, I feel it, I know it. We have not yet seen the end. This first failure will make the ultimate victory all the greater."

Gregor Strasser, the Nazi leader of Lower Bavaria, had fled with his battalion of SA after the shooting and reassembled them outside Munich to march back to Landshut. It was a grueling hike, mostly by night.

The following day, Heinrich Himmler came to the Strasser house, hoping to hide in Landshut where he had spent many years as a teenager while his father was teaching there.

Exhausted from the experience and still shocked by what had happened, the Strassers and Himmler were seated around the dining-room table, having lunch, when the doorbell rang.

It was State Police Lieutenant Georg Höfler.

"Come in," Strasser said, unaware that if his battalion had been closer to the front of the column at the Ludwig Bridge it could have been he and Höfler who almost shot each other.

"Have a bite with us. We'll set another place for you."

Höfler stood awkwardly at the door, looking with embarrassment at his brother-in-law. "I cannot, Gregor," he replied. "I am here to arrest you. Those are my orders."

Interlude VII

The News

It was still early morning in New York and Chicago when the first sketchy reports of the coup's collapse reached editorial offices.

Garbled in their facts, they reflected the confusion and turmoil reigning on the streets of Munich. Some had Hitler killed, others had him wounded, and still others claimed he had been taken prisoner.

While the *Chicago Tribune* screamed: "GERMANY UNITED BY REVOLT," a headline writer at the *New York Tribune* was saying simply: "LUDENDORFF IMPRISONED AS ROYALIST REVOLT IS CRUSHED."

Though it erroneously identified Hitler as "an ex-locksmith," the *New York World* may have come closest to the truth when it blazoned: "MUNICH UPRISING FIZZLES OVERNIGHT." Said the paper's Berlin correspondent, Arno Dosch-Fleurot:

> General von Ludendorff, the most dangerous man in Germany for the last four years, came to the end of his rope this afternoon when he was taken captive. . . . With his arrest the Bavarian revolution collapsed like a punctured balloon.
>
> Adolf Hitler escaped in the running fight in which von Ludendorff was captured. . . .
>
> The breaking down of von Ludendorff, the haughtiest, the most dramatic and also the most insolent of the old German militarists, has stirred Germany, jaded as it has been with continual crises. Driven mad by ambition and having lost all sense of proportion in his determination to reunite the Teutonic peoples into a solid fighting force which yet would conquer the world, Luden-

dorff allied himself with Hitler. When Hitler went off half-cocked last night, declaring the Fascist revolution in Munich, Ludendorff was dragged down with him.

In Rome, at midday on November 9, the papers were still carrying banner headlines about the successful coup in Munich. Kurt Lüdecke, Hitler's "ambassador" to Mussolini, was in an exuberant mood as he boarded the train which would connect in Verona with the Innsbrück-Munich express.

Lüdecke was eager to get back. He had told Hitler that it would break his heart to be out of Germany when things started to happen, that he wanted to be with everybody in the front line in Munich.

"You can fly here when it begins," Hitler had replied.

Lüdecke decided a train would do. But as it sped through the Italian countryside, he started having doubts. Toward evening he was able to buy new papers at a station stop and was disappointed to see they carried no additional information—only the terse comment that communications with Munich were interrupted.

Well past midnight, the train stopped briefly at Bologna and Lüdecke heard newspaper sellers on the platform crying "Extra! Extra!" Leaning from a window, he saw the huge black headlines "blazoning the tragic news: 'Ludendorff Arrestato!'"

It was not until he reached Verona that he managed to get a copy of the *Corriere della Sera,* which spelled out the details of the disaster at the Feldherrnhalle.

Realizing Munich was no place to go at the moment, he changed trains for Milan, where he holed up in a hotel room for two days before planning his flight to Austria. There he joined other escapees, including Hermann Esser and Putzi Hanfstaengl.

In Berlin, Chancellor Gustav Stresemann had called another cabinet meeting for noon on November 9. He, President Ebert, and their ministers were listening attentively to Germany's new dictator and commander-in-chief, General Hans von Seeckt. Haughtily, in clipped and crisp words, his ever-present monocle reflecting the light in the cabinet room, "the Sphinx" reported that Kahr, Lossow, and Seisser had repudiated the putsch, that the North Bavarian military garrisons were definitely opposed to Hit-

ler, and that both in the north and south of the state, all Reichswehr units were loyal to von Lossow and completely under his
control.

"*Meine Herren,*" von Seeckt added, "the rest of the Reich is
perfectly calm and we can assume that the revolt in Munich is a
local affair which will be put down soon. Under the circumstances, I propose lifting the ban on rail transportation and postal
communications to and from Bavaria. I also consider it advisable
to rescind all other measures that might lead to heightening of
tension or to exacerbating, the—"

He was interrupted by an aide, who handed him a slip of
paper. One might have expected at least a smile to cross his impassive face as he read it, but von Seeckt was never seen smiling.

"The Bavarian government," he continued, waving the note,
"has just reported that State Police have dispersed the rebels at
the Feldherrnhalle and that it is complete master of the situation.
General Ludendorff has been taken into custody, though Hitler
has apparently escaped in an automobile."

Friedrich Ebert and Gustav Stresemann glanced at each other
and gave an audible sigh of relief.

Later that afternoon the French ambassador asked Stresemann provocatively whether the events in Bavaria had not finally
convinced the chancellor that there were "far too many guns and
cannons around the country."

"There have been all kinds of fantastic figures bandied about,
Mr. Ambassador," Stresemann replied. "People were saying that
Hitler wanted to march on Berlin with two hundred thousand
men. Instead, he marshaled a force of perhaps two thousand, and
what was to have been a great military campaign turned out to be
nothing but a provincial putsch. Of course many people in Germany own and have kept their weapons. But my government cannot possibly search every citizen's house.

"As far as Monsieur Poincaré's concerns regarding the stability of my government and the danger of armed rebellions, please
inform him that the Munich putsch is the best demonstration of
my government's strength and authority.

"Moreover," the chancellor added, "the Bavarian movement
and the putsch would never have got started had it not been for
the fact that every Reich government since the war has been vir-

tually driven from one disaster to the next by the intolerable conditions imposed on it from abroad."

Stresemann had made his point. Of all postwar politicians, this remarkable conservative understood better than any other what was really wrong in Germany. In less than a week after that meeting, he was to introduce the new currency—the "mortgage mark"—which ended the specter of inflation and helped put Germany on the road to economic recovery and stability, at least until the next catastrophe: the 1929 crash and the subsequent depression.

But what even Stresemann did not fully understand that afternoon was the intensity of the nationalist passion in Munich and the potency of the seed of hatred that had been planted there. Adolf Hitler had not been alone in stirring the passion, though he had articulated it more effectively than anyone else. One could also blame the other reactionaries, ultra-rightists, racists, revanchists, and *condottieri* who had gravitated to the city since Kurt Eisner's 1918 "comic Opera" revolution and the armistice in order to make of Bavaria a "cell of law and order" opposed to everything the new German Republic of Weimar espoused.

22

The smoke had barely cleared and the blood not yet dried on Munich's Odeonsplatz when Hitler's seed of hatred blossomed into unprecedented violence.

By early afternoon November 9, 1923, as news of the shooting had spread and von Kahr's posters repudiating the putsch were finally up, Munich was seething and churning.

Hitler had been right. The masses were on his side. Thousands of putschists and sympathizers continued to mill aimlessly about the streets, forming new demonstration marches wherever police were not watching. Self-appointed propagandists appeared, seemingly out of nowhere, at scores of street corners and on dozens of public squares, to scream "Down with Kahr!" and "Hang the Traitors!" and then disappear again.

Wherever State Police moved in to disperse the throngs, usually on horseback with lances and steel truncheons or, when on foot, with bayonets fixed, they were jeered, insulted, spat upon, whistled at, and berated as "Jew protectors," "bloodhounds," "lackeys of Kahr," "traitors to the Fatherland," "foreign occupiers," "French swine," and "turncoats." And those "green" police were omnipresent. They manned machine guns at most major intersections and stood grimly behind chevaux-de-frise and barbed wire before all major buildings. Mounted, they charged into crowds of spectators and protesters on Marienplatz, in the Tal, on Kaufinger and Neuhauser streets, on Ludwig Strasse, Odeonsplatz, and at the Stachus. Munich was in a turmoil.

Von Kahr imposed an 8 P.M. curfew on all restaurants, theaters, cafés, taverns, and beerhalls, and gave orders to break up groups of more than three persons, but the edict did nothing to deter demonstrators.

Excerpts from the Ett Strasse blotter that afternoon and evening reveal a city in revolt:

3:35.   State Police have requested that no attempt be made to remove the dead from the Residenz before nightfall because of the unrest on Odeonsplatz.

4:15.   Precinct 20 reports that 600 to 700 Hitler people with one dead are milling about on Gollier Strasse.

4:25.   Precinct 20 reports there are 700 to 800 but they now seem to be dispersing.

5:30.   Precinct 18 reports some 300 armed National Socialists moving out on Grünwald Strasse and disappearing in Perlacher Forest.

5:55.   Some 200 National Socialists, unarmed, are marching down Sonnen Strasse toward Karlsplatz.

6:00.   Dachauer Strasse Precinct reports 1,000 Hitler people marching toward main railroad station.

8:45.   Some 1,500 to 2,000 people are assembled in front of *Münchner Neueste Nachrichten* offices and threatening action against the paper.

8:50.   Precinct 9 says there is huge crowd, mostly young men, in Schiller and Schwanthaler streets, apparently moving toward Stachus.

8:55.   Approximately 1,500 Hitler people in formation are moving through Schiller Strasse toward Pettenkofer Strasse, whistling loudly and jeering.

10:00. Precinct 5 says some 1,000 Hitlerites are moving down Ludwig Strasse to Schelling Strasse and offices of *Völkischer Beobachter*. State Police have been notified.

10:25. Large demonstration of National Socialists in front of East Side Station.

10:30. Column of unarmed National Socialists—some 1,000 strong—moving into the city from Ramersdorf. They are shouting and singing.

10:45. Precinct 17 reports 600 to 700 National Socialists marching toward Cornelius Bridge into the city. Unarmed.

11:15. Groups of 300 to 400 people continue to gather on Odeonsplatz. State Police have been notified and are moving to clear the square again.

11:30. Approximately 400 armed Hitlerites marching into city center along Prielmayer Strasse.

11:50. Agnes Auer [daughter of the Social Democratic leader] complains that large formations of singing, shouting demonstrators are parading back and forth at ten-minute intervals in front of her house on Nussbaum Strasse.

Yet the turmoil of Friday afternoon and evening only foreshadowed the popular rebellion that was to rock Munich during the next few days.

"Not since the 1918–19 revolutions have I seen the city in such an uproar," Karl Alexander von Müller noted in his diary on Saturday, November 10. "Throngs of people demonstrated through the streets, shouting 'Kahr the Judas' and 'Lossow the Traitor.'"

Some 4,000 of the demonstrators were Munich University students, screaming "Heil Hitler—Down with Kahr!" as they marched down Ludwig Strasse, placed wreaths at the Feldherrnhalle to "honor our fallen heroes," and then converged on Marienplatz, where they scuffled repeatedly with police. There were stabbings and shootings.

By late Saturday afternoon State Police had shut off virtually all downtown Munich to vehicular and pedestrian traffic.

The mood was inflamed by Fritz Gerlich's headlines and editorials in the *Münchner Neueste Nachrichten* that day and Gustav von Kahr's inane proclamations calling the putsch and the "patriotic" movement at once "utopian" and "ignoble."

Rumors were spreading, too, spurred in large measure by speculation over Hitler's whereabouts. He was reported to be amassing an army of 70,000 near Rosenheim to march on the capital. Ludendorff was said to have committed suicide, though in fact, after having been released on recognition and his "word of honor," he was safely and comfortably back in his house on Heilmann Strasse in Solln-Ludwigshöhe, making plans to attend the funeral of his servant, Kurt Neubauer. There were stories that forty-eight people had actually been killed in the fighting. And there was persistent talk about an imminent northward march into Thuringia by the irregulars on the frontier.

On Sunday, November 11th, the fifth anniversary of the 1918 Armistice, Munich was convulsed again by a paroxysm of rioting, largely by mobs of pro-Hitler youths, most of them between the ages of thirteen and seventeen. Repeatedly State Police broke up the demonstrations and, their patience wearing thin after all the insults, charged the crowds with lances, truncheons, rifle and carbine butts. Scores were injured, especially the elderly, who could not escape the onrushing formations fast enough. "It is feared," the *New York Times* correspondent cabled that afternoon, "that the disorders of the last few days may be only the prelude to further and far more serious conflicts."

The fears were well founded, for on Monday morning Munich University erupted in rebellion when four heavily armed companies of State Police converged on the Ludwig Strasse campus to halt a protest demonstration by thousands of students, the overwhelming majority of them fanatic supporters of Nationalist and Fascist movements. It was a street battle the likes of which Munich had never seen before. Speakers trying to calm the mob— among them von Müller; Dr. Ferdinand Sauerbruch, the surgery professor; and even Hermann Ehrhardt, the free-corps leader— were shouted at and shoved from the makeshift platform. When Ehrhardt called for singing "Deutschland über Alles," the crowd jeered and broke, instead, into the Nazis' favorite "Storm Song."

"We want Hitler! Where is Hitler?" the students chanted, ripping open their jackets and shirts and baring their chests to the police bayonets. "Go ahead, stab us, you dogs! Isn't that what you always do to patriots?"

A semblance of order did not return to the campus, closed

soon after by police edict, until Sauerbruch clambered onto a bench once more to shout: "Adolf Hitler was arrested last night!"

The news silenced the mob like a thunderclap.

23

Hitler had spent the first night in Uffing as Helene Hanfstaengl's "guest" in great pain from the injured shoulder and in a mood that oscillated sharply from deep depression and despondency to hysterical anger at von Kahr and Lossow's "betrayal." Wrapped in a couple of English traveling rugs that Putzi had been given by his mother in 1905 before going to study at Harvard, the Nazi Führer had been unable to sleep.

On the morning of the 10th, the house seemed to be in turmoil. Helene was worried about her husband's safety. Also there was the danger that her three-year-old son might innocently blabber to the villagers that his "Uncle Dolf" was visiting, and if not little Egon, then the excitable and gossipy maids she employed. Secrets could not be kept long in this alpine village on the shores of the Staffel Lake, where not only Hanfstaengl but his mother, Catharina, owned a chalet.

"Much as I am willing to put you up, Herr Hitler," Helene said, "you ought to find somewhere else to hide. For your own sake. Sooner or later the police will come here to look for my husband. It is too much of a risk."

Hitler understood that. But where could he go? The thought of escaping to his native Austria was repugnant to him. He hated Austria. Moreover, how could he, in his condition?

Shortly before noon that Saturday the SA's Dr. Walter Schultze returned with an assistant to set Hitler's arm properly. The injury was painful but not serious.

From Schultze he also learned some of the details of what had happened: that Scheubner-Richter was dead, Neubauer and Körner too, but that Ludendorff was alive and most of the party's top leaders seemed to have made good their escape.

He devised a plan for himself, resigned to the fact that it would have to be to Austria or nowhere. He asked Schultze to contact Helene Bechstein, wife of the piano-manufacturing mag-

324   Interlude VII: The News

nate, who had been one of his principal mentors and generous financial supporters. Would they provide him with a closed automobile in which to get across the frontier? Schultze promised to carry out the delicate assignment.

After the two physicians' departure, Hitler seemed calmer and in better spirits, trying to reassure Helene Hanfstaengl that Putzi was safe and that he himself would leave as soon as the Bechsteins sent the car he had requested.

It was still an unnerving afternoon, however. An unexpected visitor—Hermann Göring's gardener, whose loyalties to the "patriotic" and Nazi party cause Hanfstaengl had long doubted—wanted to speak to Hitler. Visibly frightened by the unexpected demand, and lying as convincingly as she could, Helene said he was not there. It took considerable persuading to get the man to leave, and when he did it was merely to take a room in Uffing's Hotel zur Post. Where, Helene wondered, had he gotten the idea that Hitler was in the house? Hanfstaengl himself was later to accuse the man of having tipped off the police.

Despite the fear of detection and arrest, Hitler slept that night—for the first time in the more than sixty hours since he had awakened on the morning of November 8, the most important day in his life, with a toothache and a splitting headache. In fact, he slept right through the persistent tolling of Uffing's church bell calling the villagers to mass on Sunday morning, November 11. It was almost noon when he finally staggered drowsily downstairs from the little attic bedroom that Helene had provided for him, dressed in white pajamas and a blue bathrobe, both belonging to six-foot-four Putzi and accordingly far too large for him. He was in a surprisingly good humor and even joked a bit.

But restlessness and despondency began overtaking him as the afternoon wore on. Looking out repeatedly at the snow-covered, picture-postcard scenery of the lakeside hamlet, he became increasingly impatient. More than twenty-four hours had passed since Schultze's departure. Where was the Bechsteins' sedan? Had they turned down his request? Had something happened to Schultze? If not, why had the car not been sent yet?

As dusk fell over the peaceful alpine landscape, he asked Helene Hanfstaengl to close the shutters and draw the drapes—people might look in and see him. Intuition seemed to tell him that his time was running out.

At 4:20 P.M., Senior Lieutenant Rudolf Belleville, commander of the State Police company in nearby Weilheim, the county seat, received a disconcerting telephone call. It was Munich on the line, Colonel von Seisser's office.

Hitler, Belleville was told, was reported very reliably to be hiding in the Villa Hanfstaengl in Uffing. Belleville was to take a strong detachment with him by truck, arrest the Nazi leader, and bring him to the fortress prison in Landsberg.

For Rudolf Belleville, twenty-nine, it was a difficult assignment to carry out—and not just because it was a Sunday afternoon with many of his men off duty, including the unit's only truck driver. There was more involved. Belleville knew Hitler well; in fact, in 1920 they had been fairly close friends and political collaborators. Moreover, during the war Belleville had been the observer and gunner in Rudolf Hess's plane, and Hess's close association with Hitler was well known to him.

Why me? Belleville thought to himself, but then reluctantly resigned himself to the fact that "orders are orders."

Putting together a force of ten policemen plus a local gendarme, and prevailing on the brewery's chauffeur—"a Social Democrat, unfortunately"—to do the driving, Belleville's posse embarked on the short 12-mile trip to Uffing. Weilheim's chief of detectives went on ahead by train to alert Uffing's gendarmerie.

"I bet you're on the way to nab that fellow Hitler," the driver remarked to Belleville, as they bumped along uncomfortably on the cobblestone road.

"What gives you that idea?" the lieutenant asked, startled.

"Oh, he's out here quite often," the chauffeur explained. "At the Hanfstaengls."

He had in mind Putzi's chalet. Belleville, however, had been told to go to the villa of Hanfstaengl's mother.

When they arrived, Belleville ordered his men to surround the house. The mass of police instantly brought out the curious villagers. Uffing had not had this much excitement in decades. After prolonged knocking, Catharina Hanfstaengl, daughter and niece of two famous Union generals in the American Civil War, opened the door.

"I am here to arrest Herr Hitler," Belleville announced officiously.

"He is not here. I have not seen him in quite some time,"

Putzi's mother said truthfully. "But you are free to go through the house if you insist."

Belleville insisted, and began a search of the villa and the surrounding grounds that lasted more than an hour. The local gendarme advised him he was looking in the wrong place; if Hitler was in Uffing, he would surely be at "the other Hanfstaengl house." But Belleville persisted.

He was just about to give up when he heard the telephone ring and one of Catharina Hanfstaengl's servants answering.

"The police are here searching," she said.

Belleville rushed into the hallway and grabbed the receiver out of her hands. "Who is this speaking?" he asked.

It was Helene.

"Where is your husband?" Belleville asked.

Helene said she had not seen him since before the putsch in Munich.

"And when did you last see Hitler?" the lieutenant pressed.

"Today," Helene replied.

Belleville did not inquire whether Hitler was still there. Hurriedly he called his men together and left for the Hanfstaengl chalet, some twenty minutes away.

Helene knew they were coming. Slowly, she walked upstairs. Hitler, in Putzi's huge pajamas and bathrobe, was standing in the hallway. Calmly she told him that the police were on their way.

"This is the end!" Hitler said hysterically, grabbing his Browning. "I will never let those swine take me. I'll shoot myself!"

What happened in that instant, according to Hanfstaengl's version in his memoirs, published many decades later, was one of those incredible oddities that changed world history. "It postponed Hitler's suicide by twenty-two years—from 1923 to 1945."

In 1909, while a senior at Harvard, Putzi had attended some jiujitsu courses given by a Boston policeman. One of the holds he was taught was how to disarm a man brandishing a pistol. Eleven years later, in 1920, when he married Helene, he instructed her in that same hold, as self-defense, in case she was ever mugged on the streets of New York. The lesson flashed back to her in that moment.

Seeing Hitler place the revolver to his temple, Helene Hanfstaengl used the Boston cop's jiujitsu grip to yank the gun out of the Nazi leader's hand. It flew across the attic hallway and landed in a barrel of flour, deep enough to disappear from sight.

"What did you think you were doing?" she berated him sharply. "How could you give up when all your followers believe in and depend on you?"

Hitler shrank back and slumped despondently onto the bed.

"The party must know what to do while you are in prison, Herr Hitler," she exhorted him. Her determination seemed to shake him out of his dejection.

Hurriedly, in the time that was left, he dictated instructions to her. He appointed Alfred Rosenberg party leader and Max Amann deputy. Hermann Esser and Julius Streicher were to serve with them on the executive committee. Hanfstaengl was to gather funds abroad and help build up the *Völkischer Beobachter*. Of Hermann Göring there was no mention.

Hiding the "legacy," Helene rushed downstairs to Belleville's insistent knocking and his calls of *"Aufmachen, Polizei!"*

"Are you the officer in charge?" she asked, opening the door.

"Yes," the lieutenant replied.

"Then may I ask you, please, first to come in alone," she said.

Belleville hesitated a moment. It could be a trap. But Helene Hanfstaengl was an attractive woman, whose request it was hard to refuse. He stepped inside.

"Bitte," she said, leading him upstairs and stopping before the attic bedroom, now closed. She looked at the police officer, signaling him. Belleville opened the door carefully and saw the man who had been his friend sitting on the bed in white pajamas, staring vacuously ahead.

"I have come to arrest you," Belleville announced, using the familiar *du*.

Suddenly, coming out of one trance and seemingly working himself into another, Hitler burst forth with a tirade of invective against von Lossow, the German officer caste, their betrayal, officialdom, von Kahr, and the "November criminals" in Berlin.

But then, seeing and recognizing Belleville, he stopped short and reached out his free hand.

"I am prepared," he said with surprising calm. "Let's make it quick, and please protect me from the mobs outside."

Refusing one of Hanfstaengl's outsized suits, he walked down-stairs in the pajamas. His trenchcoat, the Iron Cross 1st Class still pinned to it, was thrown over his shoulders. Helene handed him Putzi's English blankets to keep him warm. He thanked her for her hospitality, bade goodbye to the two maids, patted little Egon on the head, and walked out of the house to a police staff car that had been sent from Weilheim as an afterthought.

He was driven first to Weilheim, where he was formally booked. The whole town had apparently heard of the arrest, and hundreds of people, many of them Jews, lined the streets as Belle-ville set off with him for Landsberg. The lieutenant ordered the streets cleared, "especially of the Jews who were jeering Hitler."

It was 10:45 P.M. when Belleville delivered him at the fortress prison in the little city of Landsberg, 37 miles west of Munich. Count Anton Arco-Valley, the man who had assassinated Kurt Eisner in 1919, was still serving his term there—Bavaria's most prominent convict. He had to vacate his VIP cell to accommodate the Nazi Führer.

Petulantly, Hitler refused the soup that was offered him by a guard.

Early the following morning Dr. Hans Ehard, accompanied by a stenographer, arrived at Landsberg to interrogate him.

When the assistant prosecutor entered the cell, Hitler stared at him grimly and then turned to face the wall. Ehard had the feeling that "he was going to eat me, he was so angry."

"I have nothing to say, I will not talk," Hitler insisted repeat-edly, as Ehard tried to question him. "I am not going to jeopar-dize my political career by giving you a statement."

Ehard, who had gotten quite a bit out of Ludendorff, was just about to give up after an hour or so when he decided to make one more attempt by employing a different technique—an appeal to Hitler's ego.

"Look, Herr Hitler," he said, "why don't we just have a con-versation, man to man? I've always been fascinated by your politi-cal views and have wanted to meet you. There'll be no record, no protocol. In fact, I'll send the stenographer out right now. We'll just talk. You and I."

It worked, as Ehard was to say more than half a century later, "like a charm."

The minute the stenographer had left the cell, Hitler began chattering, then orating. He preached, declaimed, ranted, and soliloquized all day, without interruption except for Ehard's deft questions, intended to get the Nazi leader to incriminate himself on a charge of conspiracy to commit high treason. There were no breaks for lunch, not even to go to the toilet.

It was early evening when Ehard finally got up from the uncomfortable chair in the cell and thanked Hitler "for the illuminating interview." The Führer was drained, his voice hoarse, his brow glistening with sweat. Repeatedly he had worked himself into hysteria while talking of his plans for Germany's "rebirth" and his strategy for the putsch.

Could Ehard possibly have retained more than a fraction of the ten-hour monologue? He most certainly did. What Hitler could not have known was that Hans Ehard's mind worked like a tape recorder. He had not made a single note—indeed, he had not even kept paper and pencil in the cell. But the minute he was out, he sat down to transcribe, for hours, almost verbatim what Hitler had said. Exhausted, he returned to Munich only a few hours before dawn with an almost perfect record—the basis, he felt, for an airtight case.

On the morning of November 15, 1923, the *New York Times* reported:

MUNICH—Hitler is confined in the Fortress of Landsberg. . . .

It is by no means an unpleasant place of confinement. Prisoners are mostly political offenders and allowed a considerable amount of personal liberty: books to read, special food, and opportunities for exercises and sport, practically the only restriction being that they may not leave the grounds of the fortress.

The trial of Hitler is not likely to be held until after Christmas at the earliest. By that time public sentiment in his favor is expected to abate. When it is held, the trial will not be before a jury but before a bench of judges. If found guilty of high treason, Hitler could be sentenced to death, but it is regarded as more probable that a term of imprisonment in the fortress in which he is now confined will be considered sufficient.

Hitler's particular guards are two veteran sergeants selected for their powers of resistance to Hitler's magnetic personality.

"We have to be careful about who are his jailers," General

von Lossow, the Bavarian Reichswehr commander, is quoted as remarking, "or he will make them a speech and have them cheering for the revolution."

Everyone who has had the Bavarian Fascist leader under close observation agrees that he radiates a personal influence that is almost hypnotic.

Though conscious of his "hypnotic powers," most Germans— and the rest of the world, which had really just become aware of him and his movement—thought that the putsch had finished Hitler, that he was dead politically, and that, if remembered at all, he and his beerhall coup d'état would go down as nothing more than a footnote to history.

EPILOGUE

The putsch had ended in a bloody fiasco. The National Socialist German Workers party had been declared illegal and was being dissolved. Its newspaper, the *Völkischer Beobachter*, was banned. The party's funds and property had been confiscated—to the extent that detectives at Ett Strasse were even using the back sides of Nazi letterhead stationery as scratch paper while interrogating the more than 200 putschists who had been arrested.

Four main trials were being prepared: that of Hitler, Ludendorff, and the other top conspirators; of the Stosstrupp; of Karl Beggel and Hans Knauth for the theft of banknotes from the printing plants; and a case dealing with the raid on the weapons depot at St. Anne's Monastery.

Adolf Hitler seemed utterly discredited, his political career at an end. Yet as he brooded in his cell at Landsberg, he was already forging plans for a change in political strategy, for a new beginning.

In that genteel confinement, he confronted himself with his own mistakes. He had acted "too rashly, without adequate preparation." Cooperation with Ludendorff, he also realized, would have been "absolutely impossible" in the long run. And, although he was already envisioning how the dead at the Feldherrnhalle could be exploited as martyrs in the years ahead, he also appreciated that his attempt at an abrupt takeover of power in Germany, a march on Berlin, would have led to the "greatest of difficulties," with far more casualties than the toll at Odeonsplatz and at the war ministry.

But facing the facts of his tactical and strategic errors by no means implied that he had abandoned his quest for power or tempered his messianic, pseudo-Napoleonic sense of mission. If anything, his confidence that he was destined to be the Führer of Germany grew, and as a first step in that direction, as an instrument, he looked forward to his impending trial.

In November an unidentified Reichswehr officer had told an Associated Press correspondent in Munich, "If you are hostile to Hitler's purpose, you feel physically exhausted after resisting his talk. He takes control of the conversation from the beginning and never lets up. We dare not have a jury trial."

Well, jury trial or not, Hitler was looking forward to it, and on the eve of its opening, February 26, 1924, he was ready. He was eager to vindicate himself, to avenge the "betrayal" of Gustav von Kahr, Otto von Lossow, and Hans von Seisser and, above all, to turn the courtroom into a singular propaganda platform for himself—to make an accuser of the accused.

That he succeeded, that he was permitted to succeed, reveals how little Bavaria had changed when, in fact, so much had changed in Germany as a whole.

The chaos had come to an end and Germany was back to normalcy in a pacified world. The inflation was over, the mark had been stabilized by Gustav Stresemann and Hjalmar Schacht and was on the way to becoming one of Europe's firmest currencies. In London a committee of international financiers, chaired by Charles G. Dawes and advised by Owen D. Young, had drafted a plan to set a more realistic limit on Germany's reparations debt and a sensible schedule for its repayment. It also provided for evacuation of Allied occupation troops from the Ruhr. That which Hitler had feared as imminent had begun: a period of prosperity, relaxed tension, and more settled living conditions.

But in Bavaria, particularly in Munich, there seemed little awareness of this transformation. The most significant development had been the February 18 resignation of Gustav von Kahr, by consensus "the most hated man in the state," and Otto von Lossow's "retirement" from the Reichswehr under conditions less than honorable. Bavaria continued to view Germany and the world through distorting spectacles tinted separatist white-blue and imperial black-white-red.

On the morning of February 26, 1924, all of Germany, if not

the entire world, had its eyes focused on Munich for what was already being touted as "the trial of the age."

There had been no courtroom large enough to stage it and accommodate the 368 expected prosecution and defense witnesses, the scores of newspaper correspondents and photographers from five continents, or the hundreds upon hundreds of spectators who had reserved their seats weeks in advance. Thus, Justice Minister Franz Gürtner, none the worse for his experience as Rudolf Hess's prisoner, had arranged to produce the show in, of all places, the main lecture hall of the Infantry School. Propriety, one can suppose, precluded his renting the Bürgerbräukeller. Mars and Blutenburg streets were sealed off by two battalions of Colonel Hans von Seisser's green-uniformed State Police with chevaux-de-frise and barbed wire. The crowds being held back numbered in the thousands.

Ten defendants sat in the makeshift dock: Hitler; General Erich Ludendorff, resplendent in the uniform he had sworn never to wear again; his stepson, ex-Lieutenant Heinz Pernet; the Oberland League's Dr. Friedrich Weber; ex-Lieutenant Colonel Hermann Kriebel; Captain Ernst Röhm, also in uniform, though he had finally been removed from active duty; Munich's former police chief, Ernst Pöhner; his co-schemer, Wilhelm Frick; ex-Lieutenant Wilhelm Brückner, commander of Munich's SA regiment; and the Infantry School's Lieutenant Robert Wagner.

Notably absent were those who had escaped across the frontier or were in hiding: Hermann Göring, Rudolf Hess, Josef Berchtold, Gerhard Rossbach, Ludwig Oestreicher, Hermann Esser, and Putzi Hanfstaengl, to name a few.

The defense team consisted of a platoon of lawyers, but the prosecution's numbered only two—District Attorney Ludwig Stenglein and his assistant, Dr. Hans Ehard. It was thanks largely to Ehard's energetic efforts that the proceedings did not end with acquittals for all, for the panel of judges was most reluctant to convict.

Presiding over the trial was Justice Georg Neithardt of Nürnberg, an ardent right-wing nationalist. He was assisted by Judge August Leyendecker and three laymen—one of whom was to say during the course of the trial that "this man Hitler is a colossal fellow"—Philipp Herrmann and Christian Zimmermann, both insurance brokers, and Leonhard Beck, owner of a stationery store. At that, Neithardt was the least reluctant of the five, and at the end used all his persuasive powers to induce the panel—sympathetic to Hitler and the putschist cause—to vote for conviction and the nominal penalties imposed.

From the outset Neithardt demonstrated his partiality by favoring defense witnesses over those of the prosecution, taking sworn testimony from the former, a sign of confidence in the truthfulness of their statements under German law, and unsworn declarations from the latter, an indication that he did not believe them.

From the first day, too, Hitler directed the course of the trial with scandalous impunity. Pleading innocent, he won cheers and applause from the spectator section by declaring, "How can I be considered guilty of high treason when there is no such crime as an act of treason against the traitors of November 1918? That revolution was a stab in the back of our heroically fighting army, of the German people, German freedom, and in the back of the German nation."

With that he set the tone, the direction, and the thrust of the entire case. It was not he or the other conspirators who were on trial, but Friedrich Ebert, Gustav Stresemann, the French, the Jews, the Socialists, the Communists, the British, the banker profiteers, the Americans, the "November criminals."

How, he asked dramatically, could he be accused of a "crime" whose only purpose was to lead Germany back to honor and glory and its rightful position in the world?

He dominated the courtroom with his theatrical oratory, propagandistic monologues, and devious tactics to shift blame for the failure of the putsch on Kahr, Lossow, and Seisser. He was arrogant and supercilious when it seemed advantageous to be so; a meek, dedicated "savior of Germany" when that approach seemed more profitable. Repeatedly he cowed the judges into submission "until Neithardt's white goatee quivered with fright."

Although the warlord had been the chief defendant and the indictment read "Against Ludendorff et al.," it was Hitler who stood at center stage while the general was relegated to the role of a bit player. Magnanimously—some of his co-defendants thought condescendingly and gratuitously—he assumed all responsibility for the planning and for what had actually happened, contending that "the other gentlemen merely cooperated with me."

Simultaneously, Hitler declared that he had not wanted to rise against the state because he believed the state was with him. What had he done, he inquired in a clear, resonant baritone voice, other than what Kahr, Lossow, and Seisser themselves had wanted to do—for weeks, for months? If there had been acts of treason or betrayal, they were committed by those three men, who had turned against him and the German people after first shaking his hand in a pledge and accepting his leadership. He belittled the fact that he had extracted the pledges at gunpoint and with the backing of 600 fiercely armed storm troopers.

The triumvirs cut sorry figures as witnesses, trying to save what remained of their careers and reputations by glossing over the fact of their own ambitions and ambivalence. For Hitler they were easy prey when they were called to testify against him. Repeatedly he jumped from his bench to cross-examine and accuse them, fulminating as no prosecutor ever could. Only Seisser demonstrated a little backbone by engaging in verbal duels with Hitler.

On the rare occasions when Neithardt attempted to reprimand or rebuke him for his outbursts, disruptiveness, and interminable dramatic soliloquies, Hitler berated the judge.

"It is impossible to keep Hitler from talking," Neithardt protested, when Bavaria's Prime Minister Eugen von Knilling and Interior Minister Franz Schweyer complained about his conduct of the trial.

Nor was Ludwig Stenglein a match for the Nazi leader, even assuming that this nationalistic and ultra-conservative prosecutor wanted to be. Only Hans Ehard, who assumed almost the entire burden of the prosecution case during the last two weeks, made an honest and valiant attempt to convict Hitler and expose him for the power-hungry demagogue he was. Time after time, however, Ehard's objections and motions were overruled.

The trial became a scandal, and not only in the eyes of foreigners and non-Bavarians.

Ludwig Hümmert, who attended several sessions as a freshman law student, having graduated from *Gymnasium* that winter, saw it as "a travesty of justice, a farce, that made Bavaria the laughing stock of the world."

It was *Fasching* time in Munich, the pre-Lenten carnival season which Bavarians celebrate with a special kind of gusto and
raucousness—a period of jesting, carousing, and foolery. "The biggest jest in town," Hümmert was to recall more than fifty years
later, "was the one in that courtroom." But for Hitler it was a
triumph.

The drama lasted longer than a month, with twenty-five days
of testimony and arguments. There were numerous sessions closed
to the press and public for "security reasons"—much to Hitler's
chagrin, for without an audience his theatrics and oratory were
pointless. Hans Ehard knew that. Most "secret sessions" were
called at his behest.

On the next to the last day, March 27, the defendants were
allowed to make final statements and closing arguments. Hitler
was at his best in this long-awaited moment.

Quietly, at first, he alluded to previous testimony that he was
a man without origins, title, or virtually any education, who had
arrogated to himself the right to govern Germany, sweeping aside
all the presidents, chancellors, generals, and ministers of the government.

> This was not immodest of me. Quite the contrary, when a
> man *knows* he can do a thing, he has no right to be modest. . . . The
> art of statecraft is an art and you have to be born with it. . . . My
> opinion is that a bird sings because it is a bird, and a man who is
> born for politics must engage in politics whether in prison or at
> liberty, whether he sits on a softly upholstered chair covered with
> silk or a hard bench. . . . The man who is born to be a dictator is
> not compelled, but wills; he is not driven forward but drives him-
> self. There is nothing immodest about this. . . . The man who feels
> called upon to govern a people has no right to wait until they
> summon him. It is his duty to step forward.

The judges and the courtroom audience were aghast at this single-
mindedness. But there was more to come.

"Today's lawmakers," he intoned, working himself into the
same trance that had mesmerized audiences at his mass meetings,
"make laws without the consideration of ethics, morality, and decency. The first prerogative, if the law is to be respected again in
Germany, is for the Reich to come out of its misery and misfortune. Then, someday, a different court of justice will be established. That day will be when a prosecutor stands up in that court

and says: 'I accuse Ebert, Stresemann, and their comrades of treason. I accuse them because they have destroyed a nation of 70
million people.'

"I believe," he thundered, "that this hour will be the one in
which the masses, who today stand on the street with our swastika
banner, will unite with those who fired upon them. This blood
will not always separate us.

"The day will come. The army which *we* have formed is already growing, from day to day, and it is growing faster by the
hour. . . . One day the hour will come when those raw recruits will
form battalions, the battalions will become regiments, and the
regiments will be divisions; when the old cockade will be raised
from the mire and the old banners again wave before us."

Gesticulating dramatically, he concluded:

"*Meine Herren,* it is not you who pronounce judgment on us,
but the eternal court of history which will make its pronouncement on the charge which has been brought against us. . . . I know
what *your* verdict will be. But even if you find us guilty a thousand times over, the goddess of the eternal court of history will
tear up the prosecution's indictment and your verdict with a
smile. She will rule us innocent and speak us free."

Hitler had won, no matter how the court decided.

Judgment day, ironically, was April Fool's Day. Arriving at
the Infantry School at 10 A.M., Hitler and his co-conspirators
posed for a picture. All but Hitler, wearing a new raincoat, and
Pöhner and Frick, both looking arrogant as ever, their necks
choked by high celluloid collars, were in uniform—replete with
medals and ceremonial officers' swords. Ludendorff and Kriebel
had on gleaming, spike-tipped helmets.

The courtroom was crowded to bursting; dozens of the Nazi
leader's female admirers were present, with bouquets of flowers.

Ploddingly, Judge Neithardt read out the verdict, which had
been reached by a vote of 4 to 1. All were found guilty—Brückner, Röhm, Pernet, Wagner, and Frick on the lesser count of "aiding and abetting high treason"—with the exception of Ludendorff. The warlord indignantly denounced his acquittal as "a
disgrace which my uniform and my decorations have not
earned."

Pretrial confinement time was deducted from their sentences, so that Frick, Röhm, and Brückner could actually walk out of the courtroom as free men on probation.

Hitler, Weber, Kriebel, and Pöhner were sentenced to the minimum term of five years' "fortress confinement" and a 200-gold-mark fine apiece, with the provision that they would be eligible for parole "on probation" after serving only six months of their terms.

But then came the most important ruling of all, one that Hitler awaited with trembling hands, breath held, and face a ghostly white.

"Although Paragraph Nine, Section Two, of the Law for Protection of the Republic stipulates the mandatory deportation of a foreigner convicted of high treason," Neithardt droned, "the court is of the earnest opinion that the provision has no applicability either in its intent or the implication of its words in the case of the defendant Adolf Hitler.

"Hitler," the judge continued, "is a German-Austrian. But he regards himself as a German. The deportation clause cannot be applied to a man who thinks and feels as German as he, a man who served voluntarily in the German army during wartime for four and a half years and whose bravery in the face of the enemy won him high decorations."

A smile of relief crossed the Nazi Führer's face. Deportation was what he had feared most. Now he had a future.

The courtroom erupted with shouts of "Bravo, Bravo!" and frenetic cries of "Heil! Heil! Heil!" Piles of congratulatory flowers began mounting in the guardroom where the convicted conspirators were kept before their return to prison, and when they showed themselves at the windows, the vast crowd on Blutenburg Strasse roared with jubilation. Ludendorff's drive home to Solln-Ludwigshöhe was like a triumphal march.

Adolf Hitler, the man who had been a nobody five years earlier—whose name American newspapers had misspelled just a scant six weeks before, and whose coup d'état had been described by the *New York Times* as "Bavarian Opera Bouffe"—was now internationally known. He spent the next eight and a half months in gentlemanly confinement along with Kriebel and Weber; and later, after their conviction in separate trials, with Rudolf Hess and various members of the Stosstrupp such as Emil Maurice,

Hans Kallenbach, Walter Hewel, and Wilhelm Briemann.

It was there at Landsberg that he began writing the political autobiography and manifesto, *Mein Kampf,* which was to make him a wealthy man. Hess served as his editor, and Adolf Lenk, the Jungsturm leader, later helped Hess to type it on an Adler portable that, fifty-five years afterward, was still in Lenk's apartment on Jahn Strasse in Munich.

Hitler was paroled on probation December 20, 1924. Photographer Heinrich Hoffmann was at the fortress gate in Landsberg to meet him. As they were driving toward Munich, Hoffmann asked him what he intended to do next.

"I shall start again, from the beginning," Hitler replied.

He wasted no time making good that threat. But the beerhall putsch had taught him a lesson. Instead of attempting to overthrow the state and the democracy he hated with the force of arms and a ragtag army, he set out to subvert and undermine it, using precisely those freedoms of speech, election, and parliamentary procedure that it guaranteed him, but which he so abhorred.

Only eight years after leaving the Fortress of Landsberg, the "drummer" of Munich, the histrionic and ludicrous-looking putschist of the Bürgerbräukeller, was again wearing a swallowtail coat that gave him the appearance of a waiter—to be sworn in as Reich Chancellor and a few weeks later to become master of Germany. As he stood there, his sights were already set on a further goal: to become master of the world. The Thousand-Year Reich that he proclaimed lasted a scant dozen years, but it took the lives of fifty million people.

Each year before his reign of terror collapsed in Götterdämmerung, Hitler returned to Munich to lead the raucous co-conspirators who had been with him on November 8 and 9, 1923, in a reenactment of the march from the Bürgerbräukeller to the Feldherrnhalle, there to honor the dead rebels who had been interred in a nearby temple of honor.

The putsch failed, but its failure was the quintessential prelude to Adolf Hitler's climb to power.

APPENDIX

Some Leading Characters and Their Fates

Actors on the stage of history come and go. Some play bit parts; others leave a more lasting mark. The following is a partial list of the principals involved in or affected by Adolf Hitler's November 1923 putsch, and reports, to the extent possible, their subsequent roles in the Nazi rise to power or their fates during and after the Third Reich.

Aechter, Adolf. Born November 23, 1864. Retired lieutenant general of the Royal Bavarian Army, "military leader" of the Oberland League, arrested the night of November 8, 1923, charged but never tried for his involvement in the putsch.

Aigner, Johann. Born October 31, 1901. Servant to Dr. Max Erwin von Scheubner-Richter, Hitler's key political adviser, who was killed in the putsch. Had served in Rossbach Free Corps prior to working for Scheubner-Richter.

Amann, Max. Born in Munich November 24, 1891, died there March 30, 1957. He was Hitler's platoon sergeant during World War I, became business manager of the Nazi party and of the *Völkischer Beobachter,* his position during the putsch. He was then *Reichsleiter* of the party, subsequently president of the Reich Press Chamber, and head of the party's central publishing house in Munich, Franz Eher Nachfolger.

Arco-Valley, Count Anton. Born 1897, died 1945. Assassinated Kurt Eisner, Bavarian Socialist premier, in 1919.

Auer, Erhard. Born 1874, died 1945. Was a member of Bavarian parliament 1907–33, minister of interior 1918–19, and leader of the Social Democratic party in Bavaria. Auer was targeted for arrest by the Nazis during the putsch night but was in hiding.

Auer, Sophie. Born 1868. Wife of Erhard Auer. Was at home and molested by Nazi troopers during the putsch night.

Baldenius, Walter. Born January 1, 1898. One of Hermann Göring's adjutants at SA headquarters, he escaped to Salzburg after the putsch.

Ballin family. Jewish furniture store owners on Residenz Strasse, Munich, where Göring hid after Felderrnhalle shooting. Emigrated to the United States.

Banzer, Josef. Born 1870. Colonel of Bavarian State Police, deputy to Colonel Hans von Seisser. He was originally on Hitler's list of those officials to be arrested in the beerhall, but his name was crossed off.

Beggel, Karl. Born March 17, 1892 in Munich. A former army lieutenant, he joined the Nazi party at its beginnings in the spring of 1920. He commanded the First Battalion of the SA Regiment Munich and was in charge of banknote robberies on November 9. Later, he became disillusioned with the Nazi leadership.

Belleville, Rudolf. Born July 15, 1894 in Augsburg. State Police senior lieutenant. During World War I he was the observer in Rudolf Hess's plane, and was once a close friend and collaborator of Hitler. He commanded the State Police detachment that arrested Hitler in Hanfstaengl's chalet on November 11.

Berchtold, Josef. Born March 6, 1897, in Munich. Tobacco shop owner, former lieutenant, commander of Stosstrupp-Hitler, the Führer's bodyguard. Berchtold fled Munich after the putsch and was tried in absentia in 1924. After Hitler's release from prison, he founded the SS.

Block, Hans. Reichswehr lieutenant and student at the Infantry School, he helped line up the cadets and officer candidates for the putsch. Block was dismissed from the army after the coup but was reinstated after 1933 and became a general.

Böhm, Gerhard. Reichswehr warrant officer who was instrumental in preventing putschist takeover of 19th Infantry Regiment barracks on night of November 8. In later years he was an archive director.

Bouhler, Philipp. Born in Munich 1899, believed to have killed himself at Karinhall during Battle of Berlin in May 1945. He was assistant business manager of the party in 1923 and dealt with printers of putschist posters. After reorganization of the party, he rose to become its secretary general, then chief of Führer Chancellery. He headed the "euthanasia" program, and also served as deputy to Hans Frank, Nazi governor general of occupied Poland.

Braun, Max. A Reichswehr senior lieutenant and outspokenly anti-Nazi, he commanded a company in the battle with Röhm's men at the war ministry. After the 1933 Nazi takeover, Braun had to flee Germany.

Briemann, Wilhelm. Born March 3, 1899, in Munich. A book salesman and ex-lieutenant, he was a member of the Stosstrupp, was tried for his role in the putsch in April 1924, and sentenced to fifteen months' fortress imprisonment. Lives as pensioner in Munich.

Brückner, Wilhelm. Born December 11, 1884, Baden-Baden. A former army lieutenant, he was commander of the Munich SA Regiment, tried with Hitler and Ludendorff in 1924, and convicted. He served later as one of Hitler's adjutants.

Cantzler, Oskar. A Reichswehr captain at the Engineer Battalion barracks, his refusal to let Oberland storm troopers have their weapons on the evening of November 8 played a key role in the outcome of the putsch.

Casella, Theodor. Born August 8, 1900, in Munich. A former army lieutenant, active in Ernst Röhm's Reichskriegsflagge Society, he had an important part in Röhm's takeover of the war ministry and was killed in the fighting there November 9.

Danner, Jakob von. Reichswehr major general and commander of Munich city garrison, he was an outspoken opponent of military meddling in politics and played a key role in crushing the putsch.

Demmelmeyer, Max. State Police lieutenant, deputy commander of company posted on Odeonsplatz and at the Feldherrnhalle on the morning of November 9. He took Ludendorff prisoner.

Dietl, Eduard. Reichswehr captain and company commander in the 19th Infantry Regiment. A member of the party even before Hitler joined in 1919, he helped train Hitler's SA and develop it into a military unit. He rose to the rank of general in the Third Reich and commanded units during the invasion of Norway and on the Eastern front.

Drey, Paul. Translator and assistant to Robert Murphy at U.S. consulate general in Munich. He was with Murphy on the streets, reporting the putsch, November 8 and 9. Imprisoned at Dachau concentration camp after the Nazi takeover in 1933, he reportedly died there.

Ebenböck, Fritz. Born March 3, 1901, in Regensburg. An engineering student and deputy commander of SA's 11th Company, he still lives in Munich, retired.

Ebert, Friedrich. Born 1871, died 1925. Was first president (1919–25) of German Republic, a Social Democrat.

Eckart, Dietrich. Born 1868, died December 23, 1923, after release from Landsberg Fortress where he had been interned with Hitler. Eckart was one of the founders of the party. A writer and poet of virulently anti-Semitic and Nordic epics (and translator into German of Ibsen's *Peer Gynt*), he was one of Hitler's earliest friends in Munich and his ideological mentor.

Ehard, Dr. Hans. Born November 10, 1887, in Bamberg, died October 18, 1980, in Munich. Ehard was assistant district attorney in Munich at the time of the putsch, and the first to interrogate both Ludendorff and Hitler. He was deputy prosecutor at the putschists' trial in 1924. Despite his role as prosecutor, the Nazis did not persecute him, and he served as an appeals court judge in Bavaria from 1933 through 1945. After World War II he was one of the founders of the Christian Social (CSU) party in Bavaria, and a member of the state legislature for twenty years. He succeeded Wilhelm Hoegner as Bavarian prime minister from 1946 to 1954, was succeeded by Hoegner 1954–57, was prime minister again 1960–62, and, from 1962 until his retirement from active politics in 1966, Bavaria's minister of justice. Throughout the Third Reich, Ehard managed to preserve one of two typewritten copies of the 1924 Hitler trial record, which he gave to Bavaria's State Archives after 1945. It served as vital research material for this book. Shortly before his death in 1980, he gave the author an extensive interview.

Ehrhardt, Hermann. Ex-imperial navy commander, who led the free-corps brigade that pioneered use of the swastika symbol. Ehrhardt had a vital part in crushing Bavaria's 1919 Red Republic and in the 1920 Kapp Putsch against democratic government in Berlin. His "Organization Consul" was a sabotage and terrorist group responsible for a spate of political murders in Germany, his Viking League was a mercenary force "deputized" as auxiliary police by the Kahr regime in Bavaria. He rivaled Hitler for power, and during the November putsch refused to ally himself with Hitler and Ludendorff.

Epp, Franz von. Born in Munich 1868, died there 1946. A career officer in the Royal Bavarian Army, Epp was commander of the king's bodyguard regiment from 1914 until 1918. After the revolution, he formed a free corps in neighboring Thuringia which played a key—and brutal—part in the White terror and counterrevolution. He was named a major general in the Reichswehr, was an early supporter and crony of Hitler, and commanded the Seventh Division until his retirement in 1923 as a lieutenant general. Then he became a general in the SA. In 1928 he entered the Reichstag on the Nazi party ticket, and in 1933 Hitler appointed him Reich commissioner and plenipotentiary for Bavaria. Epp did not participate actively in the putsch, but served as intermediary between Ernst Röhm and the Reichswehr.

Esser, Hermann. Born in Röhrmoos, Bavaria, in 1900, died in Munich, 1981. After brief war service and a stint in the Social Democratic party, Esser met Hitler and Gottfried Feder in 1919 and together with Hitler joined the Nazi movement in January 1920, when it was still called the German Workers party. He became an editor of the *Völkischer Beobachter*. When Hitler took over dictatorial leadership of the party, Esser, almost as good a speaker, became its chief of propaganda and de facto Hitler's deputy. Esser played only a peripheral role in the putsch, still not having recovered from a bout of jaundice, but was instrumental in the party's reorganization after 1924. From 1929 to 1933, he was Nazi party floor leader of Munich's city council; from 1933, he was a member of the Reichstag and Bavaria's minister of economics. From 1939 to 1945, he was undersecretary for tourism in the Reich propaganda ministry. Lived, retired, in Munich until his death.

Eyre, Lincoln. Correspondent for *New York Herald*, covering the putsch.

Faust, Martin. Born January 27, 1901. A member of Röhm's Reichskriegsflagge, he was killed by machine-gun fire at the war ministry building on the morning of November 9, 1923.

Feder, Gottfried. Born 1883, died 1941. Feder was one of the founding members of the Nazi party and its economic theoretician. Brother-in-law of Professor Karl Alexander von Müller, his lecture in 1919 was what initially drew Hitler to the party, and he was the Führer's mentor in matters of finance and economics. In the putsch night he was named new Reich "finance minister." After the Nazi takeover in 1933 he was undersecretary in the Reich economics ministry, then a university professor.

Fengler, Sophie. Eldest daughter of Bavarian Social Democratic party leader Erhard and Sophie Auer. She experienced Nazi raids in the putsch night.

Fiehler brothers, Karl, Otto, and Werner. Born 1895, 1893, and 1889. Karl and Werner were in Berchtold's Stosstrupp and convicted for their role in the putsch in 1924. Otto was in the SA and implicated for his arrest of Police Inspector Otto Freiesleben on the morning of November 9. Karl Fiehler became mayor of Munich after the Nazi takeover in 1933; he was deposed in 1945.

Frank, Hans. Born May 23, 1900, executed October 16, 1946, in Nürnberg after conviction by the Allied Tribunal as a major war criminal. Frank was an early adherent of Hitler, had fought with Epp's free corps, and joined the party in 1919, even before Hitler. He was a law student in Munich at the time of the putsch, participated extensively through the night and morning, and was involved in the attempt to capture the Allied Military Control officers at the Vier Jahreszeiten Hotel. He became Hitler's lawyer in the 1920s and was elected to the Reichstag on the Nazi ticket in 1928. He was named Bavarian minister of justice in 1933, a Reich minister without portfolio in 1935, and governor general of occupied Poland in 1939, where he was responsible for the murder of millions of Jews and Poles.

Freiesleben, Otto. Munich municipal police detective, arrested by Otto Fiehler's squad of SA on morning of November 9 as an "enemy of the revolution."

Frick, Dr. Wilhelm. Born in 1877, executed October 16, 1946, after conviction by Allied Tribunal as a major war criminal. Frick was a senior Munich police official of ultra-rightist, nationalist, and racist persuasion and a protégé of Ernst Pöhner. He was one of the leading conspirators of the putsch and was installed during the night, by Pöhner, as Munich police chief. Arrested at police headquarters in the early morning of November 9, he was tried along with Hitler and the others and convicted of aiding and abetting high treason. He played a leading role in reorganizing the Nazi party, was elected to the Reichstag on its ticket, and served from 1930 to 1931 as minister of interior in Thuringia. In 1933, after Hitler became Reichschancellor, Frick was named Reich interior minister, a post he held until 1943, when he succeeded the murdered Reinhard Heydrich as "Reich Protector" of Bohemia and Moravia.

Gerlich, Fritz. Born in Stettin, February 15, 1883; murdered by the Nazis near Munich during the "Röhm Purge" on the "Night of the Long Knives," June 30, 1934. Gerlich was editor-in-chief of the moderately conservative *Münchner Neueste Nachrichten*, Munich's largest daily, and became a vociferous opponent of Hitler and the Nazis.

Gerum, Josef. Born September 22, 1888, in Munich. A Munich police detective who joined the Nazi party and became a member of Berchtold's Stosstrupp, he had a key part in the putsch, including the manning of the machine gun at the Bürgerbräukeller. He was convicted along with other Stosstrupp members in their 1924 trial.

Gessler, Otto. Born 1875, died 1955. Mayor of Regensburg, then Nürnberg, from 1911 until 1919. He was the German Republic's Reichswehr minister from 1920 until 1928, and a leading politician of the Weimar era. In Berlin during the putsch night he was instrumental in making General Hans von Seeckt temporary military dictator. He was persecuted and frequently arrested by the Gestapo during the Third Reich.

Godin, Baron Michael von. Born 1897. A State Police senior lieutenant, he commanded the company that fired the shots at the Feldherrnhalle on November 9. Godin was hounded by the Nazis in Bavaria thereafter and forced to retire from the State Police in 1926. He emigrated to Austria. In May 1933 he returned to Germany on a visit, was arrested by the Gestapo, and interrogated and tortured for eight months before being allowed to leave for Austria again. In 1938, with the German annexation of Austria, he fled to Switzerland, where he linked up with Wilhelm Hoegner and other émigrés. In 1946, after World War II, Hoegner appointed him chief of the Bavarian State Police. He retired in 1966, lives in Munich, and provided the author with a detailed description of what happened at Odeonsplatz.

Göring, Carin. Born October 21, 1888, in Stockholm as von Fock, died there October 17, 1931. Göring's first wife, she helped him escape to Innsbruck, and later to Sweden, after he was wounded in the shooting at the Feldherrnhalle on November 9.

Göring, Hermann. Born January 12, 1893, in Rosenheim, committed suicide in lieu of execution at Nürnberg, October 16, 1946, following conviction on war crimes by Allied Tribunal. A highly decorated fighter pilot and last commander of the Richthofen squadron in World War I, he did not join the Nazi party until 1923, but then rose quickly as commander of all SA troops. During the putsch, which he helped plan, he was in charge of all SA operations. After his return to Germany from Swedish exile, he became one of the top figures in the Nazi hierarchy. He entered the Reichstag on the party ticket in 1928 and became president of the parliament in 1932, a position he retained in addition to his other functions until 1945. In 1933 he also assumed the prime-ministership of Prussia and became Reich air minister as well, holding both titles until the end of the Third Reich. He was the commander-in-chief of the Luftwaffe and czar of the four-year economic plans.

Graf, Ulrich. Born July 6, 1898, died 1945. He was Hitler's personal bodyguard. A butcher by trade, he was one of the founders of the SA. He never left Hitler's side and attempted to protect him at the Feldherrnhalle, taking eleven bullets himself. Hitler never honored that loyalty but dropped the brawler from his company after getting out of prison. Graf was a Munich city councilor during the Third Reich.

Gruber, Max von. Born 1853, died 1927. Professor at Munich University and president of the Bavarian Academy of Science. Member of the audience in the Bürgerbräukeller.

Grünspann, Abisch. Jewish tobacco shop owner, a victim of the pogroms during the night of November 8–9, 1923.

Gürtner, Franz. Born 1881, died 1941. He was Bavarian minister of justice through 1932, then Reich justice minister. Though one of those arrested by Hess at the Bürgerbräukeller and kept prisoner, he was sympathetic to the Nazi movement and did much to protect Hitler in later years.

Hanfstaengl, Catharina. Mother of Ernst; her villa in Uffing was the first to be searched when police were looking for Hitler.

Hanfstaengl, Egon. Born 1920 in New York, son of Ernst and Helene.

Hanfstaengl, Erna. Sister of Ernst, she was an early Hitler supporter.

Hanfstaengl, Dr. Ernst "Putzi." Born 1887, died 1976. Harvard-educated son of a Munich art publisher and an American woman, Hanfstaengl befriended Hitler in 1921, after his return from many years in the United States, and introduced him to the city's social elite. He became "foreign press adviser" of the Nazi party, his chief role during the putsch. He helped rebuild the party and rose in its ranks as "foreign press chief" until growing disenchantment with Hitler forced him to flee to the United States in 1937. He subsequently served as an adviser to President Franklin D. Roosevelt.

Hanfstaengl, Helene. Wife of Ernst. Hitler hid in her chalet at Uffing after the putsch had failed. She prevented his committing suicide when police came to arrest him.

Heines, Edmund. Born July 21, 1897, in Munich, murdered June 30, 1934, in the "Röhm Purge." He was a mercenary, leader of various paramilitary organizations, and commander of the SA's Second Battalion. During the putsch night he was responsible for the raid on the Vier Jahreszeiten Hotel where the Allied Military Control officers lived.

Hess, Rudolf. Born in Alexandria, Egypt, in 1894. A pilot during World War I, he fought in a free-corps unit against the Red Army in Munich in 1919, was active in radical rightist circles, and joined the Nazi party in 1920. He was one of the founders of the SA and commanded a student company. He idolized Hitler, and during the putsch night arrested the Bavarian cabinet, taking them to the villa of publisher Julius Lehmann. He fled after the putsch, but returned to stand trial, joined Hitler at Landsberg, helped him to write *Mein Kampf*, and ultimately became the "Führer's deputy" until his flight to England in 1941. Tried and convicted at the Nürnberg war crimes tribunal, he was sentenced to and is still serving his life term at Spandau Prison in Berlin.

Hewel, Walter. Born in 1904; committed suicide in Berlin on May 2, 1945, two days after Hitler, by swallowing poison and shooting himself. He was a student and a member of Berchtold's Stosstrupp. As such, he was involved in all its activities during the night and morning: the raids on the *Münchener Post* and the Auer apartment, the attempt to capture police headquarters, and the arrest of the mayor and city councilors. He was tried and convicted in 1924, and served his term together with Hitler at Landsberg. Hewel later rose to prominence as a diplomat in the Third Reich, a confidant of Hitler, and, with the rank of ambassador, as the official liaison man between the foreign ministry and Hitler in the Führer Bunker in Berlin.

Himmler, Heinrich. Born in Munich, October 7, 1900; committed suicide at a British control post near Lüneburg, May 23, 1945. A friend of both Ernst Röhm and Gregor Strasser and a member of Röhm's Reichskriegsflagge Society, Himmler's participation in the putsch as a twenty-three-year-old was limited largely to his role as RKF's standardbearer and one of the troopers at the war ministry. But after Hitler's release from prison, Himmler became one of the key figures in the party, as a founding member of the SS and ultimately its chief. After the Nazi takeover he had a brief stint as Munich chief of police and then became head of the Gestapo, the SS, and Reich police chief. The Nazi Holocaust was directed by him.

Hoegner, Dr. Wilhelm. Born in Munich, September 23, 1887, died there, March 5, 1980. A deputy district attorney and Social Democratic party member, Hoegner hid the party's leader, Erhard Auer, from certain arrest by the Nazis on the night of the putsch. In 1924 he was elected to the Bavarian state parliament, serving until 1930. He co-chaired a special parliamentary committee in 1927 and 1928 investigating the putsch and its background, whose more than 1,500 pages of testimony served as crucial research material for this book. Hoegner was elected to the Reichstag in 1930 and fled Germany—first for Austria, then Switzerland—after the Nazi takeover in 1933. He returned from exile after World War II and in September 1945 was appointed prime minister of Bavaria by the U.S. military government. After Hans Ehard succeeded him in 1946, Hoegner served first as justice, then as interior minister in Ehard's cabinets, and was reelected prime minister in 1954 for a three-year term. From 1957 until 1962 he was SPD floor leader in the parliament. He was interviewed at length by the author before his death in 1980.

Hoffmann, Heinrich. Born in Fürth, Bavaria, 1885, died in Munich, 1972. A professional photographer, he was the first to take Hitler's picture and became not only his friend but "court photographer." Hoffmann's photos taken on the days of the putsch are virtually the only ones in existence.

Höfler, Georg. State Police lieutenant, friend of Himmler and brother-in-law of Gregor and Otto Strasser, he commanded the small detachment of police that was overrun by the putschists at the Ludwig Bridge on their march to the Feldherrnhalle.

Hofmann, Hans Georg. Reichswehr lieutenant colonel and commander of Ingolstadt garrison. A collaborator with Röhm and sympathizer of Hitler and Ludendorff, he sided with the putschists on November 8 and 9. Surprisingly, he was not retired from the army until 1926. When Hitler took power in 1933, he was rewarded with a high-level government position.

Hofmann, Matthäus. Munich police detective inspector and Nazi party member, who played a crucial role throughout the night of the putsch trying to implement the coup d'état and assist Hitler.

Hühnlein, Adolf. Reichswehr major, who played an important role on the putschist side and was ultimately arrested together with Ernst Pöhner at police headquarters on the morning of November 9. Dismissed from active service, he rose to the rank of general after Hitler took power in 1933.

Imhoff, Baron Sigmund von. State Police major. At police headquarters late on the evening of November 8, 1923, because he was teaching a class of younger officers, he acted on his own: was instrumental in taking measures to alert General von Danner and other officials, and in dispatching police to prevent a putschist takeover of the central telegraph office, the main telephone exchange, the railroad station, and other key power centers. More than any other single person, he contained the coup at an early hour.

Kahr, Dr. Gustav von. Born in Weissenburg, Bavaria, in 1862, murdered in gruesome fashion by Nazis during the "Röhm Purge," June 30, 1934. The son of a high-ranking Bavarian judge, Kahr was a civil servant in the royal administration and was named prefect of Upper Bavaria in 1917. An extreme rightist, monarchist, and schemer, he became prime minister of Bavaria by means of a putsch in 1920. His term lasted nearly two years. He reverted to the prefecture, and in the autumn of 1923 was appointed "general state commissioner" with emergency dictatorial powers by the cabinet of Prime Minister von Knilling. Hitler had long been trying to enlist his aid in staging a coup d'état, and the extent to which von Kahr equivocated after the events at the beerhall on November 8 has never been fully resolved. His repudiation of the putsch during the night made him "the most hated man in Bavaria." He was forced to resign his dictatorship on February 18, 1924. From then until 1927, he was chairman of the Bavarian administrative court.

Kallenbach, Hans. Born in Munich, 1897, died there in 1978. A platoon leader in the Stosstrupp Hitler, he participated in most of its actions during the night and the following morning. He was tried with other members of the group and sentenced to prison at Landsberg. In 1939 he published a detailed memoir of the putsch and his experience as a co-prisoner with Hitler.

Kautter, Eberhard. Ex-navy officer. He was deputy to Hermann Ehrhardt in command of the free corps and the Viking League, and during the night of the putsch conspired against Hitler in the hope of gaining control of the coup d'état and winning von Kahr to his side.

Kiefer, Philipp. Munich municipal police detective. He was the officer in charge of security at the Bürgerbräukeller the evening of November 8. When the storm troopers invaded, he managed to slip out of the building and get to a nearby precinct station, from where he gave the first alert.

Kiessling, Konrad. A police trainee, he had fought with the Epp Free Corps in putting down the Bavarian Red Republic, then joined the Oberland League. On the night of the putsch he was assigned to the Oberland company of Alfons Weber and the battalion of Ludwig Oestreicher involved in the attempt to capture Kahr's headquarters. Kiessling began having doubts about the legality of the coup but remained with the putschists through the day, then hurried to his job after the Feldherrnhalle shooting, "to save my career."

Kiliani, Immanuel. State Police lieutenant. During the Third Reich he was a Wehrmacht general.

Klotz, Helmut. Born in 1894. He was an associate of Julius Streicher in the Nazi leadership in Nürnberg and was active as a propaganda speaker throughout the night and morning of November 8 and 9, 1923. Klotz became disillusioned with the Nazi movement and resigned from the party before Hitler's takeover of power in 1933.

Knauth, Hans. Born in 1892. A bank clerk, like Karl Beggel, as well as a former lieutenant, Knauth commanded the SA's Third Battalion during the putsch, staged the raid on St. Anne's Monastery to obtain weapons, and then, on the morning of November 9, took quadrillions of marks in fresh banknotes from two printing plants.

Knickerbocker, Hubert R. An American newspaperman, he witnessed and reported on the putsch for the *Baltimore Sun*.

Knilling, Eugen von. Born 1865, died 1927. Bavaria's prime minister from 1922 to 1924, it had been largely at Knilling's behest that von Kahr was named dictator of Bavaria in September 1923. He was taken prisoner in the Bürgerbräukeller by Rudolf Hess on the night of the putsch.

Kressenstein, Baron Friedrich Kress von. Born 1870, died 1948. Artillery commander of the Seventh Division, he played an instrumental part in mobilizing Reichswehr units in the north of Bavaria to march on Munich to crush the putschists. He succeeded Lossow as the division's commander in February 1924.

Kriebel, Hermann. Born 1876, died 1941. A retired lieutenant colonel and former Bavarian army staff officer, he had fought with free-corps units in the White counterrevolution, and in 1923 became the "military leader" of the Kampfbund, the league of "patriotic" and fighting societies made up of Hitler's Nazi party and SA, the Oberland League, and Ernst Röhm's Reichskriegsflagge. Kriebel was, next to Hitler and Ludendorff, the key figure in the putsch, and was convicted at the 1924 trial. He served his term together with Hitler at Landsberg. After his release from prison, he maintained close ties to the Nazi party and the Oberland League, but did not benefit from Hitler's subsequent rise to power. He was dispatched to Shanghai as German consul general.

Lehmann, Julius F. A book publisher, he was one of the leading figures in the ultra-nationalist, anti-Semitic, and anti-republican movement in Munich. Lehmann was a founding member of the secret Thule Society, dedicated to Nordic culture, which was the ideological font for the counterrevolution. The father-in-law of Dr. Friedrich Weber (leader of the Oberland League), Lehmann owned the villa where Rudolf Hess kept the Bavarian cabinet and other high officials imprisoned during the putsch.

Lenk, Adolf. Born October 15, 1903. An early admirer of Hitler, Lenk was the leader of the Nazi party's Jungsturm, the precursor of the later Hitler Youth, members of which he organized for participation in the putsch. He accompanied Hitler into the Bürgerbräukeller, and together with Ulrich Graf stood guard over Kahr, Lossow, and Seisser in the side room where Hitler was pressuring the triumvirs to collaborate in the "march on Berlin." Lenk was almost killed during the march on the Feldherrnhalle. After the putsch he attempted to reorganize the youth movement and was indicted, but never tried, for trying to revitalize the then-outlawed Nazi party. Lenk never rose to prominence after Hitler took power, though he was on the Führer's staff in Berlin and at party headquarters in Munich. A disagreement with Martin Bormann led to Lenk's secret incarceration in a Munich bunker for the last two years of World War II. He resides in Munich, retired, in the same apartment where he lived with his parents at the time of the putsch.

Leupold, Ludwig. A Reichswehr colonel, he was deputy commandant of the Infantry School and sympathetic to the putschists. But it was Leupold who before dawn on November 9 warned Ludendorff that Lossow had repudiated the putsch and was planning to crush it with force.

Lossow, Otto Hermann von. Born 1868, died 1938. Reichswehr lieutenant general. Lossow was the commander of the Seventh Division and the Bavarian military district and, together with Gustav von Kahr and Hans von Seisser, one of the triumvirs ruling Bavaria in the fall of 1923. A political general and schemer, he had long toyed with taking power in the Reich and was much under Hitler's influence. His equivocation and ambivalent behavior after Hitler marched into the Bürgerbräukeller contributed to his disgraceful retirement from active duty on February 18, 1924. He went to Turkey, where he had previously served as a military adviser, and became a general in the Turkish army, returning to Germany in the early 1930s. Though threatened with retaliation by the Nazis after Hitler came to power, he enjoyed protection by the army and died of natural causes in 1938.

Lövenstein, Bernhard. Jewish businessman victimized by putschists on the night of November 9.

Löwenthal, Max. Jewish businessman whose apartment was raided by putschists on the night of November 9.

Luber, Dr. Karl and Emilie. The son-in-law and daughter of Erhard Auer, Bavaria's Social Democratic leader. Luber was taken prisoner by Berchtold's Stosstrupp the night of November 9 and kept hostage at the Bürgerbräukeller.

Lüdecke, Kurt. Born 1890. A Berlin businessman, he became enamored of Hitler in 1922, and the Nazi leader made him his "foreign policy" adviser. Lüdecke established the first contacts between Hitler and Benito Mussolini. After the putsch and dissolution of the party, he was active in raising funds for it. When Hitler came to power, however, he ordered Lüdecke locked up in Dachau concentration camp. Ernst Röhm helped him flee to the United States, where he spent the rest of his life.

Ludendorff, Erich. Born 1865, died 1937. A retired army general and key
figure, next to Hitler, in the Bürgerbräu putsch, Ludendorff had been the
German army's chief-of-staff during World War I and the principal architect of both its victories and defeats. From 1916 on, he had been virtual dictator of the Kaiser's Reich. After the 1918 Armistice, he fled to
Sweden. Returning in 1919, he played the determining behind-the-scenes
role in the 1920 Kapp Putsch, then settled in Munich, where he continued
to plot and militate against the government in Berlin, allying himself with
Hitler and the other ultra-nationalist groups in Bavaria. The march on the
Feldherrnhalle on November 9 was largely Ludendorff's idea. As Germany's greatest war hero, he was acquitted in the 1924 trial—an acquittal
which he regarded as an insult. From 1924 to 1928 he was a Nazi party
deputy in the Reichstag and, in 1925, after the death of Friedrich Ebert, a
candidate for the presidency, losing to his erstwhile superior, Field Marshal Paul von Hindenburg. He became increasingly involved with the
"Aryan" racist pseudo-religion of his second wife, Mathilde, and also
alienated from Hitler, who, he felt, had misled him. After Hitler came to
power, their relationship was largely one of charade. Ludendorff died in
Munich in 1937.

Mantel, Karl. Munich chief of police, he was arrested by Rudolf Hess in the
Bürgerbräukeller and incarcerated during the night of November 9 in the
villa of Julius Lehmann. Mantel commanded a force strongly subverted
by Nazi party members and was later blamed for having taken insuffi-
cient precautions to protect against a coup d'état.

Matt, Franz. Born 1860, died 1929. Bavaria's minister of education from 1920
to 1926 and the state's vice-premier, he was an outspoken opponent of the
Nazis and the ultra-rightist movement, as well as of Gustav von Kahr. He
had boycotted Kahr's speech in the beerhall the evening of November 8
and, as soon as he heard of Hitler's putsch, organized resistance against it,
moving, with several other cabinet members who had not attended, to
Regensburg. There he planned to establish a democratic government-in-
exile.

Maurice, Emil. Born January 19, 1897, died in Munich in 1979. A watchmaker
by trade and member of Berchtold's Stosstrupp, Maurice distinguished
himself by extreme sadism and cruelty during the elite troop's maraud-
ings on November 8 and 9, 1923, especially in the apartment of Erhard
Auer. Tried and convicted along with other Stosstrupp members, he became Hitler's intimate at Landsberg and, after their release from the prison, his chauffeur. Maurice also fell in love with Hitler's half-niece, Geli
Raubal, with whom the Führer himself was having an affair. That led to a
break between Hitler and Maurice, and to Geli Raubal's mysterious 1931
suicide.

Mayer, Father Rupert. Born January 23, 1876, died November 1, 1945. A
Jesuit priest, he had been a medical corpsman and chaplain during World
War I and was seriously wounded, losing a leg. In Munich, Father Mayer
was an outspoken opponent of the Red government. That endeared him

to the nationalist and "patriotic" movement, but after an initial flirtation with the Nazis, he broke with them and became their vociferous critic. His attempt to comfort and give last rites to the wounded and dying on Odeonsplatz after the putsch was rebuffed by all the putschists. After Hitler came to power in 1933, Father Mayer preached militantly against the Nazi regime, with the result that he was frequently arrested and imprisoned by the Gestapo and ultimately incarcerated at Oranienburg-Sachsenhausen concentration camp.

Moulin-Eckart, Count Karl-Leon du. Born November 1, 1900. He was a member of Röhm's Reichskriegsflagge and one of Röhm's closest friends and most loyal supporters. During the putsch night and while Röhm was entrenched at the war ministry, Moulin-Eckart performed numerous courier and logistic services. He was indicted for conspiracy to commit high treason along with Röhm, but charges against him were later dropped. Moulin-Eckart, a lawyer, lives in retirement in Munich.

Müller, Dr. Karl Alexander von. Born December 20, 1882, died December 13, 1964. Professor of modern history and political science at Munich University, he was an ardent nationalist, supporter of von Kahr, and contributor of essays to Cossmann's *Süddeutsche Monatshefte*. He was also the brother-in-law of Gottfried Feder. A witness to the events at the Bürgerbräukeller, he testified at Hitler's trial. His memoirs provide detailed observations of the principal characters and events.

Muxel, Wilhelm. Born 1875. A State Police lieutenant colonel, he took a leading part in the police effort to resist and quell the putsch.

Neithardt, Georg. Presiding judge at Hitler's 1924 trial.

Neubauer, Kurt. Born March 27, 1899; killed at Feldherrnhalle, November 9, 1923. An SA man and active in the Nazi party youth movement with Lenk, he worked as Ludendorff's personal servant.

Neunzert, Max. Born August 29, 1892. A former army lieutenant, Neunzert was "communications officer" of the Kampfbund. On the morning of November 9, 1923, Hitler dispatched him to Berchtesgaden to enlist the aid of Crown Prince Rupprecht as a mediator between the putschists and von Kahr. Neunzert's decision to go by train instead of by car brought him to the mountain palace too late.

Nussbaum, Albert. A Social Democratic member of the Munich city council, he was one of those arrested along with Mayor Eduard Schmid by the Stosstrupp, then held hostage and threatened with execution by Göring.

Oemler, Hans. A former army captain, he was commander of a battalion of Oberland League troopers during the putsch which attempted to take control of the 19th Infantry Regiment barracks. Oemler expressed his disillusionment with the Nazi leadership soon after, while being interrogated by police.

Oestreicher, Ludwig. Commander of the Oberland battalion that backed up Hitler's SA at the Bürgerbräukeller and which was responsible for mass arrests of Jews during the night.

Osswald, Karl. Born October 7, 1895. A former army lieutenant, Osswald was

Ernst Röhm's right-hand man as leader of the Reichskriegsflagge formations in Munich and was in command of those units' military operations during the putsch, such as the conquest of the war ministry. In the late 1920s he played an important role, together with Röhm, in the buildup of the SA.

Oswald, Heinrich. Born 1866, died 1929. Bavaria's minister of social welfare from 1920 until 1928, he was one of those cabinet members who did not attend Kahr's speech at the Bürgerbräukeller and joined forces with Franz Matt to establish a rump government-in-exile.

Pernet, Heinz. A former lieutenant and Ludendorff's stepson, he was a top figure in the conspiracy and during the putsch. He was tried along with his stepfather and Hitler in 1924, and convicted of aiding and abetting high treason.

Pöhner, Ernst. Born 1870, died 1925. As Munich's chief of police from 1919 to 1922, he had been instrumental in mounting the White terror and had covered the political murders that were shaking the fledgling German Republic. Ultra-nationalist, rabidly anti-Semitic, and closely allied with Kahr, he was one of the main plotters of the putsch, together with Hitler, and was named as Bavaria's new "prime minister" during the night. Pöhner was convicted with Hitler and the others in 1924. He was killed in a mysterious automobile accident in 1925.

Pröhl, Ilse. Rudolf Hess's fiancée at the time of the putsch, later his wife. She lives in a mountain village south of Munich.

Ried, Michael. Born February 2, 1898. A chauffeur, he was a driver for the Nazi party and involved in most of the key operations during the putsch. He brought Ludendorff to the beerhall, drove Hess and some of the hostages to the Lehmann villa, and was subsequently driver of the car that took Hitler, fleeing from the police, to the Hanfstaengl chalet in Uffing.

Röhm, Ernst. Born in 1887, murdered June 30, 1934, during the "Night of the Long Knives" and the purge named for him. A Reichswehr captain and Seventh Division ordnance officer, Röhm had been a member of the Epp Free Corps and played a vital role in the 1919 White counterrevolution in Munich. Active in a spate of monarchist, nationalist paramilitary groups, he met and befriended Hitler in 1919 and did much to introduce him to high-ranking military officers, all chafing to topple the republic. Röhm was instrumental in creating the "Black Reichswehr" in Bavaria and caching its arms. He was Hitler's military mentor, doing much to build up the SA and the other private armies in Bavaria. As leader of the Reichskriegsflagge Society of war veterans and militants, his role in the putsch was to occupy Lossow's headquarters in the old Bavarian war ministry. He was tried along with Hitler and convicted. There had been conflicts over policy and control between them before. A new one erupted in 1925 and Röhm, by then cashiered from the army, left Germany for South America for a while. In 1930, Hitler recalled him and made him supreme commander of the SA. Within a year it was a huge force, and increasingly Röhm emerged as Hitler's rival for leadership of the party. After Hitler took power in 1933, Röhm became a minister without portfolio in his government and pressed for SA hegemony over the regular army. He was accused of planning a coup against Hitler and killed in June 1934.

Rosenberg, Dr. Alfred. Born January 12, 1893; executed at Nürnberg, October 16, 1946, following his conviction by the Allied Tribunal on war crimes and crimes against humanity. A native of Reval, Estonia, and educated in Russia, Rosenberg fled to Germany after the Bolshevik revolution and became active in czarist émigré circles in Munich. A virulent anti-Semite, he met Hitler through the Thule Society and Dietrich Eckart, and joined the party in 1919. Eckart hired him for the *Völkischer Beobachter;* he became its chief editor in 1923. After the putsch, in which his main role was as propagandist and editor, his influence in the party grew strongly. He was the theoretician of the Nazi movement's anti-Semitism and racist anti-clerical platform. When Hitler took power in 1933, Rosenberg became the head of the party's foreign affairs department. In 1941 he was named minister for the occupied eastern territories. Tried and convicted as the instigator of Germany's racial hatred, he was hanged at Nürnberg.

Rossbach, Gerhard. Born 1893, he was a swashbuckling mercenary and free-corps leader who in the early 1920s enjoyed greater acclaim among the militant nationalists and rightist "patriots" than Hitler. During the putsch it was he who mobilized and led the students, cadets, and officer candidates of the Reichswehr Infantry School. He fled to Austria after the putsch and never regained prominence in the Nazi movement. He was arrested but not killed during the "Röhm Purge," and after World War II operated an export-import business near Frankfurt.

Rue, Larry. American newspaper correspondent who covered the putsch for the *Chicago Tribune*—the paper for which he worked from 1919 until his death, as its Bonn bureau chief, in 1970.

Ruith, Adolf von. Reichswehr major general, commander of the Seventh Division's infantry, who joined forces with General von Danner and General von Kressenstein to compel Lossow to repudiate the putsch.

Rupprecht, Crown Prince of Bavaria. Born May 18, 1869, eldest son of King Ludwig III, died August 2, 1955. During World War I he was commander-in-chief of the Royal Bavarian Army. He was pretender to the throne after the death of his father in 1921. His ambition was to restore the monarchy in Bavaria, but many of the figures involved with the putsch wanted to make him the new Kaiser of all Germany. Ironically, after World War II, during General George S. Patton's brief reign as military governor of Bavaria, the restoration of the Bavarian monarchy was again under consideration, and Rupprecht was asked whether he would take the throne. He told Patton he was no longer interested.

Sauerbruch, Dr. Ferdinand. Born 1875, died 1951. A famous German surgeon, he was professor of surgery and director of the teaching hospital at the University of Munich from 1918 to 1927. Sauerbruch headed the team that treated the wounded after the Feldherrnhalle shooting. Moreover, as an extreme nationalist himself, it was he who tried to calm rioting students in Munich on November 12, 1923. His assistant helped set Hitler's dislocated shoulder at the Hanfstaengl chalet when the Nazi leader was hiding there. Throughout the Third Reich, Sauerbruch ranked as an intimate of Nazi leaders.

Schacht, Hjalmar Horace Greeley. Born 1877, died 1970. A German financier, he was an executive of various banks before being named in November 1923 as commissioner of currency to implement introduction of the "mortgage" marks that ended the inflation. In December 1923 he was appointed president of the Reichsbank, a position he held until his resignation in 1930 over opposition to continued German reparations payments. By then he was a supporter of the Nazi party and Hitler, who renamed him Reichsbank president in 1933 and, in addition, minister of economics in 1934. He resigned the ministry in 1937 because he opposed Göring's four-year economic plans, and in 1939 he was dismissed as Reichsbank president for opposing Hitler's huge armaments program, which, he felt, would cause inflation. He remained a minister without portfolio until 1943, then was placed in a concentration camp in 1944 for his role in the plot to assassinate Hitler. Tried along with the other top leaders at Nürnberg, he was acquitted by the Allied Tribunal in 1946.

Schaub, Julius. Born August 20, 1898. A member of the Stosstrupp and a courier for Göring, it was Schaub who during the night of November 8 alerted Gregor Strasser and his SA forces to converge on Munich. On the morning of November 9, he, together with Heinrich von Knobloch, headed the team of storm troopers that arrested Munich Mayor Eduard Schmid and seven city councilors as hostages. After Hitler's release from Landsberg, Schaub became his bodyguard and personal adjutant, replacing Ulrich Graf, a position he held with the rank of SS general until the end. It was Schaub who burned Hitler's papers when the Führer committed suicide April 30, 1945, and who then flew to Berchtesgaden to destroy documents there.

Scheubner-Richter, Dr. Max Erwin von. Born January 9, 1884, in Riga, Latvia; killed at Feldherrnhalle, November 9, 1923. Part of the clique of émigrés from Russia in Munich, Scheubner was a close friend of Alfred Rosenberg, who introduced him to Hitler. Scheubner had participated in the Berlin Kapp Putsch and in 1920 joined the Nazi party, where he rose quickly to power and influence because of his connections to Ludendorff, the Bavarian royal family, powerful businessmen, and other radical-right organizations. He was a strategist of revolution, and the plan for the putsch is attributed as much to him as it is to Hitler. Allegedly, when Hitler was told of his death, he said, "All are replaceable, except Scheubner."

Schiedt, Adolf. Managing editor of the daily *Münchener Zeitung* and unofficial press spokesman for Gustav von Kahr. It was Schiedt, together with the *Münchner Neueste Nachrichten*'s Fritz Gerlich, who ghost-wrote the speech Kahr was giving at the Bürgerbräukeller.

Schlier, Paula. Stenographer and editorial assistant at the *Völkischer Beobachter*, the Nazi party daily. She had taken the job out of curiosity, not sympathy for the cause, and kept a diary of her time there. Though she became known in later years as a writer of religious and moral essays, her memoirs of 1923 were published in the mid-1920s and provided detailed sketches of what was happening at the newspaper office on Schelling Strasse during the hours of the putsch.

Schmid, Eduard. Social Democrat mayor of Munich from 1919 to 1924, he was taken prisoner along with seven city council members on the morning of November 9, then threatened with execution by Hermann Göring.

Schmied, Ludwig. Born in Munich, November 24, 1898. A member of Berchtold's Stosstrupp and an editor of the *Völkischer Beobachter,* Schmied spent most of the putsch night as one of Hitler's bodyguards on trips through the city. On the morning of November 9 he was assigned to the emergency car being driven by Michael Ried, which waited at the corner of Residenz and Perusa streets, and in which Hitler escaped after the Feldherrnhalle shooting. Schmied accompanied Hitler to Uffing and Hanfstaengl's house. A minor figure in the Nazi party after 1933, Schmied lives today as a pensioner in Munich.

Schreck, Julius. Born 1898, died 1936. An SA man, he was the actual founder and organizer of the Stosstrupp, Hitler's bodyguard and precursor to the SS. Schreck's role during the putsch was brief: he accompanied Major Alexander Siry to the Infantry Barracks in a futile attempt to speak to Lossow, and was arrested and kept under guard the rest of the night and the following day. In 1931, after Hitler had his falling out with Emil Maurice, Schreck became the Nazi leader's personal chauffeur.

Schultze, Dr. Walter. The staff doctor of the SA, it was he who helped Hitler escape after the shooting and treated his arm on the way to the Hanfstaengl house. Schultze remained intimately involved with the Nazi leadership, while practicing medicine in Munich. He died in November 1979.

Schweyer, Franz. Born 1868, died 1935. Bavaria's minister of interior from 1921 to 1924, Schweyer had been an early opponent of Hitler, despite his own ultra-right views, and was on the top of the list of those to be arrested by Rudolf Hess in the Bürgerbräukeller and then kept prisoner at the Lehmann villa. Schweyer was singled out for harassment by Hess.

Seeckt, General Hans von. Born 1866, died 1936. The commander-in-chief of the 100,000-man Reichswehr from 1920 to 1926, Seeckt was at times—and particularly during the period of the putsch—the most powerful man in Germany. He was named virtual military dictator of the Reich during the putsch night. A member of the Reichstag from 1930 to 1932, he was chief military adviser to Chiang Kai-shek in China from 1934 to 1935.

Seisser, Colonel Hans von. Born 1874, died 1973. The chief of Bavaria's division-sized State Police, Seisser was one of the triumvirs ruling the state. His role and attitude toward the putschists was highly equivocal, and hours passed before his subordinates knew for certain whether von Seisser was going to repudiate the coup or not. After the putsch, he was temporarily suspended from duty by the Bavarian government, but reinstated and remained chief of the State Police until his retirement in 1930. Harassed by the Nazis periodically after Hitler came to power, Seisser was briefly reinstalled as chief of the State Police by the U.S. military government in 1945, but was quickly dismissed when Wilhelm Hoegner became prime minister. Hoegner regarded Seisser as "a closet Nazi" and appointed Godin to the job.

Seydel, Josef. Born February 4, 1887. A former army captain and intimate of Ernst Röhm, he was deputy leader of the Reichskriegsflagge and played a key role in the putsch conspiracy. It was Seydel who brought Röhm the word in the Löwenbräukeller that the first part of the putsch had succeeded.

Siry, Alexander. A former army major, he attempted to mediate between Hitler and General von Lossow during the night but was placed under arrest by Lossow.

Strasser, Gregor. Born 1892; murdered June 30, 1934, in the "Röhm Purge." A Landshut pharmacist, Strasser and his brother Otto were early Fascists who envisioned the Nazi party as a movement closer to Mussolini's Black Shirt movement in Italy than what Hitler actually had in mind. Strasser's SA battalion from Landshut participated in the march on the Feldherrnhalle. He was the brother-in-law of State Police Lieutenant Georg Höfler. After the putsch was crushed and Hitler imprisoned, Strasser became de facto head of the outlawed party. When Hitler was released from prison, relations between him and Strasser became increasingly strained over policy. Strasser advocated a radical social program, as opposed to Hitler's emphasis on super-nationalism. He was forced to resign his party membership in 1932. In 1934 he was murdered along with Röhm and others on trumped-up charges of planning a coup against Hitler.

Streck, Hans. A former Reichswehr major and intimate of Röhm, he was in on the planning of the putsch, serving as liaison between the Nazi leadership and Röhm's Reichskriegsflagge.

Streicher, Julius. Born February 12, 1885; executed at Nürnberg as a major war criminal, October 16, 1946. A schoolteacher in Nürnberg, he allied himself with Hitler in 1921 and became the fledgling party's leader in Franconia. As a rabid anti-Semite, he articulated the party's racist program. Streicher's role during the putsch night and on November 9 was primarily that of propagandist and street-corner speaker. He became Nazi Gauleiter of Franconia after Hitler took power, while continuing to publish his viciously anti-Semitic sheet, *Der Stürmer.* At the Allied Tribunal he was convicted of crimes against the peace and humanity.

Stresemann, Gustav. Born 1878, died 1929. As Reich chancellor from mid-1923 until the end of that year, he was instrumental in ending the inflation and reaching an understanding with the United States, Britain, and France on the reparations question. Stresemann was named foreign minister after his chancellorship, and was the architect of the Dawes-Young Plan, the Locarno Pact, and the Kellogg-Briand Pact. He won the Nobel Peace prize in 1926. A conservative politician, he played the key role in restoring respectability and stability to Germany during the Weimar era.

Wagner, Robert. Born October 13, 1898; executed October 1946 in Strasbourg following conviction by a French military court on war crimes. A Reichswehr lieutenant and student at the Infantry School in Munich, he collaborated with Gerhard Rossbach and mobilized the 400 cadets of the school to participate in the putsch. He was convicted as one of the ten defendants in the 1924 Hitler trial. When Hitler took power, he became Gauleiter of Baden and Alsace.

Weber, Dr. Friedrich. Born January 30, 1892, he was the leader of the Oberland League and ranked along with Hitler, Ludendorff, Röhm, and Kriebel as one of the chief conspirators. Convicted at the 1924 trial, he was sentenced to a brief term in prison along with Hitler. Though he tried to keep running the Oberland organization, his political career declined, and he continued to practice veterinary medicine in Munich. When Hitler came to power, he maintained close personal contact with him and was given a lucrative veterinary position in Berlin. After World War II he continued to practice veterinary medicine. He died in 1954.

Wutzelhofer, Johann. Born 1871, died 1939. Bavaria's minister of agriculture from 1919 to 1923, he was taken prisoner by Rudolf Hess in the Bürgerbräukeller, interned at the Lehmann villa, and then harassed, along with Franz Schweyer, on the evening of November 9 as Hess drove the two into the mountains, hoping to find a ski hut where he could keep them hostage longer.

Zuckmayer, Carl. Born 1896, died 1977. A playwright, Zuckmayer was a witness to the putsch in 1923 while working as an assistant director at the Schauspielhaus in Munich. Strongly anti-Nazi, he was forced to emigrate after Hitler took power in 1933, going first to Austria, then Switzerland, and ultimately the United States. His best-known plays, among others, are *The Captain of Köpenick* and *The Devil's General*.

BIBLIOGRAPHY

Interviews and Correspondence

Josef Berchtold
Dr. Richard Bossard (Boscowitz)
Fritz Ebenböck
Dr. Hans Ehard
Frau Dr. Sieglinde Ehard
Hermann Esser
Otto Feichtmayr
Baron Michael von Godin
Dr. Otto Gritschneder
Frau Ilse Hess
Dr. Wilhelm Hoegner
Dr. Ludwig Hümmert
Frau Hans Kallenbach
Adolf Lenk
Stefan Lorant
Count Karl-Leon du Moulin-Eckart
Ludwig Schmied
Frau Dr. Walter Schultze
Ludwig Seligsberger

Documents

Bayerisches Hauptstaatsarchiv (Bavarian State Archives):

MA 103472 (Hitler Putsch Volume I)
MA 103473 (Hitler Putsch Volume II)
MA 103474 (Legal proceedings against Hitler, et al.)
MA 103475 (Newspaper articles re the Hitler Putsch)
MA 103476 (Verbatim typewritten record of the sessions of the special inves-
tigative committee of the Bavarian State Parliament regarding
the events of May 1, 1923, and the movement against the Reich
and State constitutions from September 26 to November 9, 1923.
Four volumes.)

MA 104221 (Files of the General State Commissariat—Colonel Seisser—on the events during the Hitler Putsch and in the aftermath.)
MA 104222 (Verbatim record, typewritten, of the Hitler trial from the first
MA 104223 to the twenty-fourth day, including the secret and in-chambers
MA 104224 sessions. Three volumes.)
MInn 66260 (Files of the Bavarian Ministry of Interior relating to the Hitler
   73694   Putsch and its aftermath.)
   73695
   73696
   73697
   73698
   73699
   73771
   73772

Staatsarchiv München (State Archives Munich and Upper Bavaria):

Files from Police Directorate Munich
Pol-Dir 6709 (Reports of observations November 8–9, 1923)
Pol-Dir 6710 (Reports on interrogations and depositions)
Pol-Dir 6711 (Reports on interrogations and depositions)
Pol-Dir 6712 (Reports on interrogations and depositions)
Pol-Dir 6713 (Reports on interrogations and depositions)
Pol-Dir 6715 (Hitler trial—police interrogations)
Pol-Dir 6716 (Hitler trial)
Pol-Dir 6717 (Hitler trial—signature lists demanding the release of Hitler and copies of the *Völkischer Kurier*)
Pol-Dir 6718 (Parliamentary investigative committee 1927–28)
Pol-Dir 6719 (Parliamentary investigative committee 1927–28)

Newspapers and Periodicals

Chicago Tribune: November 9–12, 1923
Frankfurter Zeitung: November 9–14, 1923
München Augsburger Abendzeitung: November 1–15, 1923
Münchener Post: November 8, 10, 27, 1923/December 16–31, 1927
Münchener Zeitung: November 1–30, 1923
Münchner Neueste Nachrichten: November 1–30, 1923/February 26–April 2, 1924
New York Daily News: November 1–15, 1923
New York Herald: November 1–15, 1923
New York Post: November 1–15, 1923
New York Times: November 1–30, 1923, and February 16–April 15, 1924
New York Tribune: November 1–15, 1923
Süddeutsche Zeitung: November 11, 1967
Vierteljahreshefte für Zeitgeschichte: 1955 and 1957
Völkischer Beobachter: November 1–9, 1923/December 16–31, 1927

Vossische Zeitung: November 1–15, 1923
Die Woche: No. 46, 1923

Munich Institutes and Libraries Used

Bayerisches Hauptstaatsarchiv
Bayerische Staatsbibliothek
Institut für Zeitgeschichte
Monacensia Section, City Library
Staatsarchiv Oberbayern
Stadtarchiv

Books

Bäthe, Kristian. *Wer Wohnte Wo in Schwabing?*, Süddeutscher Verlag, Munich, 1965.

Bennecke, Heinrich. *Hitler und die SA*, Günter Olzog Verlag, Munich-Vienna, 1962.

Bernhard, Henry (ed.). *Gustav Stresemann—Vermächtniss* (3 vols.), Ullstein Verlag, Berlin, 1932.

Bird, Eugene K. *Rudolf Hess*, Verlag Kurt Desch, Munich, 1974.

Bullock, Alan. *Hitler—A Study in Tyranny*, Harper, New York, 1953; 1964.

Bronder, Dietrich. *Bevor Hitler Kam*, Hans Pfeiffer Verlag, Hanover, 1964.

Coblitz, Wilhelm. *Theodor von der Pfordten*, Verlag Franz Eher Nachf.; Munich, 1937.

Daim, Wilfried. *Der Mann der Hitler die Ideen Gab*, Isar Verlag, Munich, 1958.

Delmer, Sefton. *Trail Sinister*, Secker & Warburg, London, 1961.

Deuerlein, Ernst (ed.). *Der Hitler Putsch, Bayerische Dokumente zum 8/9 November 1923*, Deutsche Verlags-Anstalt, Stuttgart, 1962.

Deuerlein, Ernst. *Der Aufstieg der NSDAP in Augenzeugenberichten*, Düsseldorf, 1968.

———. *Hitler, Eine Politische Biographie*, List Verlag, Munich, 1970.

Dietrich, Otto. *Mit Hitler in die Macht*, Verlag Franz Eher Nachf., Munich, 1934.

Fabricius, Hans. *Dr. Frick, der Revolutionäre Staatsmann*, Berlin-Leipzig, 1933.

Fest, Joachim C. *Hitler*, Propyläen Verlag, Berlin-Frankfurt, 1973.

Frank, Hans. *Im Angesicht des Galgens*, Friedrich Alfred Beck Verlag, Munich-Gräfelfing, 1953.

Franz-Willing, Georg. *Ursprung der Hitlerbewegung 1919–1922*, K. W. Schütz Verlag, Preussisch Oldendorf, 1974.

———. *Krisenjahre der Hitlerbewegung 1923*, K. W. Schütz Verlag, Preussisch Oldendorf, 1975.

———. *Putsch und Verbotszeit der Hitlerbewegung*, K. W. Schütz Verlag, Preussisch Oldendorf, 1977.

Friedrich, Otto. *Before the Deluge*, Harper, New York, 1972.

Frischauer, Willi. *Himmler, The Evil Genius of the Third Reich*, Belmont, N.Y., 1953.

Fügner, Kurt. *Wir Marschieren*, Ludendorffs Verlag, Munich, 1938.

Galera, Karl Sigmar de. *Geschichte Unserer Zeit—Die Krise des Reichs*, Schlüter Verlag, Leipzig, 1930.

Gilbert, G. M. *Nuremberg Diary*, Farrar, Straus and Cudahy, New York, 1947.

Gordon, Harold J. Jr. *Hitlerputsch 1923*, Bernard & Graefe Verlag, Frankfurt, 1971.

Görlitz, Walter and Quint, Herbert. *Adolf Hitler*, Steingrüben Verlag, Stuttgart, 1952.

Gritzbach, Erich. *Hermann Göring—Werk und Mensch*, Verlag Franz Eher Nachf., Munich, 1937.

Gumbel, E. I. *Verschwörer*, Malik Verlag, Vienna, 1924.

Hanfstaengl, Ernst F. *The Missing Years*, Eyre & Spottiswoode, London, 1957.

————. *Zwischen Weissem und Braunem Haus*, R. Piper & Co., Munich, 1970.

Heiden, Konrad. *Hitler* (2 vols.), Europa Verlag, Zurich, 1936.

————. *Der Fuehrer*, Houghton Mifflin Co., Boston, 1944.

Heuss, Theodor. *Hitler's Weg*, Union Deutsche Verlagsgesellschaft, Stuttgart, 1932.

Hinkel, Hans. *Einer Unter Hundertausend*, Knorr & Hirth Verlag, Munich, 1939.

Hitler, Adolf. *Mein Kampf*, Verlag Franz Eher Nachf., Munich, 1925 and 1927.

Der Hitler Prozess vor dem Volksgericht in München (Transcript of the Hitler trial), Knorr & Hirth Verlag, Munich, 1924.

Der Hitler Prozess—Auszüge aus den Verhandlungsberichten (Excerpts of the trial record), Deutscher Volksverlag, Munich, 1924.

Hoegner, Wilhelm. *Hitler und Kahr*, Landesausschuss der SPD in Bayern, Munich, 1928.

————. *Die Verratene Republik*, Isar Verlag, Munich, 1958.

————. *Der Schwierige Aussenseiter*, Isar Verlag, Munich, 1959.

Hoffmann, Heinrich. *Hitler Wie Ich Ihn Sah*, Herbig Verlag, Munich, 1974.

Hofmann, Hans H. *Der Hitlerputsch*, Nymphenburger Verlagshandlung, Munich, 1961.

Hollander, Jürgen von. *München, ein Deutscher Himmel*, Schuler Verlag, Munich, 1972.

Hollweck, Ludwig. *Unser München*, Süddeutscher Verlag, Munich, 1967.

————. *München, Liebling der Musen*, Paul Zsolnay Verlag, Vienna, 1971.

Hümmert, Ludwig. *Bayern vom Königreich zur Diktatur*, Verlag W. Ludwig, Pfaffenhofen, 1979.

Jarman, T, L. *The Rise and Fall of Nazi Germany*, New York University Press, New York, 1956.

Jonge, Alex de. *The Weimar Chronicle*, New American Library, New York, 1979.

Jünger, Ernst. *Jahre der Okkupation*, Ernst Klett Verlag, Stuttgart, 1958.

Kallenbach, Hans. *Mit Adolf Hitler auf Festung Landsberg*, Verlag Kress & Hornung, Munich, 1939.

Koch, H. W. *The Hitler Youth*, Stein and Day, New York, 1976.

Koerbling, Anton. *Father Rupert Mayer*, Schnell & Steiner Verlag, Munich, 1950.

Kotze, Hildegard and Krausnick, Helmut (eds.). *Es Spricht der Führer*, Sigbert Mohn Verlag, Gütersloh, 1966.

Krebs, Albert. *Tendenzen und Gestalten der NSDAP*, Institut für Zeitgeschichte, Munich, 1959.

Krumbach, H. J. *Franz Ritter von Epp, Ein Leben für Deutschland*, Verlag Franz Eher Nachf., Munich, 1939

Kubizek, August. *Adolf Hitler—Mein Jugendfreund*, Leopold Stocker Verlag, Graz, 1953.

Leverkuehn, Paul. *Posten auf Ewiger Wache—Aus dem Leben des Max von Scheubner-Richter*, Essener Verlagsanstalt, Essen, 1938.

Lorant, Stefan. *Sieg Heil*, W. W. Norton, New York, 1974.

Ludendorff, Erich. *Auf dem Weg zur Feldherrnhalle*, Ludendorffs Verlag, Munich, 1937.

———. *Vom Feldherrn zum Weltrevolutionär*, Ludendorffs Verlag, Munich, 1940.

———. *Ludendorff's Warnung*, Deutscher Volksververlag, Munich, 1924.

Luedecke, Kurt W. G. *I Knew Hitler*, Charles Scribner's Sons, New York, 1938.

Mann, Katja. *Unwritten Memories*, Knopf, New York, 1975.

Manvell, Roger and Fraenkel, Heinrich. *Himmler*, Ullstein Verlag, Berlin, 1966.

———. *Goering*, Ballantine Books, New York, 1972.

Maser, Werner. *Die Frühgeschichte der NSDAP*, Athenaeum Verlag, Frankfurt, 1965.

———. *Adolf Hitler*, F. A. Herbig Verlagsbuchhandlung, Munich-Berlin, 1971.

———. *Mein Kampf*, Bechtle Verlag, Esslingen, 1974.

Meier-Welcker, Hans. *Seeckt*, Bernard & Graefe, Frankfurt, 1967.

Meissner, Otto. *Staatssekretär unter Ebert-Hindenburg-Hitler*, Hoffmann und Campe Verlag, Hamburg, 1950.

Müller, Karl Alexander von. *Im Wandel einer Welt*, Süddeutscher Verlag, Munich, 1966.

Müller-Meiningen, Ernst. *Aus Bayerns Schwersten Tagen*, Berlin-Leipzig, 1923.

Murphy, Robert. *Diplomat Among Warriors*, Doubleday, New York, 1964.

O'Donnell, James P. *Die Katakombe*, Deutsche Verlagsanstalt, Stuttgart, 1975.

———. *The Bunker*, Houghton Mifflin, Boston, 1978.

Oertzen, F. W. von. *Die Deutschen Freikorps*, Bruckmann Verlag, Munich, 1936.

Payne, Robert. *The Life and Death of Adolf Hitler*, Praeger, New York, 1973.

Plümer, Friedrich. *Die Wahrheit über Hitler und Sein Kreis*, Karl Springer Verlag, Munich, 1925.

Pölnitz, Götz von. *Emir, Das Tapfere Leben des Freiherrn Marschall von Biberstein*, Verlag Georg Callwey, Munich, 1938.

Pridham, Geoffrey. *Hitler's Rise to Power*, Harper & Row, New York, 1973.

Rabenau, Friedrich von (ed.). *Seeckt—Aus Seinem Leben*, Hase & Koehler Verlag, Leipzig, 1941.

————. *Seeckt*, Gesellschaft der Freunde der Deutschen Bücherei, Leipzig, 1942.

Reich, Albert. *Dietrich Eckart, ein Deutscher Dichter*, Verlag Franz Eher Nachf., Munich, 1933.

Reitlinger, Gerald. *The Final Solution*, Beechhurst Press, New York, 1953.

Röhm, Ernst. *Die Geschichte eines Hochverräters*, Verlag Franz Eher Nachf., Munich, 1928.

————. *Die Memoirien des Stabschef Röhm*, Uranus Verlag, Saarbrücken, 1934.

Rosenberg, Alfred. *Letzte Aufzeichnungen*, Plesse Verlag, Göttingen, 1955.

————. *Kampf um die Macht*, Verlag Franz Eher Nachf., Munich, 1939.

————. *Schriften und Reden*, Hoheneichen Verlag, Munich, 1943.

————. *Blut und Ehre*, Verlag Franz Eher Nachf., Munich, 1941.

Rossbach, Gerhard. *Mein Weg Durch Die Zeit*, Vereinigte Weilburger Buchdruckereien, Weilburg-Lahn, 1950.

Sauerbruch, Ferdinand. *Das War Mein Leben*, Kindler Verlag, Munich, 1960.

Schuler, Emil. *Die Bayerische Landesplolizei, 1919–1935*, Werbedruck Rudolf Stepanek, Munich, 1969.

Schlier, Paula. *Petra's Aufzeichnungen oder Konzept Einer Jugend Nach dem Diktat der Zeit*, Brenner Verlag, Innsbrück, 1926.

Schlottner, Erich. *Stresemann, der Kapp Putsch und die Ereignisse in Mitteldeutschland und in Bayern im Herbst 1923*, Bad Homburg, 1948.

Schwarzwäller, Wulf. *Rudolf Hess*, Molden Verlag, Vienna, 1974.

Schwend, Karl. *Bayern Zwischen Monarchie und Diktatur*, Richard Pflaum Verlag, Munich, 1954.

Sendtner, Kurt (ed.). *Otto Gessler, Reichswehr Politik in der Weimarer Zeit*, Deutsche Verlags-Anstalt, Stuttgart, 1958.

Shirer, William. *The Rise and Fall of the Third Reich*, Simon & Schuster, New York, 1960.

Speer, Albert. *Inside the Third Reich*, The Macmillan Co., New York, 1970.

————. *Spandau*, The Macmillan Co., New York, 1976.

Strasser, Otto. *Aufbau des Deutschen Sozialismus*, Grunov, Prague, 1931.

————. *Hitler und Ich*, Editorial Trenkelbach, Buenos Aires, 1940.

Stülpnagel, Joachim von. *Jahre Meines Lebens*, Düsseldorf, 1960.

Toland, John. *Adolf Hitler*, Doubleday, New York, 1976.

Uecker, Bernhard. *Wie Bayern Unter die Pickelhaube Kam*, Süddeutscher Verlag, Munich, 1970.

Wilamowitz-Moellendorff, Fanny. *Carin Göring*, Verlag von Martin Warneck, Berlin, 1941.

Wilhelm, Hermann. *Nationalsozialismus im Münchner Osten 1919–1945,* Haidhauser Dokumentationsverlag, Munich, 1980.

Wolfe, Thomas. *The Web and the Rock,* Sun Dial Press, Garden City, N.Y., 1940.

Wucher, Albert. *Die Fahne Hoch,* Süddeutscher Verlag, Munich, 1963.

Wulf, Josef. *Heinrich Himmler,* Arani Verlags GmbH, Berlin, 1960.

Zimmermann, Werner. *Bayern und das Reich,* Richard Pflaum Verlag, Munich, 1953.

Zuckmayer, Carl. *Als wär's ein Stück von mir,* Fischer Taschenbuch Verlag, Frankfurt, 1969.

SOURCES

Prologue

Verbatim record of Hitler trial, MA 104222–24; Kahr's Denkschrift MA 103473; Gordon; Hofmann; Toland; Payne; Shirer; Franz-Willing; Hümmert; Schwend; Hoegner (2); Jarman; von Müller; Hanfstaengl; Maser; Röhm; Leverkühn; Ludendorff.

Interlude 1

Hollander; Hollweck; Mann; Wolfe; Hoegner.

One: The Plan in the Making

1. Hofmann; Franz-Willing; Toland; Hollweck; Ehard interview; Hoegner interview; Briemann interview; Lenk interview; Berchtold deposition in MA 103476; Himmler deposition in Pol-Dir 6713; Frischauer; Manvell-Fraenkel; Sauerbruch; Ludendorff (2); Mann; Murphy; Kahr's Denkschrift MA 103473; Mantel's report to General State Commissariat in Pol-Dir 6709 and 6710; Röhm; von Müller; Zuckmayer; Hümmert and Hümmert interview; Wilamowitz-Moellendorff; Gritzbach; Hanfstaengl; Rosenberg and Rosenberg deposition in Pol-Dir 6713; *Münchener Post*; *Münchener Zeitung*; *Münchner Neueste Nachrichten*; *Völkischer Beobachter*; *Vossiche Zeitung*; Hess testimony in MA 103476.

2. Hofmann; Gordon; Franz-Willing; Trial record MA 104222–24; Hanfstaengl; Lenk interview; Rossbach; Berchtold deposition in MA 103476; Hoffmann deposition in Pol-Dir 6712; Schlier; Toland; Kallenbach; Bennecke; Hinkel; von Müller; Neunzert deposition in Pol-Dir 6712; Imhoff deposition in Pol-Dir 6712; Mayer deposition in Pol-Dir 6712; Briemann interview; Himmler deposition in Pol-Dir 6713; Manvell-Fraenkel and Frischauer; Kiessling deposition in Pol-Dir 6709; Frank; Beggel deposition in Pol-Dir 6712; Streicher deposition in Pol-Dir 6713; Strasser; Wagner, Block, Mahler, et al. in MA 103476; Heinrich Hoffmann; Esser interview; Schreiber-Schmidt-Stiegeler-Bouhler depositions in Pol-Dir 6713; Feder documents in Pol-Dir 6713; Mantel

report Pol-Dir 6709 and 6710; Fabricius; Schuler; Von Imhoff Pol-Dir 6709 and Pol-Dir 6710; Ludendorff; Kahr's Denkschrift MA 103473; Hoegner interview; Ehard interview; Schmied interview; Alban, Christ, Bömerl, Pöhlmann, Zahner statements in Pol-Dir 6709; Hoegner interview; Brieman and Schmied interviews; Kallenbach; Berchtold in MA 103476; Stosstrupp trial documents in Pol-Dir 6712 and 6713; von Müller; Hess deposition in MA 103476; Kiefer in Pol-Dir 6709; Captain Stumpf in Pol-Dir 6709; Schreck deposition in Pol-Dir 6713; *Münchener Post, Münchener Zeitung, Münchner Neueste Nachrichten.*

Interlude II

New York Herald, Times, Tribune, World; Münchener Post; München-Augsburger Abendzeitung; Simpliccisimus; Hümmert; Schwend; Shirer; Heiden; Fest; Krumbach; Röhm; Rossbach; von Müller; Gordon; Hofmann; Franz-Willing; Hanfstaengl; Hollweck; Hollander; Schwarzwäller; Kahr's Denkschrift in MA 103473; Hoegner and Hoegner interview; Investigative committee MA 103476; Lenk interview; Briemann interview; von Gruber in MA 103476; Lehner interview in Pol-Dir 6713.

Two: The Plot as Planned

3. Franz-Willing; Schreck deposition in Pol-Dir 6712 and 6713; Ried in MA 103476; Baldenius deposition in Pol-Dir 6712; Briemann interview; Schmied interview; Lenk interview; Niederreiter deposition in MA 103476; Hewel, Maurer, Krüger, Stollwerck depositions in Pol-Dir 6713; Kallenbach; Berchtold deposition in MA 103476; Stosstrupp trial documents in Pol-Dir 6712; Rosenberg and Rosenberg deposition in Pol-Dir 6712; Toland; von Müller; Rauh, Bruckmaier, Georg Stumpf, Fritz Stumpf, Ott, Kiefer reports in Pol-Dir 6709; *Münchener Zeitung* and *Münchner Neueste Nachrichten;* Hess deposition in MA 103476; Gordon; Hanfstaengl; Lüdecke; and Trial record MA 104222–24.

4. Esser interview; Imhoff, Mayer, Ebenböck depositions in Pol-Dir 6712; Beggel deposition in Pol-Dir 6712; Gordon; Frank; Rossbach; Heines deposition in Pol-Dir 6712; Hoegner and Hoegner interview; Police blotter in Pol-Dir 6709; Böhm report in Pol-Dir 6712; Kahr's Denkschrift in MA 103473; Oemler deposition in Pol-Dir 6712; Anton Rasberger and Max Humpf in Pol-Dir 6713; Investigative committee in MA 103476; Ebenböck in Pol-Dir 6710; Seydel in Pol-Dir 6712 and 6713; Osswald in Pol-Dir 6712; Röhm; Moulin-Eckart interview; Altmann, Schmäling, and Schmäling in Pol-Dir 6709; Ludendorff; Report of State Police in Garmisch re Völk in MInn73696; Streicher deposition in Pol-Dir 6712; Kiessling deposition in Pol-Dir 6709; Berchtold in MA 103476; Lenk, Briemann interviews.

5. Trial record MA 104222–24 and *Der Hitler Prozess* transcripts; Hanfstaengl; *Münchner Neueste Nachrichten;* Kiefer report in Pol-Dir 6709; Bruckmeier report in Pol-Dir 6709; Patrolmen Zwack, Löhlen, Steiger, Winkler, Becherbauer, and Feiner in Pol-Dir 6709; Graf testimony in MA

104222–24; Kiefer in Pol-Dir 6709; Franz-Willing; Mantel's report in Pol-Dir 6710; MA 103476 on Gerum; Rosenberg; Lenk interview; Toland; Gordon; Hofmann; Kahr's Denkschrift in MA 103473; Fritz Stumpf in Pol-Dir 6709; K. A. von Müller; Büchs, Rauh, Herrmann, Gäring, Johannes Müller, Haupt, Reittinger, Singer, Ludwig Weber, Johann Schmidt reports in Pol-Dir 6709; Kress and "Confidential Anonymous" reports in Pol-Dir 6710; Mantel report in MA 104221 and MA 103473; *Chicago Tribune; New York Herald; Münchener Zeitung;* Kolb deposition in Pol-Dir 6712; Kolb, Reindl, Simmerding, Scherbauer, Max statements regarding telephones in Pol-Dir 6713 and MA 103476; Aigner and Pernet depositions in Pol-Dir 6709; Michael Ried in MA 103476; Herrmann and Hofmann in Pol-Dir 6713 on Wassermann and in MA 103476.

Interlude III

New York Times, New York Tribune, Vossische Zeitung, Nov. 8 and 9; Schlottner on Stresemann; Meissner; Bernhard (ed.) on Stresemann; Rabenau and Meier-Welcker on Seeckt; Lüdecke; *Hitler und Italien* by Pese in No. 2, 1955, and *Mussolini und Deutschland* by Rosen in Vol. 1, 1957, of *Vierteljahreshefte für Zeitgeschichte;* Oct. 11 and Nov. 18 letters of Konstantin von Neurath to Foreign Ministry Berlin in MA 103474; Memorandum Sept. 12, 1925 Bavarian ministry of interior to Bavarian ministry of foreign affairs in MA 103472; Memorandum of Reich foreign ministry to Bavarian foreign ministry dated Dec. 21, 1923, in MA 103473; three reports on Lüdecke by German Embassy in Rome to Reich foreign ministry in MA 103473.

6. Imhoff report to district attorney's office in MA 104221; Fritz Stumpf report in Pol-Dir 6709; State Police Munich report to Chief State Police (draft) in MA 104221 and investigative committee's verbatim record of same, MA 103476; Police blotters of Nov. 8 and 9, 1923, in Pol-Dir 6709; Mantel's report to Kahr and interior ministry Dec. 5 and 7, and drafts in Pol-Dir 6710; Mantel report to interior ministry April 5, 1924; Fabricius on Frick; Godin interview; Schmäling-Reithmeier reports in Pol-Dir 6709; Röhm; Toland; Franz-Willing; Gordon; Hofmann; Esser interview; Frischauer and Manvell-Fraenkel on Himmler; Himmler deposition in Pol-Dir 6713; Seydel deposition in Pol-Dir 6713; Reiner deposition in Pol-Dir 6713 and statement in MA 103476; Osswald deposition in Pol-Dir 6712; Eduard Dünkler, Heinrich Adlhoch, Heinrich Bennecke depositions in Pol-Dir 6712; Johann Tröger deposition in Pol-Dir 6709; Georg Raithel in Pol-Dir 6712 and letter dated Jan. 10, 1924; Anton Lehner, Friedrich Mayer, and Anton Zahner depositions in Pol-Dir 6713; Walther Lembert, Wilhelm Meister, Johann Will, and Herbert Müller depositions in Pol-Dir 6712; Heines deposition in Pol-Dir 6712; Hans Frank; Hoegner and Hoegner interview; Böhm report in Pol-Dir 6712; Kahr's Denkschrift MA 103473; Oemler deposition in Pol-Dir 6712; Beggel in Pol-Dir 6712; Humps in Pol-Dir 6713; Parliamentary investigative committee MA 103476; Rasberger deposition in Pol-Dir 6713; Aigner deposition in Pol-Dir 6713; Ludendorff; Trial testimony in MA 104222–24 and Der Hitler Prozess; Ried in MA 103476.

7. Kahr's Denkschrift MA 103473; Testimony of Graf, Pöhner, Kriebel,

Weber, Kahr, Lossow, Seisser in trial, MA 104222–224 and Der Hitlerprozess stenographic records; Lenk interview; Toland; Gordon; Hofmann; Franz-Willing; Maser; Fest; Hanfstaengl; Rosenberg and Rosenberg testimony in Pol-Dir 6712; K. A. von Müller; "Confidential Anonymous" report on events in hall in Pol-Dir 6710; Gruber testimony in trial MA 104222–24; Herrmann report in Pol-Dir 6709; Kress report in Pol-Dir 6712; Konrad Heiden; Singer report in Pol-Dir 6709; *Chicago Tribune* Nov. 9–12, 1923; *Münchner Neueste Nachrichten,* Nov. 9–13, 1923; Stumpf report Pol-Dir 6709; Reitinger report in Pol-Dir 6709; Ott, Johann Schmidt, Ludwig Weber, Otto Gäring, Siegfried Feistle reports in Pol-Dir 6709; Ferdinand Schreiber and Anton Schmidt depositions in Pol-Dir 6713; Parliamentary investigative committee in MA 103476; Ludendorff and Ludendorff in trial testimony; Streicher deposition in Pol-Dir 6712; Matthäus Hofmann in trial testimony MA 104222–24 and in deposition re Wassermann in Pol-Dir 6713; Herrmann in Pol-Dir 6713; Pschorr statements in Pol-Dir 6713; Wassermann statement in Pol-Dir 6713; Büchs and Bruckmeier reports in Pol-Dir 6709; Dr. Max Grassmann in Pol-Dir 6713; Zuckmayer; Ehard interview; Zettlmeier report in MInn 73694; Hess's and prisoners' statements in MA 103476; Neunzert in Pol-Dir 6712.

8. Reithmeier report in Pol-Dir 6709; Stumpf report in Pol-Dir 6709; Von Imhoff report in MA 104221 and testimony at Hitler trial in MA 104222–24; Hans Haberl, Georg Rauh, and Schmäling reports in Pol-Dir 6709; Neunzert deposition in Pol-Dir 6712; Zetlmeier in MInn 73694; Frick, Pöhner, Danner, Berchem, Bergen testimony at trial in MA 104222–224; H. H. Hofmann; Karl Wild report in MA 104221; Kahr's Denkschrift in MA 103473; Gordon; Röhm and Röhm testimony in trial MA 104222–24; Moulin-Eckart interview; Seydel deposition in Pol-Dir 6712 and 6713; Bennecke in Pol-Dir 6712; Osswald in Pol-Dir 6712; Parliamentary investigative committee MA 103476, pp. 1331–4; Tröger deposition in Pol-Dir 6709; Anton Lehner, Friedrich Mayer, and Fritz Imhoff depositions in Pol-Dir 6713; Fritz Ebenböck in Pol-Dir 6710; Mutz, Binz, Karl Hühnlein statements re Palatia house in Pol-Dir 6712; Walther Lembert deposition in Pol-Dir 6712; Oemler in Pol-Dir 6712; Max Humps and Anton Rasberger in Pol-Dir 6713 and parliamentary investigation in MA 103476 on Engineer Barracks; Esser interview; Captain Selle on Milbertshofen in Pol-Dir 6713; Paula Schlier; Heinrich Hoffmann, Hümmert interview, Hoegner interview, Godin interview; Schreiber-Schmidt-Stiegeler-Bouhler testimonies in Pol-Dir 6713; Colonel Banzer statement in MA 103473; Mantel's report in Pol-Dir 6710.

9. Statements of hostages, Rudolf Hess, Johann Niederreiter, Wilhelm Wittmer, and Michael Ried in MA 103476; Hanfstaengl; Toland; Heiden; Gordon; Hofmann; Franz-Willing; Schreck, Graf and Baldenius depositions in Pol-Dir 6712 and 6713; Ludwig Schmied interview; Röhm; Rossbach; depositions regarding Infantry School in MA 103476 and statements of Wagner, Block, and Mahler, also Wagner testimony at trial in MA 104222–24; Heines deposition in Pol-Dir 6712; Weber, Röhm, Hitler testimonies at trial in MA 104222–24; Esser interview; Johann Aigner; Ludendorff and Ludendorff testimony at trial in MA 104222–24; Kahr's Denkschrift, MA 103473; Neunzert deposition

in Pol-Dir 6712; Kiessling deposition in Pol-Dir 6709; Karl Wild report in MA 104221; Alfons Weber deposition in Pol-Dir 6712; Hans Frank.

Interlude IV

Hanfstaengl; Hans Frank; Oemler and Beggel interrogations in Pol-Dir 6712; Toland; Röhm; Gordon; Konrad Heiden; H. H. Hofmann; Heinrich Hoffmann; Wilhelm Briemann interview; Esser interview; Lenk interview; Ludwig Schmied interview; Kiessling deposition in Pol-Dir 6709; Von Imhoff report in MA 104221.

Three: The Plan Goes Awry

10. Kahr's Denkschrift in MA 103473; Testimony of Kahr, Lossow, Seisser, Pöhner, Frick, Ludendorff, Danner, Bergen, and Wagner in Der Hitler Prozess and in trial record MA 104222–24; Gordon; Hofmann; Hourly report of events at Kahr's offices in MInn 73696; Matt in record of investigative committee, MA 103476 and in protocol of Bavarian cabinet meeting Nov. 10, 1923; Ehard interview; Hoegner interview; Supplement No. 4 to Kahr's Denkschrift MA 103473 and information on role of Reichswehr in MA 103476, pp. 1300ff; Von Imhoff report in MA 104221; Mantel's report in Pol-Dir 6710; Supplement 4b to Kahr's Denkschrift in MA 103473; Karl Wild's report in MA 104221; Kiessling deposition in Pol-Dir 6709; Alfons Weber deposition in Pol-Dir 6712; Neunzert deposition in Pol-Dir 6712; Ernst Röhm; Seydel deposition in Pol-Dir 6713; Rasberger and Humps depositions in Pol-Dir 6713; Schaub deposition in Pol-Dir 6713; Statements and depositions of hostages and Rudolf Hess in Investigative committee record MA 103476; Ludendorff; *Völkischer Beobachter*, Nov. 9, 1923; *Münchner Neueste Nachrichten*, Nov. 9 and 10, 1923; Schuler; Wagner testimony in trial, MA 104222–24 and Der Hitlerprozess, and Block, Mahler statements in MA 103476; Gehrlich, Egenter, and Mündler statements in Pol-Dir 6712; Lüdecke; Texts of posters and proclamations in Pol-Dir 6711.

11. Briemann interview; Kallenbach; Verdict of Stosstrupp trial in Pol-Dir 6712; Berchtold deposition in MA 103476; Hewel, Krüger, Maurer depositions in Pol-Dir 6713; *Münchener Post*, Nov. 10 and Nov. 27, 1923; Heines deposition in Pol-Dir 6712; Hans Frank; Tauber statement in MA 103476; Sophie Auer statement in Pol-Dir 6710; Investigation report on Hübner et al. in Pol-Dir 6710; Kiessling deposition in Pol-Dir 6709; Police report on Kohn-Scheer and Engl depositions in Pol-Dir 6710; Grünspann to police in Pol-Dir 6713; Alfons Weber deposition in Pol-Dir 6712; Statements of Von Stuck and Von Bayern et al. in Pol-Dir 6713; Hümmert.

Interlude V

Schlottner on Stresemann; Bernhard (ed.) on Stresemann; Meier-Welcker on Seeckt; Rabenau (ed.) on Seeckt; Sendtner (ed.) on Gessler; Otto Friedrich;

Konrad Heiden; Gordon; Hofmann; *Vossische Zeitung*, Nov. 9 and 10, 1923, evening and morning editions; *Neue Zürcher Zeitung, Frankfurter Zeitung*, Nov. 9 and 10, 1923; Lüdecke; Von Neurath to Foreign Office in MA 103474; *New York Times, Tribune, Herald, World, Daily News*, and *Chicago Tribune*, all Nov. 8 and 9, 1923; Kahr's Denkschrift in MA 103473.

12. Gordon; Hofmann; Franz-Willing; Kahr's Denkschrift in MA 103473; Testimony of Kahr, Lossow, Seisser, Major Siry, Pöhner, Frick, von Imhoff in trial record MA 104222–24 and Der Hitler Prozess; Von Imhoff report in MA 104221; Ludendorff; Röhm; Schreck depositions in Pol-Dir 6712 and Pol-Dir 6713; *Münchner Neueste Nachrichten*, Nov. 9 and 10, 1923; Mantel's report of Nov. 23 in Pol-Dir 6710; Fabricius on Frick; Wild report in MA 104221; Parliamentary investigation commitee record MA 103476.

13. Aubele statement in Investigative committee report, MA 103476; Anna Schürz, Elsa Gisler, Karl Weiss, Philipp Bouhler depositions in Pol-Dir 6712; Streicher and Klotz depositions in Pol-Dir 6712; Esser interview; *Völkischer Beobachter*, Nov. 9, 1923; Franz-Willing; Hofmann; Gordon; Ernst Röhm; Siry testimony in trial record MA 104222–24 and Der Hitlerprozess; Lieutenant Rossmann and Lieutenant Braun testimony in trial record MA 104222–24; Seydel deposition in Pol-Dir 6712 and Pol-Dir 6713; Osswald deposition in Pol-Dir 6712; Schaub deposition in Pol-Dir 6713; Himmler deposition in Pol-Dir 6713; Walther Lembert deposition in Pol-Dir 6712; Müller, Will, Meister depositions in Pol-Dir 6712; Robert Murphy; Kriebel testimony in trial record MA 104222–24 and Der Hitlerprozess; Kressenstein testimony in trial record MA 104222–24; Ludendorff; Ludendorff testimony in trial record MA 104222–24 and Der Hitlerprozess; Mayer and Lehner depositions in Pol-Dir 6713; Paula Schlier; Rosenberg and Rosenberg deposition in Pol-Dir 6713; Heinrich Hoffmann; Anton Schmidt, Hans Stiegeler, and Ferdinand Schreiber statements and Bouhler deposition in Pol-Dir 6713; Texts of posters and proclamations in Pol-Dir 6711; Leupold's report in Supplement 4a to Kahr's Denkschrift, MA 103473; Pöhner testimony in trial record MA 104222–24; Von Imhoff report in MA 104221; Hitler's testimony in trial record MA 104222–24; Otto Strasser.

14. Gordon; H. H. Hofmann; Franz-Willing; Toland; *New York Times*, Nov. 12, 1923; Stosstrupp trial record and verdict in Pol-Dir 6712; Briemann and Schmied interviews; Hewel, Krüger, Stollwerck, Maurer, Von Knobloch depositions in Pol-Dir 6713; Kallenbach; Siry, Ludendorff, and Hitler testimonies in trial record MA 104222–24; Schreck deposition Pol-Dir 6712 and 6713; Oemler deposition in Pol-Dir 6712; Weber deposition in Pol-Dir 6712; Kiessling deposition in Pol-Dir 6709; Mayer and Lehner depositions in Pol-Dir 6713; Fritz Imhoff deposition in Pol-Dir 6713; Ebenböck deposition in Pol-Dir 6710; Beggel deposition in Pol-Dir 6712; Bennecke deposition in Pol-Dir 6712; Hans Frank; Heines in Pol-Dir 6712; Lenk interview; Wallner case as mentioned in Investigative committee report MA 103476 and in Stosstrupp depositions in Pol-Dir 6713; Streicher before International Military Tribunal in Nürnberg; Police blotter Nov. 9, 1923, in Pol-Dir 6709 and Investigative committee report MA 103476 on banknote robberies; Neunzert deposition in Pol-

Dir 6712 and statements in Investigative committee report MA 103476; Freiesleben statement in Pol-Dir 6713 and Fiehler deposition in Pol-Dir 6713; Statements on Infantry School in MA 103476; Hanfstaengl; Brückner testimony in trial record MA 104222–24.

Interlude VI

Mantel's report on posters to Bavarian interior ministry in Pol-Dir 6710; Statements of Herrmann, Schmäling, and Neeb in Pol-Dir 6710; Schiedt testimony in trial record MA 104222–24 and Der Hitler Prozess; Hofmann; Gordon; Franz-Willing; *Münchner Neueste Nachrichten, Bayerischer Kurier, Münchener Zeitung,* and *Völkischer Beobachter,* all of Nov. 9, 1923; Bennecke deposition in Pol-Dir 6712; Kiessling deposition in Pol-Dir 6709; *New York Times,* Nov. 12, 1923.

Four: The Plan Revised

15. Sauerbruch; Ehard interview; Hoegner and Hoegner interview; Hümmert interview; Koerbling on Father Mayer; K. A. von Müller; Thomas Mann diaries; Zuckmayer; Heinrich Hoffmann; Paula Schlier; Hanfstaengl; Soden, Gürtner, Hess, Ried, Niederreiter statements as contained in Investigative committee record MA 103476; Selle statement in Pol-Dir 6713; Gordon; H. H. Hofmann; Höfler report in MA 104221; Godin interview; Wilamowitz-Moellendorff on Carin Göring.

16. Gordon; H. H. Hofmann; Franz-Willing; Heiden; Toland; Fest; Berchtold deposition in Investigative committee report MA 103476; Briemann interview; Schmied interview; Depositions of Krüger, Hewel, Stollwerck, Maurer, Knobloch, Hauenstein in Pol-Dir 6713; Karl Spreng statement in Pol-Dir 6709; First supplement report of Polizeidirektion Munich to chief of State Police, Dec. 12, 1923, in MA 104221; Streicher deposition in Pol-Dir 6712; *Münchner Neueste Nachrichten,* Nov. 10, 1923; Schaub deposition in Pol-Dir 6713; Hanfstaengl; *New York Times,* Nov. 12, 1923; *Münchener Post,* Nov. 10, 1923; Kallenbach; Nussbaum testimony in trial record MA 104222–24 and in Der Hitler Prozess; Göring's statements at bridges in Investigative committee record MA 103476 and in Franz-Willing; Ludendorff; Fügner in "Wir Marschieren"; Testimony of Kriebel, Weber, Hitler, Ludendorff in trial record MA 104222–24 and Der Hitler Prozess.

17. Seydel deposition in Pol-Dir 6713; Osswald deposition in Pol-Dir 6712; Lembert deposition in Pol-Dir 6712; Röhm; Gordon; Himmler deposition in Pol-Dir 6712; Selle statement in Pol-Dir 6713; Hümmert; Supplement 4b to Kahr's Denkschrift in MA 103473; Trial record MA 104222–24; Godin statement and report in MA 104221 and Godin interview; Moulin-Eckart statement; Letter of Georg Raithel, Nov. 16, 1923, in Pol-Dir 6712; Müller, Meister, Will, and Eduard Dünkler depositions in Pol-Dir 6712.

18. Lenk interview; Toland; Franz-Willing; Heiden; Gordon; H. H. Hofmann; Strasser; Fest, Payne; Testimony in trial record MA 104222–24 and in

Der Hitler Prozess; Hans Frank; Heines deposition in Pol-Dir 6712; Schaub deposition in Pol-Dir 6713; Depositions of Knobloch, Maurer, Hewel, Krüger, Stollwerck in Pol-Dir 6713; Berchtold statements in Investigative committee report MA 103476; Esser interview; Hanfstaengl; Heinrich Hoffmann; Parliamentary investigative committee record, pp. 1344–1358, in MA 103476. Hess deposition as contained in Investigative committee report MA 103476; Neunzert deposition in Pol-Dir 6712; Nussbaum testimony in trial record MA 104222–24 and in Der Hitler Prozess; Hitler testimony in trial record MA 104222–24; Aigner deposition in MA 104221; Rosenberg and Rosenberg deposition in Pol-Dir 6712; Briemann interview; Schmied interview; Michael Ried deposition as contained in MA 103476; Hofberger deposition in Pol-Dir 6713; Höfler reports of Nov. 10 and 22, 1923, in MA 104221; Konrad Linder deposition in MA 104221; Salbey reports of Nov. 10 and 22, 1923, in MA 104221; Stosstrupp trial verdict in Pol-Dir 6712; Kallenbach; K. A. von Müller; *New York Herald*, Nov. 10, 1923; *Chicago Tribune*, Nov. 10, 1923; *Münchner Neueste Nachrichten*, Nov. 12, 1923; Robert Murphy; Zuckmayer; Siglinde Ehard interview; Hümmert interview; Paula Schlier; Fügner in "Wir Marschieren"; Ludendorff and Ludendorff in trial record MA 104222–24; Kriebel and Weber testimony in trial record MA 104222–24 and Der Hitler Prozess; Demmelmeyer report in MA 104221; Godin interview and Godin report in MA 104221.

19. Godin interview and Godin report in MA 104221; Demmelmeyer report in MA 104221; Gordon; Lenk interview; Schmied interview; Toland; Frau Dr. Schultze's confirmation; Weber testimony in trial record MA 104222–24 and Der Hitler Prozess; Kahr's Denkschrift in MA 103473; Police list of dead and injured in Pol-Dir 6710; Description of march in Investigative committee report MA 103476; Stordeur deposition in Pol-Dir 6713; Angerer deposition in Pol-Dir 6709; Kolb deposition in Pol-Dir 6712; Knobloch, Stollwerck, Hewel, Krüger depositions in Pol-Dir 6713; August Allgaier deposition in Pol-Dir 6713; Reithinger, Rommel, Abel, Schmidt, Orlowsky, Sesselmann statements, given between Dec. 12, 1923, and March 4, 1924, all in Pol-Dir 6713; Graf testimony in trial record MA 104222–24; Sauerbruch report to Kahr, Nov. 9, 1923; Franz-Willing; Ried deposition in MA 103476; Richard Bossard interview; Ludwig Seligsberger letter; Wilamowitz-Moellendorff on Carin Göring; Koerbling on Father Mayer; Rosenberg and Rosenberg deposition in Pol-Dir. 6712; Hans Frank; Kiessling deposition in Pol-Dir 6709; Aigner deposition in MA 104221; Ehard interview.

20. Koerbling on Father Mayer; Heinrich Hoffmann; Godin interview; Esser interview; K. A. von Müller; Hanfstaengl; Michael Ried deposition as contained in MA 103476; Schmied interview; Toland; Röhm; Seydel depositions in Pol-Dir 6712 and 6713; Gordon; Osswald deposition in Pol-Dir 6712; Himmler deposition in Pol-Dir 6713; Lembert deposition in Pol-Dir 6712; Meister, Will, Müller, Dünkler, and Karl Leute depositions in Pol-Dir 6712; Letter of Raithel to Reinhardt, Nov. 16, 1923, in Pol-Dir 6712; Kahr's Denkschrift in MA 103473.

21. Briemann interview; Schaub deposition in Pol-Dir 6713; Knobloch,

Hewel, Maurer depositions in Pol-Dir 6713; Berchtold in MA 103476; Nussbaum testimony in trial record MA 104222–24 and Der Hitler Prozess; Kahr's Denkschrift in MA 103473; Mantel's report of Dec. 7, 1923, in Pol-Dir 6710; Police blotter Nov. 9–14, 1923, in Pol-Dir 6709; Statements of hostages and others in Investigative committee record MA 103476, pp. 1364–88, and Hess's deposition in MA 103476; Schwarzwäller on Hess; Letter of Ilse Hess; Toland; Gordon; H. H. Hofmann; Franz-Willing; Lüdecke; Wilamowitz-Moellendorff on Carin Göring; Report of Police Captain Bomhard in MInn 73696; Report of Lieutenant Meier in Garmisch re Göring in MA 104221; Otto Strasser.

Interlude VII

New York Tribune, World, Chicago Tribune, Nov. 10, 1923; Rabenau and Meier-Welcker on Seeckt; Bernhard (ed.) on Stresemann;

22. *Münchner Neueste Nachrichten,* Nov. 10–14, 1923; *Münchener Zeitung,* Nov. 10–14, 1923; *New York Times,* Nov. 12, 1923; Sauerbruch; K. A. von Müller.

23. Hanfstaengl; Report of Weilheim court commissioner of Nov. 11, 1923, In MInn 73694; Summary of Belleville report in MInn 73696; Ehard interview; *New York Times,* Nov. 15, 1923.

Epilogue
22. Heiden; Toland; H. H. Hofmann; Franz-Willing; Ehard interview; Hümmert and Hümmert interview; *New York Times,* Nov. 15, 1923; Trial record including secret sessions MA 104222–MA 104224; *Der Hitler Prozess vor dem Volksgericht in München; Münchner Neueste Nachrichten,* Feb. 26–April 15, 1924; Hanfstaengl; K. A. von Müller; Otto Gritschneder in program on 1924 trial on Bavarian Radio Network, July 2, 1978.

INDEX